# Safeguards in a World of Ambient Intelligence

T0190419

# The International Library of Ethics, Law and Technology

## VOLUME 1

For other titles published in this series, go to
www.springer.com/series/7761

David Wright • Serge Gutwirth
Michael Friedewald • Elena Vildjiounaite
Yves Punie
Editors and Authors

# Safeguards in a World of Ambient Intelligence

Pasi Ahonen • Petteri Alahuhta
Barbara Daskala • Sabine Delaitre
Paul De Hert • Ralf Lindner
Ioannis Maghiros • Anna Moscibroda
Wim Schreurs • Michiel Verlinden
Authors

 Springer

David Wright
Trilateral Research & Consulting
London, UK

Serge Gutwirth
Vrije Universiteit Brussel
Belgium

Michael Friedewald
Fraunhofer Institute
for Systems and Innovation
Research (ISI)
Karlsruhe, Germany

Elena Vildjiounaite
VTT Technical Research Centre of Finland, Oulu
Finland

Yves Punie
Institute for Prospective
Technological Studies (IPTS)
European Commission JRC
Seville, Spain

ISSN 1875-0044
ISBN 978-1-4020-6661-0 (hardcover)
ISBN 978-90-481-8786-7 (softcover)
DOI 10.1007/978-1-4020-6662-7
Springer Dordrecht Heidelberg London New York

e-ISSN 1875-0036
e-ISBN 978-1-4020-6662-7

Library of Congress Control Number: 2010924814

Printed on acid-free paper

Springer is part of Springer Science+Business Media (www.springer.com)

# Foreword by Emile Aarts

On the morning of 22 March 2006, I was hurrying to get to Brussels in time because I had to go there to present one of my Ambient Intelligence lectures. I was invited to give a keynote at an international conference with the name SWAMI, which was organized among others by the European Commission. I did not take the effort to study the scope of the conference in detail, nor did I take the time to have a close look at the list of participants. It had something to do with ethics I was told and I took it for granted that I could present my normal introductory ambient intelligence story. So I went to Brussels and I had a unique learning experience.

When I arrived at the conference hotel, they just had a break and I had to present just after the break. I started off with my normal positive and technology-driven motivation for the need to have ambient intelligence, but I could read from the faces of the audience that they were not amused by my argumentation. So I concluded that obviously this was all common knowledge to them and I started adding more industrial evidence for the economic value of ambient intelligence by reasoning about technology innovation and business models. This, however, resulted in even less positive feedback and faces grew darker, some persons in the audience even seemed to get annoyed by my presentation and evidently I had not found the right tone so far. So again I switched content and spoke a little about applications, but this also did not help. Then I remembered that the conference was about ethical things and I skipped to the last part of my presentation where I added a few slides with philosophical statements on the role of ambient intelligence in society, but harm was done already and this could hardly turn the presentation for the better.

I decided to stop and to open the floor for a discussion with the audience. One of the first remarks was a statement made by a nice person from Austria who exclaimed that my talk was "both ingenious and ridiculous". I will never forget this remark during my entire life and I assume that the gentleman intended to emphasize that he disliked the lack of social responsibility that I expressed in my talk, and he was right. For more than half an hour, we elaborated on these social implications in a plenary setting until the chairman stopped the discussion for the sake of time. The discussions went on for another hour in the hotel corridors and after that I had to leave for another meeting, almost an hour behind schedule, but chastened.

It is my true conviction that the work this group of persons had been doing is of utmost importance. The development of ambient intelligence is going on for almost

10 years now and most of the time we have been emphasizing the technological potential of this novel and disruptive approach. We also have been largely building on the belief that user insights and user-centric design approaches should be used to come up with solutions that really matter to people, but we hardly paid attention to questions related to such important matters as trust, security, and legal aspects, nor to speak about the more ethical issues such as alienation, digital divide, and social responsibility as raised and discussed by the SWAMI community.

This book, which can be viewed as a direct outcome of the 2006 SWAMI conference, presents a very comprehensive overview of all the relevant issues and options related to the ethics of ambient intelligence. The many high-quality contributions reflect the scholarship and integrity of its authors, and some of the chapters even resemble the level of a philosophical treatise. The book approaches ambient intelligence from a unique angle and it is mandatory reading material for anyone who is professionally active in the field of ambient intelligence as it can be seen as a landmark contribution to the discussion on ambient intelligence. After almost 10 years of development, ambient intelligence can now live up to its expectation that it can change peoples' lives for the better through its novel user-centric technology. In the end, however, this will only work if we can settle the ethical issues that are connected to it, and the SWAMI effort has contributed significantly to this greater cause.

Finally, I would like to thank the SWAMI people for giving me the opportunity to have one of the most compelling learning experiences in my professional life.

Emile Aarts
Scientific Program Manager
Philips Research
Eindhoven, The Netherlands
2 February 2007

# Foreword by Gary T. Marx

## SWAMI, How I Love Ya

*For I dipt into the future, far as human eyes could see,*
*saw the world, and all the wonders that would be*

*Alfred Lord Tennyson, "Locksley Hall"*

*And you will have a window in your head.*
*Not even your future will be a mystery*
*Any more. Your mind will be punched in a card*
*And shut away in a little drawer.*
*When they want you to buy something*
*They will call you....*
*So friends, every day do something*
*That won't compute....*

*Wendell Berry, "The Mad Farmer Liberation Front"*

These poems reflect polar images of science and technology in western societies. Such contrasting views are daily expressed in our literature, popular culture, politics, policies and everyday life. We are enthralled by, and fearful of, the astounding powers new technologies may bring. We hope with Edison that "whatever the mind of man creates" can be "controlled by man's character", even as we worry with Einstein that technological progress can become "like an axe in the hand of a pathological criminal".

In our dynamic and very unequal worlds of such vast system complexity, there is much to be worried about. But there is also much to be optimistic about. This book is a welcome contrast to much of the disingenuous commentary on new information technologies offered by technical, commercial and political advocates who command the largest megaphones. The book strikes a balance between encouraging the wonders that could be, while reminding us of the dark forces of history and society, and that nature is filled with surprises. We cannot and should not stop invention, but neither should we uncritically apply it, absent the careful controls and continual evaluation the book recommends.

Before our age of avaricious, data-hungry sensors that can record everything in their path, to say that a person "really left a mark" implied that they willfully did something special. Now, merely being passively present – whether in a physical or biological sense, let alone actively communicating, moving or consuming leaves remnants as well. In an age when everyone (and many objects) will continuously leave marks of all sorts, that phrase may become less meaningful.

The topic of this book is ostensibly the embedding of low visibility, networked sensors within and across ever more environments (called ambient intelligence or AmI in Europe and ubiquitous computing or networked computing in America and Japan). But the book is about much more. It offers a way of broadly thinking about information-related technical developments. It is the most informative and comprehensive policy analysis of new information and surveillance technologies seen in recent decades.

Those wishing to praise a book often say, "*essential* reading for anyone concerned with ...". But I would go beyond that strong endorsement to say *Safeguards in a World of Ambient Intelligence* (SWAMI) should be *required* reading for anyone concerned with public policy involving new communications and surveillance technologies. This should be bolstered by frequent certifying quizzes (and maybe even licenses) for those developing and applying information technology and for those on whom it is applied. The goal is to keep ever in view the multiplicity of analytical factors required to reach judgments about technologies which so radically break with the limits of the human senses and of space and time. In encouraging caution and steps to avoid worst-case scenarios, such analysis can limit unwanted surprises occurring as a result of interactions within very complex networked systems.

How do I like this book? Let me count the ways. If this were a musical comedy, the first song would be "SWAMI, How I love Ya, How I love ya" (with apologies to George Gershwin). First, it creatively and fairly wends its way through the minefields of praise and criticism that so inform our contradictory views of technology. It avoids the extremes of technophilia and technophobia implied in the poems above and often in superficial media depictions and in rhetorical excesses of the players. It also avoids the shoals of technological, as against social and cultural, determinism. There is nothing inherent in technology or nature that means specific tools must be developed or used. The social and cultural context is central to the kind of tools developed and their uses and meaning. Yet technologies are rarely neutral in their impact. They create as well as respond to social and cultural conditions.

The book suggests a flashing yellow light calling for caution and analysis rather than the certainty of a green or a red light. This can be seen as a limited optimism or a qualified pessimism, but what matters is the call for humility and continual analysis. As with much science fiction, the dark scenarios the book offers extrapolate rather than predict. They call attention to things that could happen in the hope that they would not.

While the report is a product of 35 experts, numerous meetings, work teams and consultants, it does not read like the typical pastiche committee or team report. Rather it is smooth flowing, consistent and integrated. The product of specialists from many parts of Europe, it nonetheless offers a common view of the issues that transcend the particularities of given cultures and language. As such, it speaks to an emerging European, and perhaps global, sense of citizenship fostered by standardized technologies that so effortlessly transcend traditional national borders, as well as those of distance and time.

While the United States is the major player in the development and diffusion of new information technologies, it sadly lags far behind Europe in providing deep and comprehensive analysis of the social and ethical consequences of such technology. Not only does it lack privacy and information commissions, but there is no longer a strong national analytical agency concerned with the impact of new technologies. The short-sighted Congressional elimination of the nonpartisan analytical Office of Technology Assessment in 1995 has deprived the United States of an independent public interest voice in these matters.[1]

The book offers a very comprehensive review of the relevant literature from many fields, at least for the English language. As a historical record and chronicle of turn-of-the-century debates and concerns raised by these developments, the book will be of inestimable value to future scholars confronting the novel challenges brought by the continuing cascade of new information technologies. I particularly appreciate some of the metaphors and concepts the book uses such as data laundering, AmI technosis, technology paternalism, coincidence of circumstances, digital hermits, and the bubble of digital territory in its analysis.

Much of the extensive supporting documentation and reference material is available online, making it easy and inviting for the reader to pursue topics in more detail or to check on the book's interpretations. However, I hope this would not soon come with an AmI program that, seeing what was accessed, makes recommendations for future reading or offers discounts for related book purchases or worse sends political messages seeking to alter the assumed positions of the user/reader.

The strength of this book is in raising basic questions and offering ways of thinking about these. Answers will vary depending on the context and time, but the social factors and trade-offs that must be considered remain relatively constant. Rules and regulations will differ depending on the setting and the phase. A given use can be approached through a temporal process as we move from the conditions of collection to those of security and use. Or settings can be contrasted with respect to issues such as whether individuals should be given maximum, as against no, choice regarding the offering/taking of their personal data; questions around the retention or destruction of personal information; and whether the data should be seen as the private property of those who collect it, those about whom it is collected, or as a public record. A related issue involves whether AmI systems are viewed as public utilities in principle available to all or are viewed as private commodities available only to those who can afford them and/or who qualify.

---

[1] In a blatantly partisan and socially destructive move, the 104th Congress withdrew funding for OTA and its full-time staff of 143 persons. Copies of OTA publications are available from the Superintendent of Documents, P.O. Box 371954, Pittsburgh, PA 15250-7974. As this book notes, the National Research Council has stepped in to partially fill the void, most recently with the Committee on Privacy in the Information Age, *Engaging Privacy and Information Technology in a Digital Age*, 2007.

It has verisimilitude both in its treatment of the policy issues and in its scenarios. It offers an encyclopedia of safeguards and calls for a mixture of available means of regulation. While the book gives appropriate attention to technical controls and those involving legislation and courts at many levels (national, European community, international) and notes the role of markets, it stands apart from the voluminous policy literature in attending to civil society factors such as the media, public awareness and education, cultural safeguards and emerging tools such as trust marks, trust seals and reputation systems. The informal, as well as the formal, must be part of any policy considerations and analysis of impact.

An aspect of the book's reality check is its consideration of the trade-offs and tensions between conflicting goals and needs. In spite of the promises of politicians and marketeers and the fantasies of children, we cannot have it all. Hard choices must often be made and compromises sought.

In the rush to certainty and in the pursuit of self-interest, too much discussion of technology shows a misguided *either/or* fallacy. But when complex and complicated topics are present, it is well, with Whitehead, not to find clarity and consistency at the cost of "overlooking the subtleties of truth". We need to find ways of reconciling, both intellectually and practically, seemingly contradictory factors.

In considering issues of computers and society, there are enduring value conflicts and ironic, conflicting needs, goals and consequences that require the informed seeking out of the trade-offs and continual evaluation the book recommends.

These can be considered very abstractly as with the importance of liberty and order, individualism and community, efficiency and fair and valid treatment. When we turn to AmI, we see the tensions more concretely.

Thus, the need for collecting, merging and storing detailed personal information in real time, on a continual basis across diverse interoperable systems, is central for maximizing the potential of the AmI. But this can cause tension between the goals of authentication, personalized service and validity and those of privacy and security (the latter two can, of course, also be in tension, as well as mutually supportive). The generation of enormous databases presents monumental challenges in guarding against the trust-violations of insiders and the damage that can be wrought by outsider hackers. How can the advantages of both opacity and transparency be combined such that systems are easy to use and in the background and hence more egalitarian and efficient, while simultaneously minimizing misuse and encouraging accountability and privacy? As the song says, "something's got to give". Personalization with its appreciation of the individual's unique needs and circumstances must be creatively blended with impersonalization with its protections of privacy and against manipulation. We need solutions that optimize rather than maximize with a keen awareness of what is gained and what is lost (and for whom under what conditions) with different technical arrangements and policy regimes.

Under dynamic conditions, the balance and effort to mange competing needs must be continuously revisited. Some changes are purposive as individuals and organizations seek to undermine AmI as its operation becomes understood, others involve growth and development as individuals change their preferences and behavior, and environmental conditions change.

The dark scenarios are particularly refreshing given the predominance of good news advocacy stories in our culture. The bad news stories offered here are hardly the product of an unrestrained dystopian imagination rambling under the influence of some banned (or not yet banned) drug. Rather, they reflect a systematic method relying on cross-observer validation (or more accurately review and certification). This method should be in the toolkit of all analysts of new technology. Unlike the darkness of much science fiction, these stories are reality-based. The methodology developed here involves both a technology check (are the technologies in the stories realistic given current and emerging knowledge and technique?) and an actuality check (have the outcomes to some degree actually occurred, if not all at the same time or in exactly the same way as the story describes?).

These restrictions give the scenarios plausibility absent in fiction bounded only by the imagination of an author. However, for some observers, requiring that similar events have actually happened might be seen as too stringent. For example, by these standards the Exxon oil spill (prior to its occurrence) could not have been a scenario. This is because something like it had never happened and the chance of it happening was so wildly remote (requiring the coming together of a series of highly improbable events), that it would have been deemed unrealistic given the above methodology.

## An extension or reversal of George Orwell?

The aura of George Orwell lies behind many of the critical concerns this book notes. In some of its worst forms (being invisible, manipulative and exclusionary, not offering choice, furthering inequality and ignoring individuality and individual justice in pursuit of rationality and efficiency across many cases), ambient intelligence reflects *1984*. It could even bring horrors beyond Orwell where surveillance was episodic, rather than continual, and relied on fear, lacking the scale, omnipresence, depth, automatism and power of ambient intelligence. With the soft and unseen dictatorship of design, the individual could face ever fewer choices (e.g., being unable to pay with cash or using an anonymous pay telephone) and if able to opt out and do without the benefits, becomes suspicious or at least is seen as someone who is socially backward as a result of nonparticipation. Rather than mass treatment which, given its generality, left wiggle room for resistance, the new forms drawing on highly detailed individuated information could greatly enhance control.

Orwell's treatment of language can be applied. With "Newspeak" and phrases such as "peace is war", Orwell's satire emphasizes how concepts can euphemize (or maybe euthanize would be a better term) meaning. To call this book's topic "ambient intelligence" brings a positive connotation of something neutral and supportive in the background, maybe even something warm and fuzzy. Ambience is popularly used to refer to a desired environmental condition. Like surround sound, it envelops us, but unlike the latter, we may be less aware of it. Ambient has been used as the name of a popular pill that induces somnolence. What feelings would be induced if the book's topic was instead called "octopus intelligence" or, given a record of major failures, "hegemonic stupidity"?

But there are major differences as well. In Orwell's Oceania, the centralized state is all-powerful and the citizen has neither rights nor inputs into government. Mass communication is rigidly controlled by, and restricted to, the state. There are no voluntary associations (all such organizations are directly sponsored and controlled by the state). The standard of living is declining and all surplus goes into war preparation rather than consumption. Society is hierarchically organized, but there is little differentiation, diversity or variety. Everything possible is standardized and regimented. Individuals are isolated from, and do not trust, each other. Private communication is discouraged and writing instruments are prohibited, as are learning a foreign language and contact with foreigners.

Yet empirical data on communications and social participation for contemporary democratic societies does not generally reflect that vision, even given the restrictions and enhanced government powers seen since 9/11. Indeed in its happier version, ambient intelligence can be seen as the antidote to a 1984-type of society – networked computers relying on feedback going in many directions can bring decentralization and strengthen horizontal civil society ties across traditional borders. Differences – whether based on space and time or culture – that have traditionally separated persons may be overcome. The new means vastly extend and improve communication and can offer informed end-users choices about whether or not, or to what degree, to participate. Pseudonymous means can protect identity. In the face of standardized mass treatment, citizens can efficiently and inexpensively be offered highly personalized consumer goods and services tailored to their unique needs.

The potential to counter and avoid government can protect liberty. On the other hand, privatization can bring other costs including insulation from regulation in the public interest and increased inequality. Those with the resources who do not need the advantages the technology offers in return for the risks it brings may be able to opt out of it. Those with the right profiles and with the resources to participate, or to pay for added levels of security, validity and privacy for their data, will benefit, but not others.

In many ways, we have moved very far from the kind of society Orwell envisioned in 1948. His book remains a powerful and provocative statement for a 19th-century kind of guy who never rode on an airplane and did not write about computers. Yet, if forced to choose, I would worry more (or at least as much) about the threat of a crazily complex, out-of-control, interventionist society that believes it can solve all problems and is prone to the errors and opaqueness envisioned by Kafka than about Orwell's mid-20th-century form of totalitarianism. Hubris was hardly a Greek invention.

While there is societal awareness of mal-intentioned individuals and groups to the extent that "Orwellian" has become clichéd, yet the threat posed by rushing to technologically control evermore aspects of highly complex life through constant data collection and feedback, interaction and automated actions is less appreciated and understood. The emergent dynamism of the involved interdependent systems and the difficulty of imagining all possible consequences must give us great pause.

The book's scenarios offer a cornucopia of what can go wrong. Ideally, we wish to see well-motivated people and organizations using good and appropriate technology. The book's dark scenarios suggest two other forms to be avoided:

**Bad or incompetent people and/or organizations with good technology.** The problem is not with the technology, but with the uses to which it is put. There may be an absence of adequate regulation or enforcement of standards. Individuals may lack the competence to apply the technology or end users may not take adequate protection and may be too trusting. As with identity theft, the wrongful cleansing and misuse of legitimately collected data, and machines that are inhuman in multiple ways, malevolent motivation combined with powerful technologies is the stuff of our worst totalitarian nightmares. But consider also the reverse:

**Good people and/or organizations with bad or inappropriate technology.** This suggests a very different order of problem – not the absence of good will, competence and/or legitimate goals, but of technology that is not up to the job and spiraling expectations. Achieving the interoperability and harmonization among highly varied technical and cultural systems that AmI networks will increasingly depend on can bring new vulnerabilities and problems. For technical, resource or political reasons, many systems will be incompatible and varying rates of changes in systems will affect their ability to co-operate. Technology that works in some settings may not work in others or may be neutralized in conflict settings. Here we also see the issue of "natural" errors or accidents that flow from the complexity of some systems and the inability to imagine outcomes from the far-flung interactions of diverse systems. Regular reading of the *Risks Digest* (http://www.csl.sri.com/~risko/risks.txt) can not only give nightmares, but also make getting out of bed each day an act of supreme courage.

From one standpoint, there are two problems with the new communication and information technologies. The first is that they do not work. The second is that they do. In the first case, we may waste resources, reduce trust, damage credibility and legitimacy and harm individuals. Yet, if they do work, we risk creating a more efficient and mechanical society at the cost of traditional human concerns involving individual uniqueness and will. Given power and resource differentials, we may create an even more unequal society further marginalizing and restricting those lacking the resources to participate and/or to challenge technical outcomes. There will be new grounds for exclusion and a softening of the meaning of choice. The failure to provide a detailed profile, or of a country to meet international standards, may de facto mean exclusion.

The book notes the importance of (p. xxvi) "focusing on concrete technologies rather than trying to produce general measures". Yet, in generating specific responses, we need to be guided by broad questions and values and the overarching themes the book identifies. These change much more slowly, if at all, than the technologies. That is of course part of the problem. But it can also be part of the solution in offering an anchoring in fundamental and enduring human concerns.

An approach I find useful amidst the rapidity and constancy of technical innovation is to ask a standard set of questions. This gives us a comparative framework for judgment. The questions in Table 1 incorporate much of what this book asks us to consider.[2]

A central point of this book is to call attention to the contextual nature of behavior. Certainly these questions and the principles implied in them are not of equal weight, and their applicability will vary across time periods depending on need and perceptions of crisis and across contexts (e.g., public order, health and welfare, criminal and national security, commercial transactions, private individuals, families, and the defenseless and dependent) and particular situations within these. Yet, common sense and common decency argue for considering them.

Public policy is shaped by manners, organizational policies, regulations and laws. These draw on a number of background value principles and tacit assumptions about the empirical world that need to be analyzed. Whatever action is taken, there are likely costs, gains and trade-offs. At best, we can hope to find a compass rather than a map and a moving equilibrium instead of a fixed point for decision making.

For AmI, as with any value-conflicted and varied-consequence behavior, particularly those that involve conflicting rights and needs, it is essential to keep the tensions ever in mind and to avoid complacency. Occasionally, when wending through competing values, the absolutist, no-compromise, don't-cross-this-personal line or always-cross-it standard is appropriate. But, more often, compromise (if rarely a simplistic perfect balance) is required. When privacy and civil liberties are negatively affected, it is vital to acknowledge, rather than to deny this, as is so often the case. Such honesty can make for better-informed decisions and also serves an educational function.

These tensions are a central theme in this book, which calls for fairly responding to (although not necessarily equal balancing of) the interests of all stakeholders. Yet, it only implicitly deals with the significant power imbalances between groups that work against this. But relative to most such reports, its attention to social divisions that may be unwisely and unfairly exacerbated by the technology is most welcome.

In a few places, the book lapses into an optimism (perhaps acceptable if seen as a hope rather than an empirical statement) that conflicts with its dominant tone of complexity and attention to factors that should restrict unleashing the tools.

---

[2] Adapted from G.T. Marx, "Seeing Hazily, But Not Darkly, Through the Lens: Some Recent Empirical Studies of Surveillance Technologies", *Law and Social Inquiry*, Vol. 30, No. 2, 2005. A related factor is to identify the background assumptions and tacit empirical and moral beliefs that underlie attitudes toward technology. In a presentation to the 2006 SWAMI conference in Brussels where various parts of this book were presented, I identified 38 such beliefs. Perhaps the most important is not confusing data with knowledge, nor technique with wisdom. "Rocky Bottoms: Techno-Fallacies of an Age of Information", *International Political Sociology*, Vol. 1, No. 2, 2007. In G.T. Marx and G. Muschert, "Personal Information, Borders, and the New Surveillance Studies", *Annual Review of Law and Social Science*, Vol. 3, 2007, we discuss value conflicts and ironic and conflicting needs, goals and consequences. These and other related articles are at garymarx.net and G.T. Marx, *Windows Into the Soul Surveillance and Society in an Age of High Technology*, University of Chicago Press, forthcoming.

**Table 1** Questions for judgment and policy

1. *Goals* – Have the goals been clearly stated, justified and prioritized? Are they consistent with the values of a democratic society?
2. *Accountable, public and participatory policy development* – Has the decision to apply the technique been developed through an open process and, if appropriate, with participation of those to be subject to it? This involves a transparency principle.
3. *Law and ethics* – Are the means and ends not only legal, but also ethical?
4. *Opening doors* – Has adequate thought been given to precedent creation and long-term consequences?
5. *Golden rule* – Would the controllers of the system be comfortable in being its subject, as well as its agent? Where there is a clear division between agents and subjects, is reciprocity or equivalence possible and appropriate?
6. *Informed consent* – Are participants fully apprised of the system's presence and the conditions under which it operates? Is consent genuine (i.e., beyond deception or unreasonable seduction or denial of fundamental services) and can "participation" be refused without dire consequences for the person?
7. *Truth in use* – Where personal and private information is involved does a principle of "unitary usage" apply, whereby information collected for one purpose is not used for another? Are the announced goals the real goals?
8. *Means–ends relationships* – Are the means clearly related to the end sought and proportional in costs and benefits to the goals?
9. *Can science save us?* – Can a strong empirical and logical case be made that a means will in fact have the broad positive consequences its advocates claim (the does-it-really-work question)?
10. *Competent application* – Even if in theory it works, does the system (or operative) using it apply it as intended and in the appropriate manner?
11. *Human review* – Are automated results with significant implications for life chances subject to human review before action is taken?
12. *Minimization* – If risks and harm are associated with the tactic, is it applied to minimize these showing only the degree of intrusiveness and invasiveness that is absolutely necessary?
13. *Alternatives* – Are alternative solutions available that would meet the same ends with lesser costs and greater benefits (using a variety of measures not just financial)?
14. *Inaction as action* – Has consideration been given to the "sometimes it is better to do nothing" principle?
15. *Periodic review* – Are there regular efforts to test the system's vulnerability, effectiveness and fairness and to review policies and procedures?
16. *Discovery and rectification of mistakes, errors and abuses* – Are there clear means for identifying and fixing these (and in the case of abuse, applying sanctions)?
17. *Right of inspection* – Can individuals see and challenge their own records?
18. *Reversibility* – If evidence suggests that the costs outweigh the benefits, how easily can the means (e.g., extent of capital expenditures and available alternatives) be given up?
19. *Unintended consequences* – Has adequate consideration been given to undesirable consequences, including possible harm to agents, subjects and third parties? Can harm be easily discovered and compensated for?
20. *Data protection and security* – Can agents protect the information they collect? Do they follow standard data protection and information rights as expressed in documents such as the Code of Fair Information Protection Practices and the expanded European Data Protection Directive?

This book (p. 8) sets for itself the "difficult task of raising awareness about threats and vulnerabilities and in promoting safeguards *while not undermining the efforts to deploy AmI*" and it suggests (p. 6) that "the *success* of ambient intelligence will depend on how secure its use can be made, how privacy and other rights of individuals can be protected, and, ultimately, how individuals can come to trust the intelligent world which surrounds them and through which they move". The book argues (p. xxii) that "matters of identity, privacy, security, trust and so on need to be addressed in a multidisciplinary way *in order for them to be enablers and not obstacles* for realizing ambient intelligence in Europe" (italics added).

Is the task of the public interest analyst to see that public policy involves "enablers not obstacles for realizing ambient intelligence in Europe"? Should the analyst try to bring about the future, guard against it (or at least prevent certain versions of it), or play a neutral role in simply indicating what the facts and issues are?

Certainly, where the voluntary co-operation of subjects is needed, the system must be trusted to deliver and to protect the security and privacy of valid personal information. Showing that people will be treated with dignity can be good for business and government in their efforts to apply new technologies. Yet, the book's call to implement the necessary safeguards will often undermine (if not prevent) "the efforts to deploy AmI".

Here, we must ask "what does success mean?" One answer: AmI is successful to the extent that the broad value concerns the book raises are central in the development of policy and practice. But another conflicting answer, and one held by many practitioners with an instrumental view, is that AmI is successful to the extent that it is implemented to maximize the technical potential and interests of those who control the technology. The incompatibility between these two views of success needs to be directly confronted.

Emile Aarts, who has played an important role in the development and spread of ambient intelligence, notes in the other foreword to this book that the technology's promise will "only work if we can settle the ethical issues that are connected to it". Yet, we must always ask just how well do we want it to work, what does "to work" mean, who does it work for and under what conditions? Furthermore, the day we *settle* the ethical and social issues we are in deep yogurt. Given the inherent conflicts and trade-offs and dynamic and highly varied circumstances, we need to continually encounter and wrestle with unsettling and unsettled issues. This book offers us an ideal framework for that ongoing process.

Gary T. Marx
Professor Emeritus
Massachusetts Institute of Technology
Cambridge, MA, USA
http://www.garymarx.net
7 May 2007

# Acknowledgements

We express special thanks to Laurent Beslay, who is now with the European Data Protection Supervisor (http://www.edps.europa.eu), for his initial contributions to our project. We also thank Marc Langheinrich of the Institute for Pervasive Computing at the Swiss Federal Institute of Technology, Zurich, Erkki Kemppainen of STAKES, Helsinki, and Jean-Marc Dinant, Head of the technology and security research unit in the Center for Research in Law and Computer Sciences (CRID) at the University of Namur for their excellent, independent review of our project deliverables.

We thank the following experts for their participation and useful comments at our workshops:

**Achilles Kameas**, Research Academic Computer Technology Institute, Patras, Greece
**Albrecht Schmidt**, University Duisburg Essen, Germany
**Bart Walhout**, Rathenau Instituut, The Hague, The Netherlands
**Gregory Neven**, KU Leuven, Belgium
**Ian Brown**, Foundation for Information Policy Research, London, UK
**Irene Lopez de Vallejo**, University College London, UK
**Jan Möller**, Federal Ministry of the Interior, Germany
**Lorenz Hilty**, Swiss Federal Materials Testing Agency, St. Gallen, Switzerland
**Maddy Janse**, Philips Research, Eindhoven, The Netherlands
**Marc Langheinrich**, ETH Zürich, Switzerland
**Marco Conte**, CE Consulting, Rome, Italy
**Mario Hoffmann**, Fraunhofer SIT, Darmstadt, Germany
**Markus Hansen**, Independent Data Protection Centre Schleswig-Holstein, Kiel, Germany
**Michael Lyons**, BTexact Technologies, Ipswich, UK
**Michael Vanfleteren**, Office of the European Data Protection Supervisor, Belgium
**Miriam Lips**, Tilburg University, The Netherlands
**Norbert Streitz**, Fraunhofer IPSI, Darmstadt, Germany
**Pertti Huuskonen**, Nokia Research Centre, Tampere, Finland
**Sandro Bologna**, Italian National Agency for New Technologies, Energy and the Environment, Rome, Italy

**Spyros Lalis**, University of Thessaly, Greece
**Stefaan Seys**, KU Leuven, Belgium

Finally, we acknowledge that although this book is based on a project funded by the European Commission, the views expressed herein are those of the authors alone and are in no way to be interpreted as those of the European Commission. We are grateful to our project officer, Inmaculada Placencia-Porrero, in the Directorate General for Information Society and Media, for her concurrence in the publication of this book.

# Preface

This book is a warning. It aims to warn policy makers, industry, academia, civil society organisations, the media and the public about the threats and vulnerabilities facing our privacy, identity, trust, security and inclusion in the rapidly approaching future world of ambient intelligence (AmI).

The book has several objectives. First, as mentioned above, it aims to be a warning. Second, it aims to illustrate the threats and vulnerabilities by means of what we have termed "dark scenarios". Third, it sets out a structured methodology for analysing the four scenarios, and we believe that our methodology will serve others who seek to construct or deconstruct technology-oriented scenarios. Fourth, it identifies a range of safeguards aimed at minimising the foreseen threats and vulnerabilities. Fifth, it makes recommendations to policy-makers and other stakeholders about what they can do to ensure that we all benefit from ambient intelligence with the inevitable risks of negative consequences minimised as far as reasonably possible.

While we intentionally set out to display and illuminate the dark side of ambient intelligence in this book, we do not wish to be regarded as doomsayers or scaremongers, stridently opposed to AmI. We are as convinced of the social, political, economic and individual benefits of AmI as any of the enthusiasts. However, our enthusiasm is tempered by our concerns for the impacts on privacy, identity, security and so on. The threats and vulnerabilities can be minimised, if not eliminated. If AmI is to be a European success story, as it should be, we believe urgent action on a multiplicity of fronts is necessary. Delaying action until AmI is fully deployed will be too late.

The book grew out of the SWAMI project (Safeguards in a World of Ambient Intelligence), which began in February 2005 with funding from the European Commission under its Sixth Framework Programme of research and technological development. The SWAMI consortium comprises five partners, namely Fraunhofer Institute for Systems and Innovation Research (Germany), the VTT Technical Research Center of Finland, Vrije Universiteit Brussel (Belgium), the Institute for Prospective Technological Studies (IPTS, Spain) of the EC's Joint Research Centre, and Trilateral Research and Consulting (UK).

In addition to our co-authors, we offer our special thanks to Emile Aarts, Vice President of Philips, and Gary T. Marx, Professor at MIT, for agreeing to write the forewords for this book.

The editors

# An Executive Summary for hasty readers

Ambient Intelligence (AmI) describes a vision of the future Information Society as the convergence of ubiquitous computing, ubiquitous communication and interfaces adapting to the user. In this vision, the emphasis is on greater user-friendliness, more efficient services support, user empowerment and support for human interactions. People are surrounded by intelligent intuitive interfaces embedded in all kinds of objects and an environment capable of recognising and responding to the presence of different individuals in a seamless, unobtrusive and often invisible way.[1]

While most stakeholders paint the promise of AmI in sunny colours, there is a dark side to AmI as well. In a way, this dark side is inherent in many technologies including AmI, where intelligence is embedded in the environment and accessible anywhere and at any time including by those on the move. In this future, virtually every product and service – our clothes, money, appliances, the paint on our walls, the carpets on our floors, our cars, everything – will be embedded with intelligence. With networking microchips tinier than a pinhead, personalised services can be provided on a scale dwarfing anything hitherto available. Taken together, these developments will create a profoundly different information landscape from the one with which we are familiar today and that will have the following key characteristics[2]:

- *Complexity*: As hardware capabilities improve and costs reduce, there is continuing pressure to attempt to build systems of ever greater scope and functional sophistication.
- *Boundary-less nature of the systems and interconnectedness*: Few systems have a clear-cut boundary. They are subdivided into systems within systems.
- *Unpredictability*: All nodes, connected through a common infrastructure, are potentially accessible from anywhere at any time, which may result in unpredictable emergent behaviours.

---

[1] IST Advisory Group, K. Ducatel, M. Bogdanowicz, F. Scapolo, J. Leijten and J.-C. Burgelman, "Scenarios for Ambient Intelligence in 2010", Institute for Prospective Technological Studies (IPTS), EC-JRC, Seville, 2001; Punie, Y., "The Future of Ambient Intelligence in Europe: The Need for More Everyday Life", *Communications and Strategies* 57, 2005, pp. 141–165.

[2] Riguidel, M., and F. Martinelli, "Beyond the Horizon – Thematic Group 3: Security, Dependability and Trust", Report for Public Consultation, 2006. http://www.beyond-the-horizon.net

- *Heterogeneity and blurring of the human/device boundary*: For example, wearable and/or implantable devices will become more widely available and drop in cost.
- *Incremental development and deployment*: Systems are never finished; new features (and sources of system faults and vulnerabilities) are added at a continuous pace.
- *Self-configuration and adaptation*: Systems are expected to be able to respond to the changing circumstances of the ambient intelligence environment where they are embedded.

The scale, complexity and ever-expanding scope of human activity within this new ecosystem present enormous technical challenges for privacy, identity and security – mainly because of the enormous amount of behavioural, personal and even biological data (such as DNA, fingerprints and facial recognition) being recorded and disseminated. Moreover, many more activities in daily life, at work and in other environments, will depend on the availability of AmI devices and services. Questions of ownership and governance of infrastructures and services will thus loom large. The growing autonomy and intelligence of devices and applications will have implications for product liability, security and service definition. There will also be new and massive economic activity in the trading of those techniques that make things smart. One can expect vigorous discussions of who has rights over what information and for what purpose. Finally, there will be a constant struggle to defend this world of ambient intelligence against attacks from viruses, spam, fraud, masquerade, cyber terrorism and so forth. The risk of new vulnerabilities may prove to be one of the biggest brakes on the deployment and adoption of new capabilities and needs to be mitigated.[3]

This book considers how and to what extent it is possible or could be possible in the future to overcome the problematic implications of the dark side of ambient intelligence through the implementation of various safeguards and privacy-enhancing mechanisms, the aim of which is to ensure user control and enforceability of policy in an accessible manner and the protection of rights for all citizens in the Information Society.

There is an urgent need for realising these objectives. Matters of privacy, identity, trust, security and so on need to be addressed in a multidisciplinary way in order for them to become enablers and not obstacles for realising ambient intelligence in Europe. As often happens, technology is progressing faster than the policy-building process that might otherwise assuage public concerns about the potential for new encroachments on privacy and engender trust in our technological future.

These concerns are reflected in the four scenarios contained in this book. Scenarios are not traditional extrapolations from the present, but offer provocative glimpses of futures that can (but need not) be realised. Scenario planning provides a structured way to get an impression of the future and to uncover the specific steps and challenges in technology that have to be taken into account when anticipating the future. Most scenarios are developed so as to demonstrate the benefits of new technologies. By contrast, our scenarios are "dark" since they include applications that go wrong or do not work as expected. Our four scenarios are the following:

---

[3] Sharpe, B., S. Zaba and M. Ince, "Foresight Cyber Trust and Crime Prevention Project. Technology Forward Look: User Guide", Office of Science and Technology, London, 2004.

**Dark scenario 1 (the AmI family)** presents AmI vulnerabilities in the life of a typical family moving through different environments. It introduces dark situations in the smart home, at work and during a lunch break in a park.

**Dark scenario 2 (a crash in AmI space)** also references a family but focuses more specifically on senior citizens on a bus tour. An exploited vulnerability in the traffic system causes an accident, raising many different problems related to both travel and health AmI systems.

**Dark scenario 3 (what is a data aggregator to do?)** involves a data-aggregating company that becomes victim of theft of the personal data which it has compiled from AmI networks and which fuel its core business. Given its dominant position in the market, the company wants to cover this up but ends up in court two years later. The scenario draws attention to the digital divide between developed countries with AmI networks and developing countries that do not have such networks.

**Dark scenario 4 (an early morning TV programme reports on AmI)** portrays an AmI risk society from the studios of a morning news programme. It presents an action group against personalised profiling, the digital divide at a global scale and related to environmental concerns, the possible vulnerabilities of AmI-based traffic management systems and crowd control in an AmI environment.

The four scenarios deal with issues that need to be addressed for the successful deployment of ambient intelligence, among which are the following:

- **Privacy** – It is important to be aware of the implications of AmI for private life and personal data and to take adequate social, technical, economic and legal measures to protect privacy. The scenarios show different facets of privacy invasion, such as identity theft, the "little brother" phenomenon, data laundering, disclosure of personal data, surveillance and risks from personalised profiling.
- **Security** – This is a key challenge for successful AmI implementation. The scenarios depict security issues in different contexts: security imposed for telework, biometrics used for authentication or identification, human factors and security, malicious attacks, security audits, back-up security measures, security risks, access control, the illusion of security and viruses. The possible impacts that arise when there is a lack of security or unsuitable security measures are also underlined.
- **Identity** – The different components of identity, i.e., information related to legal identity, identification, authentication and preferences, play important roles in determining the feasibility of the AmI environment. The scenarios expose and detail the consequences when identity-based data are misused, erroneously used or incompletely processed.

- **Trust** – The notion of trust has technical aspects as well as social, cultural and legal aspects. In the scenarios, trust is raised in different connections: trust and confidence, lack of trust (from loss of control, unwillingness to provide some data, contextual misunderstandings) and honesty.
- **Loss of control** – This is one of the main issues in the dark scenarios and stems from different factors, for instance, when there is a lack of trust on the part of the citizen/consumer in the AmI infrastructure and its components. It can also emerge when the complexity level of AmI devices or services is too high and consequently does not enable users to get what they want. Strategies should be defined in order to compensate for the complexity and to weaken this feeling of loss of control.
- **Dependency** – This issue emerges directly from the usage of a technology by the user and the prospects (benefits and alternative solutions) for the technology. The scenarios mainly highlight its social impacts. Several situations are described, such as dependence on personalised filtering, on seamless and ubiquitous communications, on AmI systems (e.g., health monitoring and traffic management systems) and users' feeling of dependence and frustration when the technology does not work as expected.
- **Exclusion** (vs inclusion) – Exclusion may be voluntary, for instance, when a user switches off, but usually it is outside people's own will. The scenarios acknowledge that equal rights and opportunities for all need to be built into the design of new technologies since they are not achieved automatically. Exclusion can also be the result of lack of interoperability, denial of service, inadequate profiling and data mismatches.
- **Victimisation** – Citizens have a democratic right not to be treated as criminals (unless they are criminals, of course), otherwise, they will be unfairly victimised. The scenarios illustrate victimisation as an AmI impact by describing a disproportionate reaction based on unfounded suspicions and emphasise the difficulty in being able to act anonymously (anonymity is regarded as suspicious behaviour) and without being subject to anonymity profiling.
- **Surveillance** – Every citizen/consumer leaves electronic traces as the price of participation in the ambient intelligence society. These traces enable new and more comprehensive surveillance of our physical movements, use of electronic services and communication behaviour. These traces will make it possible to construct very sophisticated personal profiles and activity patterns. Although the justification for installing surveillance systems has a strong public interest dimension, i.e., for the safety and security of society, surveillance raises ethical, privacy and data protection issues. There is a clear need to delineate and define the boundaries between the private and public spheres.
- **Identity theft** – Without appropriate security, the AmI environment may provide malicious persons many opportunities to steal identity information and to use it for criminal purposes. The scenarios offer a picture of identity theft in AmI space and a new kind of crime, which is data laundering.
- **Malicious attacks** – Every new technology is plagued by known and/or unknown weaknesses, which threaten to serve as the backdoor for malicious

attackers. Some possible consequences and impacts are considered in the scenarios.

- **Digital divide** – AmI technology has the potential (because of its foreseen user friendliness and intuitive aspects) to bridge some aspects of the current digital divide but this same technology could also widen other aspects with regard to unequal access and use.
- **Spamming** – This encompasses several issues such as profiling, disclosure of personal data and malicious attacks.

In addition to the scenarios, this book presents an analytical approach we devised for both constructing and deconstructing the dark scenarios, but this approach, this methodological structure, could also be applied to many other technology-oriented scenarios. Our structured approach consists of several elements: the context describes the scenario situation (its purpose, a very brief resume), the technologies referenced in the scenario, the applications, the drivers (what factors impel the scenario), the issues raised, including a legal analysis of the issues, and our conclusions.

In addition to our scenario analysis *structure*, the book describes the *process* we followed to construct the scenarios. The process is depicted in Fig. 1.

Essentially, as shown in Fig. 1, we made an extensive review of existing AmI-related projects and studies, with particular reference to the scenarios. We held an experts workshop to discuss the most important threats and vulnerabilities posed by AmI. At an internal workshop, we brainstormed until we agreed the rough outlines of four contrasting scenarios. We then developed these outlines into scenario stories or scripts, and did a "technology check" (are the technologies referenced in the scenarios probable?) and a "reality check" (are there press reports of events similar to those mentioned in the scenarios?). Each of the partners reviewed all of

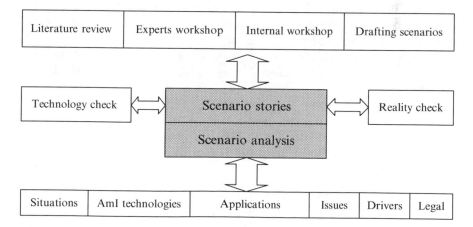

**Fig. 1** The process of constructing the four dark scenarios

the scenarios in order to eliminate doubtful points, unnecessary wordage, irrelevancies, etc., and to sharpen them to illustrate the points we wanted to emphasise. Once the scenarios were "stable", we performed our analysis of them (following the structured approach as described above), the last part of which was the legal analysis, which was able to consider not only the scenarios, but also the analyses.

In addition to submitting our scenarios and analyses to the Commission, we presented the scenarios at a second workshop in order to benefit from the comments of other experts.

The scenarios and their analyses are followed by a chapter on threats and vulnerabilities and a chapter on safeguards, before arriving at the final chapter which contains our recommendations and conclusions, specifically addressed to the European Commission, Member States, industry, academia, civil society organisations and individuals. The main recommendations are these:

1. The European Commission and Member States, perhaps under the auspices of the European Network and Information Security Agency (ENISA), should initiate a formalised risk assessment/risk management process with regard to the risks posed by AmI to security and privacy. The assessment and decision-making process should be open, transparent and inclusive. Stakeholder groups should be identified and contacted and encouraged to take part in the process. Individuals should also be given an opportunity to express their views.
2. The Commission and Member States should invest in an awareness campaign specifically focused on AmI, the purpose of which would be to explain to all stakeholders, including the public, that AmI is on its way, that it offers great benefits, but also poses certain security and privacy challenges.
3. The Commission and Member States should review and address the inadequacies and lacunae in the existing legal and regulatory framework with respect to AmI.
4. Legal instruments should not prohibit new technological developments (even if it were possible to do so), but should "channel" them (such as by data protection and security measures). Focusing on concrete technologies rather than trying to produce general solutions seems to be more appropriate for AmI, an environment that adapts and responds to changes in context, and in which privacy and other legal issues are also context-dependent.
5. The Commission and Member States should be proactive in the development of a more comprehensive international co-operation framework that would take AmI technologies and capabilities into account as a matter of urgency.
6. The European Commission should ensure that projects that it funds take questions of privacy, security and trust into account. It should require project proposals to specifically speculate what privacy or security impacts might arise from their projects and what measures could be taken to address those. Member States should adopt a similar approach.

Sooner or later, we will live in an ambient intelligence type of world. For ambient intelligence to be a success story, in human terms, according to democratic principles, and not to be an Orwellian world, all stakeholders must be cognisant of the threats and vulnerabilities and work together to ensure that adequate safeguards exist.

Certainly, industry should become more active in creating applications that are secure and privacy enhancing since this is the major way to create consumer trust and make ambient intelligence fruitful to *all* participants. Industry should not view privacy, security, identity, trust and inclusion issues as regulatory barriers to be overcome. Rather, they should regard such measures as necessary, justified and, in the end, crucial to ensuring that their fellow citizens will use ambient intelligence technologies and services. In the meantime, we encourage all stakeholders to be vigilant.

# Contents

# Chapter 1
# Introduction

## 1.1 From ubiquitous computing to ambient intelligence

The brave new world of ambient intelligence is almost upon us. Ambient intelligence is the phrase coined to describe a world in which "intelligence" is embedded in virtually everything around us. It has been called an Internet of things, where radio frequency identification (RFID) tags are attached to all products. It is a world of smart dust with networked sensors and actuators so small as to be virtually invisible, where the clothes you wear, the paint on your walls, the carpets on your floor, and the paper money in your pocket have a computer communications capability. It is a 4G world where today's mobile phone is transformed into a terminal capable of receiving television, accessing the Internet, downloading music, reading RFIDs, taking pictures, enabling interactive video telephony, and much more. It is a world of convergence, where heterogeneous devices are able to communicate seamlessly across today's disparate networks, a world of machine learning and intelligent software, where computers monitor our activities, routines and behaviours to predict what we will do or want next. In the brave new world of ambient intelligence, we will never have to worry about losing track of our children because they will have a location device implanted under the skin or, if they are squeamish about that, then at least they will have one in their wristwatch.

Different descriptors have been used to refer to this brave new world. In Europe, we use ambient intelligence (AmI), a term adopted by the European Commission. In America, its equivalent is ubiquitous or pervasive computing. In Japan, they use ubiquitous networking. Some have referred to the disappearing computer or invisible computing, but essentially all these terms mean much the same thing: Researchers in Europe, the United States and Japan are all exploring and developing similar technologies and dealing with similar issues.

In the European vision of ambient intelligence, the emphasis is on greater user friendliness, more efficient services support, user empowerment and support for human interactions. People are surrounded by easy-to-use interfaces that are embedded in all kinds of objects and by an everyday environment that is capable of recognising and responding to individuals in a seamless, unobtrusive and invisible way.

D. Wright et al. (eds.), *Safeguards in a World of Ambient Intelligence*.
© Springer 2010

This future world was first described in 1991 by Mark Weiser, chief scientist at the Xerox Palo Alto Research Center (PARC) in California, when he published a paper in *Scientific American* entitled "The computer for the 21st century". In it, he introduced his vision of a third generation of computing systems to a mass readership. Essentially, the vision described the historical transition from the large mainframe computers of the 1960s and 1970s to the standalone desktop personal computer (PC) of the 1980s and 1990s, and finally towards the networked computing appliance of the future. He presented third-generation computing as an integrated system of advanced computing devices, intelligent interface design, and anytime, anywhere data communications.[1]

Weiser used the term "ubiquitous computing" to describe this third wave of computing systems, which marked the initial articulation of a vision of a future information society. What is most significant about Weiser's vision is that while it pre-dated the mass diffusion of the Internet by a few years, it clearly embodies the idea of pervasive networked computers, assuming all kinds of shapes and located in all kinds of unconventional settings. Essential to the vision is networking, for without the ability of these computing devices to communicate with one another, the functionality of such a system would be extremely limited. In 1993, Weiser stated that the next-generation computing environment would be one "in which each person is continually interacting with hundreds of nearby wirelessly connected computers".[2] At the time, such forms of wireless networking were still in their infancy, but today with wireless LAN, WiMAX and Bluetooth, the possibilities for such dense local area networks are entering the realm of commercial reality.

While researchers in the United States were working on the vision of ubiquitous computing, the European Union began promoting a similar vision for its research and development agenda. Ambient intelligence has a lot in common with Weiser's ubiquitous computing vision, while perhaps giving more emphasis to human-centred computing and to the convergence of innovations in three key technologies: ubiquitous computing, user interface design and ubiquitous communication.[3]

In May 2000, the Information Society Technologies Advisory Group (ISTAG) commissioned the creation of four scenarios "to provide food for thought about longer-term developments in Information and Communication Technologies", with the intent of exploring the social and technical implications of ambient intelligence. Among other things, the scenarios suggested a set of "critical socio-political factors" that were considered crucial for the development of ambient intelligence, including the issue of security and trust. ISTAG said that "a key aspect is management of privacy: more open systems tend to lower privacy levels [where] technological developments are outpacing

---

[1] Weiser, M., "The Computer for the 21st century", *Scientific American* 265, No. 3, 1991, pp. 94–104.

[2] Weiser, M., "Some Computer Science Issues in Ubiquitous Computing", *Communications of the ACM* 36, No. 7, 1993, pp. 75–85.

[3] For an overview, see Punie, Y., "The future of Ambient Intelligence in Europe: The need for more Everyday Life", *Communications and Strategies* 57, 2005, pp. 141–165.

regulatory adjustments".[4] The scenarios developed for and assessed in the ISTAG report were regarded as a first step towards the creation of a research agenda in the European Union that would contribute to the development of "trust and confidence enabling tools" for the management of privacy within an ambient intelligence context. The ISTAG vision became a major focus of the "Disappearing Computers" component of the EC's Fifth Framework Programme and provided a point of departure for structuring IST research under the Sixth Framework Programme.

The Japanese have adopted the term "ubiquitous network society" to describe a vision that in many respects is being transformed into concrete action plans. They have put in place an initiative under the label "u-Japan Strategy" to replace the previous "e-Japan" policy framework.[5] Japan has been addressing a range of issues similar to those that underpin the European Union's ambient intelligence research programme.[6]

While IBM is credited with coining the term "pervasive computing" to refer to a shift in corporate computing systems, Philips chose the term "ambient intelligence" to describe its new paradigm for home computing and entertainment. One of the first prototypes developed by Philips is a system that supports "smart home" applications based on the collection and use of personal information that enables user preferences and creates user profiles for customising entertainment and other applications.[7]

Whereas companies such as Philips are engaged in an ambitious vision that involves the private domain within the walls of the home, more mundane scenarios marking an important step towards the ubiquitous network society are being implemented today, often crossing into public space. One example is the growing use of RFID tags (radio frequency identification tags) to enable supply chain and inventory management in the private and public sectors.[8] Representing an early entry point into pervasively networked environments, these tags contain radio-enabled microchips, attached to objects, which can be read out wirelessly. The growing use

---

[4] IST Advisory Group, K. Ducatel, M. Bogdanowicz, et al., *Scenarios for Ambient Intelligence in 2010*, EUR 19763 EN, EC-JRC, Institute for Prospective Technological Studies (IPTS), Seville, 2001. http://www.cordis.lu/ist/istag-reports.html

[5] Murakami, T., "Establishing the Ubiquitous Network Environment in Japan: From e-Japan to U-Japan", NRI Paper 66, Nomura Research Institute, Tokyo, 2003. http://www.nri.co.jp/english/opinion/papers/2003/pdf/np200366.pdf

[6] See, for example, (MPHPT) *Information and Communications in Japan: Building a Ubiquitous Network Society that Spreads Throughout the World*, White Paper, Ministry of Public Management Home Affairs Posts and Telecommunications of Japan, Economic Research Office General Policy Division, Tokyo, 2004. http://www.johotsusintokei.soumu.go.jp/whitepaper/eng/WP2004/2004-index.html

[7] Aarts, E., and S. Marzano (eds.), *The New Everyday: Views on Ambient Intelligence*, Uitgeverij 010 Publishers, Rotterdam, 2003.

[8] See Weis, S.A., S.E. Sarma, R.L. Rivest and D.W. Engels, "Security and Privacy Aspects of Low-Cost Radio Frequency Identification Systems", in D. Hutter, G. Müller et al. (eds.), *Security in Pervasive Computing*, First International Conference, Boppard, Germany, March 12–14, 2003, Springer (Lecture notes in computer science, 2802), Berlin and New York, 2004, pp. 201–212; Oertel, B., M. Wölk, L.M. Hilty et al., *Risiken und Chancen des Einsatzes von RFID-Systemen: Trends und Entwicklungen in Technologien, Anwendungen und Sicherheit*, SecuMedia, Ingelheim, 2004.

of RFID for supply chain management, access control and other applications indicates that the construction of the ambient intelligence (AmI) environment has already begun. The dramatic reduction in the cost of computing and communications and the rise of wireless broadband communications will facilitate the exchange of information among these early AmI devices and contribute to laying the foundations for the scenarios envisaged for the future. Above all, the networking of the proliferating devices in recent years demonstrates that the future, despite the still remaining formidable technological challenges, is not so far off.

While the technologists have been at work, goaded on by new and "old" high-technology industries, concerns relating to identity, privacy, security, trust, social inclusion and other issues are beginning to get more airtime, too. The fears conjured up by the impact of an Orwellian Big Brother only complicate the apparent lack of trust, which hinders the full flowering of the Internet for e-commerce, e-government, e-health and much else. In November 2003, some 30 privacy advocacy groups joined together to produce a position paper calling for a halt to the deployment of radio frequency identification tags (RFIDs) until certain public policy issues are resolved.[9] Their concerns reflected a few of the more numerous and even more complex issues raised by ISTAG in its June 2002 position paper entitled "Trust, dependability, security and privacy for IST in FP6".[10]

## 1.2    Challenges from the deployment of ambient intelligence

Ambient intelligence should be seen as an emerging property (and not as a set of specific requirements) requiring a proper balance of a complex diversity of interests and values related to protection of identity, protection against intrusions by public and private actors, protection of the individual sphere (i.e., security), trust, protection against discrimination, access to information, free speech and so on. Such a balanced approach should take into account the different social, economic, legal and technological dimensions, but also has to reflect many possible relevant perceptions and definitions of AmI. It also needs to embrace broader concerns such as, for example:

• The increasing concern for security after 11 September 2001
• Technological innovations, their dissemination and consequences, only some of which can be foreseen (the invisibility of networked "intelligent" devices, ubiquity of computer communications, anonymity and privacy impacts, user friendliness, price, accessibility, etc.)

---

[9] See, for instance, Albrecht, K., "Supermarket Cards: The Tip of the Retail Surveillance Iceberg", *Denver University Law Review*, No. 79, 2002, pp. 534–539, 558–565.

[10] IST Advisory Group, *Trust, dependability, security and privacy for IST in FP6*, Office for Official Publications of the European Communities, Luxembourg, 2002. http://www.cordis.lu/ist/istag-reports.html

- The general tendency towards privatisation of governance (the weakening of public power to control and steer the evolutions as a result of the increasing power of private actors both at local and global level).

Apart from the security concerns, AmI will directly affect our lives in many ways. Every one of us goes through life playing several different roles, which in essence could be reduced to three main ones – that of the private individual, the professional and the public participant.

Private individuals are mindful of their pursuits and/or responsibilities as parents or members of a family. They also have personal requirements in terms of entertainment, leisure and other activities such as shopping and may have special concerns in terms of health and/or education. According to the promoters of AmI, living in a world of ambient intelligence will greatly reduce the demands on their time to pursue any of these things and greatly increase the richness of daily experience.

Similarly, the professional's ability to communicate with his or her peers, either in the same office or on the other side of the world, to have an infinite world of information and intelligence at his or her fingertips to facilitate decision-making, will greatly expand with ambient intelligence.

In their public roles, citizens will participate in social and political activities, perhaps lobbying for or supporting this or that cause. In each of these roles, the citizen's level of trust and confidence in supporting technology and in those with whom he or she might be in contact will vary.

Citizens' demands for privacy, security, trust (or confidentiality) will also vary according to the situation, and the situations may be very fluid, changing many times in the course of a day. At times, they may be unaware of the computing, monitoring and networking going on around them. Nevertheless, they must be alert to the possibility of social engineering and threats to their space, to their digital well-being. Individuals will need verifiable assurances that they can perform their various roles according to the level of privacy, security, trust, confidentiality and anonymity that they dictate. To understand the dimensions of this new world of ambient intelligence, to understand how it impacts them, what their rights and responsibilities are, how they can benefit from it, how they can control it, is one of the objectives of this book.

Before ambient intelligence technologies do indeed become ubiquitous, our political decision-makers – indeed all stakeholders, including the public – need to consider policy options based on research addressing:

- Issues such as privacy, anonymity, manipulation and control, intellectual property rights, human identity, discrimination and environmental concerns
- New societal responsibilities and the ethics of digital behaviour
- Protection of rights for all citizens in all their roles (private and professional) in the Information Society
- Safeguards and privacy-enhancing mechanisms to ensure user control, user acceptance and enforceability of policy in an accessible manner
- Equal rights and opportunities of accessibility to the Information Society and its ambient intelligence environment.

## 1.3   Challenges from ambient intelligence for EU policy-making

The definition of, and provision for, safeguards can be seen as critical for the rapid deployment and the further development of ambient intelligence in Europe. Instead of making people adapt to technology, we have to design technologies for people.

Taking the human factor into account is crucial in the construction of safeguards in a world of ambient intelligence. The success of ambient intelligence will depend on how secure its use can be made, how privacy and other rights of individuals can be protected and, ultimately, how individuals can come to trust the intelligent world which surrounds them and through which they move.

In a networked world, best symbolised by the Internet, in which communications and computing capabilities know no borders, international co-operation is a must if the privacy and rights of individuals are to be protected. Many risks and vulnerabilities to Europeans emanate beyond our borders, hence social and policy options must include a global outlook. The Cybercrime Convention was an important step in this direction since its 34 signatories include more than just the Union's Member States. In addition, representatives from the European Commission, Member States and European industry participate in many standards-setting bodies concerned with cyber security and with a nominally global outlook. Nevertheless, more initiatives are needed in that direction.

There is a clear need to consider ambient intelligence technologies and developments in the context of how the rights of individuals can best be protected and to formulate adequate policy options. Even those in scientific and technical projects should take on board such considerations. It is already obvious that realising the vision of ambient intelligence will require more than just technology and, as has happened throughout history, especially in the last decade or so, significant technological advances almost always raise policy issues.

This book examines the adequacy of the existing policy and regulatory framework in the context of the emerging technologies, capabilities and properties that are embedded in ambient intelligence.

While the world of ambient intelligence will undoubtedly bring many benefits, trust and security should be designed into this world rather than inserted as an afterthought into an already constructed world of smart spaces. Already it may not be possible to achieve this goal, at least not completely, because there are already islands of ambient intelligence and, in any event, the notion of "absolute security" is not feasible. AmI networks, like existing networks such as the Internet, are such that they evolve as new software and many different people and entities add technologies. Thus, building trust and security into networks inevitably involves an effort of trying to create trustworthy systems from untrustworthy components. The success of this brave new world will depend on its acceptability by citizens and on the measures taken to address concerns about further encroachments upon their privacy, safety and security.

What is new in AmI is that devices with embedded intelligence are being networked and their numbers are set to increase by orders of magnitude. That has alarmed major privacy advocacy groups who, as briefly mentioned above, have called for a halt in the use of RFIDs until key issues are resolved. Meanwhile, companies such as Wal-Mart in the United States, the Metro Group in Germany, Tesco in the United Kingdom and others are proceeding with their plans for a massive increase in the use of RFIDs, even before some standards issues have been resolved.

Similarly, location aware services have prompted concerns, even though they also offer many benefits. The increasing use of GPS in mobile phones in the United States in conjunction with services such as uLocate and Wherify Wireless enables those with mobile phones to be tracked wherever they go. While helping parents to know where their children are, the risks of unwanted and unwarranted surveillance have been highlighted by privacy advocates and others. In an AmI world, embedded intelligence will be able to detect our whereabouts at all times. But who should have access to such data and under what circumstances? Should businesses be able to bombard us with individualised advertising when they detect we are near one of their shops? Should governmental security services be able to track our movements (or only those of suspected terrorists)? These and similar examples highlight the need for urgent research in regard to the emerging world of ambient intelligence and, in particular, matters of privacy, security, trust, identity and so on.

The lack of consumer trust is often cited as the reason why e-commerce (and e-health and e-government) via the Internet have yet to realise their full potential. Attacks via the Internet are no longer confined to big name targets such as the military or credit card companies. These days, everyone and anyone's personal computers are being attacked or used as the staging platform for distributed denial of service attacks. Attacks are not only becoming more numerous, they are becoming much more sophisticated. The software security firm Symantec observed that, in July 2001, the Code Red worm spread to 250,000 systems within 6 hours and the worldwide economic impact was estimated to be US$2.62 billion. Code Red's spread was fast enough to foil immediate human intervention and the ramifications were huge. But now, already we can see the emergence of attackers who use advanced scanning techniques to infect vulnerable servers on the Internet in a matter of minutes or even seconds.[11] Such threats undermine trust and confidence.

Security must be regarded as an enabler for the development of new markets, not an inhibitor. As an example of where security contributes to market development, one need look no further than the cars that we drive or the homes in which we live. Automobile manufacturers promote their products' various security features in marketing campaigns. Similarly, the insurance premiums we pay on our homes are diminished if we have installed security devices. In electronic commerce, some forms of business activities require or are facilitated by a particular level of trustworthiness (i.e., security is an enabler). The availability of secure

---

[11] Schwarz, J., Statement of John Schwarz, President, Symantec Corporation on Worms, Viruses and Securing Our Nation's Computers, House Government Reform Subcommittee on Technology, Information Policy, Intergovernmental Relations and the Census, Washington, DC, 2003. http://reform.house.gov/UploadedFiles/Schwarz-v5.pdf

socket layer (SSL) encryption for Web traffic has given comfort to some consumers about sending their credit card details across the Internet.

ISTAG observed that "Security policies in this [AmI] environment must evolve, adapting in accordance with our experiences. Such approaches may be very different from present approaches to computational security policies, but may better embody our approaches to real-world person-to-person trust policies. This is the main new feature of the new paradigm for security in AmI Space."[12] In the future AmI world, new approaches to security, trust, privacy, etc., will be required and it is urgent that such new approaches be considered before AmI becomes a reality, otherwise we, as a society, will be faced with a future akin to trying to squeeze toothpaste back into the tube. It will be difficult to embed retroactively new security and trust paradigms in AmI when those technologies have been deployed. The early definition of safeguards can contribute to the development of such new approaches.

## 1.4   The challenges of this book

In this book, we provide a state-of-the-art overview of the key social, legal, economic, technological and ethical implications with regard to identity, privacy and security of ambient intelligence.

Especially by means of four dark scenarios and the analysis of those scenarios, we aim to identify some of the key threats and vulnerabilities facing us all in the deployment of AmI technologies. We examine the adequacy of the existing legal and regulatory framework, identify lacunae and propose the adoption of technological, socio-economic and legal safeguards to minimise the identified threats and vulnerabilities.

We do not believe it is possible to completely eliminate the risks, but even so implementing safeguards is a matter of prudence. We do not seek to exaggerate the threats and vulnerabilities, nor do we seek to characterise ambient intelligence as dangerous or insidious to society. We are convinced of the benefits of ambient intelligence and convinced too that Europe must go "full steam ahead" in developing the necessary technologies and architectures in order to remain competitive against our rivals in the United States, Japan, Korea and elsewhere. (At the same time, of course, there is considerable merit in collaborating with them, especially in ensuring an international legal regime that protects the individual citizen.)

Thus, this book has a difficult task in raising awareness about threats and vulnerabilities and in promoting safeguards while not undermining the efforts to deploy AmI.

It is perhaps useful to point out here that the word "security" used in this book has two, somewhat different meanings. We trust that the context makes clear in which sense the word is being used. In some instances, security refers to the efforts made to protect individuals, technologies and networks against malicious attacks

---

[12] ISTAG, 2002, p. 11.

and vulnerabilities. In other instances, security may be seen as an excuse to violate or erode the rights and liberties of the individual in order to protect society against terrorists and criminals. We could envisage certain politicians, law enforcement authorities and intelligence agencies as saying "We need to know everything about you and to keep track of what you are doing, saying and thinking at all times in order to protect you. If you have nothing to hide or fear, you should have no objection." While such an articulation might be a bit exaggerated, we fear that it nevertheless reflects a reality (a paranoia) in our society today.

Hence, an issue that runs throughout this book is the trade-off or balance between security and privacy, between the individual and society. There are no simple solutions to striking the right balance, just as there are no simple solutions to making sure that AmI benefits citizens and consumers as well as industry and government. Unfortunately, many safeguards are necessary because there are many threats and vulnerabilities, some of which are known today, others of which will only emerge in the years to come. There is no alternative to addressing each of them one by one, step by step. We need to see the big picture as well as the details (of ambient intelligence). That's the main challenge of this book: to show the reader what we see, to identify some of the principal threats and vulnerabilities and enlist the reader's collaboration in implementing the necessary safeguards.

Not everyone uses the Internet, but even so, it is patently obvious that the Internet has transformed our economy and society. Ambient intelligence will have a transformative impact many times greater. Although AmI is more than just an "Internet of things", such a characterisation gives a good indication of just how transformative AmI will be. When every product is embedded with intelligence, everyone must (or should) be involved in safeguarding his or her privacy, identity, trust, security and inclusiveness in a world of ambient intelligence.

# Chapter 2
# The brave new world of ambient intelligence

This chapter provides an overview of ambient intelligence in order to set the stage for the subsequent identification and discussion of threats, vulnerabilities and safeguards.

In this chapter, we provide a somewhat high-level description of the key technologies that are crucial to the development and deployment of ambient intelligence.

The development and deployment of AmI are being propelled by certain visions of the future, which we reference in this chapter. For the most part, the development and deployment are taking place in a rather structured context composed of visions, scenarios, roadmaps, strategic research agendas, platforms and projects. We highlight the most important of these.

## 2.1 Enabling technologies

In this section, we present the most frequently mentioned technologies that enable AmI services together with a critical examination of associated threats posed by and vulnerabilities in such technologies.

### 2.1.1 Ubiquitous computing

A common vision of ubiquitous computing is that computers will be everywhere, invisibly integrated into everyday life and providing proactive support to people in their diverse activities.[1] The main components of this vision are:

- Highly reliable hardware with long-lasting power supplies and of different sizes, from smart dust to huge public screens

---

[1] "In an AmI world, devices operate collectively using information and intelligence that is hidden in the network connecting the devices." Aarts, E.H.L., J.L. Encarnação (eds.), *True Visions: The Emergence of Ambient Intelligence*, Springer, Berlin, Heidelberg, 2006, p. 1.

D. Wright et al. (eds.), *Safeguards in a World of Ambient Intelligence.*
© Springer 2010

- Pervasive wireless communications between computers
- Intuitive interfaces which everybody can easily use, e.g., a natural speech interface
- Embedded intelligence capable of controlling interfaces and communications, self-configuring and self-repairing, reasoning about people and the world around us and doing all this unobtrusively.

Inevitably, this vision implies enormously increased autonomy of computers, both in the sense that computers will need less (direct) user input than today and in the sense that users should not care about what is going on inside computers. From the privacy point of view, hardware as such is of less interest than other components of the vision. The main privacy threats presented by hardware are: first, the smaller intelligent devices become, the harder it is for people to even notice them, let alone remember that they are observing us.

Second, the smaller smart personal devices are, the easier it is to lose (or steal) them. It is easier to steal a mobile phone than a laptop computer, and the growing amount of data stored in small phones makes them increasingly valuable. In the near future, even toys will store a lot of information about their owners, and toys can be lost or stolen just as easily as phones.

Ubiquitous computing systems cannot function properly without collecting data about the users, and this accumulation of personal information is already threatening privacy. However, the main privacy threat arises from the possibility of linking data about the user accumulated in and/or from different parts of the system. To minimise this danger, users' identities should be hidden as much as possible, and interactions with different subsystems should happen under pseudonyms or anonymously.

Essentially, threats arising from the pervasiveness of ubiquitous computing depend on several things:

- What kind of information about people is stored
- What kind of information is transmitted between system components
- What kind of information is presented by the system to people
- How long-term usage of AmI and growing dependence on it affects humans.

All these issues need to be taken into account in future technology development, and safeguards should be built into enabling technology from the beginning rather than adding them later as an afterthought.

## 2.1.2   Ubiquitous communications

Almost all scenarios require ubiquitous communications, and it will be mainly wireless communications connecting literally everything: people (more precisely their personal devices), pets, objects (cameras in parking lots, food products, clothes, home appliances, cars, passports, wallets and so on endlessly) and organisations (e.g., hospital, city administration, bank and border control system). Moreover, wireless connections will be virtually available everywhere and maintained seamlessly on the move with sufficient bandwidth to provide fast access to large quantities of data and fine-resolution images and videos. A high density of communicating nodes will not be a problem.

This vision requires interoperability between all kinds of short-range and long-range wireless and wired networks (body area networks, personal area networks, virtual home environment, ad hoc, cellular, sensor, satellite networks, etc.) and their convergence into all-IP all over the world.[2] Ubiquitous communications present challenging problems for privacy protection.

Privacy can be protected by:

- Reducing the amount of transmitted personal data (embedded intelligence will have the task to process as much personal data as possible in the personal device and to decide which data to transmit).
- Encrypting the transmitted data.
- Designing the system in such a way that all parts are secure. Security expert Bruce Schneier has stated that cryptography is not magic security dust and that "Security is not a product, but a process." To prove his point, he has cited impressive examples of broken cryptographic algorithms.[3]

At least the first two approaches are already widely accepted as required functionalities, and researchers are working actively on their implementation. However, this is protection at the application level, but protection should start from the lowest network levels such as communication protocols, and current communication protocols are rather more concerned with efficiency of data delivery than with privacy protection. Moreover, privacy and security are sometimes contradictory requirements. For example, the report of the Wireless Security Center of Excellence[4] recommended that security of GPRS networks (used currently for Internet access by mobile phones) be strengthened by storing device logs, which is a risk for privacy.

Communications between people and organisations fall into two major categories: first, communications that require the ability to link data to the user identity; second, communications that do not require such linkage. Communications of the first type might require linkage for different reasons, such as billing the right person. Other examples can be of an employee who wants to confirm that his superior set a given task. Or if a person sells something via the Web but does not deliver the goods after receiving a payment, there should be means to find this person. Thus, in communications of the first type, the main goal is to hide the user's identity from everybody except authorised persons, and currently in many aspects, it is trusted to operators and service providers.

In communications of the second type, the main goal is to hide the user's identity completely. For example, if a person buys something and pays immediately, or

---

[2] Alahuhta, P., M. Jurvansuu and H. Pentikäinen, "Roadmap for network technologies and service", *Tekes Technology Review* 162/2004, Tekes, Helsinki, 2004.

[3] Schneier, B., "Risks of Relying on Cryptography", in *Communications of the ACM* 42, No. 10, 1999, p. 144.

[4] Whitehouse, O., *GPRS Wireless Security: Not Ready for Prime Time*, Research report, Stake, Boston, MA, 2002. http://www.atstake.com/research/reports/acrobat/atstake_gprs_security.pdf

simply surfs the Web having paid in advance, this does not present a danger to anybody. Unfortunately, because unique identifiers are used in communication protocols (IP addresses, MAC addresses, Bluetooth physical device ID, UIDs of RFID tags, IMEI code of mobile phones), tracking the communication links between devices is relatively easy, and this raises a question about whether pseudonymity and anonymity are achievable at all. In the case of mobile phones, unique identifiers allow tracking of personal location not only by GSM cell, but also by point of IP access and Bluetooth communication.

Communications between objects also commonly features in AmI visions. Currently, the main enabling technology is RFID tags embedded into objects. RFID tags do not need batteries and are small enough to be embedded into objects of all kinds, making computing truly ubiquitous. Since the primary purpose of RFID technology is inexpensive and automated identification, current RFID communication protocols present very high threats to privacy. In low-cost tags (those most likely to be embedded into personal belongings), communication between reader and tag is unprotected, that is, tags send their UIDs without further security verification when they are powered from a reader.[5] Thus, tracking a person by reading the UID of his glasses, keys or wallet becomes possible. Second, even those high-end ISO 14443 tags that provide access control to the memory (currently, ISO 14443 is used in Malaysian second-generation e-passports[6]) still use UIDs in collision avoidance protocols. Thus, if a passport's UID was once associated with a user's identity (e.g., the user was recognised by his facial features), then the next time the user shows the passport, he will be recognised by the passport's UID without there being a need to read the protected memory of an RFID tag.

Ubiquitous communication as an enabling technology requires not only universal coverage with high bandwidth, scalability for high density of communicating nodes and seamless connections between different networks, but also privacy-preserving mechanisms at all communication layers.

## 2.1.3   User-friendly interfaces

AmI scenarios describe highly advanced user-friendly interfaces, the most popular of which are speech interfaces capable of understanding a person's natural speech (i.e., users are not restricted to a set of commands and can use any words and phrases when talking to an AmI system) and video interfaces capable of understanding and presentation of three-dimensional pictures, including tracking of users' movements. There might be many people moving and talking to an AmI

[5] Knospe, H., and H. Pohl, "RFID Security", in *Information Security Technical Report* 9, No. 4, 2004, S. 30–41.

[6] Juels, A., D. Molnar and D. Wagner, "Security and Privacy Issues in E-passports", ePrint Archive Cryptology Report 2005/095. http://eprint.iacr.org/

system; the system should be capable of understanding who has done or said something. Recognition of users' emotions by voice processing, image processing or physiological measurements is also often mentioned in existing AmI scenarios. Privacy threats here depend on the context in which the interface is used, on what the system is doing with the user data and whether the interface is to a public or personal device.

Interaction with large public screens is often mentioned in scenarios as a user convenience. Public screens present privacy threats because users do not have any control over the logging of their interactions with a public device. Thus, public interfaces should have built-in capabilities to hide user interactions from everybody but authorised persons.

## 2.1.4 *Embedded intelligence*

An incomplete list of embedded intelligence functions[7] includes context recognition, data mining, pattern recognition, decision making, information fusion, personalisation, adaptivity, ontologies and security.

The term "embedded intelligence" denotes the system's capabilities to infer the user's context from whatever input is available and to reason about how to use data about the inferred context: in proactive suggestions to the user or in acting autonomously on the user's behalf. Embedded intelligence needs to learn about the user's personality from observations of the user's behaviour, and to store the acquired data for future use. Storage of personal data presents privacy risks in cases when these data can be accessed, either when the device is with the owner or not (it could be lost or stolen). Privacy protection in this case is closely linked to security, but security alone is not sufficient to protect the user's privacy.

Since it is improbable that users will devote significant effort to control a flow of their personal data, it should be the task of embedded intelligence to select which privacy policy is appropriate in a particular context and to minimise storage and transmission of personal data. For example, of many possible data mining algorithms, the ones that store selected features should be preferred over those that store raw data. Fule has proposed that sensitive patterns in data mining be detected automatically and treated cautiously.[8]

Current security mechanisms are mainly concerned with protection of personal data during transmission (e.g., by encryption), from being intercepted when the device is with the owner (by not allowing execution of external untrusted code) and

---

[7] By "embedded intelligence", we mean that part of an ambient intelligence system which performs reasoning.

[8] Fule, P., and J.F. Roddick, "Detecting Privacy and Ethical Sensitivity in Data Mining Results" in V. Estivill-Castro (ed.), *Computer Science 2004*, Twenty-Seventh Australasian Computer Science Conference (ACSC2004), Dunedin, New Zealand, January 2004, Australian Computer Society (CRPIT, 26), 2004, pp. 159–166.

with protection of the personal device from being switched on by someone other than the owner (authentication by PIN codes, passwords and biometrics is currently done only when the user logs in). Apart from the fact that "password crackers can now break anything that you can reasonably expect a user to memorize",[9] these security measures are not user-friendly, which means that they are used more or less randomly. Indeed, how often does a user in practice enter a PIN code or touch a fingerprint sensor?

Personal devices are often lost or stolen in an "on" state (after the owner has logged on) when personal data are not protected. Thus, in addition to the need to improve existing security methods, new security mechanisms that perform continuous recognition of the owner should be developed, and personal data should be stored encrypted.

With the increased autonomy of computer devices of all kinds, the security of content becomes a major issue. One of the main tasks of embedded intelligence is personalisation, which to a great extent means filtering incoming information according to a user's personal preferences and capabilities. Since current security mechanisms are mainly directed against theft of personal data, however, they do not really check how trustworthy incoming data are. This allows manipulation of content received by the user. Another example of how acceptance of untrustworthy incoming data can cause harm is phishing. To prevent phishing, security mechanisms are needed to check the legitimacy of incoming data.

Embedded intelligence should also provide a user with the means to understand its functions, and to switch those functions off easily if the user dislikes something.

### 2.1.5 Sensors and actuators

The AmI world will be populated with positioning, biometric authentication, physiological and health condition sensors. The most popular position determination technology outdoors is satellite-based, such as that provided by the Global Positioning System. The most popular position determination technologies indoors are ultrasound-based, WLAN-based and RFID tag-based. Privacy threats in these technologies depend on where the position is actually calculated, in the personal device or in the infrastructure, and on use of unique identifiers of people or objects inside the system. Further development of positioning technology requires an increase in positioning precision and wider coverage (for example, currently, GPS does not work well in so-called urban canyons). Further development also requires applications that do not disclose users' locations to third parties, but this is the task of embedded intelligence.

Biometrics as an enabling technology is not mature yet. The main privacy concern in biometric applications is prevention of identity theft. One important

---

[9] Schneier, B., "Customers, Passwords, and Web Sites", in *IEEE Security and Privacy Magazine*, Vol. 2, No. 5, 2004, p. 88.

direction of development is "aliveness" detection – security against spoofing the sensor by artificial biometrics, such as fake fingerprints. Another important direction of development is unobtrusive identification, that is, identification which does not require an active effort on the part of the user and which can be performed continuously. Currently, unobtrusive biometrics (e.g., face, voice and gait recognition) are not reliable enough, while using reliable biometrics (e.g., fingerprint or iris recognition) is time consuming. Another important research problem is storage of biometric data in such a way that they cannot be stolen, for example, in the form of encrypted templates which would prevent restoration of raw data. Yet another problem is interoperability between different biometrics systems, which means standards are needed for biometric data storage and exchange.

Physiological sensors could be used for recognising user emotions, but they could easily violate privacy in the sense that people often hide their emotions behind neutral or fake facial expressions. Thus, revealing a person's true emotions even to a computer could be dangerous, since data protection is not perfect yet and would not be in the near future.

AmI sensors for evaluating health conditions will be tiny, very sophisticated (the "lab on a chip" capable of performing various physiological tests) and capable of continuous monitoring and detection of anomalies, including life-threatening ones such as heart attacks. Another group of sensors will be used for driving safety. Apart from precise positioning, these sensors detect obstacles, estimate road conditions, sliding and grip.

Actuators will function invisibly in the background, switching on and off diverse home and office appliances, health maintenance systems, transportation systems (e.g., taking care of driving safety) and access control systems, and there needs to be plenty of them, all reliable and invisible. They will have a power over people's lives when they give medicines or control cars. Personal identification sensors and health-related sensors and actuators are often envisioned as implants.

## 2.2  AmI visions

These and other AmI technologies are the subject of hundreds of projects and studies in Europe, the United States, Japan and elsewhere. We reviewed many of these (more than 100 projects and an even greater number of papers, articles, reports and studies on AmI) to see to what extent they have taken into account the issues of concern to us – i.e., privacy, identity, trust, security and the digital divide. In this section and those that follow, we summarise (really summarise) our review with a few examples categorised according to their visions, scenarios, roadmaps, research agendas, platforms and projects. The linkage between these has been nicely depicted in Fig. 2.1 in the Embedded Systems Roadmap.[10]

---

[10] See p. 4 of the Embedded Systems Roadmap at www.stw.nl/progress/ESroadmap/index.html

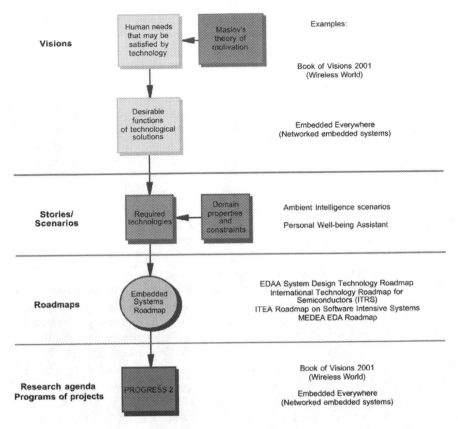

**Fig. 2.1** The linkage between visions, scenarios, roadmaps, research agendas, platforms and projects. (Reproduced with permission from Dr. Frank Karelse, STW/Progress.)

Many projects have visions of what they want to do or, more expansively, of the future world of ambient intelligence. However, most such visions are not elaborated to any great extent. Nevertheless, several important visions of AmI have been produced.

Perhaps the best-known vision document, the one most elaborated, is *The Book of Visions*, which provides a vision of our technological future, or at least our wireless technological future. It resulted from an initiative of several large European companies and Motorola who came together to form the Wireless World Research Forum (WWRF). *The Book of Visions* includes ambient intelligence within its scope. The first version of the Book appeared in 2001.[11] The vision was of a future 10–15 years away.

There is some interesting discussion in *The Book of Visions* about profiling users, especially in the context of personalisation of services, security and privacy.

---

[11] www.wireless-world-research.org/general_info/BoV2001-final.pdf. The most recent version of the *Book of Visions* was published in April 2006 by Wiley. http://www.wireless-world-research. org/general_information/book_of_visions.php

It observes that without access to user-related context data many mobile services would not exist and that the issue of incomplete context information (or profile data) must be solved.

ISTAG produced a vision of the AmI future in a September 2003 report entitled *Ambient Intelligence: from Vision to Reality*. In its vision, it saw "significant opportunities" for AmI in relation to:

- Modernising the European social model particularly in terms of: improving civil security; providing new leisure, learning and work opportunities within the networked home; facilitating community building and new social groupings; providing new forms of health care and social support; tackling environmental threats; supporting the democratic process and the delivery of public services.
- Improving Europe's economy in terms of: supporting new business processes; increasing the opportunities for teleworking in the networked home; enhancing mobility and improving all forms of transport; supporting new approaches to sustainable development.[12]

While ISTAG has a generally sunny outlook with regard to AmI, it does see at least one dark patch. It says the anticipated benefits of ambient intelligence may be numerous but the enabling technologies can also facilitate monitoring, surveillance, data searches and mining, as a result of which AmI deployment is likely to be of great concern to citizens, civil liberties groups, governments and industry. Addressing the balance between privacy and security will, it says, be a core challenge for the future.[13]

It's been said that the *Embedded Everywhere* report published by the National Academy of Sciences (NAS) is a vision document, but in fact it is explicitly a research agenda.[14] Nevertheless, as its title suggests, it does contain some visions of the future. For example, with networking sensors embedded everywhere, it foresees the day when we will have an Internet of things.[15]

The authors of the *Embedded Everywhere* opined that "Privacy may be at much greater risk than at any previous time in history." Alarming, at least for some, many people do not seem that bothered. They are quite willing, especially post 11 September 2001, to forego some of their right to privacy in exchange for better security. However, some of the same profiling and data mining technologies that

---

[12] IST Advisory Group, *Ambient Intelligence: From Vision to Reality*. For participation – in society and business, Office for Official Publications of the European Communities, Luxembourg, 2003, p. 9. http://www.cordis.lu/ist/istag-reports.html

[13] ISTAG 2003, pp. 11 et seq.

[14] Estrin, D. (ed.), *Embedded, Everywhere: A Research Agenda for Networked Systems of Embedded Computers*, National Academy Press, Washington, DC, 2001.

[15] The phrase "Internet of things" comes from an article with the same title by Chana R. Schoenberger in *Forbes* magazine, 18 March 2002. The author quotes Kevin Ashton, an executive at Procter & Gamble who heads the Auto ID Center at MIT: "We need an internet for things, a standardized way for computers to understand the real world." www.forbes.com/global/2002/0318/092.html

can be used to improve security can also be used for surveillance and to bombard people with unwanted advertising. Accordingly, the erosion of personal privacy, identity theft and other downsides of the brave new world we live in have inspired some ubiquitous computing projects and studies in the United States, just as they have in Europe.

Japan's vision of or strategy for a ubiquitous network society has been shaped by, especially, three documents (or rather sets of documents). The first are the NRI Papers produced by the Nomura Research Institute. The Ministry of Internal Affairs and Communications (MIC)[16] chose an NRI managing director, Teruyasu Murakami, to chair the policy roundtable that generated the December 2004 report on which Japan's current ubiquitous network society strategy is based. In addition to the NRI Papers and the MIC's own reports, the Mobile IT Forum produced a vision document, which is also a roadmap and a platform, all rolled into one, called the *Flying Carpet* report.

Nomura Research Institute (NRI) has published about a dozen papers on ubiquitous networking in Japan, including one entitled "Establishing the Ubiquitous Network Environment in Japan – from e-Japan to u-Japan", published in July 2003. In this paper, Teruyasu Murakami proposes a u-Japan strategy. Murakami distinguishes between the concept of ubiquitous computing, as coined by Mark Weiser, and his concept of ubiquitous networking. In the instance of the former, he concludes that physical computers are hidden in the background and people are not necessarily aware of their presence, while with ubiquitous networking, its fundamental basis is the idea of better person-to-person connecting (as well as person-to-object and object-to-object networking). Murakami distinguishes two phases in ubiquitous networking (I and II). In the first phase, the network is "highly vulnerable from the viewpoint of security". The routes for potential security breaches are many and diverse. Only after overcoming this vulnerability do we arrive at Ubiquitous Network II.

The Flying Carpet report[17] was produced by the Mobile IT Forum. The first version came out in 2001 and a second version in 2004. It visualises how future mobile communication systems (4G for fourth generation) will be used in social activities around 2010. As in Europe and the United States, mobile communications are envisaged as integral part of the ubiquitous network society. The report says 4G mobile systems will not only serve as media for communications, but also provide means for connecting users with home appliances and various systems via the home network, etc. In other words, the system itself is required to function as a highly advanced interface system. In a ubiquitous network environment, it says, any product or device may become an object of communications.[18]

---

[16] The Ministry of Public Management, Home Affairs, Posts and Telecommunications (MPHPT) changed its English name in September 2004. www.soumu.go.jp/english/index.html

[17] Kato, U., T. Hayashi, N. Umeda et al. (eds.), *Flying Carpet: Towards the 4th Generation Mobile Communications Systems*, Version 2.00, 4th Generation Mobile Communications Committee, 2004. Flying Carpet was chosen for the report's name because the authors thought "with its magical power to fly the sky, we might be able to foresee our new lives and the underlying mobile technologies a decade from now." See www.mitf.org/public_e/archives/index.html

[18] Kato et al., p. 60.

The Japanese government has embraced the notion of ubiquitous networking, the Japanese buzz phrase equivalent to ambient intelligence, and has set a target date for achieving it. The u-Japan policy is built on three pillars or goals:

1. Preparation of ubiquitous networks
2. Advanced use of ICT
3. Preparation of an environment for ICT use.

More details of the government's strategy to achieve the u-Japan vision can be found in an MIC White Paper, published in 2004, with the somewhat grandiose title "Building a Ubiquitous Network Society That Spreads Throughout the World".[19] The White Paper provides an indication of people's expectations of ubiquitous networks generated from a survey.[20] Both individuals and businesses believe that ensuring information security including the protection of personal information is the most important issue. The survey found that the most frequently mentioned concern regarding the use of ubiquitous networks was "fraud and unscrupulous methods of business" followed by "leaks and improper use of personal information in the possession of businesses" and "improper access to and use of personal information".[21]

From our review of AmI visions produced in Europe, the United States and Japan, we found some slight differences (e.g., Japan is less focussed on the "invisibility" of embedded intelligence), but overall, they are similar in their view of ubiquitous computer networking and the wonders that lie in wait for us in the next decade or so. But these wonders are not unalloyed. They also are in accord in seeing threats to privacy and the difficulties in dealing with the policy issues raised by the ubiquity of the new technologies and how they could be used by the less than scrupulous.

## 2.3   Scenarios

Scenarios are a form of story-telling, but with a very specific purpose. In the last few decades, scenarios have provided a way of analysing the implications of alternative futures, especially as they might be impacted by new technologies. They are also expected to stimulate discussion of the economic, social, political and other drivers that underlie these alternatives. The results of such analysis and discussion are used in preparing roadmaps (how do we get from here to the future we want) and setting strategic research agendas (what must be developed).

---

[19] MPHPT, Information and Communications in Japan: *Building a Ubiquitous Network Society that Spreads Throughout the World*, White Paper, Ministry of Public Management Home Affairs Posts and Telecommunications of Japan, Economic Research Office, General Policy Division, Tokyo, 2004. http://www.johotsusintokei.soumu.go.jp/whitepaper/eng/WP2004/2004-index.html

[20] MPHPT 2004, p. 18.

[21] MPHPT 2004, p. 31.

Military organisations were among the first to design and develop scenarios, which were (and are) played out in "war games".[22] Today, industry, environmentalists and others also develop and use scenarios for planning and strategic purposes. In the wake of the oil crisis of 1971–1972, the Shell Group used scenarios to help work out its corporate response.[23] The International Panel for Climate Change (IPCC) has devoted considerable effort to developing scenarios about the impacts of global warming on our planet.[24] Even religious groups are using scenarios for considering their future.[25]

Scenario planners systematise the perceptions of alternative futures and help to develop a strategy for an uncertain future.[26] Unlike other methods (e.g., the Delphi method) that produce a single forecast, scenario planners have developed many scenarios to account for all major "drivers" of the future. More recently, some scenario planners have favoured a limitation on the number of scenarios by generating several orthogonal futures based on a matrix containing four quadrants. Each quadrant represents a permutation of the future by combining major drivers or factors indicated by the x- and y-axis. For example, in the ISTAG scenarios, the two axes are efficiency versus sociability and individual versus communal. They contrast technology applications that serve to optimise efficiency (whether in business or in society) against those that emphasise human relationships, sociability or just having fun. They also underline the place of ambient intelligence in serving society and the community as well as individuals.[27]

The major steps in creating such orthogonal scenarios (or futures) have been set out as follows:

- Identify a focal issue and determine the time frame
- Identify key factors
- Search for the unknown driving forces behind the key factors
- Organise forces in scale of importance and uncertainty
- Pick important and uncertain forces and create a scenario matrix or a few scenarios by combining forces

---

[22] Mietzner, D., and G. Reger, "Scenario Approaches – History, Differences, Advantages, and Disadvantages", in Fabiana Scapolo and Eamonn Cahill, *New Horizons and Challenges for Future-Oriented Technology Analysis*, Proceedings of the EU-US Scientific Seminar, New Technology Foresight, Forecasting and Assessment Methods, 13–14 May 2004, European Commission DG JRC-IPTS, Seville, 2004. http://www.jrc.es/projects/fta/

[23] See http://www.shell.com/ and in particular its "Scenarios" web page.

[24] IPCC Special Report on Emissions Scenarios. http://www.grida.no/climate/ipcc/emission/036.htm

[25] Inayatullah, Dr. Sohail, "Alternative Futures for the Islamic Ummah", Metafuture.org (undated). http://www.metafuture.org/Articles/AltFuturesUmmah.htm

[26] Noteworthy scenario planners include Peter Schwartz (*The art of the long view*, Doubleday, New York, 1991; *Inevitable Surprises: Thinking Ahead in a Time of Turbulence*, Gotham Books, June 2003), Gill Ringland (*Scenario Planning: Managing for the Future*, Wiley, 1998), Kees van der Heijden (*The Art of Strategic Conversation*, Wiley, 1996; *The Sixth Sense: Accelerating Organisational Learning with Scenarios*, Wiley, 2002) and Mats Lindgren (*Scenario Planning: The Link Between Future and Strategy*, Palgrave, Macmillan, 2002).

[27] [ISTAG] Ducatel, K., M. Bogdanowicz, F. Scapolo, J. Leijten and J.-C. Burgelman, *Scenarios for Ambient Intelligence in 2010*, IPTS, Seville, 2001. http://cordis.europa.eu/ist/istag-reports.htm

- Evaluate the focal question in each scenario
- Identify indicators that tell in which direction the environment is heading.[28]

As many different groups use scenarios, it is not surprising that there are different types of scenarios (and different terminologies to describe each type). Among them are the following:

*Trend scenarios* (sometimes called *reference, extrapolative* or *predictive* scenarios) start from the present and project forward on the basis of to-be-expected trends and events (*forecasting*). They are intended to be realistic rather than, for instance, normative or extreme.

*Normative scenarios* are developed to evaluate how a specific outcome can be reached. They are designed on the basis of a set of desirable features or "norms" that the future world should possess. The exercise then consists of tracing backwards (*backcasting*) a viable path from such an outcome to today – pointing the way to reaching that desirable future. Normative scenarios often reflect more radical discontinuities; they can be combinations of technological possibilities and political ambitions or targets.

*Explorative scenarios* address the question: What could happen? The scenarios are thus explorations of what might happen in the future.[29] They are based on identifying critical uncertainty factors and on different expectations of technical and/or policy developments over the short to medium term.

Additional types of scenarios can be derived from these three major types of scenarios as follows.[30]

## *Trend extrapolation vs contrasting*

Trend scenarios attempt to follow what is thought to be most probable and surprise-free. They avoid discontinuities. Contrasting scenarios display divergence, i.e., a number of scenarios are compared which are quite different, but all "possible".

## *Descriptive vs normative*

Descriptive scenarios simply posit a set of possible events or circumstances, without positive or negative value judgements being made. Normative scenarios are either teleological – i.e., directed towards certain desirable ends – or they involve positive and negative value judgements concerning the events or circumstances described.

---

[28] Björk, Staffan, "Designing Mobile Ad Hoc Collaborative Applications: Scenario experiences with Smart-Its", www.smart-its.org. These steps are based on those in Schwartz, Peter, *The art of the long view*, Doubleday, New York, 1991.

[29] Börjeson, Lena, Mattias Höjer, Karl-Henrik Dreborg, Tomas Ekvall and Göran Finnveden, "Towards a user's guide to scenarios – a report on scenario types and scenario techniques", Version 1.1b, Department of Urban Studies, Royal Institute of Technology, Stockholm, 2005. http://www.infra.kth.se/fms/pdf/ScenarioRapportVer1_1b.pdf

[30] Ducot, C., and G.J. Lubben, "A Typology for Scenarios", *Futures*, Vol. 12, February 1980.

## *Explorative vs anticipatory*

Explorative scenarios are "synthetic", in that they proceed from a given set of circumstances and attempt to draw conclusions about possible effects – i.e., they describe a future from a given present (forecasting, predictive). Anticipatory scenarios are "analytic", i.e., they proceed from a defined future set of circumstances (effect) and attempt to draw conclusions about the possible causes or processes that could lead to such a future (backcasting, diagnostic).

Scenarios started to appear in ambient intelligence (AmI) projects and studies soon after the term ambient intelligence was brought into common currency by Emile Aarts of Philips in 1999.[31] Probably the best-known AmI scenarios are those produced for the European Information Society Technologies Advisory Group (ISTAG), a group with about 30 members from industry and academia, which advises the European Commission's Information Society Directorate General.

ISTAG has described scenario planning as a tool for inventing our future.[32] In May 2000, ISTAG commissioned the creation of four scenarios "to provide food for thought about longer-term developments in Information and Communication Technologies", with the intent of exploring the social and technical implications of ambient intelligence. The ISTAG scenarios were actually developed by the Institute for Prospective Technological Studies (IPTS), which is part of the European Commission's Joint Research Centre, in collaboration with about 35 experts from across Europe. The aim was to describe what living with ambient intelligence might be like for ordinary people in 2010.

The four ISTAG scenarios are entitled and can be summarised as follows:

1. *Maria – Road Warrior* – This scenario is about a young woman travelling to a far eastern country where she is to make a sales pitch. Less than a decade ago, she had to carry a collection of different personal computing devices (laptop PC, mobile phone, electronic organisers and sometimes beamers and printers). Her computing system for this trip is reduced to one highly personalised communications device, her "P–Com" that she wears on her wrist.

2. *Dimitrios and the digital me (D-Me)* – Dimitrios, a 32-year-old employee of a major food multinational, is taking a coffee at his office's cafeteria. He is wearing, embedded in his clothes, a voice-activated digital avatar of himself, known as a "D-Me" or "Digital Me". A D-Me is a device that learns about Dimitrios from his interactions with his environment, and acts on his behalf offering

---

[31] "The term Ambient Intelligence was originally suggested by a consultant Eli Zelkha during a workshop held at Philips Research in 1998. The first official publication that mentions the term was by Appelo and myself and appeared in 1999 in a Dutch journal. The first international publication that uses the term appeared in the ACM proceedings called *The Invisible Future* edited by Peter Denning in 2001 and was written by Harwig, Schuurmans and myself." Emile Aarts in an e-mail to the authors, 10 October 2006.

[32] [ISTAG] Ducatel, K., M. Bogdanowicz, F. Scapolo, J. Leijten and J.-C. Burgelman, *Scenarios for Ambient Intelligence in 2010*, IPTS, Seville, 2001. http://cordis.europa.eu/ist/istag-reports.htm

communication, processing and decision-making functionality. Dimitrios' D-Me converses with and provides helpful information to the D-Me of an older person (whom Dimitrios does not know, but who suffers from a similar heart condition).

3. *Carmen: traffic, sustainability and commerce* – Carmen plans her day with the help of AmI, to find a non-smoker with whom she could drive downtown. Her e-fridge helps her in planning the meal for some guests that evening. Her driver's car, equipped with a dynamic route guidance system, warns the driver of long traffic jams up ahead due to an accident and calculates alternative routes. On the way to the office, her wearable personal area network (PAN) alerts her to an offer on her preferred Chardonnay wine. On her way home, pollution levels have risen, and the city-wide engine control system automatically lowers the maximum speeds for all motorised vehicles. AmI suggests she telework from home the next day as a big demonstration is planned for downtown.

4. *Annette and Solomon in the ambient for social learning* – This scenario describes the meeting of an environmental studies group. With the help of an "ambient", members of the group, ranging from 10 to 75 years old, contribute to and learn from the meeting. During the day, individuals and subgroups located in appropriate spaces in the ambient to pursue learning experiences at a pace that suits them. An expert, several thousand miles away, joins the meeting via videoconference to answer some questions.

Among other things, the ISTAG scenarios suggested a set of "critical socio-political factors" considered crucial for the development of ambient intelligence, including the issue of security and trust. The scenarios were regarded as a first step toward the creation of a research agenda.

In the *Embedded Everywhere* report, there are three scenarios relating to the use of Emnets (as they are called) in the automotive, agricultural and defence sectors. They do not map out alternative futures, so much as show how the new technologies can be used. In fact, those scenarios are firmly grounded in today's technologies. They merely extend what is available today to what's likely to be available tomorrow.

A few of the projects reviewed for this chapter do carry scenarios akin to those of the ISTAG studies among others in Europe. The Oxygen project at MIT is one such example. The AURA project at Carnegie Mellon University also uses scenarios.[33] Another is the Portolano project which comes not only with a "screenplay" and analysis, but even with cartoons.[34]

The *Who Goes There?* report (see Section 2.4) has two very good scenarios to illustrate the ways in which identification and authentication arise in everyday life and

---

[33] Garlan, D., D. Siewiorek, A. Smailagic and P. Steenkiste, "Project Aura: Toward Distraction-Free Pervasive Computing", *IEEE Pervasive Computing*, Vol. 21, No. 2, 2002, pp. 22–31.

[34] http://portolano.cs.washington.edu/scenario/

to highlight some of the important issues associated with new systems.[35] The first scenario describes the life of Joseph K as he goes on a business trip. The second describes a token-based authentication system used by Laura on a visit to a hospital.

Few scenarios appear in papers about Japan's ubiquitous networking projects, at least, not scenarios developed to the extent that one finds in (especially) European and American projects. Not all scenarios need to be written, of course. The Ministry of Internal Affairs and Communications prepared a briefing package for the overseas press which has several "images" of the ubiquitous network society. On KDDI's web site, one can find several ubiquitous network scenarios in video format.[36]

From our review of AmI scenarios by other researchers, we found some very good scenarios, but almost none that could be regarded as "dark" or that focus on the impact and use of AmI on "our" key issues of privacy, identity, trust, security and the digital divide. Nor did we find a structured approach to constructing and deconstructing scenarios like the approach we have developed.

## 2.4   Roadmaps

Roadmaps follow on from scenarios – i.e., to realise a scenario, a roadmap sets out what steps must be taken. Roadmaps have become a strategic planning tool in many industries and even in international diplomacy, e.g., the (now defunct) US-brokered Middle East roadmap. Roadmaps provide an overview of technology development by mapping out gaps, barriers and bottlenecks to be overcome in order to bring about the future envisaged in one or more scenarios.

Roadmaps were developed during the 1980s as a strategic planning tool by (mainly American) corporations and use of the tool was later extended for the purposes of entire industry sectors. In recent years, roadmapping has also been applied to an increasingly broad range of areas such as transdisciplinary high-tech common goals or the provision of intelligence for science and technology policy-making.[37]

There are several European AmI-relevant roadmaps. One of the first was the PROGRESS Embedded Systems Roadmap produced in 2002 by the Dutch embedded systems community at the behest of the Technology Foundation STW, the Dutch funding agency for university research.[38]

None of the roadmaps is specifically focused on the key issues discussed in this book.

---

[35] Kent, S.T., and L.I. Millett (eds.), *Who Goes There? Authentication Through the Lens of Privacy*, National Academies Press, Washington, DC, 2003, pp. 21–27.

[36] See the "Knock! Knock! Ubiquitous" video streaming scenarios at www.kddi.com/english/index.html

[37] Da Costa, O., M. Boden, Y. Punie and M. Zappacosta, "Science and Technology Roadmapping from Industry to Public Policy", in *The IPTS Report* 73, 2003, pp. 27–32.

[38] PROGRESS is the acronym for PROGram for Research in Embedded Systems and Software. The roadmap can be found at www.stw.nl/progress/ESroadmap/index.html

## 2.5 Strategic research agendas

From roadmaps, research agendas can be developed which indicate what areas must be researched in order to bring visions into reality. Quite a few European projects have developed research agendas important to AmI. Among those are the following:

ARTEMIS, a European group with representatives from industry, governments, regulators and academia, has produced a strategic research agenda.[39]

The eMobility platform (see the section on platforms below) has also published a strategic research agenda.[40] The latest version, available on its website, is dated November 2005. Major sections of its research agenda deal with ambient services, ambient connectivity, security and trust.

The US National Academy of Sciences (NAS) has published several important reports that have served as research agendas for embedded systems and ubiquitous computing. Among them are the *Embedded Everywhere* report,[41] which is undoubtedly the best known, *Who goes there? Authentication through the lens of privacy*,[42] *Trust in Cyberspace*[43] and, most recently, a summary report from a workshop on *Radio Frequency Identification Technologies*.[44]

By far the best of the strategic research agendas, in the context of the issues that concern us, is the *Embedded Everywhere* report. Even though it is now several years old, it still rewards those who read it. Many of the issues raised there still await resolution. We like to think, however, this book goes some distance to addressing those issues and proposing workable solutions.

## 2.6 Platforms

There are many players in AmI development in Europe. To harness their efforts and ensure congruence, some organisational arrangements must be put in place. That is essentially the function of a platform. Technology platforms bring together a wide

---

[39] ARTEMIS, Strategic Research Agenda, 1st Edition, March 2006. http://www.artemis-office. org/DotNetNuke/PressCorner/tabid/89/Default.asp

[40] http://www.emobility.eu.org/research_agenda.html

[41] Estrin, D. (ed.), *Embedded, Everywhere: A Research Agenda for Networked Systems of Embedded Computers*, National Academy Press, Washington, DC, 2001. http://www.nap.edu/

[42] Kent, S.T., and L.I. Millett (eds.), *Who Goes There? Authentication Through the Lens of Privacy*, National Academies Press, Washington, DC, 2003.

[43] Schneider, F.B. (ed.), *Trust in Cyberspace*, National Academy Press, Washington, DC, 1999. http://newton.nap.edu/html/trust/

[44] Committee on Radio Frequency Identification Technologies, *Radio Frequency Identification Technologies: A Workshop Summary*, Computer Science and Telecommunications Board, National Research Council, National Academies Press, Washington, DC, 2004. http://books.nap. edu/catalog/11189.html

range of stakeholders, including key industrial players, small and medium enterprises, the financial world, national and regional public authorities, the research community, universities, non-governmental organisations and civil society to define R&D priorities, timeframes and action plans.

A strong commitment to openness and transparency is key to the success of a European Technology Platform (ETP). Each platform must have clear "rules of the game" to ensure that it is founded on broadly based agenda-setting and does not become dominated by narrow industry groupings or other stakeholder lobbies, nor become a "closed shop".[45]

The Commission began promoting European technology platforms in 2003 and encouraged interested parties to come together and set up platforms at European level. The Commission continues to emphasise the importance of platforms as vehicles for public–private partnerships in stimulating competitive research while ensuring the complementarity of action at national, transnational and European level.

The Commission has a web site devoted to European technology platforms across many research areas[46] and of those, two especially relevant to AmI, namely those of ARTEMIS (embedded systems) and eMobility (mobile and wireless communications technology).

ARTEMIS[47], launched in 2004, is a sort of public–private partnership which aims to mobilise and co-ordinate private and public resources to meet business, technical and structural challenges in embedded systems and to ensure that systems developed by different vendors can communicate and work with each other via industry standards.

eMobility is a mobile and wireless communications technology platform, established by industry and operators in 2004.[48] Its objective is to reinforce Europe's leadership in mobile and wireless communications and services and to master the future development of this technology.

Neither has working groups dealing with the issues of concern in this book, although we can assume they are aware of their importance. There is a brief reference to some of "our" key issues in the ARTEMIS Strategic Research Agenda, in which it is stated that "In most application areas, the design, implementation and operation of Embedded Systems are constrained by European or international regulations concerning safety, security, digital trust, and the environment. These regulations have strong cost impacts on the design and engineering processes especially for software. ... ARTEMIS will ... forge links with the regulation authorities to

---

[45] European Commission, *European Technology Platforms*: Moving to Implementation, Second Status Report, Office for Official Publications of the European Communities, Luxembourg, May 2006. ftp://ftp.cordis.europa.eu/pub/technology-platforms/docs/ki7305429ecd.pdf

[46] http://cordis.europa.eu/technology-platforms/home_en.html

[47] ARTEMIS is the acronym for Advanced Research and Development on Embedded Intelligent Systems. www.cordis.lu/ist/artemis

[48] http://www.emobility.eu.org

overcome regulatory barriers to the introduction of the new ARTEMIS technologies." This does not strike us as a particularly constructive approach to resolving the privacy and other related concerns of consumers and citizens.

In addition to ARTEMIS and eMobility, three other European platforms, not quite so advanced as ARTEMIS and eMobility, could contribute to the deployment of AmI:

- NESSI (Networked European Software and Services Initiative) says it aims to provide a unified view for European research in services architectures and software infrastructures that will define technologies, strategies and deployment policies fostering new, open, industrial solutions and societal applications that enhance the safety, security and the well-being of citizens.[49]
- NEM (the Networked and Electronic Media Initiative) is focused on an innovative mix of various media forms, delivered seamlessly over technologically transparent networks, to improve the quality, enjoyment and value of life. NEM represents the convergence of existing and new technologies, including broadband, mobile and new media across all ICT sectors, to create a new and exciting era of advanced personalised services.[50]
- ENIAC (European Nanoelectronics Initiative Advisory Council) aims to provide a strategic research agenda for the nanoelectronics sector, to set out strategies and roadmaps to achieve this vision and to stimulate coherent public and private investment in R&D.[51]

## 2.7 Projects

As noted above, hundreds of AmI projects and studies have been initiated in Europe. The first lot of projects inspired by the ISTAG vision of ambient intelligence were those in the "Disappearing Computers" component of the EC's Fifth Framework Programme (1998–2002). The Sixth Framework Programme greatly increased the funding and number of projects.

To have some idea of the scale of European AmI projects, it is useful to note that of the 100 or so projects reviewed by the authors,[52] the largest project (WEARIT@ WORK) in euro value has a budget of €24 million and the smallest (STORK) had a budget of €200,000. The average value was €4.7 million. Nine had a budget of more than €10 million. Twelve had a budget of less than €1 million.

---

[49] http://www.nessi-europe.eu/Nessi/AboutNESSI/Overview/tabid/152/Default.aspx

[50] http://www.nem-initiative.org/

[51] http://cordis.europa.eu/ist/eniac/home.html

[52] For a review of AmI projects in Europe, the United States and Japan, see Wright, D., "The dark side of ambient intelligence", *Info*, Vol. 7, No. 6, October 2005, pp. 33–51. www.emeraldinsight.com/info

These numbers indicate that hundreds of millions of euros are being spent on AmI, and hundreds of European companies, universities and others are participating collaboratively in taking AmI from vision to reality. Virtually all of the European AmI projects reviewed have been undertaken by consortia. The number of partners varies from three to 36, with an average number of 11 partners per project. Consortia typically comprise partners from different countries and different sectors, especially universities and industry.

The United States, Japan and other countries also have been exploring pervasive computing and ubiquitous networking (their comparable buzz words) in many projects too, often through collaborative efforts between government, industry, universities, research institutes and other stakeholders. Most projects are undertaken by universities and industry, often with support from federal funding agencies such as the US Defense Advanced Research Projects Agency (DARPA), National Science Foundation (NSF), NASA, etc.

Smart Dust was a project at the University of California at Berkeley supported by the DARPA, among others. The project started in 1997 and finished in 2001,[53] but many additional projects have grown out of it. The project developed tiny sensors, dubbed "smart dust", or motes, with wireless connectivity capable of organising themselves into flexible networks. The aim was to develop a complete sensor network node, including power supply, processor, sensor and communications, in a single cubic millimetre.

The Portolano project[54] at the University of Washington is tagged as "An Expedition into Invisible Computing". Invisible computing is a term coined by Donald Norman to describe the coming age of ubiquitous task-specific computing devices.[55] The devices are so highly optimised to particular tasks that they blend into the world and require little technical knowledge on the part of their users. The Portolano project, with funding from DARPA, is researching how to make computing devices ubiquitous, to make computer electronics and computation an integral part of all manufactured goods.

There are quite a few ubiquitous network projects in Japan. Little information is available on the sources and amounts of funding. Many of the projects have been undertaken by research laboratories. There seems to be no projects on the scale of the largest European and American projects and none with large consortia of partners, as one finds in the United States and especially Europe. Furthermore, none of the projects has been specifically dedicated to privacy, security, identity, trust and the digital divide. Nonetheless, protection of personal information and security are of concern to the Japanese and these issues are frequently mentioned in the projects and other documents.

---

[53] http://robotics.eecs.berkeley.edu/~pister/SmartDust/

[54] http://portolano.cs.washington.edu

[55] In his 1998 book, *The Invisible Computer*, Norman says computer and technology companies are too focused on the technology, whereas he wants these companies to think about human beings first. In his vision, the computer and its software would fade into the background, become "invisible" and be replaced with simple, task-centred devices.

Examples of Japanese ubiquitous network society projects are the following:

The Ubila project[56], sponsored by the Ministry of Internal Affairs and Communications (MIC) of Japan in co-operation with industry, academia and government, aims to realise ubiquitous networking, where computers and networks are present in all aspects of daily life. Its specific focus is on control management technologies for ubiquitous networks.

Project STONE was initiated at the University of Tokyo in 1999 (and is continuing) to develop an innovative network architecture for supporting future ubiquitous computing applications. STONE provides service discovery, context awareness, service synthesis and service mobility.[57] The STONE project developed an authentication process so that even appliances could establish the identity of different users. Authentication of appliances also is designed to prevent impersonation attacks on the network. In the project, all communications over the network were encrypted by secure sockets layer (SSL) encryption to make the system resistant to tampering.

The official name of the Yaoyorozu project (August 2002–March 2005)[58] is "Research on Ubiquitous Information Society based on Trans-Disciplinary Science". The project has several partners including Hitachi, the University of Tokyo, Keio University, the National Institute of Media Education and Tokyo University of Technology and UDIT. It has received support from the Ministry of Education, Culture, Sports, Science and Technology (MEXT). Its principal research goal is desirable institutional systems and core technology for the ubiquitous information society in 2010. The Yaoyorozu project, for example, is asking questions about whether existing privacy protections are sufficient. The teams are examining ethics in the ubiquitous information society, increasing privacy consciousness as well as enhancing secure and versatile connectivity. One of the project's four themes is the examination of appropriate policies for handling privacy and clarifying the basic requirements.

## 2.8 Prospects

Of the various European projects reviewed, we were encouraged to find about a fifth of them are devoted to privacy, identity and (personal) security issues or treat these issues in a substantive way. Of these, the four biggest projects (PISA, PRIME, FIDIS and GUIDE) had or have substantial budgets, ranging from €3.2 million and nine partners (PISA) to €13.14 million and 21 partners (PRIME). In addition to these four projects, also supported by the EC's Framework Programme, we can also mention the PAW project, which has funding from Dutch sources.

---

[56] Participants include the University of Tokyo, Kyushu Institute of Technology, NEC Corporation, Fujitsu Limited, KDDI R&D Laboratories, Inc. and KDDI Corporation. www.ubila.org

[57] Kawahara, Y., M. Minami, S. Saruwatari, et al., "Challenges and Lessons Learned in Building a Practical Smart Space", in *The First Annual International Conference on Mobile and Ubiquitous Systems: Networking and Services*, Boston, MA, 22–26 August 2004, pp. 213–222.

[58] The project's web site is www.8mg.jp/en/outline_goals01.htm

The PISA project (January 2001–2004)[59] focused on development of new privacy-enhancing technologies (PETs) for electronic business and demonstration of PETs as a secure technical solution to protect the privacy of individuals when they use intelligent agents.

The GUIDE project (January 2004–June 2005),[60] which sought to speed up the adoption of e-government across Europe, rightly took the view that services must be citizen-centric, user-driven and technology-enabled, but also recognised the specific needs of Europe based upon the social, ethical and legislative differences regarding privacy and data protection.

The Dutch PAW project (October 2003–2007)[61] is developing a privacy protecting architecture to protect the user's privacy in an ambient world. The project takes a two-tier approach. To prevent unwanted collection of data about a user and his actions, techniques from secure computing are extended to provide private computing. To control the authorised dissemination of data about a user, licensing techniques similar.

The PRIME project (March 2004–February 2008)[62] is a follow-on to PISA. PRIME aims to develop solutions for privacy-enhancing identity management for end users. The PRIME consortium expects to help citizens manage their privacy and to support business in its compliance with privacy data-processing requirements.

The FIDIS project (April 2004–March 2009),[63] a network of excellence, operates from the point of view that the European Information Society requires technologies that address trust and security yet also preserve the privacy of individuals. The FIDIS consortium has proposed a preliminary vision of decentralised identity management. This vision seems to go a bit further than the PRIME proposal.

These and other projects (including the SWAMI project, of course) are important, not only on their merits, but because they show that there is concern about the key issues of privacy, identity, trust, etc., that researchers from industry and academia are joining forces to find solutions and that there is financial support for such initiatives. As dissemination activities are an important part of every EC-supported project, each one of them contributes to raising public awareness as well as exchanging findings among the research community. While AmI poses severe challenges to privacy, identity, trust and so on, researchers are rising to those challenges.

---

[59] PISA is the acronym for Privacy Incorporated Software Agent. The project had a budget of €3.2 million and nine partners. Its web site is www.pet-pisa.nl/pisa_org/pisa/index.html

[60] GUIDE is the acronym for Government User IDentity for Europe. The project has a budget of €12.47 million and 23 partners. Its web site is http://istrg.som.surrey.ac.uk/projects/guide

[61] PAW is the acronym for Privacy in an Ambient World. The project is funded by the Dutch Ministry of Economic Affairs through the IOP GenCom programme managed by Senter. PAW is additionally supported by funds from TNO Telecom. It has four partners. Its web site is www. cs.ru.nl/~jhh/paw/index2.html

[62] PRIME is the acronym for Privacy and Identity Management for Europe. The project has a budget of €13.14 million and 21 partners. Its web site is www.prime-project.eu.org

[63] FIDIS is the acronym for the Future of Identity in the Information Society. The project has a budget of €6.10 million and 24 partners. Its web site is at: www.fidis.net

# Chapter 3
# Dark scenarios

In this chapter, we present four "dark scenarios" that highlight the key socio-economic, legal, technological and ethical risks to privacy, identity, trust, security and inclusiveness posed by new AmI technologies. We call them dark scenarios, because they show things that could go wrong in an AmI world, because they present visions of the future that we do *not* want to become reality. The scenarios expose threats and vulnerabilities as a way to inform policy-makers and planners about issues they need to take into account in developing new policies or updating existing legislation.

Before presenting the four scenarios and our analysis of each, we describe the process of how we created the scenarios as well as the elements in our methodology for analysing the scenarios.


## 3.1 Creating and analysing dark scenarios

The process we followed in constructing the four dark scenarios is depicted in Fig. 3.1.

As indicated in Fig. 3.1, we made an extensive review of existing AmI-related projects, studies and scenarios, with a view to understanding their implications in terms of the key issues. While most existing scenarios describe the brave new world of AmI, how great it will be living and working in an AmI-enabled future, we often found that the technological marvels had some negative aspects to which little attention had been given.

Following a workshop with other AmI experts to discuss the most important threats and vulnerabilities posed by AmI, we had our own internal workshop where we brainstormed until we agreed the rough outlines of four contrasting scenarios. We then developed these outlines into scenario stories or scripts. To ground our scenarios in reality – to ensure that they were not too far-fetched – we did a "technology check" (are the technologies referenced in the scenarios probable?) and a "reality check" (are there press reports of events similar to those mentioned in the scenarios?). Then, all of the partners reviewed all of the scenarios in order to eliminate doubtful points, unnecessary wordage, irrelevancies, etc., and to sharpen them

D. Wright et al. (eds.), *Safeguards in a World of Ambient Intelligence.*
© Springer 2010

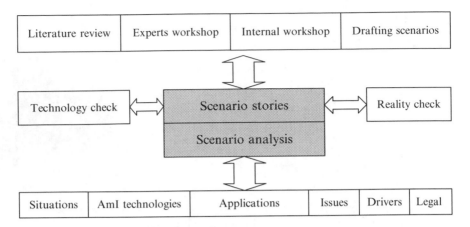

**Fig. 3.1** The process of constructing the four dark scenarios

to illustrate the points we wanted to emphasise. Once the scenarios were "stable", we performed our analysis of them, including a legal analysis. We presented the scenarios and our analyses at a second workshop in order to benefit from the comments of other experts.

We devised a methodology, an analytical structure for both constructing and deconstructing scenarios, not only our own scenarios, but many other technology-oriented scenarios. Our analytical structure comprises the following elements or activities:

### 3.1.1  Framing the scenario

This first step summarises the scenario in question and explains its context – who are the main actors in the scenario, what happens to them or what do they do, how far into the future is the scenario set, where does it take place and in what domain (home, office, on the move, shopping, etc). It identifies the type of scenario (trend, normative and explorative) and key assumptions (e.g., intelligent technologies will be embedded everywhere in rich countries, but not in poor countries).

### 3.1.2  Identifying the technologies and/or devices

Next, we identify the most important AmI technologies and/or devices used and/or implied in the scenarios.

### 3.1.3  Identifying the applications

We consider the applications that emerge in each scenario and that are supported by the technologies mentioned in the previous step.

### 3.1.4 Drivers

At this step in the analysis, we identify the key drivers that impel the scenario or, more particularly, the development and use of the applications. Drivers are typically socio-economic, political or environmental forces (e.g., in our third scenario, the Data Mining Corporation seeks a global monopoly, economic disparities are inflaming poor countries, the world is becoming a hothouse) or personal motivations (e.g., greed).

### 3.1.5 Issues

Next, we identify and explicate the major issues raised in each scenario. The issues of concern, as mentioned above, are privacy, identity, trust, security and inclusiveness (or its opposite, the digital divide). A discussion of the issues considers the threats and vulnerabilities exposed by the scenario.

### 3.1.6 Legal synopsis

We present the legal and regulatory issues, especially in the context of today's legislation, and point out lacunae in today's legal framework and how those lacunae need to addressed to deal with issues that will be prevalent in an AmI future.

### 3.1.7 Conclusions

The final step is a reality check of the scenario itself (how likely is it? are the technologies plausible?) and a consideration of what should be done to address the issues it raises. One might conclude that a range of socio-economic, technological and legal safeguards are needed in order to minimise the risks posed by the threats and vulnerabilities highlighted by the scenario.

## 3.2 Scenario 1: The AmI family

### 3.2.1 The scenario script

#### Scene 1: At home and at work

The Sebastianis are a middle-class family who make intensive use of their smart AmI home. Both parents work full time but with flexible hours. The father (Paul) mainly works from home for a private security company. His work concerns remote surveillance of company premises. His wife Maruja works for a real estate company in the city. They have two teenage children (Ricardo and Elena).

*Paul has been called out for a meeting at the security company. Such meetings where security agents have face-to-face contacts are organised only occasionally. Although he likes working from home, Paul also enjoys actually meeting the colleagues with whom he collaborates on a daily basis.*

*He forgot to close the door of his highly protected study when he left the house. Usually, this is not a problem. The room knows when Paul leaves because embedded sensors in the room detect inactivity. Unfortunately, the door with its fingerprint reader did not close automatically because a carpet was displaced and folded accidentally. It prevented the door from closing.*

*Paul receives an alarm signal on his Personal Wrist Communicator (PWC). There is an intruder in the house. "How is that possible?" he asks himself. He knows that his son Ricardo is home. He had invited some friends to play a new virtual reality game (for which Ricardo has a licence) from the entertainment centre downstairs. Paul checks the home surveillance system remotely but only gets a still image from 30 minutes ago. There is no live image available from the front and back door cameras, nor is Paul able to play back who has passed in front of the doors today. Ricardo does not answer his calls. "What's happening? Where is he?"*

*Paul contacts the neighbourhood security service and asks them to check visually on his house and children. From the outside, nothing seems to be wrong except that all curtains and windows are closed. Moreover, it seems that all security systems are blocked and the security agents on the spot cannot get access to the security surveillance logs. Paul is informed of the situation and decides to call the police. In the past, AmI security systems alarmed the police automatically but because of too many false alarms, this procedure has been stopped.*

*Paul is just leaving the office to return home when his boss calls, "Come in, Paul. I'm glad you are still at the office. It seems we have a small problem. ... I've just been contacted by the police who have asked for access to all the data we have on you. I understand this is just an informal request so we do not have to give them anything, but, as you know, as a security company, we cannot afford any suspicions of our staff."*

*Paul is astonished and does not understand what is happening. First the home problem, now this. "Surely, this must be some kind of mistake. I don't know why they'd want my data – although I have heard lately of cases where the police have been investigating innocent people based on inadequate profiling."[1]*

*"Yes, I know, Paul," she says. "And I trust you, but you must understand that under such circumstances, I can't go to the board of directors meeting tomorrow with a proposal for your promotion at a time when you are being investigated by the police. I'm sorry, but we'll just have to wait until this situation is clarified."*

---

[1] Singel, Ryan, "Nun Terrorized by Terror Watch", *Wired News*, 26 September 2005. http://www.wired.com/news/privacy/0,1848,68973,00.html

*"Okay, sure, I understand,"* Paul replies. *He is disappointed to miss a promotion now, but he is confident that the opportunity will come around again. "I really don't know what the police could be after, but, of course, the best thing to do is to co-operate and let's clear up this misunderstanding." This is what he says, but what he thinks is "This is not my best day, but first I need to find out what's happening at home."*

*Paul receives multiple messages on his PWC the moment he leaves his boss's office.[2] He had all incoming communications on hold from the moment he entered her office. This is a company default setting. There is one message that immediately attracts his attention. "If you want your house systems to work again, click on the following link ..."*

*"What? I'm being blackmailed! So that's why I couldn't get access to my home systems, nor could the local security agent. That's why I got the intruder message,"* he thinks, slightly reassured, *since that probably means that his children at home are OK.*

*Ricardo is indeed enjoying himself with his friends in Paul's study. They were able to enter because the door was still open. At last, he has the opportunity to check whether the print-out he has of his father's iris can fool the iris scanner which it must do if Ricardo is to unlock his father's computer. It does because Paul still has an old-fashioned model without liveness testing![3] With his father's profile and identity, Ricardo can circumvent the parental control system that governs use of the Internet by all terminals in the home. It's time for some fun. Ricardo places a bet on a sports gambling site, downloads some xxx-rated movies and games on his personal space on the family server and checks out his father's online favourites.[4] "Hmmm, I didn't know the old man likes erotic poetry. And I see he's just bought some pretty pricey lingerie. ... Well, I hope it's for mum," Ricardo laughs.* But he won't be laughing when his father finds out that Ricardo has spent 200 euros from his account.

*While one of his friends goes to the entertainment room to start a multiplayer virtual reality game, Ricardo goes to the kitchen to prepare some gin and tonics. The cupboard containing the alcohol can only be opened by a numerical code, but Ricardo figured that out long ago. The code is the date of his parents' wedding anniversary.[5]*

---

[2] Alahuhta, P., M. Jurvansuu and H. Pentikäinen, "Roadmap for network technologies and service", *Tekes Technology Review* 162/2004, Tekes, Helsinki, 2004.

[3] Daugman, John, "Iris Recognition: Anti-spoofing Liveness Testing, Stable Biometric Keys, and Further Research Directions", BioSecure 1st Residential Workshop, Paris, August 2005; Maghiros, I., Y. Punie, S. Delaitre, et al., *Biometrics at the Frontiers: Assessing the Impact on Society*, Study commissioned by the LIBE Committee of the European Parliament, EC – DG Joint Research Centre, Institute for Prospective Technological Studies (IPTS), Seville, 2005.

[4] A recent study indicates that spyware risks are highest for broadband users and for those who visit pornographic sites or play games online: http://news.bbc.co.uk/1/hi/technology/4659145.stm

[5] Not everything in the smart house is accessed via biometric verification. But then, the human tendency to use easy-to-guess passwords and/or access codes continues to constitute a possible security weakness. For more on the security weakness of passwords, see Schneier, B., "Customers, Passwords, and Web Sites", in *IEEE Security and Privacy Magazine*, 2, No. 5, 2004.

## Scene 2: Shopping while being at work

*Across town, Paul's wife Maruja needs to find a funny (farewell to girlhood!) present for her best friend. Because she is busy at work, she decides to try her new Shopping Assistant Software (SAS), which, according to the hype, is supposed to have intelligent search capabilities and an advanced speech interface.[6] But Maruja is not impressed. The SAS's suggestions seem too ordinary, so she instructs the SAS to keep searching "until you find something really funny".[7] On her way back to the office, Maruja notices that she has received a message from her daughter Elena on her Personal Wrist Communicator (PWC) for a special offer on the new "Real Magic Experience" (RME) she wants for her next birthday. Elena knows her mother would never buy her such an expensive game but with in view of a really good online offer, she might. The snag is that the offer is only valid for one hour. What Maruja does not know is that this new version of RME will allow Elena to play it at school without the teacher's noticing it.*

*Neither Maruja nor Elena is aware that the web site with the attractive offer contains a powerful spyware program that looks for personal data and preferences, so that users can be targeted with personalised advertising. The spyware helps to reveal a person's attitude towards privacy and spam.[8] Companies are paying a lot of money for personal and group profiles.[9] This phenomenon is known as "data laundering". Similar to money laundering, data laundering aims to make illegally obtained personal data look as if they were obtained legally, so that they can be used to target customers.*

*Maruja receives the message from her daughter just before a business meeting starts. She looks at the message in a hurry and, attracted by the discount price, she buys the game. Turning her thoughts to the meeting, she is confident she will be able to convince her prospective client, a construction company, to invest in the land held by her company. If she's right, she expects a big annual bonus.*

*While giving her presentation, Maruja receives, much to her surprise, because she thought she had banned incoming messages, a "Most Funny Wedding Present" advertisement. She accidentally activates the message and displays it on the big screen. It shows an ad for a sex-related product. Flustered and embarrassed,*

---

[6] Garate, A., I. Lucas, N. Herrasti and A. Lopez, "Ambient Intelligence Technologies for Home Automation and Entertainment", in EUSAI 2004, Workshop "Ambient Intelligence Technologies for Well-Being at Home", 2004.

[7] Dey, A., and J. Mankoff, "Designing Mediation for Context-Aware Applications", *ACM Transactions on Computer-Human Interaction*, Special issue on Sensing-Based Interactions 12(80), Issue 1, March 2005, pp. 53–80.

[8] Krebs, Brian, "Hacked Home PCs Fueling Rapid Growth in Online Fraud", *Washington Post*, 19 September 2005. http://www.washingtonpost.com/wp – dyn/content/article/2005/09/19/AR2005091900026.html

[9] Vijayan, Jaikumar, "ID Theft Continues to Increase. More than 13 million Americans have been victimized, new study reveals", *Computerworld*, 30 July 2003. http://www.pcworld.com/news/article/0,aid,111832,00.asp; Zetter, Kim, "TSA Data Dump Leads to Lawsuit", *Wired News*, 14 July 2005. http://www.wired.com/news/privacy/0,1848,68560,00.html

*Maruja apologises and continues with her presentation, but she never really gets back on track after that.*

*An audio track of the meeting is recorded and converted to a document, as is normal practice in Maruja's company (thanks to AmI, nobody needs to write and distribute "meeting minutes" anymore!). Next day, Maruja's boss, surprised by the partners' decision to postpone financing of a joint project, checks the meeting report and gets the impression that Maruja did not prepare her presentation well enough. She will probably not get the annual bonus she was counting on. The reason for Maruja's embarrassment was not recorded to the "meeting minutes" since it was a video message, not an audio advertisement.*

### Scene 3: In the park

*After the terrible business meeting experience she has had, Maruja leaves the office for a lunch break. She decides to buy a takeaway sandwich and walks towards the park. She is receiving almost continuously messages on the flexible screen on her sleeve.[10] She likes the blouse she borrowed from her friend to test the on-screen possibilities of this smart piece of clothing. The screen shows there is a tai-chi gathering on the east side of the park. She might want to join because of her interest in relaxation exercises and in Eastern philosophies.*

*"Not today," she thinks, "and I am certainly not having lunch in the Chinese restaurant around the corner, despite its interesting price. I do not like Chinese food. My avatar should know that and I already have a sandwich. ... Damn, I should have indicated that I already had lunch. You have to think of everything here." The avatar could not know that she already has a sandwich, because she paid cash for it.*

*Another ad appears: "Special offers from the bookshop next door." Maruja gets annoyed by the location-based spam[11] and decides to switch off almost completely, only allowing incoming emergency messages.*

*Later, she finds out that her boss has phoned twice. She also misses a proximity message that a good friend was sitting in a nearby pub. She feels deprived and angry because it is so difficult to get the thresholds of her avatar right. It seems there will always be grey zones where intelligent agents are not able to take the most intelligent filtering decisions. "I should have been more open to the physical environment," she thinks, because then she would probably have noticed that she had passed one of her friend's favourite bars.*

*Maruja thinks about her friend Claire who is always fast in adopting new electronic gadgets such as this blouse. Maruja likes it. It seems really practical.*

*Claire, however, at that moment, is having a rather bad experience. She is working at home when burglars break into her apartment. The burglars are surprised to*

---

[10] Espiner, T., "Philips unfurls prototype flexible display", ZDNet UK, 2 September 2005. http://news.zdnet.co.uk/hardware/emergingtech/0,39020357,39216111,00.htm

[11] Paciga, M., and H. Lutfiya, "Herecast: An open infrastructure for location – based services using WiFi, Wireless and Mobile Computing, Networking and Communications", WiMob'2005, IEEE International Conference, 2005, pp. 21–28.

*find Claire at home. In the ensuing confrontation, Claire is punched in the face. The burglars get away with only her PWC, her wallet and some jewels that were lying on the table but the experience of getting robbed will haunt Claire for a much longer time. Moreover, she will now have to train her new PWC from scratch because she did not want to store her profile online, and because the burglars have destroyed her home computer which Claire had used to back up her PWC.*

*The burglary and mugging occurred because of an unlucky coincidence of circumstances, i.e., Maruja was wearing Claire's blouse when she went to the park where the criminal gang happened to be operating. As she was passing by, the gang "read" the RFID tag embedded in the blouse. As a result, the gang found out that the blouse had been sold at a certain shop. The gang hacked the client database to discover Claire's profile (a well-off woman living alone in the richer part of the city).[12] On the assumption that Claire was wearing the blouse, the criminals decided to break into the flat and to steal whatever luxury goods they could find.*

*After passing by the gang, Maruja is stopped by a young foreign woman. "Excuse me," she asks. "I want to go to the town hall in the central market square. Can you tell me which exit from the park to take?"*

*"Sure, let's look it up." Maruja clicks on the city map that locates their position and in the blink of an eye, they find that is the right exit on the upper-east side. "Thank you," the young woman replies and walks on.*

*Maruja wonders why this woman does not have her own location device. She would feel completely lost without hers.*

*The location device is not perfect, as Maruja knows from her experience last week when some thugs forced her to hand over her "smart" purse which did not require any authentication in order to make small payments. Maruja had forgotten to authorise an update of the location-based software and found herself walking in an area of the city frequented by drug addicts and criminals. Because there are so many surveillance cameras everywhere these days, criminal gangs and other bad sorts now move quickly from one area to another, taking advantage of the fact that the security information system only gets updated once a month and that only subscribers receive these updates.*

### 3.2.2   Analysis

### 3.2.3   The context

Scenario 1 presents three different environments to depict AmI-related privacy and security weaknesses: at home, at work and in an open public space. There are differences between these environments but the distinction between them is blurring. Already today,

---

[12] Knospe, H., and H. Pohl, "RFID Security", *Information Security Technical Report* 9, No. 4, 2004, pp. 30–41.

ICTs enable work to be brought home and contact with the home at work. This trend will continue with AmI, although it can lead to some problems as shown in the scenario.

### Scene 1: At home and at work

Although many people could be teleworking in the future, the scenario shows that face-to-face contacts are still important. Ricardo is able to make use of his father's absence to enter the study before the smart room door closes. Paul's employer has imposed certain security measures to enable Paul to work at home. One of these is the fingerprint scan needed to open the study door. Another is the biometric protection via iris recognition but Ricardo is able to spoof that with a picture of Paul's iris because iris scanners are inexpensive. Ricardo is able to use his father's identity to bypass the parental control system and to shop online. Another security weakness is the easy-to-guess passwords or codes. The scenario also shows that different security systems are used for different purposes.

Later, at work, Paul receives alarming information that something is wrong at home, but he does not know what. This obviously creates a feeling of loss of control. He soon finds out that he is being digitally blackmailed (a new crime, or rather an existing crime in new clothes). Then, Paul meets his boss following an informal police check caused by inadequate profiling. The search for all digital information on Paul highlights a disproportionate reaction to a suspicion based on an inaccurate profile.

### Scene 2: Shopping at work

Scene two tells the story of Maruja's preparing for a business meeting while communicating with her daughter and with Shopping Assistant Software (SAS). It provides examples of AmI vulnerabilities within a commercial context. In the first instance, the SAS does not find a suitable gift. In the second instance, it misinterprets the notion of funny in relation to a farewell present for a girlhood friend and gives sex-related suggestions. These suggestions would normally only be visible on Maruja's PWC, but she accidentally projects them on the big screen during her business meeting. Not only is this embarrassing but also it leads to Maruja's losing a client and, consequently, an end-of-year bonus. The complexity of the technology in relation to the value the user gets from using it is in question here.

More vulnerabilities pop up when Maruja accepts a special offer, suggested by her daughter, to buy a computer game. Because they didn't have the time to check out the web site properly, Maruja is afflicted by powerful spyware that captures her personal data without her knowing about it. That was exactly the purpose of the special offer on the computer game. It is a manifestation of a new crime called data laundering.

Another issue is related to control as shown in the situation where children seek to circumvent parental and teacher control over playing computer games at school and the work situation where staff are "controlled" during business meetings to the extent that what is said is automatically recorded. The latter instance, however, can result in a decision taken on the basis of incomplete information, i.e., information that is not recorded.

### Scene 3: At the park

Scene three starts with Maruja's going to a park for her lunch break to disconnect from her disastrous business meeting. Unfortunately, she gets spammed continuously with location-based advertising as a result of a misinterpretation of her personal profile. The avatar makes mistakes (Chinese food), is not informed (sandwich lunch) or gets influenced (low price restaurant). It shows that people can be irritated and annoyed by certain AmI applications. Maruja decides to switch off temporarily but later she regrets having missed a call from her boss and not being aware of the nearby presence of a friend.

Her friend Claire goes through a much worse situation because she is robbed while working in her apartment. The high-tech criminals did not expect her to be at home. By reading the RFID tags on Claire's blouse and by hacking[13] the client database of the shop that sold the blouse, they were able to determine the location of her apartment. The criminals did not know that Maruja, not Claire, was wearing the blouse. Claire not only suffers physically and financially from the crime, but also needs to invest time in retraining her PWC again because she did not have her profile stored online. Although it was saved locally on her PC, the burglars wrecked her machine.

In the park, Maruja encounters a foreign visitor asking for the whereabouts of the central market. Maruja is surprised by the request because she (Maruja) would never go abroad without her location device. Maruja does not realise that this woman did not have a choice because of a lack of a roaming agreement between their respective service providers. Another issue is raised in the last situation in which Maruja reflects on theft of her electronic purse in a dangerous neighbourhood. While AmI technologies allow the update of neighbourhood crime rates and guide users out of such places, they still depend on the business models supporting such applications. Maruja did not know because she forgot to authorise the update of her location software.[14]

## 3.2.4   AmI technologies and devices

The  scenario makes reference to several AmI or AmI-related technologies:

- Sensors and actuators
    - Embedded in the environment and in objects, such as the sensors in Paul's study used to monitor physical presence and actuators that close the door after a while for security reasons
    - RFID tags attached to clothing (readable from a distance) with backward traceability to the shop which sold it
- Indoor and outdoor positioning devices
- Biometrics including a fingerprint reader to open the door of the study and an iris scanner to authenticate online identity (which Ricardo manages to spoof because the model did not yet contain liveness testing)

---

[13] Krebs, Brian, "Teen Pleads Guilty to Hacking Paris Hilton's Phone", *Washington Post*, 13 September 2005. http://www.washingtonpost.com/wp–dyn/content/article/2005/09/13/AR2005 091301423.html

[14] See recent experiments with so-called Map Mash-Ups, combining geographical visualisation tools such as Google Maps with other data such as local crime statistics: Wade Roush, Killer Maps, www.technologyreview.com, October 2005.

- Interfaces
    - Smart clothing, e.g., the blouse that has an integrated flexible screen
    - Speech and voice recognition
- Intelligent algorithms
    - For data mining (e.g., used by police)
    - Speech recognition
    - Web search algorithms
- A Personal Wrist Communicator which is a multi-functional (phone, watch, camera, colour display) personal intelligent device
- Wireless, wireline and broadband communications networks

### 3.2.5   AmI applications

The AmI technologies referenced in the scenario are used in various applications:

- Security – restricted and authenticated access to Paul's study via a fingerprint reader and to his online profile via an iris scanner; automatic closing of a door when the absence of a person is detected
- Remote surveillance of the home and other premises
- Digital rights management (DRM), e.g., a licence fee associated with an IP number to prevent illegal copies
- Audio tracking of meetings and automated transcription into text
- Shopping Assistant Software (SAS) with intelligent search capabilities for e-commerce
- Powerful spyware programmes to detect personal profiles
- Personalised advertising
- Seamless migration of content on different platforms/screens, from a PWC to big screens but only when explicitly authorised (and this went wrong in the case of Maruja as a result of a hasty decision)
- New crimes such as digital blackmail, determining the presence or absence of people by reading RFID tags incorporated in clothing and other objects, crime information networks (e.g., Google Earth combined with local crime statistics)
- Temporary online offers for quick decision-makers
- Location-based services
    - Automated priority settings on incoming messages (e.g., Paul in his boss's office; Maruja during her business meeting)
    - Advertising.

### 3.2.6   Drivers

Drivers for the AmI technologies and/or dark situations elaborated in the scenario are the following:

- *Telework* (working from home) – Although telework's importance and prevalence have been predicted for some decades, AmI might give a boost to it, not only because of the availability of high-bandwidth infrastructures, but also of its user-friendliness, media richness and proximity to face-to-face interactions (although these are still needed, as mentioned in the scenario).
- *Convenience* – The AmI home addresses human weaknesses (via sensors and actuators) such as forgetting to close a door or window or to put out the lights or to turn off the cooker, etc.
- *Parental control* – The adoption of AmI technologies may be stimulated by those who seek greater parental control of children and, in particular, their access to services, drinks, entertainment, etc. On the other hand, clever children such as Ricardo may try to circumvent control mechanisms in order to engage in ID theft within the family.
- *Crime* – Criminals may see AmI as offering opportunities for new forms of old crimes such as blackmail (on a small scale involving many people for small amounts of money) by intervening into personal and home networks; data laundering (personal profiles for which people are willing to pay money); robbery (of, e.g., electronic purses or by means of the remote detection of the presence/absence of wealthy individuals); exploiting weaknesses in AmI crime information networks such as a well-known weakness in the security of personal and home networks when rebooting.
- *Security* – Individuals, groups and societies will see AmI-based services such as remote surveillance as enhancing protection of physical premises as well as protecting their online identities.
- *Personalisation* – AmI will be driven by, inter alia, companies who see opportunities for better market penetration through the provision of personalised services such as suggestions for shopping (e.g., Shopping Assistant Software); for eating (e.g., restaurants) and for matching personal profiles with location-based information. Personalisation is also likely to be an important driver for individuals as well, who will enjoy the benefits of services specifically tailored to their interests, needs and desires.

## 3.2.7   Issues

The scenario raises several issues by showing what can go wrong with AmI in everyday life. Many of them have to do with human factors such as failing to take adequate measures and feelings of loss of control.

### 3.2.7.1   Human factors and security

Human factors such as excitement can cause people to forget things (closing the door to the study), but AmI can help address the consequences (closing the door, locking access to online services). As studies show repeatedly, however, human errors constitute major security weaknesses. AmI will certainly help to overcome this problem, but it would be naïve to assume that human failings could be factored out completely. Since not everything in the smart home will be accessed via biometric verification only, people will continue to use easy-to-guess or accessible passwords and/or access codes.

Remote surveillance of the smart home is not enough to secure it. Security requires on-the-spot checks and back-up systems if something goes wrong. False "automatic" alarms could be an issue in the future to the extent that they become counterproductive and ignored.

The scenario depicts other vulnerabilities: Maruja accepts a special offer, suggested by her daughter, to buy a computer game on a web site that they did not check out properly because of lack of time.

### 3.2.7.2   Loss of control

Dark feelings can range from irksome to burdensome and entail annoyance and embarrassment. Although AmI is supposed to be seamless and only visible when we want it to be, it can be assumed that it also occupies our minds since settings have sometimes to be confirmed or changed. AmI cannot know everything. It has to be fed information, which places a burden on people. Also, when AmI does not function as it should, people will get annoyed, possibly leading to their temporarily rejecting it (switching off). Annoyance can be foreseen when AmI does things that are not expected or wanted, even if authorised (willingly or unwillingly). All this contributes to a feeling of loss of control.

Scene 1 shows a loss of control when Paul receives an alarm from his home system but without details on what is happening. He depends on his AmI system, but it does not behave as expected. More examples are raised in scene 2. Maruja gets an unexpected message on the same screen as her business presentation. The sex-related message came from an AmI service (Shopping Assistant Software), which had misinterpreted her desire for a "funny" gift. She is annoyed and embarrassed. In scene 3, Maruja is irritated because her avatar was not able to take into account her preferences.

Loss of control is also depicted when children seek to circumvent parental and teacher prohibitions over playing computer games at school. At work, employees are subjects controlled by automatic recording of what is said in meetings which in turn can lead to decisions taken on the basis of incomplete information, i.e., information that is not recorded.

### 3.2.7.3.   Disproportionate reaction to suspicions

The scenario shows a weakness in profiling which leads to a disproportionate reaction to (unjustified) suspicions. Paul's boss informs him that he is being checked out by the police who have found that he seems to match one of their profiles of criminals. AmI systems generate lots of publicly available data on individuals, so the police can check out people before seeking a search warrant. But profiling systems also generate false positives, and Paul's case is one such. Unfortunately for Paul, being subject to police scrutiny has negative consequences. He is under a cloud at work and misses out on a promotion.

#### 3.2.7.4  Insider ID theft

Ricardo is able to use his father's identity to bypass parental controls and to shop and gamble online. The scenario shows that ID theft is possible without criminal intentions, that people who know each other can also breach privacy (the "little brother" phenomenon) and that once an ID is misappropriated, it is easy to spend money because payments are automated, at least up to a limit.

#### 3.2.7.5  Exclusion

Not all AmI services will be available to everyone, of course. In scene 3, the foreign woman in the park does not have access to personalised location-based services because of a lack of an agreement between service providers.

### 3.2.8  Legal synopsis

#### 3.2.8.1  Working from home

The first scene of this scenario highlights the important issue of privacy protection. Privacy is not only a social expectation, but it is also expressed in legal terms. Within the western legal system, privacy is primarily an issue of international and constitutional law, protected by explicit provisions, both in international human rights treaties and in the distinct national constitutions. The first provision to mention is Article 12 of the 1948 **Universal Declaration of Human Rights**,[15] although, strictly speaking, it has no legally binding force. Article 17 of the 1966 **International Covenant on Civil and Political Rights (ICCPR)** also seeks to protect privacy.[16] And finally, Article 8 of the

---

[15] Article 12 of the Universal Declaration of Human Rights (United Nations, 1948): "No one shall be subjected to arbitrary interference with his privacy, family, home or correspondence, nor to attacks upon his honour and reputation. Everyone has the right to the protection of the law against such interference or attacks."

[16] Article 17 of the International Covenant on Civil and Political Rights (United Nations, 1966): "1. No one shall be subjected to arbitrary or unlawful interference with his privacy, family, home or correspondence, nor to unlawful attacks on his honour and reputation. 2. Everyone has the right to the protection of the law against such interference or attacks."

**European Convention on Human Rights (ECHR)**[17] confers respect for private life. Both the ICCPR and the ECHR are binding treaties. Article 17 of the ICCPR and Article 8 of the ECHR[18] directly affect national legal systems. Both can be invoked and applied by national judges. The **Charter of Fundamental Rights of the European Union** also protects privacy (Article 7) and personal data (Article 8) of individuals.[19]

The protection of the private home together with the protection of privacy is guaranteed at the European level by Article 8 of the ECHR.[20] There is no explicit mention of a right to have data protected in the ECHR, but the case law of the European Court of Human Rights (the Strasbourg Court) leaves no mistake about this right being incorporated in the more general right to protection of privacy. Issues regarding violations of the home are also seen as privacy issues and vice versa. These rights are not absolute. Exceptions are possible (Article 8(2)), however, they have to fulfil several criteria: the restriction must be foreseen by law (the formal criterion); it must be necessary in a democratic society (the necessity criterion); it can only be used to achieve one of the specific and limited goals set out in Article 8 of the ECHR, including public security and the safeguarding of rights and freedoms of others (the legitimacy criterion). The Strasbourg Court has ruled that any action must be useful, indispensable and proportionate to achieve the set goal (the proportionality criterion). The last standard implies that the established goal could not be reached through measures that would have had a lesser impact on the guaranteed freedom of the individual concerned.

Article 8 of the ECHR has weaknesses. For instance, it does not apply to the private sector in a straightforward manner: you cannot take firms to Strasbourg; instead, you have to sue the Member State(s) responsible for human rights violations of private actors. The protection of personal data by privacy rights is not complete: the right to a private life, as interpreted by the Court, does not necessarily include all personal data; and the right of access to personal data is not covered by this Article, nor is the right to correct erroneous personal data.[21] These limitations explain why it was

---

[17] Council of Europe – European Convention on Human Rights of 4 November 1950.

[18] The ICCPR is overshadowed by the ECHR because the latter is older, has a strong supranational judicial control mechanism and the Strasbourg Court has issued an impressive list of judgments on privacy.

[19] Charter of Fundamental Rights of the European Union, *Official Journal* C 341, 18 December 2002. Article 7 says, "Everyone has the right to respect for his or her private and family life, home and communications"; Article 8 says, "Everyone has the right to the protection of personal data concerning him or her. Such data must be processed fairly for specified purposes and on the basis of the consent of the person concerned or some other legitimate basis laid down by law. Everyone has the right of access to data that has been collected concerning him or her, and the right to have it rectified. Compliance with these rules shall be subject to control by an independent authority."

[20] Article 8 of the European Convention on Human Rights states: "1. Everyone has the right to respect for his private and family life, his home and his correspondence. 2. There shall be no interference by a public authority with the exercise of this right except such as is in accordance with the law and is necessary in a democratic society in the interests of national security, public safety or the economic well-being of the country, for the prevention of disorder or crime, for the protection of health or morals, or for the protection of the rights and freedoms of others."

[21] Maghiros, I. (ed.), *Security and Privacy for the Citizen in the Post-September 11 Digital Age: A Prospective Overview,* Report to the European Parliament Committee on Citizens' Freedoms and Rights, Justice and Home Affairs (LIBE), IPTS Technical Report, Institute for Prospective Technological Studies, Seville, 2003. ftp://ftp.jrc.es/pub/EURdoc/eur20823en.pdf

necessary to create an independent set of data protection regulations at the level of the Council of Europe and the European Union. Unlike the ECHR privacy protection, the European Data Protection Directive[22] applies to the processing of personal data in both the private and public sectors (with limited exceptions).

The coexistence of privacy and data protection regulations can be understood as follows. According to Article 8 of the ECHR and its interpretation by the Court of Strasbourg, privacy is a legal concept to ensure non-interference in individual matters by the state and other powerful actors. It works as a shield to protect the opacity (anonymity) of the individual. Opacity is linked to the recognition of human rights, individual autonomy and self-determination. Normative in nature, opacity tools can be distinguished from transparency, which aims not against the power, but at channelling or controlling the power of the state and others. Transparency tools provide for a system of checks and balances and procedural safeguards. Interference into one's autonomy is then allowed, but under control.[23] This is the standpoint of the data protection laws, which also aim at protecting privacy. In sum, data protection is not prohibitive. The data protection regulations created a legal framework whereby the processing of personal data is in principle allowed and legal[24] (and therefore mainly belongs to tools of transparency) subject to safeguards protecting individuals, promoting accountability by government and private data holders, and providing data subjects with an opportunity to contest inaccurate or abusive record-holding practices. The rationale behind data protection in the public sector is the knowledge that authorities can easily infringe privacy and that in all administrative systems is an urge to collect, store and use data, an urge which must be curtailed by legal regulation. A similar rationale explains the European option to regulate data processing in the private sector.

The basic principles of data protection are spelled out by various international institutions, such as the Organization for Economic Cooperation and Development (**OECD Guidelines**[25]), the Council of Europe (**Treaty 108**[26]), the

---

[22] Directive 95/46/EC of the European Parliament and of the Council of 24 October 1995 on the protection of individuals with regard to the processing of personal data on the free movement of such data, *Official Journal* L 281, 23 November 1995. This Directive has been supplemented by data protection provisions in other, more specific directives.

[23] For more on opacity and transparency, see De Hert, P., and S. Gutwirth "Making sense of privacy and data protection. A prospective overview in the light of the future of identity, location based services and the virtual residence" in Maghiros, I. (ed.) *Security and Privacy for the Citizen in the Post-September 11 Digital Age*, op. cit.

[24] An outright processing ban effectively applies only to special categories of sensitive personal data concerning racial or ethnic origin, political opinions, religious or philosophical beliefs, trade union membership, health or sex life.

[25] OECD Guidelines Governing the Protection of Privacy and Transborder Flows of Personal Data, 23 September 1980.

[26] Convention for the Protection of Individuals with Regard to Automatic Processing of Personal Data, *European Treaty Series – No. 108*, Strasbourg, 28 January 1981.

**UN Guidelines**[27] and the European Union (the Data Protection Directive). The European Union has also included the right to data protection in the European Charter of Fundamental Rights (see supra).

Within the European Union, the main source of regulation in the field is the **Data Protection Directive**,[28] together with legislation implementing it nationally. The Directive applies to the processing of data relating to an identified or identifiable natural person or "personal data".[29] Anonymous data do not fall under the scope of the Directive.[30] The Directive grants every person the right not to be subject to a decision that produces legal effects concerning him or significantly affects him and that is based solely on automated processing of data.[31]

The Directive applies to both the private and public sectors. It does not apply to processing of personal data by a natural person for purely personal and domestic purposes, and to data concerning legal persons. It also does not apply to processing carried out for purposes of public security, defence and national security or in the course of State activities in areas of criminal law and other activities that do not come within the scope of Community law.[32]

The Data Protection Directive and national data protection laws in general provide for a number of requirements in order to legally process personal information.[33] Those are twofold: on the one hand, there exists a series of rights for individuals[34] such as the right to receive certain information whenever data are collected, the right

---

[27]The United Nations Guidelines for the Regulation of Computerized Personal Data Files, adopted by General Assembly resolution 45/95 of 14 December 1990, are a more recent international instrument. We do not discuss these UN guidelines, because they are overshadowed by the other regulations in Europe.

[28]Directive 95/46/EC.

[29]It is not always clear what should be understood as "personal data" or when data are anonymous. See Chapter 5, section 5.3.4, subsection on "Data protection and profiling: a natural pair".

[30]However, the problem of anonymous data can be relative in some circumstances: the notion of "identifiable" in the European Directive is, unlike other international data protection texts, very extensive. Data that at first glance do not look like personal data can very often lead to an individual. Even if a processor wants data to be anonymous, they may not. The definition of "identifiable" is so broad that data can be considered personal as long as the controller himself is still able to identify the persons behind the data. Staying out of reach of European data protection is only possible through maximum anonymity.

[31]The Data Protection Directive, Article 15. See also sections 3.2.8.4 and 3.5.8.1 as well as Chapter 5, section 5.3.4, subsection on "Data protection and profiling: a natural pair".

[32]The Data Protection Directive, Article 3. There is now a debate about whether to extend data protection to third pillar issues: See Proposal for a Council framework decision on the protection of personal data processed in the framework of police and judicial co-operation in criminal matters, COM (2005) 475 final of 4 October 2005. http://eur – lex.europa.eu/LexUriServ/site/en/com/2005/com2005_0475en01.pdf

[33]For an overview, see Gutwirth, S., *Privacy and the information age*, Rowman & Littlefield, Lanham/Boulder/New York/Oxford, 2002, pp. 83–112.

[34]See the discussion on the right to be informed in sections 3.2.8.4, 3.2.8.7 and 3.4.8.4; the right to consult the data, the right to have data corrected and the obligation on data controllers to collect and keep relevant, correct and up-to-date data in sections 3.2.8.2, 3.3.8.3 and 3.5.8.2 and the right to object to certain types of data processing in section 3.5.8.1.

of access to the data and, if necessary, the right to have the data corrected and the right to object to certain types of data processing. Also, data protection law generally demands good data management practices by the data controllers and imposes a series of obligations[35]: the obligation to use personal data for specified, explicit and legitimate purposes (finality or purpose specification principle), the obligation to guarantee the confidentiality and security of the data against accidental or unauthorised access or manipulation and, in some cases, the obligation to notify a specific independent supervisory body before carrying out certain types of data processing. These laws provide specific safeguards or special procedures to be applied in the case of transfers of data abroad. Any processing of personal data must be lawful and fair to the individuals (fairness principle). All data must be adequate, relevant and not excessive in relation to a purpose for which they are collected and/or further processed (proportionality principle). There is also a prohibition on processing sensitive data. To be legitimate, personal data may only be processed if the data subject has unambiguously given his consent. It may be processed without his consent under limited conditions provided by law.[36]

The challenge for data protection law in relation to AmI mainly concerns the reconciliation of the principles of data protection law with the concept of AmI. This challenge emerges because AmI and its supporting technologies need personal data and profiles to work. In order to provide people with information (enhanced goods and services), AmI needs to process personal information.[37] The decreasing cost of these technologies as well as the increasing emergence of customers willing to pay for these services are already noticeable trends.

The **Privacy & Electronic Communications Directive**[38] contains specific legal, regulatory and technical provisions for electronic communications. It applies only to

---

[35] See the discussion on the finality and purpose specification principle in sections 3.2.8.2 and 3.2.8.7, the confidentiality and security obligation in sections 3.2.8.3 and 3.3.8.3, the obligation to notify the supervisory body and the fairness principle in sections 3.2.8.2 and 3.5.8.2, the proportionality principle in sections 3.2.8.2 and 3.3.8.4, the prohibition on processing sensitive data in sections 3.3.8.4 and 3.5.8.1, and the specific safeguard to be applied in the case of transfer of data abroad in section 3.4.8.1.

[36] When the processing is necessary for (1) the performance of a contract to which the data subject is party or in order to take steps at the request of the data subject prior to entering into a contract, or (2) compliance with a legal obligation to which the controller is subject, or (3) protecting the vital interests of the data subject, or (4) the performance of a task carried out in the public interest or in the exercise of official authority vested in the controller or in a third party to whom the data are disclosed, or (5) the purposes of the legitimate interests pursued by the controller or by the third party or parties to whom the data are disclosed, except where such interests are overridden by the interests for fundamental rights and freedoms of the data subject (Data Protection Directive, Article 7). The issue of consent is further discussed in sections 3.3.8.4 and 3.4.8.2.

[37] However, this means that not only should concepts, scenarios, practices and techniques of AmI be tested on their compliance with data protection law, but also data protection law itself can and should be put into question if necessary, e.g., where some data protection rights cannot be reconciled on a reasonable ground with good practices and techniques of AmI that are preferable and desired by the user.

[38] Directive 2002/58/EC of the European Parliament and of the Council of 12 July 2002 concerning the processing of personal data and the protection of privacy in the electronic communications sector (Directive on privacy and electronic communications), *Official Journal* L 201, 31 July 2002, pp. 37–47.

public communication services, whereas the Data Protection Directive applies to both public and non-public services. The Privacy & Electronic Communications Directive not only protects fundamental rights and freedoms of natural persons, but also the legitimate interests of legal persons, whereas the Data Protection Directive only offers protection to natural persons. Neither of the directives applies to activities concerning public security, defence, state security and the activities of the state in areas of criminal law. The Privacy & Electronic Communications Directive stipulates that Member States may, for reasons of national security, defence, public security and the prevention, investigation and prosecution of criminal offences, enact legislation providing for the retention of traffic and location data pertaining to all forms of electronic communications by telecommunications operators.[39] It imposes security and confidentiality obligations on service providers[40] and foresees specific rules for traffic[41] and location[42] data and provides for limits in processing such information.

---

[39] Directive 2006/24/EC of the European Parliament and of the Council on the retention of data generated or processed in connection with the provision of publicly available electronic communications services or of public communications networks and amending Directive 2002/58/EC, *Official Journal* L 105, 13 April 2006. This retention possibility has been firmly criticised by EPIC (www.epic.org) and Privacy International (www.privacyinternational.org): "Although this data retention provision is supposed to constitute an exception to the general regime of data protection established by the Directive, the ability of governments to compel Internet service providers and telecommunications companies to store all data about all of their subscribers can hardly be construed as an exception to be narrowly interpreted. The practical result is that all users of new communications technologies are now considered worthy of scrutiny and surveillance in a generalized and preventive fashion for periods of time that States' legislatures or governments have the discretion to determine." See Andrews, S., *Privacy and human rights 2002*, produced by the Electronic Privacy Information Center (EPIC), Washington, DC, and Privacy International, London, 2002, p. 44. http://privacyinternational.org/survey/phr 2002. These privacy invasive retention schemes were devised in the aftermath of 11 September 2001. Critics also come from Internet service providers who are confronted with the storage and security costs, and from other human rights organisations like Statewatch (www.statewatch.org) and EDRI (http://www.edri.org). See also Article 29 Working Party, *Opinion 4/2005 on the Proposal for a Directive on the retention of Data processed in connection with the Provision of Public Electronic Communications Services and Amending Directive 2002/58/EC* (http://ec.europa.eu/justice_home/fsj/privacy/workinggroup/index_en.htm). The Data Retention Directive is also discussed under section 3.2.8.4.

[40] See also sections 3.2.8.3 and 3.3.8.3.

[41] " '[T]raffic data' means any data processed for the purpose of the conveyance of a communication on an electronic communications network or for the billing thereof" (Article 2). The level of protection of traffic data depends on the purpose of the processing: (1) transmission of communication, (2) billing or (3) marketing electronic communication as well as providing of value-added services, e.g., tourist information, route guidance, traffic information and weather forecasts, and generally may be processed by the service provider to the extent and for the duration necessary for that purpose. In any of these cases, processing of traffic data must be restricted to what is necessary for the purposes of such activities and must be restricted to persons acting under the authority of the network or service provider. In any of these cases, if data are processed for a longer time than for the transmission, the user or subscriber must be informed of the duration of such processing (Article 6 of the Privacy & Electronic Communications Directive).

[42] " 'Location data' means any data processed in an electronic communications network, indicating the geographic position of the terminal equipment of a user of a publicly available electronic

AmI will cause a blurring of the boundaries between spaces and activities. The first scenario gives an example of a father, working for a security company mostly from his private home. New communication technology facilitates teleworking and makes it possible to deal with private business from an office. Boundaries between what is private and what is professional will become less distinctive and more permeable than today. What are the consequences of such ambiguous situations from a privacy point of view? How can a distinction still be made between private and professional, private and public? Such situations result in doubts about the extent to which privacy is legally protected in professional contexts, especially when employees work outside the office.

The European Court of Human Rights has clarified that the protection of private life does not exclude the professional life, and that it is not limited to the life within the home or family. In *Niemitz* v. *Germany* (23 November 1992), the Court stated that there is no reason why the notion of "private life" should be taken to exclude activities of a professional or business nature. Moreover, the Court added that this view is supported by the fact that "it is not always possible to distinguish clearly which of an individual's activities form part of his professional or business life and which do not." In *Halford* v. *United Kingdom* (27 May 1997), the Court introduced the criterion of "reasonable expectations of privacy". Accordingly, Miss Halford, a senior officer whose telephone calls were intercepted without warning, was granted privacy protection in her office space, although not absolutely. The protection of privacy at work remains one of the grey areas in European human rights law. The case of Halford, a senior officer with privileges, is in itself not a typical case. More case law is needed to clarify the reasonable expectation of privacy in the workplace. It should also be borne in mind that surveillance of the individual after a suspicion has been raised raises fewer concerns than the general surveillance at workplace, in a public building or at home. It is unclear how and if the reasonable expectation of privacy would apply in AmI situations as described in Scenario 1. While being always online, would we be able to talk with any expectation of privacy at all?

An additional problem is the lack of clarity regarding the consequences of privacy violations. The European Court of Human Rights is unwilling to reject evidence obtained through privacy violations. In cases such as *Khan* (2000) and *P.H. & P.G. against the United Kingdom* (2001), the Strasbourg court decided that a violation of Article 8 of the ECHR had taken place, but it nevertheless accepted the evidence found in violation of Article 8 of the ECHR in a criminal process.

---

communications service" (Article 2). Location data may only be processed (a) when they are made anonymous or (b) with the consent of the users or subscribers to the extent and for the duration necessary for the provision of a *value-added service*. When consent has been obtained, the user shall be given the possibility to *withdraw his consent* for the processing of such data at any time and must continue to have the possibility, using a simple means and free of charge, of *temporarily refusing* the processing of such data for each connection to the network or for each transmission of a communication (Article 9 of the Privacy & Electronic Communications Directive).

Some national courts have followed this line of reasoning. In Belgium, there are examples of the erosion of privacy law in the workplace: The Belgian Data Protection Act (1992, revised in 1998) and the Collective Labour Agreement 68 of 16 June 1998 foresee that strict procedures of information and negotiation must be followed when cameras are installed in the workplace. Thus, employees must be informed when an employer installs cameras. The *Cour de Cassation*, the highest Belgian court, argued in a recent case that Articles 6 and 8 of the ECHR do not necessarily mean that the infringement of the information and negotiation procedure laid down in data protection law voids the evidence obtained with a hidden camera (in this case, a theft by an employee).[43]

Most probably AmI will challenge our understanding of the terms "home" and "communication" and require a reinterpretation of the term private life, since the distinction between private and professional life might become further blurred. It is unclear how and if the criterion of "reasonable expectations of privacy" will be applied further by the European courts. It is equally unclear how this criterion will apply in an AmI world. If the privacy case law does not offer sufficient and clear privacy protection of AmI environments, additional legal and constitutional protection may be warranted.

### 3.2.8.2   Digital rights management

The scenario gives an example of using online content and accessing online services by unauthorised individuals, who manage to spoof the technical access control. It also shows a new model of consuming the content legally by accessing it from a given location in accordance with the licence provisions (Ricardo's friends play an online game for which Ricardo has a licence). Licence provisions (stipulating how the content might be used, on which device, or how many times) will most probably be governed by digital rights management (DRM) systems.

In order to manage access rights, some digital rights management mechanisms would probably be used. If intrusive DRMs are chosen, systems might require identification and authentication of users having rights to the content, and might monitor how many times users access the work, how long they consume the content, what other content they like, etc. Such DRM systems allow content holders not only to process personal data (user behaviour), but also to construct (group) profiles, building statistics, consumer behaviour, etc. Here again, personal data are stored for a longer period and for purposes of which the user may not always be aware. This issue bears on the protection of privacy and personal data.

---

[43] See also De Hert, P., and M. Loncke, "Camera Surveillance and Workplace Privacy in Belgium", in Sjaak Nouwt, Berend R. de Vries and Corien Prins (eds.), *Reasonable Expectations of Privacy? Eleven Country Reports on Camera Surveillance and Workplace Privacy*, T.M.C. Asser Press, The Netherlands, 2005, pp. 167–209. See also the judgment of the Belgian *Cour de Cassation* of 2 March 2005 at http://www.juridat.be.

Creating profiles via DRM systems may conflict with some principles expressed in Article 6 of the Data Protection Directive,[44] like, inter alia, fairness and lawfulness, purpose specification and finality, data accuracy and proportionality. For example, the proportionality criterion laid down in Article 6 obliges policy-makers to consider alternative, less infringing ways of reconciling intellectual property rights with privacy rights.

DRMs are protected against circumvention under the **Copyright Directive**,[45] even if they impede data protection provisions. Member States must grant protection against any person knowingly performing without authority acts such as: "(a) the removal or alteration of any electronic rights-management information; (b) the distribution, importation for distribution, broadcasting, communication or making available to the public of works or other subject-matter protected under this Directive or under Chapter III of Directive 96/9/EC from which electronic rights-management information has been removed or altered without authority" (Article 7).

The Directive harmonised the legal protection against circumvention of effective technological measures (and against provision of devices and products or services aiming at circumvention), which effectively restrict acts not authorised by the holders of any copyright, rights related to copyright or the *sui generis* right in databases.[46] Notwithstanding this legal protection, Member States shall take appropriate measures to ensure "that the right holders make available to the beneficiaries of an exception or limitation provided for in national law the means of benefiting from that exception or limitation, to the extent necessary to benefit from that exception or limitation and where that beneficiary has legal access to the protected work or subject-matter concerned" (Article 6(4)).

---

[44] Article 6 says, "1. Member States shall provide that personal data must be: (a) processed fairly and lawfully; (b) collected for specified, explicit and legitimate purposes and not further processed in a way incompatible with those purposes. Further processing of data for historical, statistical or scientific purposes shall not be considered as incompatible provided that Member States provide appropriate safeguards; (c) adequate, relevant and not excessive in relation to the purposes for which they are collected and/or further processed; (d) accurate and, where necessary, kept up to date; every reasonable step must be taken to ensure that data which are inaccurate or incomplete, having regard to the purposes for which they were collected or for which they are further processed, are erased or rectified; (e) kept in a form which permits identification of data subjects for no longer than is necessary for the purposes for which the data were collected or for which they are further processed. Member States shall lay down appropriate safeguards for personal data stored for longer periods for historical, statistical or scientific use; 2. It shall be for the controller to ensure that paragraph 1 is complied with."

[45] Directive 2001/29/EC of the European Parliament and of the Council of 22 May 2001 on the harmonisation of certain aspects of copyright and related rights in the information society, *Official Journal* L 167, 22 June 2001.

[46] Article 6 of the Directive states: "Member States shall provide adequate legal protection against the circumvention of any effective technological measures, which the person concerned carries out in the knowledge, or with reasonable grounds to know, that he or she is pursuing that objective."

Another instrument providing for legal protection of the technological measures is the **Software Directive**.[47] The Directive obliges Member States to provide appropriate remedies against a person committing any act of putting into circulation, or the possession for commercial purposes of, any means the sole intended purpose of which is to facilitate the unauthorised removal or circumvention of any technical device which may have been applied to protect a computer program.[48] An important difference between this Directive and the Copyright Directive is that this Directive requires that the "sole" intended purposes is circumventing the technical device, while the Copyright Directive requires that it would be "primarily" designed for this purpose. The Software Directive only protects against the putting into circulation of devices that have no other function than circumventing protective measures, which is an important limitation. Another important difference is that the Software Directive only protects against the putting into circulation, possession of these devices and not against the act of circumventing as such. It would be advisable to have a uniform solution which includes the protection of privacy-enhancing technologies.

**The Directive on the protection of services based on conditional access**[49] should be also mentioned here. This Directive deals with the legal protection of all of those services whose remuneration relies on conditional access, such as television broadcasting, radio broadcasting and especially information society services. Many services in an AmI world will rely on conditional access and it is important to provide sufficient protection of those services. The Directive obliges the Member States to prohibit (a) the manufacture, import, distribution, sale, rental or possession for commercial purposes, (b) the installation, maintenance or replacement for commercial purposes, and (c) the use of commercial communications to promote devices, which enable or facilitate without authority the circumvention of any technological measures designed to protect the remuneration of a legally provided service. A similar legal protection could be provided for privacy-enhancing technologies.

DRM systems might also prevent users from anonymously "consuming" (reading, viewing, listening to) "information". The argument of freedom of expression will probably prove to be one of the more powerful in the future, next to privacy and data protection arguments, against such rights management systems, based on individual identification. General principles of data protection and freedom of expression and thought oppose digital rights management systems and applications that rely on unnecessary individual monitoring or that are used for purposes other than DRM, such as profiling, especially when these other uses are imposed in a

---

[47]Council Directive 91/250/EEC of 14 May 1991 on the legal protection of computer programs, *Official Journal* L 122, 17 May 1991.

[48]Privacy-enhancing technology might be protected against their circumvention under this provision, since they are often software.

[49]Directive 98/84/EC of the European Parliament and of the Council of 20 November 1998 on the legal protection of services based on, or consisting of, conditional access, *Official Journal* L 320, 28 November 1998, pp. 54–57.

non-negotiable way. Possible solutions may be found in e-commerce and consumer protection law, by giving, for example, more legal (and technological) possibilities to consumers to negotiate use of their personal data.

### 3.2.8.3   ID theft and liability

As we saw in the scenario, it was not difficult for Ricardo to obtain access to his father's profile and preferences, as well as to access to his father's professional and confidential documents. Who is responsible for the fact that Ricardo could enter the office and obtain his father's profile? Was the system developed in a way sufficient to prevent manipulation of the kind described in the scenario? Was the father careful enough or did he put the confidential information in his office in jeopardy?

The Data Protection Directive imposes a number of obligations on the data controller, such as those on confidentiality and security of data. Appropriate technical and organisational measures must be taken, at the time of the design of the processing system and at the time of the processing itself to ensure an appropriate level of confidentiality and security, taking into account the state of the art and the costs of their implementation in relation to the risks represented by the processing and nature of the data to be protected (Articles 16 and 17). Analogous security obligations of the service providers are included in the Privacy & Electronic Communications Directive.[50] Compliance with such security obligations is not clearly regulated. When Paul works at home or at any place in the AmI environment and processes personal data of data subjects, for example, his employer's clients, strict compliance with the Data Protection Directive is needed. It is not clear, however, how far the obligations

---

[50] Article 4 says: "(1) Service providers should take appropriate technical and organisational measures to safeguard the security of their services, if necessary in conjunction with the network provider and having in regard the state of the art and the cost of their implementation." According to recital 20, they also have the obligation to take, at their own cost, appropriate and immediate measures to remedy any new, unforeseen security risks and restore the normal security level of the service. See also in the same Article: "(2) In case of a particular risk of a breach of the security of the network, the service provider must inform the subscribers of such risk and, where the risk lies outside the scope of the measures to be taken by the service provider, of any possible remedies, including an indication of the likely costs involved." This information must be free of charge. According to recital 20 of the Directive, the service provider must also inform the users and subscribers of Internet communication services of measures they can take to protect the security of their communications, for instance, by using specific software or encryption technologies.

Article 5 obliges Member States to guarantee the *confidentiality* of communication through national regulations prohibiting any unauthorised listening, tapping, storage or other kinds of interception or surveillance of communications and the related traffic data by persons other than users, without the consent of the users (except when legally authorised to do so or when legally authorised for the purpose of providing evidence of a commercial transaction). In any case, the subscriber or user concerned is provided with clear and comprehensive information in accordance with the Data Protection Directive. The confidentiality of communications applies both to the contents of communications and to the data related to such communications.

of both the "data controller" and the "data processor" (acting under the responsibility of the data controller) go. Who is responsible for the security of the home network used for telework? Is the employer obliged to secure at his risk and at his cost the employee's home-work environment? Who – the employee or the employer – is responsible if personal data relating to customers are copied, altered or stolen through the employee's home network as a consequence of a lack of security? How can the security of the home system network be controlled by a third party? When is the employer liable when something goes wrong with personal data, and when the employee?

All controllers and processors must be aware of the security and confidentiality requirements. National laws should be harmonised to organise data protection and security measures in telework conditions and clear policies should be agreed.

Many Member States have no criminal sanctions for violation of the duty to foresee sufficient security safeguards. Especially when unique identifiers are being collected and processed, lack of protection could be considered as a criminal act. One can foresee specific measures on the use of biometric data and to prohibit badly protected or too risky use of biometrics.[51]

Ricardo was able to enter his father's office and profile relatively easily. Perhaps he was able to hack the profile and view the confidential information (both private and professional information) due to defects in the security system (hardware or software). The question is whether the provider of the security software can be held liable and to what extent this liability can be waived in general contractual terms and conditions. Today, software products' licence agreements clearly indicate that the software is purchased without liability for the loss of information. In this scenario, it is not clear if the defects, if any, are linked to the software or to the hardware. On the basis of actual regulation, this is important: Article 1 of the **Directive on liability for defective products**[52] provides that the producer of a product is liable for damage caused by a defect in his product. A product, however, is only defective when it does not provide the "safety which a person is entitled to expect taking all circumstances into account, including: (a) the presentation of the product; (b) the use to which it could reasonably be expected that the product would be put; (c) the time when the product was put into circulation. A product shall not be considered defective for the sole reason that a better product is subsequently put into circulation."[53] A product is defined as "all movables, with the exception of primary agricultural products and game, even though incorporated into another movable or into an immovable".[54] It is

---

[51] De Hert, P., "Biometrics: legal issues and implications", Background paper for EC JRC – Institute of Prospective Technological Studies, Seville, January 2005.

[52] Council Directive 85/374/EEC of 25 July 1985 on the approximation of the laws, regulations and administrative provisions of the Member States concerning liability for defective products, *Official Journal* L 210, 7 August 1985.

[53] Article 6 of the Directive on liability for defective products.

[54] Article 2 of the Directive on liability for defective products.

unclear today whether this Directive applies to defective software and/or hardware, and whether the Directive could be invoked in the case of ICT products. Also, it is not clear if and to what extent economic damages fall under the concept of damage (injury) in the sense of the Directive.[55]

From a consumer perspective, there are reasons to argue in favour of a full application of the Directive to the issues mentioned in the preceding paragraph. The strict liability regime of the Directive on liability for defective products facilitates establishing the producer's liability, since no proof of fault is required: demonstrating that the product is defective is sufficient. Since the security system did not prevent the son from using his father's profile, we could consider the system to be defective. An important question is, of course, which producer caused the defect and how to find him. Article 3 of the Directive provides for the joint liability of producers and suppliers. It states clearly that, when the producer of a product cannot be identified (which might be a serious problem in an AmI world), the supplier is liable unless "he informs the injured person, within a reasonable time, of the identity of the producer or of the person who supplied him with the product". On the basis of Article 5, two or more persons shall be liable jointly and severally when they are liable for the same damage. This implies that if several service providers are coresponsible for the defect, the victim can claim the total damages from one of them, probably his direct supplier.

In certain specific situations, defined in Article 7, the producer can limit his liability. A producer cannot invoke the fault of others to escape his liability when his product was defective.[56] He can reduce his liability when the victim was coresponsible,[57] as in this case where the father has been negligent. Article 12 does not allow provisions excluding or limiting liability arising from this Directive.

### 3.2.8.4 Inadequate profiling

Paul is astonished because the police request access to his personal data. He has heard that the police have been investigating innocent people because their suspicions were based on inadequate profiling. Paul does not understand why the cyber police suspect him of a certain crime. Probably the cyber police treat him as a suspect, because a small part of his profile fits with that of a perpetrator of a crime. The decision to ask for information from his employer on the basis of this small match is a decision based solely on the automated processing of data intended to

---

[55] See section 6.3.8.

[56] Article 8 (1) of Directive on liability for defective products states: "The liability of the producer shall not be reduced when the damage is caused both by a defect in the product and by the act or omission of a third party."

[57] Article 8 (2) of Directive on liability for defective products states: "The liability of the producer may be reduced or disallowed when, having regard to all the circumstances, the damage is caused both by a defect in the product and by the fault of the injured person or any person for whom the injured person is responsible."

evaluate certain personal aspects relating to him, such as his reliability and conduct. In order to be able to defend himself against these accusations, Paul will need to know which personal data the cyber police collected and processed. The data protection laws traditionally grant rights to the data subject, enabling him to safeguard his interests in the collection and processing of his personal data, including the right to access and correct, the right not to be subject to a decision which produces legal effects concerning him or significantly affects him and which is solely based on such an automated processing of personal data. Such rights are explicitly granted by the Data Protection Directive.[58] However, the Directive does not apply to activities in areas of criminal law (nor, as mentioned above, public security, defence and state security. These services are governed by national data protection laws, which have not been harmonised by an instrument of the European Union. At the same time, threats to security as well as new policing and antiterrorism strategies are paving the way for the acceptance of police practices based on profiling. The principle of availability, for example, included in the European Union's Hague Programme[59] gives greater data protection flexibility to the police.

It is also clear that the longer electronic communications traffic data are retained, the greater are the possibilities for the police to collect and process personal data and to build and use profiling techniques. According to the Privacy & Electronic Communications Directive, electronic communication data must be deleted when they are no longer needed for the provision of the service or for the billing thereof. However, like the Data Protection Directive, the Privacy & Electronic Communications Directive does not apply to activities in areas of criminal law, nor to public security, defence or state security.

That does not mean there is a complete lack of protection and individual guarantees. National data protection rules may provide some safeguards (e.g., the Belgian national data protection law is applicable in such circumstances). National data protection rules have to be in line with the Council of Europe Convention for the Protection of Individuals with regard to Automatic Processing of Personal Data no. 108. With regard to police, security and defence issues, however, the provisions of the 1981 Convention are very sober. The 1981 Convention contains no provision comparable to Article 15 of the Data Protection Directive providing the right not to be subject to a decision that produces legal effects concerning the data subject or significantly affects him and that is solely based on such an automated processing of personal data. This is only partly compensated for in Recommendation No. R (87)15

---

[58] Articles 6, 12 and 15 of the Data Protection Directive.

[59] In the Hague Programme of October 2005, the Commission proposed to substitute the principle that data can only be transmitted to another Member State on the conditions established by the state that holds the information with the "principle of availability". Under the latter principle, the authorities of any Member State would have the same right of access to information held by any other authority in the Union as applies to state authorities within the state where the data are held. According to the Hague Programme, the Commission made a proposal for a Council Framework Decision on the exchange of information under the principle of availability, COM (2005) 490 final. http://europa.eu.int/eur – lex/lex/LexUriServ/site/en/com/2005/com2005_0490en01.pdf

regulating the use of personal data in the police sector (17 September 1987). The recommendation, a "soft law" instrument developed by experts in the context of the 1981 Council of Europe Convention, is not legally binding and was conceived in an era that was unaware of (or unwilling to accept) new forms of systematic and intelligence-led policing. If our police forces were to apply the recommendation today, they would have no choice except to collect data only when there are sufficient grounds to do so and to destroy such data as soon as possible. Clearly, this is not in line with current policing and antiterrorism policies and strategies.

In addition to national laws and international instruments, there are some initiatives at European level relevant to protection of personal data with regard to police, security and defence issues. The **Data Retention Directive**[60] provides for at least six months and a maximum of two years for data retention necessary for the purpose of investigation, detection and prosecution of serious crime. The data to be retained are the traffic and location data necessary to identify the subscriber or registered user. It applies to legal entities and natural persons both. However, it does not apply to the content of communication.[61] The Directive does not indicate what is regarded as a serious crime, except to say that it applies to serious crimes as defined in national laws. It also states that the necessity and proportionality principles must be defined in national laws in accordance with international rules.[62] The respect for the freedoms and fundamental rights of persons concerned are expressed in recitals to the Directive.[63] The Directive also sanctions the access to and transmission of the retained data, which is not permitted under national laws adopted pursuant to this Directive, and provides for the right to compensation in case of damages caused by any unlawful processing of data.[64]

Moreover, the European Commission has proposed a third-pillar data protection instrument.[65] There is a strong need for a coherent instrument for the protection of personal data under the fields now covered by Titles V and VI of the EU Treaty covering current police practices such as profiling. A framework favourable to profiling practices as described in the scenario is not unthinkable, although it should be balanced with adequate guarantees for the data subjects. Defining the rights of the data subject in the context of data processing in a criminal investigation is one of the aims of the draft Framework Decision on the protection of

---

[60] Directive 2006/24/EC.

[61] Articles 1 and 6 of the Data Retention Directive.

[62] Article 4 of the Data Retention Directive.

[63] Recitals 9, 16, 17, 22 and 25 of the Data Retention Directive.

[64] Article 13 of the Data Retention Directive.

[65] Proposal for a Council Framework Decision on the protection of personal data in the framework of police and judicial cooperation in criminal matters, COM(2005) 475 final of 4 October 2005. http://eur – lex.europa.eu/LexUriServ/site/en/com/2005/com2005_0475en01.pdf. The European Union was founded on three pillars. First pillar issues fall within the domain of the European Community. The second pillar concerns matters of common foreign and security policy. The third pillar concerns criminal matters within the domain of police and judicial co-operation.

personal data in the framework of police and judicial co-operation in criminal matters.[66] Such rights are defined in Chapter IV of the proposal. The proposal envisages a data subject's right to information,[67] when data are collected with his knowledge as well as when such data are not obtained from him or are collected without his being aware of such collection.[68] Necessarily, there are some restrictions on such disclosures.[69]

The proposal also foresees the right of access, rectification, erasure or blocking of data,[70] also subject to some restriction.[71] This provision, analogous to Article 12 of the Data Protection Directive, should allow Paul to know why he is suspected by the police and might allow him to prove he is not the person for whom the cyber police are searching. Moreover, the right to rectification, blocking and erasure of data would allow him to correct his profile as created by the cyber police. Article 22 of the proposal would require that any rectification, erasure or blocking be notified to third parties to whom the data have also been disclosed, such as Paul's employer or other state agencies. In addition, the proposal contains provisions relating to the principles of fairness and lawfulness, purpose specification, legitimacy and proportionality, and to data quality.[72]

The obligation to ensure the high quality of data is crucial in order to make sure profiles built on those data are correct and effective as a tool of modern investigation practices.

The above safeguards are essential to protect data subjects against victimisation and abusive commercial practices.

---

[66] See recital 14 of the proposal.

[67] Articles 19 and 20 of the proposal. Some information must be provided, including the identity of the controller, the purposes of the processing the recipients of the data.

[68] Some additional conditions are imposed. See Article 20 (1) of the proposal.

[69] Article 19 (2) and Article 20 (2) of the proposal.

[70] Article 21 (1) states: "(a) without constraint, at reasonable intervals and without excessive delay or expense: confirmation as to whether or not data relating to him are being processed and information at least as to the purposes of the processing, the categories of data concerned, the legal basis of the processing and the recipients or categories of recipients to whom the data have been disclosed; communication to him in an intelligible form of the data undergoing processing and of any available information as to their source; (b) as appropriate, the rectification, erasure or blocking of data the processing of which does not comply with the provisions of this Framework Decision, in particular because of the incomplete or inaccurate nature of the data; (c) notification to third parties to whom the data have been disclosed of any rectification, erasure or blocking carried out in compliance with (b), unless this proves impossible or involves a disproportionate effort."

[71] Article 21 (2) – (4) of the proposal.

[72] Article 4 (1) (d) of the proposal states that personal data must be "accurate and, where necessary, kept up to date. Every reasonable step must be taken to ensure that data which are inaccurate or incomplete, having regard to the purposes for which they were collected or for which they are further processed, are erased or rectified. Member States may provide for the processing of data to varying degrees of accuracy and reliability in which case they must provide that data are distinguished in accordance with their degree of accuracy and reliability, and in particular that data based on facts are distinguished from data based on opinions or personal assessments."

### 3.2.8.5   Monitoring behaviour

Paul and Maruja installed a system to monitor the digital movements of their children. It does not function, since the son has disabled the system, but should the parents be entitled to do so in an AmI world (even outside the private home)? Has Ricardo the right to protect his privacy, especially in his own home? Article 8 of the ECHR protects the private life of every natural person and thus that of Ricardo. Paul may have certain rights to control what his children are doing, but these rights are to be balanced.

**The United Nations Convention on the Rights of the Child**[73] contains a specific privacy right for children. Without denying parental rights, this UN Convention adds more weight to the privacy rights of children. The Convention also sets up monitoring instruments such as National Children Rights Commissioners. "New" problems such as the digital monitoring of children will thus also have to be taken up by National Children Rights Commissioners. It is unclear what the outcome of this balancing act will be. Permanent monitoring infringes on children's privacy rights, but it might be looked upon as a way of or price for granting more physical liberty to children.

### 3.2.8.6   ID theft and payments

Ricardo accessed his father's profile to download movies and make online payments. What is the status of a contract concluded by a minor (probably not capable of concluding contracts independently)? What is the status of contracts concluded by someone who has infringed another's private profile? Ricardo misleads the system, but we can ask how much effort the service supplier should make to ensure that he verifies who the real customer is.

There are two main legal texts relevant to electronic contracts.[74] The first is the **Distance Contract Directive**.[75] It applies to consumer contracts concluded under an organised distance sales or service-provision scheme run by a supplier by means of distance communication. The Directive obliges the supplier to provide to the consumer specific information related to a contract in good time prior to its conclusion. This obligation, created to protect the consumer, also refers to the protection of those unable to give their consent, such as minors. The supplier is obliged to identify himself and the main stipulations of the contract (characteristics of goods or services, price, including all taxes, delivery costs, arrangements for payment, the period for which the offer remains valid and so on). In order to obtain a certain AmI service, many service providers may be involved and it may not be feasible

---

[73] United Nation Convention on the Rights of the Child of 20 November 1989.

[74] On consumer protection, see section 3.3.8.3.

[75] Directive 97/7/EC of the European Parliament and of the Council of 20 May 1997 on the protection of consumers in respect of distance contracts, *Official Journal* L 144, 4 June 1997.

for all of them to provide the required information. How to solve this problem? How can electronic contracts be concluded through intelligent agents? How can conditions, such as consent, provision of information prior to the contract, approval of the goods, etc., be fulfilled?

Article 6 of the Distance Contract Directive provides for a right of withdrawal within at least seven working days. Where the right of withdrawal has been exercised by the consumer, the supplier must reimburse the consumer free of charge. In principle, the father could use this right to cancel the contract. However, he cannot exercise this right where services (such as downloading X-rated movies) are provided before the withdrawal period concludes, or for the supply of goods made to the consumer's specifications or clearly personalised, or for the supply of audio or video recordings or computer software which were unsealed by the consumer or for certain other services such as online betting.[76] It is likely that the goods or services bought by Ricardo fall under one of these exceptions which will be true for many AmI services too. Thus, the right of withdrawal may not be very helpful in an AmI future.

Also, even if Paul were entitled to exercise his right of withdrawal, the refund of sums already paid might be difficult to achieve in practice, especially when goods or services are delivered from outside the European Union. The Distance Contract Directive will not offer much assistance in such cases. What could help is the creation of a trusted third party that receives the payments on behalf of the service provider, while keeping the amount of the payment automatically in a temporary account, until the right of withdrawal has expired.

The Directive also provides for specific information requirements and a written confirmation or confirmation in another "durable medium" that must be made available to the consumer. Among the requirements are information on the right to withdrawal, the supplier's geographical address, after-sales services and guarantees, and the conclusion for cancelling the contract, where it is of unspecified duration or exceeding one year.[77] Again a problem might arise when several suppliers are involved.

The **Directive on electronic commerce** protects consumers in the domain of e-commerce.[78] It applies to information society services defined as "any service normally provided for remuneration, at a distance, by electronic means and at the individual request of a recipient of services".[79] Insofar as they represent an

---

[76] Article 6(3) of the Distance Contract Directive. The Directive also mentions goods that, by reason of their nature, cannot be returned or are liable to deteriorate or expire rapidly.

[77] Article 5 of the Distance Contract Directive.

[78] Directive 2000/31/EC of the European Parliament and of the Council of 8 June 2000 on certain legal aspects of information society services, in particular electronic commerce, in the Internal Market ("Directive on electronic commerce"), *Official Journal L* 178, 17 July 2000.

[79] Article 2 (a) of the Directive on electronic commerce in relation to Article 1(2) of the Directive 98/34/EC of the European Parliament and of the Council of 22 June 1998 laying down the procedure for the provision of information in the field of technical standards and regulations and on rules on information society services, *Official Journal* L 204, 21 July 1998, p. 37. The Directive was amended by the Directive 98/48/EC *(Official Journal* L 217, 5 August 1998, p. 18).

economic activity, they also extend to services which are not remunerated by those who receive them, such as online information or commercial communications or tools for search, access and retrieval of data. Information society services also include the transmission of information via communication networks, providing access to a communication network or hosting information provided by a recipient of the service.

Electronic mail or equivalent individual communications used by natural persons acting outside their business, trade or profession is not regarded as an information society service. The contractual relationship between employers and employees is excluded. Activities that, by their very nature, cannot be carried out at a distance and by electronic means, such as medical advice requiring the physical examination of a patient, also cannot be considered as information society services. In an AmI world, more services will be carried out at a distance and the definition of information society services might change dramatically.

The Directive on electronic commerce imposes important information obligations on the service provider,[80] especially if the contract is concluded by electronic means.[81] Those additional rules, however, do not apply to contracts concluded *exclusively* by exchange of electronic mail or equivalent individual communications. In any case, the contract terms and conditions must be made available to the recipient in a way that allows him to store and reproduce them.[82] Although such provisions might appear useful when contracting online, the Directive does not provide a direct solution in cases where contracts are concluded in abuse of personal profiles.

Ensuring the security of contracts was one of the objectives of the **Directive on electronic signatures**.[83] This Directive creates a legal framework for electronic signatures and for certain certification services. Electronic signatures might

---

[80] Article 5 of the Directive on electronic commerce obliges service providers to provide at least the following information: his name, geographic address, e-mail address, the trade register in which the service provider is entered and his registration number, VAT number, the particulars of the relevant supervisory authority. If the service provider is in a regulated profession, he must identify the relevant professional body with which he is registered, its professional title and make reference to applicable professional rules in the Member State of establishment and the means to access them.

[81] Article 10 (1) of the Directive on electronic commerce states that in such a case, the service provider must supply the following information in a clear, comprehensible and unambiguous way prior to the order being placed: (a) the steps to be followed to conclude the contract; (b) whether or not the concluded contract will be filed by the service provider and whether it will be accessible; (c) the technical means for identifying and correcting input errors prior to the placing of the order; and (d) the languages offered for the conclusion of the contract. Article 11 requires the service provider to acknowledge the receipt of the recipient's order without undue delay and by electronic means and has to provide effective and accessible technical means allowing the recipient to identify and correct input errors, prior to the placing of the order.

[82] Article 10 (2–4).

[83] Directive 1999/93/EC of the European Parliament and of the Council of 13 December 1999 on a Community framework for electronic signatures, *Official Journal* L 013, 19 January 2000.

enhance the security of electronic transactions in an AmI world.[84] To make electronic signatures reliable, they should be certified by professional organisations that can ensure they fulfil the necessary requirements. That is why the Directive tries to promote the establishment of certification service providers. To further enhance the trust in electronic signatures, the Directive enumerates the requirements for secure signature-creation devices to ensure the functionality of advanced electronic signatures. The Directive also deals with the legal effects of electronic signatures[85] and the liability of certification service providers.

### 3.2.8.7  Spyware, personal preferences and the illegal collection of data

When Maruja purchases the game for her daughter on the Web, a powerful spyware program is active, searching personal data and preferences.

The use of spyware clearly constitutes an infringement of the basic principles of data protection. Article 6 of the Data Protection Directive provides that personal data must be processed "fairly and lawfully", a provision linked to the principle of transparency in processing. Moreover, according to the purpose specification principle, personal data must be collected for previously specified, explicit and legitimate purposes and not further processed in a way incompatible with those purposes. The use of techniques such as spyware runs counter to the rights conferred on the individual by the data protection law. In principle, data subjects have to be truly and fully informed about all phases and contexts of the processing procedure.[86] Such transparent information is a *conditio sine qua non* for subsequent controls on data processing. It specifically applies to the gathering of personal data, which should

---

[84] They are also important in an AmI world, since they might allow the use of pseudonyms: Only the certification provider needs to know the identity of the signatory. The party who receives the document with an electronic signature can rely on the certification provider and in case of a legal conflict, the certification provider can exceptionally make the identity of the signatory public.

[85] The legal effects of electronic signatures depend on whether they are advanced electronic signatures according to the criteria laid down by Article 5 of the Directive.

[86] The right to be informed is granted by Articles 10 and 11 of the Data Protection Directive. In collecting data from the data subject, the controller must always provide the data subject with (1) the identity of the controller or his representative and (2) the purposes of the processing for which the data are intended. Some additional information should be provided if necessary to guarantee a fair processing, such as (1) the recipients or categories of recipients of the data, (2) whether replies to the questions are obligatory or voluntary, as well as the possible consequences of a failure to reply [this refers to the question as the data collection technique] and (3) the existence of the right of access and the right to rectify the data concerning the data subject. When the data have not been obtained from the data subject himself but from a third party, the controller or his representative must at the time of undertaking the recording of personal data or, if a disclosure to a third party is envisaged, no later than the time when the data are first disclosed, also provide the data subject with information as described above, including the indication of the categories of data concerned.

not be based on secret, hidden or sly methods. The secret, hidden gathering and processing of personal data or the hidden use of microphones, cameras, listening devices, detectors and programmes are in principle prohibited. No openness, no legitimacy. To be legitimate, according to Article 7 of the Data Protection Directive, personal data may only be processed if the data subject has unambiguously given his consent or if the processing is necessary in certain situations which are clearly not covered in the case of spyware.

**The Cybercrime Convention**[87] is an international instrument that obliges the contracting parties to create both substantive and procedural legislation related to certain offences. The use of spyware programs (installing and spying) is a criminal offence since it involves illegal access (Article 2) and illegal interception (Article 3) when there is, in the latter case, an interception, without right, made by technical means, of non-public transmissions of computer data to, from or within a computer system.

Not only is the use of spyware a criminal offence, the Cybercrime Convention also incriminates the following misuses of devices: "when committed intentionally and without right (a) the production, sale, procurement for use, import, distribution or otherwise making available of a device, including a computer program, designed or adapted primarily for the purpose of committing an illegal access or interception or a data or system interference." Simple possession might constitute a criminal offence (Article 6).

The Convention also provides – under certain conditions – for corporate liability for the above-mentioned offences.

The Convention contains specific procedural rules about expedited preservation of stored computer data, production order, search and seizure of stored computer data, real-time collection of computer data and jurisdiction. General principles are set out concerning international co-operation, extradition, mutual assistance and spontaneous information. In an AmI world, countries will have to co-operate to deal effectively with criminal offences. However, some question such efficiency under the Cybercrime Convention and point out the unsatisfactory status of ratification and the problems with enforcement.

### 3.2.8.8  Data laundering

Companies are paying a lot of money for personal and group profiles, although their origin is not always very clear. As a matter of fact, the illegal origin (illegal collection) of personal data can be camouflaged via a large number of transactions and operations. This phenomenon is known as "data laundering". By definition, data laundering is a violation of data protection legislation, since it hides the fact that personal data were illegitimately processed. Persons and companies involved in or assisting data laundering should be subject to penal sanctions.

Especially companies are prone to participate in data laundering. A way to prevent data laundering could be an obligation on those who buy or otherwise

---

[87] Council of Europe, Cybercrime Convention of 23 November 2001.

acquire databases, profiles or significant amounts of personal data to check diligently the legal origin of these data. Without checking the origin and/or the legality of the databases and profiles, one could consider the buyer equal to a receiver of stolen goods.

Another possibility is to apply the rules of money laundering in a similar way to data laundering, for example, by the obligation to notify the national data protection officer when, how and from whom personal data are acquired. Data laundering via large uncontrolled (commercial) traffic of individual profiles and personal data could become one of the "escape routes" in the struggle against data protection infringements. There are no clear provisions for this in criminal law, but there could be, making it a criminal offence to acquire obviously illegally collected personal data.

### 3.2.8.9    Location-based advertising and spam

Maruja receives lots of targeted advertisements. With new communication possibilities, location-based advertisements and spam grow to new levels. As she gets annoyed with advertisements, Maruja switches off almost completely, cutting herself off from potentially useful information.

Unsolicited electronic communications for the purposes of direct marketing is prohibited, although exceptions exist, for example, in an existing customer relationship. In principle, however, the Privacy & Electronic Communications Directive establishes an opt-in regime, implying the prior consent or wish of the subscriber (Article 13). Other obligations are that the identity of the sender may not be disguised or concealed and that each message must contain an electronic address so that the receiver can easily opt out.

The "unsolicited communications" chapter of the Privacy & Electronic Communications Directive may not apply in some situations. First of all, it will not protect the user against the advertisements for which he did opt in, even though his consent is being abused. In such a case, the user would need to exercise his opt-out right, as mentioned above (which still can lead to frustration and disappointment on the part of the user). Secondly, the article is about commercial communications (see recital 40), so that non-commercial communications fall outside the scope of Article 13. Moreover, the opt-in rule is applicable only to the use of automated calling systems without human intervention (automatic calling machines), facsimile machines (fax) and electronic mail for purpose of direct marketing.

But, in addition, in order to apply the opt-in rule, it must be a commercial "communication". A "communication" is defined in Article 2 (d) of the Privacy & Electronic Communications Directive as "any information exchanged or conveyed between a finite number of parties by means of publicly available electronic communications service. This does not include," continues the definition, "any information conveyed as part of broadcasting service to the public over an electronic communications network except to the extent that the information can be related to the identifiable subscriber or user receiving the information."

One can argue that the opt-in obligation does not apply when the messages are sent to (displays or other embedded devices on clothing, like Maruja's blouse, or other devices that belong to) anonymous persons. In that case, the information cannot be related to an identifiable subscriber or user receiving the information. One can also argue that, if messages are broadcast to everybody who enters a certain area or walks in a certain park or street with his device on, this case falls outside the scope of the Directive as well: There is a constant broadcast in Elm Street and every person walking in Elm Street with his device on can be compared to a person switching his TV from channel X to channel Y.

United States case law has confirmed that pop-ups (small windows separately popping up when visiting a web site, often containing commercial information) do not infringe anti-spam law.[88]

Article 13 of the Privacy & Electronic Communications Directive also provides for an opt-out mechanism in some circumstances. When electronic contact details of consumers are obtained in the context of the sale of a product or a service, these electronic contact details may be used by the same entrepreneur for direct marketing of his own similar products or services, provided, however, that customers clearly and distinctly are given the opportunity to object, free of charge and in an easy manner, to such use of electronic contact details when they are collected and on the occasion of each message in case the customer has not initially refused such use. The opt-out mechanism has several disadvantages. The data subject has to declare specifically that he does not want to receive these messages, which puts a burden on him. He might not know who sends the information[89] and he might have to opt out from a number of personalised message systems. When he opts out, he might also lose important information and services. This limits his freedom to opt out to a great extent. People are even considered suspicious when they decide not to use certain services. Some solution to the above-mentioned problems with location-based communication are foreseen by Article 9(2) of Privacy & Electronic Communications Directive which says that the user has to be able to temporarily refuse processing of location data using simple means and free of charge. That would allow the user to shield himself from location-based (commercial) communication, while still being able to receive other useful information. However, this provision does not protect users against broadcast advertisements, nor does it provide a solution for not losing other location-based information (e.g., "locate my friend" applications) when using the possibility afforded by Article 9(2) to protect oneself against commercial messages.

---

[88] Utah Court of Appeals, *Jesse Riddle* v. *Celebrity Cruises*, 30 December 2004. http://www.droit – technologie.org/1_2.asp?actu_id=1038)

[89] It should be mentioned, however, that the Directive on electronic commerce 2000/31/EC contains an information obligation in the case of commercial communication. The Directive states that, among other information requirements, natural or legal persons on whose behalf the commercial communication is made must be clearly identifiable (Article 6 (b)). As already mentioned, similar provisions facilitating opt-out are contained in Article 13 (4) of the Privacy & Electronic Communications Directive.

The **Directive on electronic commerce 2000/31/EC** also contains important provisions on commercial communications. Article 6 of the Directive obliges the provider of commercial communications, even when they are solicited, to ensure that commercial communications are clearly identifiable as such; to identify the person on whose behalf the commercial communications are made; to ensure that promotional offers and promotional competitions are clearly identifiable as such, and their conditions are easily accessible and presented clearly and unambiguously. Providing this information should allow users to understand the aim of the messages they receive and to distinguish useful from manipulated information. Article 7 of this Directive sets out additional conditions for unwanted commercial communications.

Service providers undertaking unsolicited commercial communications by e-mail should consult regularly and respect the opt-out registers in which natural persons not wishing to receive such commercial communications can register themselves. Consumers should be better protected against spam and unsolicited communications through enforcement. Opt-out registers seem to be insufficient and impractical.

Spam laws, spam filters and other mechanisms have not stopped spam, which already accounts for most of the traffic on the Internet today. Europeans confronted with spam have great difficulties in undertaking civil actions because they cannot find the spammer and, even if they were able to do so, they cannot prove the damage (which is indeed low, from an individual point of view) in a procedure which is too expensive.[90] In the United States, fixed civil remedies (e.g., US$10 per spam received) are built into laws of states such as Arizona, Arkansas, Connecticut, Illinois, Minnesota, New Mexico and North Carolina. Legal certainty should exist in the enforcement of spam law and in new methods and applications targeting people with commercial communications in an AmI world.

In the Distance Contracts Directive,[91] an opt-in rule (prior consent) is provided for use of faxes or automated calling systems, while an opt-out possibility for users must exist for all other means of communication through which distance contracts can be concluded.[92] The opt-in rule for unsolicited communication is important to ensure respect for the consumers' privacy. It should, however, not be limited to faxes and automated calling systems. Opt-out mechanisms for unsolicited communication are less effective.

### 3.2.8.10 An RFID-tagged blouse

Burglars "read" the blouse worn by Maruja. The blouse contains an RFID chip with information about the shop where it was bought. The thieves hack the shop's database

---

[90] But some actions have been successful. A small claims court in Colchester awarded £270 damages against Media Logistics UK for spamming after the complaint took on the company. See Lewis, Paul, "Court victory hailed as spam stopper", *The Guardian*, 28 December 2005. http//www.guardian.co.uk/uk_news/story/0,,1674316,0,0.html

[91] Directive 97/7/EC of the European Parliament and of the Council of 20 May 1997 on the protection of consumers in respect of distance contracts, *Official Journal* L 144, 4 June 1997.

[92] Article 10 of Distance Contract Directive.

to find out where the buyer of the blouse lives. Because the blouse was borrowed from a friend, the burglars confront this friend when they break into the house.

The personal data contained and processed in the RFID-embedded blouse fall under the rules and conditions of data protection law which does not allow secret and unfair collection of personal data. The RFID tag that identifies the object links the purchase data that identify the subject, which is sufficient to regard information on the tag as "personal data".[93]

Moreover, when the burglars accessed the information in the blouse, they committed offences defined by the **Cybercrime Convention**, such as illegal access, possibly illegal interception. The Cybercrime Convention defines illegal access as "when committed intentionally, the access to the whole or any part of a computer system without right". Illegal interception is "when committed intentionally, the interception without right, made by technical means, of non-public transmissions of computer data to, from or within a computer system, including electromagnetic emissions from a computer system carrying such computer data".

The **Council Framework Decision 2005/222/JHA** of 24 February 2005 on attacks against information systems[94] defines illegal access, data and system interference. Article 3 (illegal system interference) obliges Member States to "take the necessary measures to ensure that the intentional serious hindering or interruption of the functioning of an information system by inputting, transmitting, damaging, deleting, deteriorating, altering, suppressing or rendering inaccessible computer data is punishable as a criminal offence when committed without right, at least for cases which are not minor".

It is important to have a common definition of these criminal activities, since they often have a cross-border dimension. The Convention gives participating countries the option to set extra conditions for described actions to be a criminal offence. This freedom limits harmonisation of Member States' laws.

The Council Framework Decision 2005/222/JHA obliges Member States to take measures to comply with the provisions of this Framework Decision by 16 March 2007. Thus, Member States are more bound by this instrument than by the Cybercrime Convention. The Framework decision is limited, however, both in scope and territory, since it only defines a limited number of crimes and is only applicable to EU Member States.

It could also be argued that the RFID chip (hardware) and the embedded protection software were defective products, causing damage to Maruja, because they were easy to access while the user does not have any control over such access. This could bring the Directive on liability for defective products into play, as discussed above.

---

[93] However, it is not always clear what constitutes "personal data" in the context of RFIDs, and whether all RFIDs contain "personal data", which would trigger application of the Data Protection Directive. See also Chapter 5 on Safeguards and, in particular, section 5.3.4.

[94] Council Framework Decision 2005/222/JHA of 24 February 2005 on attacks against information systems, *Official Journal* L 069, 16 March 2005, pp. 67–71.

### 3.2.9   Conclusions

This scenario depicts AmI vulnerabilities in the life of a typical family, in different environments – at home, at work and in a park. It indicates some of the potential benefits of AmI services but also shows dark aspects, including human failings in security measures, identity theft, loss of control, inadequate profiling, spyware and spamming, data laundering, illegal interception and so on. Additional legal measures will be needed to address some of these issues, but legal safeguards alone cannot fix all problems. Improved security measures will be necessary. Consumers will also need to adjust their behaviour, e.g., to be sceptical of special offers, to make sure their personal devices reflect their preferences, to be more conscious of what they can and should do to improve the security of the systems and services they use.

## 3.3   Scenario 2: A crash in AmI space

### 3.3.1   The scenario script

#### 3.3.1.1   Introduction

Martin and Barbara Schmitt have lived for more than 10 years in an AmI-equipped alpine village specifically designed for senior citizens. For their age (Martin is 77, his wife is 75), both are healthy. Their daughter Heike lives in northern Germany. Heike sees her parents only once or twice a year, but maintains contact during the rest of the year by means of AmI.

In this scenario, the Schmitts are in a group of senior citizens touring Florence.

**Scene 1: News from the police report: Senior citizen dies after bus accident**

Florence – Twenty-four senior citizens were injured, one fatally, in a bus accident on a sightseeing trip on Friday afternoon.

According to Florence police reports, the bus was on a sightseeing trip with 46 senior tourists from Germany and Austria when for unknown reasons the traffic lights at a major intersection went to green for all directions. The bus driver avoided a collision with the oncoming traffic but knocked down some traffic signs, went off the street and finally crashed into a lamppost.

Fifteen of the passengers on the bus had minor injuries but nine were more seriously injured and had to be treated at the Careggi Hospital. Though the emergency service arrived quickly, the severe internal injuries of an 84-year-old woman from Austria remained undetected because she used an outdated health monitoring system. She died on the way to the hospital.

*Heike Lengbacher-Schmitt is sitting in the subway on her way home when she suddenly receives two alarm messages on her personal wrist communicator (PWC). Her parents' health monitoring devices (HMD) issued the alarms, indicating that a critical situation had occurred.*

*Of course, Heike becomes concerned. She had picked up similar messages before from one of her parent's HMD, and in all of these instances things eventually turned out to be fine. But this was the first time she received alarms from both parents at once. Moreover, she knows that her parents are on a bus tour, making the situation even more worrisome.*

*Heike's attempts to call her parents are not successful. As she learned later that day, in an emergency situation, the HMDs by default block any incoming communications from people not directly involved in the rescue efforts in order not to disrupt the immediate rescue process. And during the examinations at the hospital, mobile communication devices are to be turned off.*

*Over the course of the next three hours, she leaves numerous messages at her parents' digital communication manager, urging her parents to return her calls as soon as possible.*

*In addition, Heike accesses her father's personal data storage. The system recognises her and, because she was granted comprehensive access rights beforehand, releases the travel information she requests such as her parents' itinerary, stopovers, etc. Eventually, she finds out that her parents are at the Careggi Hospital in Florence. After phoning the hospital, Heike is informed that her parents are receiving medical treatment.*

*After Martin Schmitt has been thoroughly examined, he is allowed to leave the emergency room and turn on his communication devices again.[95] He immediately calls his daughter.*

*Heike: Hello? Oh, it's you, dad. Thank goodness! Are you all right? How's mom? What happened?*

*Martin: Our bus had an accident, and your mom was slightly injured, nothing serious. She has a slight concussion and I have a few scratches. Nothing to worry about, believe me.*

*Heike: Can I talk to her?*

*Martin: Sorry, honey, but she's still being treated and the doctors said she should not be disturbed.*

*Heike: By the way, Aunt Anna called me just a few minutes ago. She was totally freaking out because she received the same alarm messages as me. Apparently she became so excited that her HMD even alarmed her doctor!*

*Martin: Oh no, I forgot to take Anna off the list of people to be automatically notified in an emergency. Please call her and try to calm her down. Listen, I want to go back to your mother. I'll call you later. Just wanted to let you know everything's okay.*

*As it is already past midnight when Martin finally leaves the hospital, he decides to send a video message to his daughter instead of calling her. In his hotel room, Martin sets up his mobile phone in front of him and starts recording his*

---

[95] At the moment it is debated if wireless technology can be banned from hospital any longer or if "wireless tagging is 'inevitable'". Carr, S., "Wireless tagging in hospitals is 'inevitable': Prepare to be chipped …", silicon.com, 7 December 2004. http://hardware.silicon.com/storage/0,39024649,39126387,00.htm

*message. He also attaches a short clip showing Barbara in the hospital, saying a few words to reassure her daughter. Martin had ignored the ban on using mobile recording devices in the hospitals and filmed a short video-sequence of his wife anyway.*

*Dear Heike! As you can see, I'm absolutely fine. And your mother is recovering quickly. She will be released tomorrow morning. But let me tell you what happened from the beginning.*

### Scene 2: Travel preparation and check-in procedure for public transportation

*Your Mom and I had completed travel preparations way ahead of time. So there was no need to get stressed out. And thanks to the travel-assistance procedure of the AmI environment in our home in Murnau, this time we even thought of recharging our PWCs and HMDs early enough to avoid losing "our identity" like on our last trip.*

*In Munich, I experienced an awkward situation after I located a former colleague of mine using the "friend-locator" function (LBS) of my PWC.[96] I just wanted to say "Hi", but when I walked up to him, I was surprised to see that he had a good-looking, younger woman with him who obviously was not his wife. He blushed, mumbled a few words and disappeared in the crowd. It seems difficult to keep secrets these days ...*

*At Munich station, we met our old friends Brigitte and Peter as planned. The four of us proceeded to meet up with the travel group in the new bus terminal, just next to the station.*

*Alessandra, our Italian tour manager, introduced herself and welcomed us to the tour and we finally started to pass through the security gates in order to board the bus.*

*I guess I'll never feel comfortable with all these safety measures you have to endure when travelling: biometric ID verification,[97] detectors for drugs and explosives, etc., especially if they reject you erroneously.[98] One of our fellow travellers, Michael from Baden-Baden, was denied access to the boarding area of the terminal, even though he had a valid ticket and had the receipt from his travel agent![99] Apparently, some kind of data mismatch between his personal ID, the e-ticket and the information stored on the central server had caused the problem.*

*The security personnel at the terminal were absolutely stubborn and unwilling to make an exception, despite several interventions by Alessandra and Peter, who is a good friend of Michael. The officials urged Alessandra to accept the situation*

---

[96] Paciga, M., and H. Lutfiya, 2005.

[97] Bolle, R.M., J.H. Connell, S. Pankanti, N.K. Ratha and A.W. Senior, *Guide to Biometrics*, Springer, New York, 2004.

[98] Maghiros, I., Y. Punie, S. Delaitre et al., 2005.

[99] Schneier, Bruce, "Identification and Security", *Crypto-Gram Newsletter*, 15 February 2004. http://www.schneier.com/crypto–gram–back.html

*and told her to leave without Michael. But they hadn't reckoned on the solidarity of the whole group – we made it unequivocally clear that we wouldn't leave behind a member of the group.*

*According to the law, Michael was obliged to receive a "possible risk status for an unlimited time" because he is causing more security risks than normal. He has to accept this "possible risk status", granted to him by the officer, which means that all his actions and movements are tracked and stored.*

*To make a long story short, it took another hour before Alessandra had worked out an agreement with one of the senior officials. The solution was that the tour manager and all passengers had to sign a statement discharging the bus terminal of any responsibility for possible damages that Michael might cause. Pretty ridiculous if you ask me, especially considering that once you leave the terminal, anybody can hop on the bus without any security checks at all!*

### Scene 3: Traffic supported by ambient intelligence

*After a pleasant stopover in Bolzano, we continued our journey the next day. The ride through Upper Italy was uneventful. Some of us were watching on-demand videos or reading books on their portable screens.[100] And Alessandra turned on the interactive tour guide of the bus that explains what we could have seen outside the bus if it had not been so foggy in the Po lowland. Instead, some videos of the scenery were projected onto the windowpanes.*

*Later on, our bus driver managed to by-pass a major traffic jam on the highway near Modena. Well, actually he just had to follow the instructions he received on his on-board navigation system. We learned that the traffic monitoring system had detected a severe accident about 30 km ahead of us, and within seconds of the disruption of the traffic flow, a traffic warning was issued and an alternative route suggested.*

*Thanks to the intelligent filtering system, our driver was able to take the decision at the right moment without being distracted by too much information while driving.*

*Luckily, the bus company we were travelling with had subscribed to one of these expensive premium traffic information schemes. Many other people travelling in the same direction weren't as fortunate.*

*In Florence, traffic volume was pretty high, but considering the rush hour, we moved along quite smoothly. The electronic road signs told us that inbound traffic was given priority. In addition, our bus had permission to use the lane reserved for public transport. Paying tolls is always a pain, but these urban traffic management systems seem to pay off.*

---

[100] Espiner, T., "Philips unfurls prototype flexible display", ZDNet UK, 2 September 2005. http://news.zdnet.co.uk/hardware/emergingtech/0,39020357,39216111,00.htm

### Scene 4: Emergency situation

*But then again, traffic management systems are far from secure: We learned later that the accident we were involved in was caused by a kid who had managed to hack into the Florence traffic management system.[101]*

*All of a sudden, cars coming from the right entered the junction at high speed. In order to avoid a collision, our bus driver pulled to the left and we ran into the central reserve, hitting all kinds of signs and objects. Finally, we crashed into a large lamppost and came to a brutal and sudden stop.*

*It took me a few moments to realise what had happened and to regain orientation. Your Mom was unconscious. So I checked her HMD immediately. The display indicated that an emergency call had already been issued. Thank goodness, all vital parameters such as blood pressure and pulse rate were okay.*

*I looked around and saw the mess we were in. You should see the camera images taken in the bus (as you know, the cameras in the bus record everything constantly), but they were not immediately available because the bus company gave commercial exclusivity to a television station. ... So we have to wait until the police give us a copy, if we ever get one.*

*What I did not know was that some passengers were using HMDs that are not compatible with the Italian system. Thus, they were not able to download the health information of a couple of people on the bus and the semi-automatic rescue co-ordination centre assumed there were only 32 people on board and sent too few ambulances. This did not have severe repercussions since many of us were not seriously hurt.*

*The police, ambulances and fire brigade arrived rather quickly. The fire brigade, however, was not needed. It was called because the alarm signal stopped after three minutes due to a power shortage in the vehicle and the rescue centre interpreted this as an indication that the bus might have caught fire – the travel organisation will have to pay for this service, but who wants to grouse?*

*On their way, the paramedics had checked the medical records of the passengers and the HMD signals and set up a list of people with more serious injuries and those with private health insurance.[102] Apparently, they were given priority treatment and transport to the hospital. Too bad we didn't opt for such insurance and had to wait for more than half an hour before being examined.[103]*

---

[101] In summer 2005, the US government outlawed the possession of "traffic signal-pre-emption transmitters" after hackers had used them to manipulate traffic lights. Poulsen, K., "Traffic Hackers Hit Red Light", *WiredNews*, 12 August 2005. http://www.wired.com/news/technology/0,1282,68507,00.html

[102] Michahelles, F., P. Matter, A. Schmidt, B. Schiele, "Applying Wearable Sensors to Avalanche Rescue: First Experiences with a Novel Avalanche Beacon" in *Computers & Graphics* 27, No. 6, 2003, pp. 839–847.

[103] Carr, Sylvia, "Wireless tagging in hospitals is 'inevitable'. Prepare to be chipped ...", Silicon.com, 7 December 2004. http://hardware.silicon.com/storage/0,39024649,39126387,00.htm

*My neighbour on the bus had two narrow escapes. He escaped from the bus crash without a scratch but he was almost given an injection just because he had picked up someone else's HMD and not his own.*

*But something really tragic occurred with Monika Klein, a nice 84-year-old lady from Salzburg. She was one of those whose health insurance refused to pay for an update of the HMD to the latest model; the paramedics had neither her patient record nor her current vital data. When one of the paramedics walked around and talked to those who were not on his automatically-produced list, she told him that she was not in pain, only exhausted. Because there weren't enough ambulances at the scene, they left her sitting on a bench next to the road. Since the introduction of HMDs, these guys depend too much on the technology. They are not even able to practise the simplest diagnosis. Otherwise they would have diagnosed that Mrs Klein had internal bleeding. I heard that when they finally decided to take her to the hospital, one of the last to go, she suddenly lost consciousness and passed away before the ambulance reached the hospital.*

### Scene 5: Ambient intelligence and medical care

*After we arrived at the hospital, I had a fierce argument with the lady at the reception who complained that she was not able to get full access to my health and insurance record. The doctors, she said, were unable to help me if I wouldn't disclose my complete data to the hospital.*

*Heike, you probably remember that I had forbidden the health services to give away certain data because I had been spammed with so many drug adverts last year after that scandal over the illegal trading of personal health data. I saw no necessity to give the hospital complete access since I only had some scratches. However, I had to sign a statement that the hospital is not liable for any impairment resulting from their treatment.*

*I really wonder if the benefits of automated health care are really worth this mess. I promise to keep you posted. Say hi to George and hug the kids for us!*

*Bye for now!*

## 3.3.2    Analysis

## 3.3.3    The context

The scenario presents three different environments that reveal possible weaknesses in public or semi-public infrastructures and the trade-off between economically efficient procedures as implemented in AmI services and the variety of individual needs.

Citizens must be able to trust and rely on unfailing operation of these infrastructures – especially for vital functions. Fair access and user-friendliness are needed to prevent an ambient intelligence divide. While equal and fair access is the basic requirement for public utilities, user-friendliness is a critical consideration regarding actual use of AmI services. In this respect, disabled and elderly people have special requirements that need to be factored in.

*Scene 1: Framework situation: AmI-supported communication*

This scene depicts communication links between a senior citizen and his daughter who lives far away.[104] Synchronous and asynchronous communication using text, phone or video from basically any location is assumed to be standard. For both the father and daughter, these communication possibilities are part of everyday life, including receiving all kinds of information automatically issued by personal agents such as HMDs. In an emergency situation, however, automatic alerts can actually cause more harm than good unless they inform the recipient adequately about the situation.

*Scene 2: Travel preparation and check-in procedure for public transportation*

This scene shows the senior citizens' preparations for their bus trip to northern Italy. The scenario assumes that the couple remain healthy and active up to an advanced age and are supported by AmI technology in their daily activities.[105] AmI-enabled services can remind users not to forget important things (like an HMD).

In the aftermath of 11 September and other terrorist attacks in recent years, boarding public transportation usually involves more or less extensive procedures of identification, control and surveillance. People have to get used to it. Flaws in technologies and/or applications periodically lead to nuisance and sometimes even to open insubordination when results are *obviously* faulty and authorities deny services. An open issue in this respect is the trade-off between public security and individualism.[106]

*Scene 3: Traffic supported by ambient intelligence*

This scene explores the delicate balance between market- and supply-driven approaches to many new mobile services enabled by the availability of personal information in fields that are considered public utilities today. This development may result in a decreasing relevance of free and publicly available services and in a growing disparity between those who can afford the benefit offered by ambient intelligence and those who cannot.

---

[104] As presented in Cabrera Giráldez, M., and C. Rodríguez Casal, "The role of Ambient Intelligence in the Social Integration of the Elderly" in G. Riva, F. Vatalaro et al. (eds.), *Ambient Intelligence: The Evolution of Technology, Communication and Cognition Towards the Future of Human – Computer Interaction*, IOS Press (Studies in New Technologies and Practices in Communication, 6), Amsterdam, 2005, pp. 265–280.

[105] See, for instance, Cabrera Giráldez and Rodríguez Casal, 2005, and Korhonen, I., P. Aavilainen and A. Särelä, "Application of ubiquitous computing technologies for support of independent living of the elderly in real life settings" in *UbiHealth 2003: The 2nd International Workshop on Ubiquitous Computing for Pervasive Healthcare Applications*, Seattle, 8 October 2003.

[106] See, for instance, Fujawa, J.M., "Privacy Made Public: Will National Security Be the End of Individualism?", *Computers and Society*, 35, No. 2, 2005.

Extrapolating from current developments, we can assume that bus drivers (like other traffic participants) will be supported by numerous AmI applications to make driving more efficient and less stressful. Avoidance of traffic jams will be one of the most popular applications (which would not be surprising considering the experiences made in the late 20th century). As some of these services lend themselves to business models, quality and speed of traffic information services differ according to the price consumers are willing to pay.

AmI technology also supports passenger activities such as individualised enter-tainment (video, music, interactive games) and "edutainment" like an electronic tour guide, which gives explanations about the scenery outside (augmented by videos and other multimedia).

AmI technologies will be an important element in large cities' efforts to come to grips with unbearably high traffic volumes and recurrent congestion. Traffic management systems constantly monitor and manage traffic flows according to predetermined parameters through centrally controlled traffic signs, traffic lights and other electronic means of traffic management. Certain vehicles such as ambu-lances, streetcars, buses and taxis are granted priority rights. Traffic management systems can be deceived, however, by illegal hardware and software.

### Scene 4: Emergency situation

Public authorities have established AmI-supported emergency systems with automated information chains from the individual person and vehicle to the emergency services (police, ambulances, hospital).[107] This has become a complex system, since heterogene-ous actors and systems have to communicate seamlessly. Given the fast development of technology, different national standards and health systems, this system remains imper-fect – services cannot be offered to all citizens in the same way. In addition to the prob-lems associated with operating efficiency, health and emergency services become increasingly differentiated from basic to premium services, creating an "AmI divide". For whatever reasons (e.g., because they are using older equipment, live in regions without technical coverage, or even have opted out), people who remain outside the system are at risk of not being provided with the most basic services.

As for other applications, AmI-enabled emergency systems may be driven by market forces making differences between people who can afford a premium serv-ice and those who cannot. While this is already taking place in the existing health insurance system, it is a sensitive issue who is actually driving the development: the insurance companies and health care suppliers who are under constant pressure to act economically and efficiently or citizens (represented by the government) who set the rules and define boundaries for AmI health care services.

---

[107] Savidis, A., S. Lalis, A. Karypidis et al., *Report on Key Reference Scenarios*, 2WEAR Deliverable D1, Foundation for Research and Technology Hellas, Institute of Computer Science, Heraklion, 2001.

In addition, identities can easily be mixed up if the link between a person and his/her personal device is dissociated (e.g., by picking up the wrong HMD).

### Scene 5: Ambient intelligence and medical care

This scene reveals vulnerabilities like those in the emergency situation. Hospitals ask for a complete disclosure of health information (regardless of the need for the actual treatment) in order to be on the safe side and avoid liability. This raises a question about who is in control of the system and who establishes the rules that apply to denial of services.

In order to reduce possible interference with medical procedures and to protect patients' privacy, all mobile communication devices are required to be turned off within hospitals.

## 3.3.4 AmI technologies and devices

This scenario makes reference to several AmI technologies:

- Sensors and actuators

  - Embedded in the environment and in objects and attached to people, such as an impact sensor for accident detection and body sensors measuring the vital parameters of the elderly (or people with health risks)
  - Detectors of drugs and explosives
  - Positioning
  - Biometrics

- Interfaces

  - Portable screens
  - Augmented reality displays (such as bus windows)

- Intelligent algorithms for

  - Priority-based traffic routing
  - Routing of network traffic in emergency situations
  - Processing of health data in real time
  - Detection of persons with highest health risks or best insurance

- Communications networks enabling seamless service by heterogeneous devices with or without central control providing greater coverage (especially for emergency communication):

- (Personal) Health Monitoring Devices (HMDs), which are health-related personal intelligent devices and which could be combined with other multifunctional devices such as Personal Wrist Communicators.

### 3.3.5   AmI applications

Scenario 2 refers to various AmI-enabled applications including the following:

- *Personal communication management system*, like that described in ISTAG's "Dimitrios Scenario",[108] controls the communication of the elderly couple based on the context, e.g., it denies communication in the emergency when communication with the authorities has priority and at the hospital where mobile communication devices are not allowed. On the other hand, it proactively sends messages to family members and recognises people close by ("friend locator").
- *Support system for elderly people* helps to enable an independent life to an advanced age. This system reminds users about tasks to be done and objects to taken with them. When coupled to a health monitoring system, it also supports a healthy lifestyle.
- *Check-in and security procedures* for public transportation are technically integrated to a large extent, combining access controls with identification procedures (supported by biometrics and central databases) and security protocols. If operating accurately, the system speeds up regular check-in procedures and helps to detect potential security risks.
- *Personal health monitoring systems* survey vital parameters of people with certain risks such as high blood pressure or diabetes. The collected data can be used either by a physician for routine examination or in an emergency. The personal health monitoring system may be linked to a health insurance database and a communication system.
- *Public traffic management systems* collect information about the current traffic and support road users either collectively or individually. The business models may vary from free public information to pay-per-advice models.
- *Automated emergency alarm systems* can detect accidents and the urgency of the situation (especially if coupled with the personal health monitoring devices of the drivers and passengers). The rapid alarms and automated requests for assistance improve the quality of the medical system and help to reduce traffic casualties.
- In a *seamless medical information system*, all relevant information is collected, including personal medical history items such as prior illnesses, treatments and medication as well as up-to-date vital information and information about health insurance.

### 3.3.6   Drivers

Each of the AmI technologies mentioned in the scenario has been driven by a set of two or more interdependent factors. Analytically, the following drivers can be distinguished:

---

[108] ISTAG, Scenarios, 2001.

- *Political* – The introduction of some of the most important AmI applications in the scenario has largely been driven by political objectives such as reducing the risk of terrorism (security), improving the efficiency of the health care system (emergency), and the improvement of the traffic situation in urban areas (public infrastructure).
- *Commercial* – Numerous AmI services such as the "friend-locator", multimedia applications on the tour bus, individually tailored traffic information and automated communication links are primarily driven by profit motives and the (successful) development of business models.
- *Diffusion* – Especially in mass consumer markets, high penetration levels of basic communication technologies constitute an important vantage point for the demand for complementary services such as video-based communication or automated and personalised information exchange.
- *Accountability* – Both the boarding procedures at the bus terminal, which proved to be quite humiliating for one of the group members, as well as the fact that hospital patients are required to disclose their complete personal health data are based on the institutions' objective to reduce liability as far as possible.
- *Illegitimate personal advantages* – As AmI technologies regulate access to scarce goods, people may be motivated to seek personal advantages by circumventing standard procedures and/or by using technical solutions to deceive the system (in the scenario, a young person hacks into the traffic management system). Perpetrators might take into account possible hazardous consequences (because they seek to cause those consequences) or they might not (because they are ignorant of the consequences).

### 3.3.7  Issues

In view of the above-mentioned vulnerabilities of ambient intelligence in travel/ mobility and health care applications, we can identify certain issues that are critical for AmI applications that rely on large-scale public infrastructure and have largely the character of a public utility:

#### 3.3.7.1  Dependence

Automated alerts are not necessarily beneficial – they may even cause more confusion because alerts reach the addressee immediately, but direct communication with the victim is often no longer possible.[109] The promise of permanent accessibility leaves the user helpless when communication is needed but not possible.

---

[109] Savidis et al. assume in their scenarios that the personal communication device is deactivated for public communication in order not to disrupt emergency relief activities.

### 3.3.7.2  Privacy

What is the necessary degree of disclosure of information? In a normal situation even the disclosure of simple data (e.g., location) may violate privacy, whereas in other cases, the revelation of more information of the same kind may be warranted. Thus, the degree of information disclosure depends on the person, context and situation, which poses a challenge for the design of adequate communication rules.[110]

### 3.3.7.3  Loss of control

If certain activities rely on the proper operation of technical systems, a feeling of uneasiness and loss of control may occur if it is not transparent to the citizen why a certain decision is made, especially when common sense suggests a different decision.

### 3.3.7.4  Risk and complexity

If AmI systems that are vital for the public (such as in emergencies) are known to be vulnerable or that do not cover the whole population, a "conventional" back-up system, which provides at least a basic level of service, is needed.

### 3.3.7.5  Safeguards

Responsibility is moved to the weakest link in the chain, normally the citizen. In cases in which users do not adapt fully to the system requirements (e.g., provision of data), a liability may be generally refused – even if it has nothing to do with a certain damage or harm.

### 3.3.7.6  Exclusion

Services regarded as public utilities today may become commercialised tomorrow. Even if the common welfare is increased, there is a risk of more inequality and even a loss of benefits for certain social groups.

### 3.3.7.7  Identity

The loss and/or confusion of identity may not only be the result of malicious identity theft, it can also occur by mistake if the identification of a person is merely based on a detachable personal device.

---

[110] This issue is discussed extensively in Waldo, James, Herbert S. Lin and Lynette I. Millett (eds.), *Engaging Privacy and Information Technology in a Digital Age*, National Academies Press, Washington, DC, 2007. http://books.nap.edu/openbook.php?isbn=0309103924.

### 3.3.7.8    Crime and complexity

Complex and distributed technical systems may offer new opportunities for illegal activities. This not only applies to property offences and terrors, but also to misdemeanours and regulatory offences as well. Especially in those cases in which sensitive elements of the public infrastructure (e.g., traffic management) increasingly rely on AmI technology, even minor violations of the rules can unintentionally cause severe damage.

## 3.3.8    Legal synopsis

### 3.3.8.1    Bus accident caused by hacker

The traffic accident in Scenario 2 is caused by a kid who illegally used software for priority vehicles like ambulances and police cars. The scenario raises interesting questions about who is liable and to what extent, since many actors are involved: the kid who hacked into the traffic management system, the developer of the hacking tools, the traffic system controller, service providers, the bus driver and still others. The scenario also raises question about the applicable jurisdiction for prosecuting those liable.

Criminal law aspects

Currently, there is no binding European regulatory framework determining jurisdiction in criminal matters. Member States are free to choose their own rules. The rule of territory is basic: states incriminate actions that happen on their territory. The notion of territory is, however, open to interpretation. Many Member States broaden their jurisdiction by using expansive criteria such as the criterion of ubiquity. The result is that for transborder crime, several Member States find themselves competent at the same time for the same facts. This process is not a process of legislation, but of case law.

   There is a tendency in the case law of national judges to interpret the principle or ground of territorial jurisdiction extensively. Belgian judges, for example, are not, except for explicit statutory provisions, competent in extraterritorial cases. Legal practice shows that judges give great leeway to Belgian legal authorities when crimes are committed outside Belgium territory but impinge on Belgium interests. The legal situation in Belgium and the Netherlands, and a country such as Chile that also belongs to the civil-law tradition is very similar. In all these countries, there are several accepted theories, criteria or answers to the *locus commissi delicti* question, namely, the question to what extent a wrongful act can be considered to fall within the territorial jurisdiction of a state. Within the Dutch and Belgian traditions, the following accepted criteria are applied:

- Activity criterion – the territory where the activity took place is the relevant one
- Criterion of the instrument of the crime
- Criterion of the constitutive consequence
- Ubiquity criterion – the *locus delicti* is every country where one of the constitutive elements of the crime can be located; thus, an offence may fall within the jurisdiction of more than one country.

Unlike in Germany and France, neither the Dutch nor the Belgian Criminal Codes contains a real choice for one of these criteria; the issue is left to the courts. An analysis shows that whatever criterion is applied, it is almost always easily possible for a judge to declare himself or herself competent and to hold that the events took place on "his" or "her" territory. The ubiquity criterion, in particular, by now the most successful criterion within the civil-law tradition, enables a flexible approach towards the *locus commissi delicti* question. It allows countries to prosecute persons spreading computer viruses or racist information from computers abroad, or persons who "call" in by telephone from abroad when this conversation forms the starting point for a crime. The flexibility of the ubiquity criterion explains without any doubt the total absence of jurisdiction provisions in the Belgian and Dutch Computer Crime Acts.

To avoid conflicts of jurisdiction, an international solution is preferable. Currently, there is no such thing as a stringent set of rules with regard to determining territory. A small paragraph in the Cybercrime Convention tries to remedy this conflict by imposing a guideline that "the Parties involved shall, where appropriate, consult with a view to determining the most appropriate jurisdiction for prosecution".[111] A bit firmer is Article 10 paragraph 4 of the **2005 EU Framework Decision 2005/222/JHA on attacks against information systems**, requiring the Member States concerned to co-operate in order to decide which of them will prosecute the offenders with the aim, if possible, of centralising proceedings in a single Member State. "To this end, the Member States may have recourse to any body or mechanism established within the European Union in order to facilitate co-operation between their judicial authorities and the co-ordination of their action. Sequential account may be taken of the following factors:

- The Member State shall be that in the territory of which the offences have been committed according to paragraph 1(a) and paragraph 2
- The Member State shall be that of which the perpetrator is a national
- The Member State shall be that in which the perpetrator has been found."

Although these guidelines are not legally binding, there is some wisdom in them. Future experiences will indicate whether more stringent rules are needed.

It is also important to focus on the different possible defendants. The hacker can be difficult to track. He commits criminal offences defined in the Cybercrime Convention, such as "illegal access", "illegal interception", "data and system interference" and possibly "computer-related fraud". The producer, seller or distributor

---

[111] See Article 22 of the Cybercrime Convention.

of hacking software might also fall under the scope of the Cybercrime Convention which provides for criminal offences including the misuse of devices, i.e., the intentional production, sale, procurement for use, import, distribution or otherwise making available of a device, including a computer program, designed or adapted primarily for the purpose of committing an illegal access or interception or a data or system interference. Simple possession of such devices might also constitute a criminal offence (see Article 6 of the Cybercrime Convention).

Both the Cybercrime Convention and the Framework Decision 2005/222/JHA provide for the criminal liability of legal persons. Article 8 of the Framework Decision obliges each Member State to take the necessary measures to ensure that legal persons can be held liable for offences defined in a framework decision, also when committed due to lack of adequate supervision by a person under its authority. Article 9 contains specific penalties for legal persons.

Determining the applicable jurisdiction in criminal affairs is still a complex affair, waiting for an international solution.

Civil law and liability aspects

In the scenario, a number of service providers are involved in the accident, such as the traffic light network provider/operator. The traffic management system company had to guarantee that its system was sufficiently protected against hacking attacks. Since a minor was able to hack into the system, the question arises whether the company did enough in that respect.

It will be difficult to determine which of the various service providers involved in the traffic management system should be held responsible for the security problem. Normally, the person harmed by the security failure would have to find the specific provider who did not provide sufficient protection and to prove that this provider committed the fault, which caused the specific damage. This is difficult to prove. The strict liability regime under the Directive on liability for defective products,[112] however, allows the victim only to prove that the product (here the traffic management system) was defective and that it caused a damage. Since it was relatively easy for a hacker to access the system, the condition of proving defect might be fulfilled. Moreover, the Directive on liability for defective products contains rules that allow the victim to react against the supplier of the defective good, when the producer cannot be found. When the damage is caused by defects in the products or services of different suppliers, Article 5 makes it possible to claim all of the damage from one of the suppliers. This is important since it would be difficult for the victim to prove to what extent the different producers are responsible for the damages and to act against every producer involved. However, the Directive is not applicable to services.

As far as the European legal framework for liability is concerned, harmonisation at EU level is very limited. Thus, the national law will apply in most cases. However, some specific provisions on the liability of electronic service providers

---

[112] See section 3.2.8.3. above for more on strict liability under the Directive.

have been established in the Directive on electronic commerce.[113] This Directive limits the liability of intermediary service providers in three specific situations. Article 12 provides that in case of mere conduit (the transmission in a communication network of information provided by a recipient of the service, or the provision of access to a communication network), the service provider is not liable for the information transmitted. In the case of "caching" (i.e., when an information society service is provided that consists of the transmission in a communication network of information provided by a recipient of the service), the service provider is not liable for the automatic, intermediate and temporary storage of that information, performed for the sole purpose of making transmissions of information to other recipients more efficient upon their request. In the case of "hosting" (i.e., when an information society service is provided that consists of the storage of information provided by a recipient of the service), the service provider is not liable for the information stored at the request of a recipient of the service. Liability is excluded in such cases, unless certain conditions are broken.[114] Article 15 provides that the intermediary service providers have no general obligation to monitor the content of the information transmitted.

The exceptions to the general liability rules apply only in the case of transmissions of information via a network. The exceptions will not be applicable when a system malfunctions because of a security flaw.

The law on liability is only partially harmonised on the European level (e.g., by the Directive on liability on defective products). Thus, liability is mostly regulated by national laws of the Member States. The question then arises which Member State's laws are applicable to the liability cases arising from the cross-border situations.[115] In the case of the accident in this scenario, we might have to deal with both, the extra-contractual liability (e.g., of the hacker or the traffic management system company) and the contractual liability (e.g., also of the traffic management system company).

As far as the contractual liability is concerned, the law applicable is indicated by the **Rome Convention on the law applicable to contractual obligations**.[116]

According to the Convention, the parties to the contract can choose which law will be applicable (Article 3 of Rome Convention) under the contract. Usually, the service providers impose the choice.

If the law applicable to the contract has not been chosen by the parties, the contract is governed by the law of the country with which it is most closely connected. The Rome Convention in Article 4 contains the presumption that the contract is most closely connected with the country of habitual residence (or central administration) of the party who is to effect the performance of the contract. Specific rules cover the carriage of goods. An AmI service supplier could have his habitual residence or central administration anywhere in the world and he could choose this place based on how beneficial the law is for him.

---

[113] Directive 2000/31/EC, pp. 0001–0016.

[114] See Articles 12–14 of the Directive on electronic commerce.

[115] On private international law issues (applicable law, jurisdiction), see section 5.3.11.2.

[116] Convention of Rome on the law applicable to contractual obligations opened for signature in Rome on 19 June 1980 (80/934/EEC), *Official Journal* L 266, 9 October 1980.

There are, however, exceptions to these general rules in case of specific contracts such as consumer contracts and individual employment contracts.

Article 5 of the Rome Convention deals with consumer contracts. It reiterates the principle that consumers cannot be deprived from their national consumer protection by the choice of law made in a contract. The consumer enjoys the protection afforded to him by the mandatory rules of the law of the country in which he has his habitual residence, though under conditions: "(1) if in that country the conclusion of the contract was preceded by a specific invitation addressed to him or by advertising, and he had taken in that country all the steps necessary on his part for the conclusion of the contract, or (2) if the other party or his agent received the consumer's order in that country, or (3) if the contract is for the sale of goods and the consumer travelled from that country to another country and there gave his order, provided that the consumer's journey was arranged by the seller for the purpose of inducing the consumer to buy." Article 5, however, does not apply to a contract of carriage or for the supply of services where the services are to be supplied to the consumer exclusively in a country other than that in which he has his habitual residence. It shall, however, apply to a contract that, for an inclusive price, provides for a combination of travel and accommodation. This article is clearly built on the notion of habitual residence. In an AmI world, however, the notion of habitual residence might be flexible, which might make it difficult to apply these rules.

If the bus driver made a mistake, he might be liable towards his employer. Presumably both are situated in the same country, Germany, so German law would be applicable. If not, Article 6 of the Rome Convention contains specific rules on labour contracts. The European Union has recently adopted a regulation which unifies the rules on the law applicable to non-contractual obligations, the so-called Rome II Regulation.[117] The basic rule under the Regulation is that the law applicable should be the law of State where the direct damaged occurred (*lex loci damni*).[118] However, the Regulation allows for exceptions to this general rule. Such "escape clauses" seek to provide a more adequate solution in cases when the tort or delict is mostly connected with the country other than the one of the *lex loci damni*. This will be the case when both parties have their habitual place of residence in the same State. Moreover, if it is clear from the circumstances of the case that the tort or delict is manifestly more closely connected with the law of the country other than that of the *lex loci damni* or of habitual residence, the law of this other country should apply.[119]

Special rules apply in the case of some specific torts or delicts, e.g., in the case of product liability or in the case of infringements of intellectual property.

---

[117] Regulation (EC) No 864/2007 of the European Parliament and of the Council of 11 July 2007 on the law applicable to non-contractual obligations (Rome II) *Official Journal* L 199, 31 July 2007, pp. 40–49

[118] Article 4 (1) of the Rome II Regulation.

[119] Article 4 (3) of the Rome II Regulation.

The parties can choose the law by agreement, though some limitations are provided.[120]

The Rome II Regulation excludes from its application a number of fields, inter alia, the law on companies and non-contractual obligations arising out of the violation of privacy and rights relating to personality, including defamation.[121]

The Regulation shall apply from January 2009.

The competent court in this scenario would be determined by the **Brussels Regulation**.[122] As in the case of applicable law, the parties have the possibility to determine in their contract which courts will be competent (Articles 23 and 24). The basic principle of this Regulation is that a defendant can be sued in the Member State of his domicile (Article 2). If the defendant is domiciled outside the European Union, this Regulation will not provide a solution for problems of jurisdiction (Article 4). In such situations, national legislation will determine the adequate forum. Article 2 has another disadvantage. When a user wants to sue an AmI services supplier, the service supplier will have the advantage of being sued at home. He might determine his domicile to ensure a beneficial jurisdiction.

In addition to this general principle, the Regulation contains a number of special jurisdiction rules, including those applicable to contracts, tort, and consumer and labour contracts. In matters relating to a contract, a person may be sued in the court of the place of the performance of the obligation in question (Article 5). In an AmI world, it will be difficult to determine the place of performance. In a certain sense, the contract is performed worldwide and this does not allow one to determine the competent court. Article 5 section 1 (b) specifies that in the sale of goods or services, this term should be understood as the place in a Member State where, under the contract, the goods are delivered or services provided (or should have been delivered/provided). In an AmI future, it might be difficult to determine where the goods or services were delivered and thus difficult to determine one single competent court. This scenario provides a case in point, i.e., a tour bus and its customers travelling around different countries.

The court competent to deal with extra-contractual issues, such as the liability of the hacker and the traffic management company towards the users, is the court of the place where the harmful event occurs (Article 5(3) of the Brussels Regulation).[123]

The damage caused by the hacker is not limited to Italy. Hacking is a criminal offence and Article 5(4) of the Brussels Regulation provides that a civil claim for damage or restitution which is based on an act giving rise to criminal proceedings

---

[120] Article 14 of the Rome II Regulation.

[121] Article 1 of the Rome II Regulation.

[122] Council Regulation (EC) No 44/2001 of 22 December 2000 on jurisdiction and the recognition and enforcement of judgments in civil and commercial matters, *Official Journal L* 012, 16 January 2001.

[123] See also ECJ, Case 21/76 *Bier* v. *Mines de Potasse d' Alsace* [1976] *ECR* 1735, where the European Court of Justice stated that the place where the harmful event occurred should be understood as the place where the damage occurred or the place where the event having the damage as its sequel occurred.

can be brought in the court seized of those criminal proceedings, to the extent that that the court has jurisdiction under its own law to entertain civil proceedings. Since several persons might be coresponsible for the accident, there could be several parallel proceedings. Since this would make the issue more complex and expensive for the parties, Article 6 provides for the possibility of consolidating claims so closely connected that it is expedient to hear and determine them together to avoid the risk of irreconcilable judgments resulting from separate proceedings, in the court of domicile of any of the (many) defendants. This allows the plaintiff to sue the different defendants before one single court. However, not all claims from the same factual situation may fulfil conditions set up by the Article 6. To offer an extra protection to the consumer, Article 16 of the Brussels Regulation provides that: "A consumer may bring proceedings against the other party to a contract either in the courts of the Member State in which that party is domiciled or in the courts for the place where the consumer is domiciled." The bus customers can start proceedings in their own courts, which can be an important advantage. Provisions on the jurisdiction for consumer contracts apply when both parties are domiciled in EU Member States. However, the jurisdiction may also be established if the dispute arises out of the operation of a branch, agency or other establishment of the dependent in the Member State.[124] Despite such provisions broadening the scope of application of the Regulation, a substantial number of businesses offering services to EU consumers stay outside the reach of the Brussels Regulation.

Specific jurisdiction rules are provided in case of individual employment contracts.

### 3.3.8.2   Lack of interoperability

Seniors are involved in the accident while travelling through Italy. A woman dies because her health monitoring system is not compatible with the local health network system and her injury is not detected in time. In an AmI world, interoperability is crucial.

To ensure that information society systems and networks are compatible, international standards are created. An important legal instrument to ensure the creation of uniform standards and technical regulations is the **Directive on technical standards and regulations**,[125] which regulates some aspects of standardisation in the Union. It provides that national authorities and the European Commission should inform each other about new initiatives in the field of technical standards and norms (Articles 2–4). This should guarantee the necessary level of transparency between

---

[124] Article 15(2) of the Brussels Regulation. It is possible that, in the future, the localised web page would be understood as the establishment in the undertaking of this particular provision. See Schaub, Martien, "European legal aspects of E-Commerce", *Europa Law*, Groningen, Netherlands, 2004, p. 147.

[125] Directive 98/34/EC of the European Parliament and of the Council of 22 June 1998 laying down a procedure for the provision of information in the field of technical standards and regulations, *Official Journal* L 204, 21 July 1998.

the different competent bodies in the European Union. The Directive also established a standing committee, consisting of representatives of the Member States and, as chairman, a representative of the Commission, to ensure that the national interests of Member States are taken into consideration in new standards initiatives. Technical standards and regulations could, however, constitute barriers to the free movement of AmI services. That is why they are only allowed "where they are necessary in order to meet essential requirements and have an objective in the public interest of which they constitute the main guarantee". The Directive foresees a detailed information procedure that aims at meeting those criteria.

Member States also have the obligation to ensure that their standardisation bodies do not take any action that could prejudice European standardisation initiatives. When a Member State wants to create new technical regulations, Articles 8 and 9 provide detailed information and co-operation procedures, to ensure compatibility with EU and other national initiatives.

All of this should guarantee that the European Commission and the Member States work together in the most efficient way and are aware of each other's initiatives. If it were to work optimally, all national systems should interoperate and be based on compatible standards and regulations. Similar standardisation initiatives exist at the international level.[126] The issue of standardisation and interoperability is of major importance for AmI applications. When standards have been achieved, stringent regulations should be imposed, at least on sensitive AmI services such as health and general alarm systems, to ensure compliance with the standards and regulations throughout the European Union.

Regarding the important – for AmI, necessary – interoperability of software programs, the **Software Directive**[127] obliges Member States to protect computer programs by copyright and asserts that only a specific expression and not the underlying ideas and principles of any element of the computer program are protected. Some limited exceptions to the exclusive right of the rights-holders are foreseen.[128] The Directive also contains a provision on decompilation in order to

---

[126] Important standardisation initiatives regarding privacy have been taken by the Platform for Privacy Preferences (P3P) and Open Profiling Standard (OPS) of the World Wide Web Consortium seeking to develop a single vocabulary through which a user's privacy preferences and the site's practices are articulated, enabling the negotiation of privacy requirements between them, and to provide for secure transmission of a standard profile of personal data. See WP 29 Opinion 1/98 on Platform for Privacy Preferences (P3P) and Open Profiling Standard (OPS), adopted 16 June 1998.

[127] Council Directive 91/250/EEC of 14 May 1991 on the legal protection of computer programs, *Official Journal* L 122, 17 May 1991.

[128] Exceptions to the exclusive rights of the copyright holders are: (a) reproduction, translation, adaptation, arrangement and any other alteration of a computer program and the reproduction of the results thereof, where these acts are necessary for the use of the computer program (…) including for error correction; (b) making a back-up copy; (c) to observe, study or test the functioning of the program in order to determine the ideas and principles which underlie any element of the program (Article 5 of the Directive). These exceptions seem to be insufficient to allow the free use of computer programs required in an AmI world. Also, they can only be invoked by the lawful acquirer, which is a vague term and which could lead to important restrictions.

avoid a situation where copyright could hinder interoperability. Article 6 says that the authorisation of the rights-holder shall not be required where reproduction of the code and translation of its form are indispensable to obtain the information necessary to achieve interoperability between an independently created computer program and other programs, subject to conditions, inter alia: these acts are performed by the licensee or by another person having a right to use a copy of a program, or on their behalf by a person authorised to do so, and these acts are confined to the parts of the original program necessary to achieve interoperability. Information acquired in accordance with these provisions should not be used for goals other than to achieve the interoperability, and should not unreasonably prejudice the rights-holder's legitimate interests.

There has not been much case law based on this Directive. A Dutch court, however, recently decided that the Dutch copyright law (implementing the Software Directive) obliges application service providers to copy the data, which are processed in one program, to a script that makes it possible to process the same data in another program. In this case, a school wanted to change the software program without losing the data, and the Court decided that the first software provider was obliged to make a script that translates the data into the other program.[129] There have been many criticisms of this judgment because the Software Directive focused on the interoperability of software, not the interoperability of data. But this exactly highlights an interesting issue for AmI: to what extent are licensors of software programs compelled to deliver the data, processed in their programs, in a script that allows processing the data in another program? This is also important from the data protection perspective, in particular for the data subjects who, according to Article 12 of the Data Protection Directive, have an access right to the data, namely, a right to communication "in an intelligible form of the data undergoing processing and of any available information as to their source". This is also important for anyone who needs to use (personal) data and other information processed in any other processing system.

Another case that relates to interoperability is the Commission Decision of 24 March 2004 relating to a proceeding under Article 82 of the EC Treaty (Case COMP/C-3/37.792 Microsoft) in which the Commission decided that on the basis of Article 82, Microsoft abused its dominant position "by deliberately restricting interoperability between Windows PCs and non-Microsoft work group servers, and by tying its Windows Media Player (WMP), a product where it faced competition, with its ubiquitous Windows operating system". The Commission imposed a fine of €497 million and the following remedies on Microsoft: (1) the obligation to offer an unbundled version of Windows (a version of Windows without Windows Media Player) ("unbundling of WMP" remedy); (2) the obligation to make available to its competitors certain technical interface information necessary to allow non-Microsoft work group servers to achieve full interoperability with Windows PCs; this having to be done on reasonable and non-discriminatory terms ("interoperability remedy"). The findings of the Commission were upheld by a judgment of

---

[129] Rb. Leeuwarden 25 May 2005 Openbaar onderwijs Zwolle/Pendula. http://www.rechtspraak.nl.

the Court of First Instance in September 2007.[130] Such similar, specific interoperability remedies might be necessary in AmI. Lack of interoperability can preclude individuals from obtaining the services they wish to enjoy and result in serious harm to them, as shown in the scenario.

There is no doubt that the technology can facilitate the life of the individuals. Well functioning emergency systems may save lives. On the other hand, creating standards is costly and raises the question of who will bear the costs of such developments. Companies might be less willing to contribute to the development of standards because they will not receive the expected return on investment and might still be liable for the good functioning of their standardised product. In the scenario, a woman was not provided with a compatible device. In more extreme situations, a whole country or continent may not be able to afford these technologies. This highlights the digital divide issues of affordability and discrimination, which may be reinforced by the introduction of new and costly technologies. Sensitive AmI services and technologies could be treated as public or universal services, which should be available to all. The topic is high on the European agenda. There have been research activities relating to accessibility, under the eEurope 2002 Action Plan.[131] The Council also adopted a resolution on e-accessibility in December 2002. The eEurope 2005 Action Plan[132] seeks to ensure that peoples with disabilities and other disadvantaged groups can participate in and have equal access to major innovations in online public services, covering e-government, e-learning and e-health, and to create a dynamic, accessible e-business environment.

The **Universal Service Directive**[133] recognises the need to provide universal services to citizens at an affordable price. Such affordable price is set within each Member State and may depart from those resulting from market conditions. Member States are obliged to ensure access to those services (at affordable prices) to all end-users. However, the scope of the Directive is limited to electronic communication networks and services (and a few other services, e.g., the Directive mentions access to public pay telephones and uninterrupted access to the emergency services free of charge). They include the guarantee that at least one undertaking provides access to the public telephone network following a reasonable request of the quality allowing speech and data communications (including Internet access), and takes into account prevailing technologies available to the majority of end-users. Member States may decide to make additional services publicly available on their own territory.

The Directive makes provision for a review of the services in light of economic, social and technological developments. Any change of scope in universal services is subject to availability of services to the substantial majority of the population,

---

[130] Case T-201/04, Microsoft [2007].

[131] http://ec.europa.eu/information_society/eeurope/2002/action_plan/pdf/actionplan_en.pdf

[132] http://europa.eu.int/information_society/eeurope/2002/news_library/documents/eeurope2005/eeurope2005_en.pdf

[133] Directive 2002/22/EC of the European Parliament and of the Council of 7 March 2002 on universal service and users' rights relating to electronic communications networks and services, *Official Journal* L 108, 24 April 2002.

and must consider whether the lack of availability of such services creates the risk of social exclusion of those who cannot afford them. Changes in the scope of the universal services or in the technology cannot produce disproportionate financial burden on the undertakings providing services. Costs of such changes must not fall unfairly on consumers in the lower income brackets.

The scope of this Directive is limited and obviously not adjusted to the AmI environment. Nevertheless, consideration should be given to vital AmI services and technologies, such as those that may play an important role in future emergency service being available to all individuals in a non-discriminatory, reasonable and safe way.

### 3.3.8.3 Access refusal as a result of data mismatch

One of the seniors, who wanted to participate in the journey, was refused transport because of problems with his identification.

In the AmI world, new tools and methods for identification will be developed, manufactured and implemented. In the scenario, the public transport relies on biometric identification. No identification system, however, is perfect; each is subject to errors to a greater or lesser extent. The data controller takes the risk for and bears (some of) the consequences of the errors. Today, errors seem to be accepted as a fact of life, however undesirable, as they can cause harm to people, especially when identification systems become much more prevalent than they are today.

The problem spotlighted by this scenario is caused by a mismatch between personal data held by the individual and information held on a central server. We do not know why such an incompatibility of information occurred. The information on the central server has been collected, acquired and processed under the responsibility of the data controller. It might be difficult, however, to identify who is the data controller in such a situation, and thus who is liable. One should again examine the obligations of the data controller under the Data Protection Directive to see if they provide for legal protection in such a situation. Article 17 of the Directive obliges the data controller to protect the data against destruction or accidental loss, alteration, unauthorised disclosure or access, and against all other unlawful forms of processing of such data.[134] A mismatch does not automatically imply destruction, loss, alteration, unauthorised disclosure or access. So it is difficult to find protection in the security and confidentiality obligations of the Directive (and of the Privacy & Electronic Communications Directive).

The Data Protection Directive also requires collected information to be accurate and up to date. Compliance with those requirements is an important protection of the

---

[134] Article 17 says that "the data controller must implement appropriate technical and organizational measures to protect personal data against accidental or unlawful destruction or accidental loss, alteration, unauthorized disclosure or access, in particular where the processing involves the transmission of data over a network, and against all other unlawful forms of processing. Having regard to the state of the art and the cost of their implementation, such measures shall ensure a level of security appropriate to the risks represented by the processing and the nature of the data to be protected."

data subject's privacy. Correctness of the processed data is obviously crucial. Be that as it may, however, the obligation to keep personal data accurate and up to date is difficult to achieve but crucial for an AmI world where the accuracy of the processing depends on the accuracy of the data. The mismatch in this case could be a consequence of an update of Michael's personal data that occurred just an hour before. Lack of interoperability may also cause mismatch that lies outside the responsibility of particular data controllers. Indeed, the scenario shows that the data controller tries to avoid any responsibility and puts the burden on the users of the system.

Refusal to provide the service (to Michael) may also be the consequence of defective services, hardware or software. It causes harm to the data subject. Who is liable for such damage? In the scenario, the security personnel try to eliminate their liability for the damage caused by shifting the liability to the group. The problem, however, might have been the result of an error in the central server of the security service itself. Article 12 of the **Directive on liability for defective products** states that the liability of the producer of a defective product (the security control system) may not be limited or excluded by a provision limiting or exempting him from liability. The Directive may provide the grounds for Michael's claiming damages if he had been refused and not permitted to participate in the trip, and if the refusal had been caused by a malfunction of the server.

The protection of the consumer[135] against unfair provisions in contracts is provided by the **Directive on unfair terms in consumer contracts**.[136] This Directive covers "the abuse of power by the seller or supplier, in particular against one-sided standard contracts and the unfair exclusion of essential rights in contract". It only applies to contracts between sellers or suppliers and consumers (natural persons) and, in particular, only to contractual terms that have not been individually negotiated by the parties. In an AmI world, consumers will become increasingly dependent on services and there is a significant risk that the suppliers of AmI services will obtain an even stronger power position and will abuse it. Thus, the supplier should also not be allowed to unfairly limit his liability for security problems in the service he provides to the consumer. This supplier should not be allowed to set out privacy conditions that are manifestly not in compliance with the generally applicable privacy rules and that disadvantage the consumer.

The Directive imposes mandatory rules for consumer protection, inter alia, that contracts should be drafted in plain, intelligible language, that the consumer should be given an opportunity to examine all of the terms and that, if the terms are in doubt, the interpretation most favourable to the consumer should prevail. It might be difficult, however, to implement those mandatory rules in an AmI world where a large number of transactions will be concluded instantly and continuously. The Directive includes provisions to avert the risk that the consumer may be deprived of protection under the Directive when the other contracting party designates the law of a non-member country as the law applicable to the contract. The Directive contains a list of examples of

---

[135] Some issues of consumer protection are also covered in section 3.2.8.6.

[136] Council Directive 93/13/EEC of 5 April 1993 on unfair terms in consumer contracts, *Official Journal* L 095, 21 April 1993.

unfair terms. Although consumer protection organisations can ask for the annulment of unfair terms before the competent courts, the Directive does not, however, entail prior verification of the general conditions in individual economic sectors.

### 3.3.8.4.  Disproportionate request for personal information

After the accident, medical help is given to the seniors. A hospital requires mandatory access to the complete medical record of a slightly injured patient. When the patient refuses to give access to his complete record, he is obliged to sign a statement waiving the hospital of any liability for any impairment from the treatment.

This part of the scenario highlights two major problems of data protection in AmI. First, the principle of "proportionality" (a cornerstone of data protection law) is questioned. Second, the concept of "consent" and how consent takes place should be examined in the context of AmI, which may curtail our freedom of choice in many situations.

The Data Protection Directive endorses the principle of proportionality, laid down in the first internationally binding document regarding data protection, namely Treaty 108 of the Council of Europe (1981). The principle of proportionality in the Data Protection Directive states that "the data must be adequate, relevant and not excessive in relation to the purposes for which they are collected and/or further processed".

Despite its importance, this principle risks being eroded in a fast society with constant data processing and systems capable of intelligent processing and using large amounts of personal data. In other words, disproportionate data processing often takes place. There is not much case law in which one can find out what "proportionate" data processing is and what it is not. In addition, it is very difficult to define the exact meaning of "proportionate". On the one hand, there are too many diverse situations in which processing takes place, so that one particular situation might require more data processing for one reason or another. On the other hand, a definition of what is proportionate and what is not, somehow takes away the right of an individual to decide himself who can have access to his personal data and how long they may be stored and processed. Some persons might even find advantages in a vast and extensive processing and storage of their personal data.

Data protection officers do not often use the possibility to check the proportionate character of data processing by data controllers. Actually, there might well be too much data processing taking place in AmI to realise an effective control. In addition, many data controllers are exempted from notification of the processing to the data protection office, so that a priori control of the data controller seems to be very complicated.

This brings us to the second issue, which is that of the consent of the data subject: Processing of personal data must be "legitimate". This is stated explicitly in Article 7 of the Directive. Beyond a series of exceptions that we will not address here (processing necessary for the performance of a contract or for compliance with a legal obligation to which the controller is subject or in order to protect the vital interests of the data subject), legitimacy is based on three general principles.

The first concerns processing operations to help fulfil government tasks and pursue the public interest by the authorities themselves or others working for them. A government data processing has to meet the criteria of the legal framework of the specific administrative authority and comply with its statutory powers. On top of that, each action by the authorities has to meet the criteria of the public interest. Mutatis mutandis, this also applies to the processing operations that the authorities manage or delegate. As a result, government data processing is not justified when it is not necessary for the exercise of a specific power of the administration concerned. It is just as unjustified when government data processing operations constitute a disproportionate invasion of privacy, since protection of privacy is, to a great extent, part of the public interest. There should be less invasive methods available to achieve the same goal. In addition, governmental data processing also has to respect Article 8 of the ECHR. The restrictions set out in the second paragraph of that article fully apply. This implies, that apart from the aforementioned legality and proportionality requirement, governmental data processing must be necessary in a democracy and be "in the interest of national security, public safety or the economic well-being of the country, for the prevention of disorder or crime, for the protection of health or morals or the protection of the rights and freedoms of others". This means that a processing operation is not justified simply because it is executed by or for the government. National rules need to make this meticulously clear. They have to ensure and encourage that the judges and the specially created supervisory authorities consider the interests of every side in every situation.

A second legitimacy principle primarily concerns the private processing of personal data. Article 7(f) of the Directive says that "processing is necessary for the purposes of the legitimate interests pursued by private interests, except where such interests are overridden by the interests for fundamental rights and freedoms of the data subject". Again, two aspects intertwine. In the first place, the ultimate purpose of the processing should be lawful. If the processing is undertaken by a legal person, its corporate purposes will be taken into account as an additional touchstone. Legal persons can only undertake actions to achieve the goals laid out in their articles of association. The processing operation has to be congruent with those. Second, the processing operation must be clearly necessary and indispensable to achieve the set purpose of the processor. Is it possible to achieve that purpose through other means? In regard to privacy, is this the least harmful way? Proportionality is essential. The interests at stake have to be carefully balanced. In each case, the concrete interests facing each other have to be carefully evaluated. A purely commercial purpose that results in an invasion of privacy (e.g., the processing of personal data for direct marketing sales) has to be judged differently (and more severely) than data processing necessary to maintain public health, freedom of speech or, for that matter, the running of a sports club.

The third legitimacy principle is consent. Article 7 (a) states that "personal data may be processed only if the data subject has unambiguously given his consent". Consent is taken to mean "any freely given specific and informed indication of his wishes by which the data subject signifies his agreement to personal data relating to him being processed" (Article 2 (h)).

Processing personal data is thus justified if the data subject clearly gives his/her consent after being informed of all aspects of the processing operation: the delineated and justified purpose of the processing operation, the categories of personal data to be processed, possible third parties that will have access to the information, who is responsible, his/her rights, etc. The unambiguity and specificity of the consent and the complete information on which it is based will need to be proved by the processor in case of conflict.

The consent criterion engenders a number of difficulties. First, the freedom of choice is often limited and relative in reality. Not everyone in our society has the same possibilities. Data processing is mostly entrenched in relationships in which the data subject is the weak party and the data flow is often one-way. Most of the time, the data subject needs something (e.g., credit, health insurance) and is almost forced to give consent. In the end, consent is often turned into a pure formality without offering any guarantee. Second, the general framework of the Data Protection Directive leaves doubt about what processing operations can be justified solely based on the consent of the data subject. If no consent is given, the other legitimacy grounds in themselves seem to span the whole range of possibilities (especially Article 7 (f) discussed above). Unless one assumes that such consent would legitimise disproportionate and illegitimate processing – which is questionable. It is problematic to invoke the consent of a data subject in order to justify a disproportionate processing. In penal law, the consent of a victim does not erase the criminal character of an action. Mandatory secrecy is not affected when a party gives consent to make something public. The mutual consent between parties on illegal agreements does not yield a legal agreement. As a result, the unambiguous consent of the data subjects is only one of the aspects that affect the considerations of the different interests.

Where sensitive personal data are involved, such as health-related data, things are even more complex because the Data Protection Directive has created a special regime. Indeed, Member States must *proscribe* the processing of "personal data revealing racial or ethnic origin, political opinions, religious or philosophical beliefs, trade-union membership, and the processing of data concerning health or sex life" (Article 8(1) of the Data Protection Directive). In those cases, a fundamental data processing prohibition applies because it endangers not only privacy, but also the principle of non-discrimination. Yet this fundamental ban also allows for exemptions. The processing of sensitive data is then possible, inter alia, when the data subject has given his explicit consent.[137] Thus, the "explicit consent" to the processing of such sensitive information would make it legitimate. The hospital example shows that this consent is often not

---

[137] Article 8 allows other exceptions for processing of sensitive data, i.e., those where the processing is necessary for the purposes of carrying out the obligations and specific rights of the controller in the field of employment law; or is necessary to protect the vital interests of the data subject; or is carried out, with appropriate guarantees, by a foundation, association or other non-profit-seeking body with a political, philosophical, religious or trade union aim and on condition that the processing relates solely to its persons or those who have regular contact with it in connection with its purposes and that the data are not disclosed to a third party without consent; or relates to data made public by the data subject or is necessary for legal claims. The Member States can add extra exemptions to the general prohibition.

freely given because the data subject is in a subordinate situation. He is subject to the power of the data processor and controller, who possess a good or a service one wants. In this scenario, the data subject is dependent on the hospital (and therefore will mostly give disproportionate access to his personal data), but also the hospital is dependent on the insurance companies that require hospitals to enforce access to the complete records of their patients (and therefore the hospitals will mostly ask for disproportionate access to the personal data).

Article 8 of Data Protection Directive provides the rule that the prohibition on processing of sensitive data does not apply in a case "where processing of the data is required for the purposes of preventive medicine, medical diagnosis, the provision of care or treatment or the management of health-care services, and where those data are processed by a health professional subject under national law or rules established by national competent bodies to the obligation of professional secrecy or by another person also subject to an equivalent obligation of secrecy". That might imply that a patient would need to grant access to his medical records by the hospital, to enable the latter to provide him with the treatment. In any event, the hospital is still obliged to respect the proportionality principle and not to process more data than necessary. However, the hospital is deciding what is proportionate under the circumstances rather than the patient. In an optimal situation, the hospital treating minor injury should be able to obtain access to only a portion of the patient's medical record as necessary to treat the case.

The non-discrimination principle is well established in the European law. Articles 21 and 23 of the Charter of Fundamental Rights of the European Union prohibit discrimination based on grounds such as sex, race, colour, nationality, ethnic or social origin, genetic features, language, religion or belief, political or any other opinion, membership of a national minority, property, birth, disability, age or sexual orientation.[138] The non-discrimination principle is also in the EU Treaties (Article 6 of the Treaty on European Union by reference to respect fundamental rights, as guaranteed by the European Convention for the Protection of Human Rights and Fundamental Freedoms,[139] Articles 7, 12 and 13 of the Treaty establishing the European

---

[138] The Charter of Fundamental Rights of the European Union is not legally binding, but it is already referred to in the case law of the Court of Luxembourg. See García, R.A., "The General Provisions of the Charter of Fundamental Rights of the European Union", Jean Monnet Working Paper 4/02, www.jeanmonnetprogram.org.; Eriksen, E.O., J.E. Fossum and A.J. Menéndez (eds.), *The Chartering of Europe: The European Charter of Fundamental Rights and its Constitutional Implications*, Verlag, Nomos, Baden-Baden, 2003; Peers, S., and A. Ward (eds.), *The European Union Charter of Fundamental Rights*, Hart Publishing, Oxford, 2004; Heusel, W. (ed.), *Grundrechtcharta und Verfassungsentwicklung in der EU*, Bundesanzeiger, Köln, 2002; Band 35 in Schriftenreihe der Europäischen Rechtsakademie Trier.

[139] This Convention, signed in Rome on 4 November 1950, recognises the principle of equal treatment in Article 14, which prohibits the discrimination on any grounds such as sex, race, colour, language, religion, political or other opinion, national or social origin, association with a national minority, property, birth or other status in enjoyment of rights protected by the Convention. All Member States are Contacting Parties to the Convention. Any discrimination on the basis of the same grounds in enjoyment of rights set forth by law is also forbidden under Protocol No. 12 to the Convention. According to the protocol, no one shall be discriminated against by any public authority on any grounds such as those mentioned above.

Community) and in a wide range of EU legislation implementing those provisions. Non-discrimination is a fundamental principle of the European Union. Provisions establishing this principle prohibit using some of the characteristics (grounds for prohibited discrimination as enumerated in the legal documents) in decision-making. This principle would apply to decisions taken in the AmI environment as well, including automated decisions. Non-discrimination provisions do not prohibit the use of such data for other purposes (data collection, profiling), nor do they address possible use of such characteristics, but only the decision actually made. Those aspects are remedied to some extent, however, by data protection legislation, which establishes a prohibitive and more severe regime for the processing of sensitive data not as an expression of the will to protect privacy, but to remedy the danger of discrimination that may arise from the processing of such sensitive data. On the other hand, antidiscrimination law could also have the ability to fill gaps in the legal provisions of more specific instruments (such as data protection law). Prohibition of discrimination applies to all situations based on the forbidden criteria, not only in the case of identifiable individuals (which is a limitation the data protection law) but also anonymous members of a group (group profiling).[140]

## 3.3.9   Conclusions

The scenario about ambient intelligence in travel and health applications makes clear that even in fields with a quasi-public character, it is not self-evident that all citizens will benefit from the deployment of ambient intelligence as envisioned by policy-makers and scientists.[141] In fact, the complexity of large-scale technological systems for traffic management and public health shows that careful steps have to be taken in order to balance public and private interests – ranging from government, commercial network and service providers to the individual citizen and civil society as a whole.

It is a great challenge to avoid unjustified and excessive drawbacks or benefits for any of the affected parties. The challenge requires a blend of legal, organisational and technical measures. On the technological level, interoperating systems with a high degree of dependability (supplemented in part by independent fallback systems) are needed when the individual or society as a whole depends on an operating system. On the organisational level, measures are needed to make (public) services transparent and trustworthy. Finally, the legal framework and the

---

[140] Custers, B., *The Power of Knowledge, Ethical, Legal and Technological Aspects of Data Mining and Group Profiling in Epidemiology*, Wolf Legal Publishers, Nijmegen, 2004, pp. 164–165.

[141] See, for example, IST Advisory Group, *Ambient Intelligence: From Vision to Reality*, Office for Official Publications of the European Communities, Luxembourg, 2003. http://www.cordis.lu/ist/istag – reports.html. See also Emiliani, P.L., and C. Stephanidis, "Universal access to ambient intelligence environments: opportunities and challenges for people with disabilities", *IBM Systems Journal* 44, No. 3, 2005, pp. 605–619.

regulation of important public services have to be adjusted to new circumstances. This also means that existing networks and constellations of societal actors need to respond accordingly.

## 3.4    Scenario 3: What's an AmI data aggregator to do?

### 3.4.1    The scenario script

#### 3.4.1.1    Introduction

The Data Mining Corporation (DMC) has an almost perfect business model. It collects data about individuals from hundreds of sources[142] and then sells the aggregated data back to many of those sources. Its principal sources (and clients) include insurance companies, retail chains, media conglomerates, credit-reporting agencies, mobile phone companies, law enforcement agencies, customs and immigration authorities, and intelligence agencies.

The advent of ambient intelligence technologies – including RFIDs, networks of sensors and actuators, fourth-generation (4G) mobile, surveillance and biometric technologies, and software that learns from our past behaviour and preferences to predict what we will want or will do[143] – has enabled DMC to construct detailed files on virtually every person in the United States, western Europe and other developed countries.[144] DMC knows what products we buy, services we use, who we are in contact with, where we are at any point in time, and so on. DMC can confirm whether we are who we say we are and what sort of activity we've been engaged in. Linking together many different databases and processing the acquired data using its own proprietary algorithm has enabled DMC to create such fine-grained profiling that it is the envy of its few remaining competitors.

Although DMC is a relatively new company, it has grown quickly. Among the ways it has managed to sidestep legislative and regulatory constraints on transfers

---

[142] Data aggregators today mine data from thousands of sources. For example, see O'Harrow, Robert, *No Place to Hide*, p. 124: "LexisNexis, a subsidiary of the UK-based Reed Elsevier Group, maintains billions of records, including media reports, legal documents, and public records collected from thousands of sources around the world."

[143] cf. Biever, Celeste, "RFID chips watch Grandma brush teeth", NewScientist.com news service, 17 March 2004: "Tiny computer chips that emit unique radio-frequency IDs could be slapped on to toothbrushes, chairs and even toilet seats to monitor elderly people in their own homes. Algorithms on the PC use 'probabilistic' reasoning to infer what the person is doing. For some tasks, merely picking up an object such as a toothbrush is enough."

[144] See, for example, O'Harrow, p. 222: "HNC ... monitors 90 per cent of all credit cards in the United States and half of those in the rest of the world ... using artificial intelligence to seek out indications of fraud and deceit." See also Solove, Daniel J., *The Digital Person*, p. 20: "Wiland Services has constructed a database containing over 1,000 elements, from demographic information to behavioural data, on over 215 million people."

of personal data is through mergers with or acquisitions of companies with their own extensive databases. It is headquartered in Miami, but now has major subsidiaries in London and Tokyo. It is listed on the New York and London Stock Exchanges and is considering a listing on the Tokyo Stock Exchange.

### Scene 1: Management board meeting

*The company secretary places his hand on a fingerprint reader outside the boardroom and then stands close to the iris scanner. The boardroom door opens and he enters. As he does so, the lighting and the air conditioning automatically come on and are set at his comfort levels, which are known from his previous activity in the room. A second later, the door slides open and the DMC president walks in. The sensors and actuators in the boardroom slightly adjust the air conditioning and lighting to the midpoint between the president and secretary's preferences. The president nods a slight greeting to the company secretary who can see his boss is preoccupied. A few seconds later, the vice presidents enter one by one and take their seats, and the lighting and air conditioning sensors and actuators make further adjustments to the collective mid-point levels.*

*The vice president for media relations has not arrived. The president is petulant. "Where's MacDonald?" she barks at Alvin, the holographic embodiment of DMC's embedded intelligence. The boardroom video screen switches from the agenda and shows MacDonald's office. He is heard and seen finishing off a telephone conversation with a journalist. He gets up from his desk and leaves his office. As he does so, another camera in the hallway shows him going down a corridor. His position co-ordinates, accurate to less than a metre, shown in the lower left-hand corner of the boardroom screen, change as MacDonald approaches the boardroom. He is seen putting his hand to the fingerprint reader, but the reader does not respond. He tries unsuccessfully to rub some ink from his finger, and then leans close to the iris scanner, which does respond, but he is still not admitted to the boardroom since he must have positive responses from both systems. The impatient president commands Alvin to open the door and finally McDonald is admitted.*

"Okay, let's get on with it," says the president. "Show me today's agenda," she instructs the computer. The agenda appears on a large wafer-thin video screen on the wall opposite the president. Three items are listed:

Data from developing countries. (Switzer)
Theft of data, 29 June 2017. (Perrier)
Considerations re listing on the TSE. (Hausmann)

*Kevin Switzer, vice president for operations, speaks. "We've had complaints from the Customs and Immigration folks about the shortage and reliability of our data on people coming into the States.*[145] *It mainly concerns people from*

---

[145] See O'Harrow, p. 48: "For years, the credit bureaus had been dogged by complaints. Information in their reports was chronically incorrect. They routinely failed to correct mistakes, and seemed arrogant when individuals called."

*developing countries. With our profiling technologies, we are able to identify anyone who might be a security risk or disposed to anti-social behaviour. Unfortunately, most developing countries have no AmI networks, which makes it impossible to build up the same kind of detailed profiles of individuals like we can here in the US, Europe or Japan. So the immigration authorities have been making threatening noises about refusing entry to people from countries without AmI networks."*

*"So what are you doing about it?" asks the president.*

*"Well, I think we have a golden opportunity here. We can offer to set up AmI networks in those countries as long as we, I mean DMC, are the ones to collect and process the data. You'd think most countries would jump at the chance to have networks put in place at virtually no or little cost to them, but some of the countries are quibbling with us."*[146]

*"Quibbling?" asks the president, "What do you mean?"*

*"Quibbling about control of the data. They say if we control the data, it's tantamount to signing their sovereignty over to us. But we've been working on a deal where we copy for them the data we collect... well, some of it, at least. Our intelligence agencies would not want us to hand over everything, and we don't have to either. We can offer the raw data to the developing countries, but certainly not the processed data. Developing countries will never know how we've processed the data, especially since we do the processing here in the United States or in the UK, i.e., outside their jurisdiction. They'll have to settle for what we give them."*

*"Okay, that sounds good to me. Any objections?" she asks the others who remain silent. "No? Okay, then, Jacques, it's your turn. What's the latest on the theft or whatever it was at our London office?"*

*But before Jacques Perrier, vice president for security, can respond, the company secretary leans over and whispers something to the president. "Yes, you're right." The secretary stops the boardroom monitoring systems from recording more of the discussion on this subject.*

*Perrier shifts uncomfortably in his chair. "Well, as everyone here knows, we have a regular monthly audit of DMC's data processing activity. From the last audit two weeks ago, we discovered that there had been a second back-up of data immediately after the first. These back-ups are made every day. Sometimes there's a problem and a second back-up is made. It's not that unusual, but since it's not supposed to happen, we always check them out. The second back-up was anomalous too because it wasn't the whole of the database and didn't get backed up to the usual destination. In other words, we assume it was backed up locally ..."*

---

[146] See O'Harrow, p. 186: "On June 1 [2004], the government granted the contract for a massive expansion of US Visit to Accenture. The deal, worth up to $10 billion, will bring together an array of information and surveillance industry contracts. ... In the coming years, Accenture will be helping to build sprawling computer networks and identity systems to enable the government to track foreign visitors to the United States. The company aims to create digital folders containing visitors' fingerprints, photographs, and details about their travels. The new systems will also rely on radio frequency identification and face recognition software."

Hausmann intervenes, "By locally, you mean to another computer here in the building?"

"Yes, except that none of the computers here show any evidence of having been the destination for the second back-up. That means some portable device with an optical connector was used."

"You mean like a memory stick?"

"Something like that."

"I presume you know who made the second back-up?" asks the president.

"Umm ... uh ... yes. It seems likely that it was three of my staff who were responsible for doing the regular back-ups that night. We wanted to ask them about this second back-up, but they had left on holidays a few hours after the second back-up was made. They were supposed to have returned from holidays three days ago, but they haven't reported for work and they haven't answered our calls."

The president is getting angry. "So you mean your staff have copied part of our database and walked off with it?"

Perrier is visibly squirming in his seat. "That's what it looks like."

"And how many records do you think were copied?" she asks.

"Uh ... It's bad, I'm afraid." Perrier coughs. "My guys think about 16 million."

"Outrageous," says the president, slapping the table. "And why don't you know where they are? Surely you can track them via their location implants. Everybody has to have a location implant. It's a condition of employment in our company, just like any critical infrastructure like banks, nuclear power companies, etc."

"Yes, we've been checking their location data, but so far nothing," says Perrier.

"They could have been surgically removed," says Switzer. "What about the data from the AmI systems? Have you checked the sensor networks in the homes and cars of those three employees?"

"Yes," says Perrier. "Like other employees, they've agreed that we can check their home systems and we've done that. There's obviously nobody in their apartments, and their cars have been stationary since they left on holidays ..."

"And what about the surveillance systems?" asks the president. "You can't go anywhere in London without being caught by surveillance cameras hundreds of times a day."

"Yes, we've been reviewing the data from the surveillance systems too," says Perrier. "But they haven't shown up on those either. We've also been checking with the airlines and railways and car rental agencies to see where they might have gone on holidays. Now we know they left for Costa Rica, but then the trail goes cold. As Kevin has just pointed out, the developing countries don't have the kind of AmI infrastructure needed to track people, so they could really be anywhere. We've also been checking with the mobile telecom companies too, but so far, there's been no data recovered on use of their mobiles."

"I don't understand how they could have got past our own security systems," says the president. "We have access control to prevent employees from unauthorised copying or manipulation of data."

"That's true," says Perrier. "The snag is that they were authorised. Quite a few employees have partial access, so if three or four with access to different bits *collaborate, as these three appear to have done, they are able to get virtually full access to the data.*"[147]

"*Even so,*" *asks the president,* "*how did they get the data outside our headquarters?*"

"*With today's technology, it's easy to copy vast amounts of data in seconds onto high capacity optical storage devices no larger than a deck of playing cards, which makes them easy to conceal on the way out of the building. It's hard to break into DMC offices, but it's not hard to get out.*"

*The president:* "*Are there any indications yet of what they might do with all this data?*"

*Perrier:* "*No, not yet, but there are several likely possibilities, of course. They could use the identity information to commit all kinds of fraud on a huge scale without leaving any trails retraceable to them. Or they could simply sell it. There are lots of digital sites that deal in stolen data. You can easily get $100 these days for each ID.*[148] *Or they could sell it to an insurance company or an intelligence agency, although we've pretty much already cornered those markets. Or they could sell it to some terrorist organisations. Or they could try to blackmail us, and we'd either have to pay up or risk the bad press we'd get if people find out just how much data we've been able to collect about them since AmI technologies became so widespread, and some of that data, as you know, has not always come from legitimate sources. Or they could blackmail victims with the knowledge they've derived from our profiles.*"

"*Or maybe they won't do any of those things,*" *adds MacDonald.* "*Maybe they just want to make a political statement.*"

"*What do you mean?*" *asks the president.*

"*They may feel they have a social obligation to show how extensive our data aggregation practices have become since the introduction of AmI networks and how easy it is to pilfer the data we collect,*" *says MacDonald.* "*If we were exposed, it would be a complete disaster. Among other things, it would show our clients that the profiles of our own people were not reliable because we were not able to predict that these few rogue employees were going to abscond with copies of our files.*"

*The president snorts.* "*If they have 16 million records and they could get $100 for each record, I doubt they're very interested in political statements.*"

*Max Court, DMC's general counsel, speaks up.* "*If we were exposed? Are you suggesting we should withhold information about this theft from the police and those whose files have been copied?*"[149]

---

[147] A Computer Security Institute study found that 70 per cent of all computer attacks came from insiders. See Schneier, Bruce, *Secrets & Lies*, p. 189.

[148] See Zeller, Tom Jr., "Black Market in Stolen Credit Card Data Thrives on Internet", *The New York Times*, 21 June 2005: "A 'dump', in the blunt vernacular of a relentlessly flourishing online black market, is a credit card number. And what ZoOmer is peddling is stolen account information – name, billing address, phone – for Gold Visa cards and MasterCards at $100 apiece."

[149] Some state governments in the United States have passed legislation recently (e.g., California law SB1386, effective July 2003) that forces organisations to inform individuals whenever there has been a privacy breach, and makes organisations liable for improper use of information. In October 2005, a US Senate committee was considering new legislation for a Personal Data Privacy and Security Act. The bill requires that, on discovering a data breach, any agency or business entity that "uses,

*"Of course," says MacDonald. "It's obvious, isn't it? I'd hate to imagine what it would do to our share price and our plans for a listing on the Tokyo Stock Exchange."*

*The president takes a deep breath, as if she were trying to control her temper. "You've got to find those three," she says to Perrier.*

*"Yes, mam. I know."*

*She turns to Frank Hausmann, her chief financial officer. "Okay, Frank, what's your advice about the listing on Tokyo?"*

*MacDonald interrupts before Hausmann can respond. "I'm sorry to interrupt again, but I was just talking to a journalist from* The Financial Times. *That's why I was a bit late for the start of the meeting. She rang about our intentions re the listing on Tokyo. I don't know how she knew that we were even thinking about it. I didn't confirm or deny anything. Then, she asked whether we were complying fully with the Safe Harbour Agreement. Of course, I said we were, but then she posed some very pointed questions about the security of our data. I began to wonder whether she knew about the theft ..."*

*"So, Madame President, before I give my views on the Tokyo listing, I'd like to know if we are going to put out a statement about this theft. It'll make a difference about the timing," says Hausmann. "Are we going to inform those people whose records have been compromised? Are we going to tell the media?"*

*"We can't inform the individuals, because we don't know, at least not yet, whose records have been compromised," says Perrier.*

*"It's for you to decide what we should do," says MacDonald to the president.*

### Scene 2: The Old Bailey, two years later

*BBC 1 news presenter: "And now we go to our reporter, Miles Davenport, who's been at the Old Bailey today, attending the trial involving the Data Mining Corporation and its directors. What's the latest, Miles? Has the jury returned with a verdict?"*

*Miles Davenport: "Thanks, Serena. No, the jury hasn't returned yet, but an announcement is expected in the next few minutes."*

*BBC presenter: "Miles, can you just recap for our viewers what this trial's been all about? And why is it so important?"*

*Miles: "Sure, Serena. As you know, this case has had all the elements of a Jeffrey Archer thriller. It's involved high technology, secretive corporations, the world of intelligence, consumer activists, and high-level calls between the president of the United States and our prime minister. Even the European Commission has got into the act.*

*"It all started about two years ago when* The Financial Times *broke a story about the theft of personal information on 16 million people in the United States and the UK. All these personal data were held by the Data Mining Corporation, an Anglo-American conglomerate most people had never even heard of.*[150] *DMC had*

---

accesses, transmits, stores, disposes of or collects sensitive personally identifiable information" notify "without unreasonable delay" any US resident whose data were subject to intrusion. As of mid-2007, the bill had not yet been adopted by the Senate.

[150] See O'Harrow, p. 34: "Acxiom is not a household name. But as a billion dollar player in the data industry, with details about nearly every adult in the United States, it has as much reach into American life as Pepsi or Goodyear. You may not know about Acxiom, but it knows a lot about you."

*been growing like a powerhouse through mergers and acquisitions, until it had become the world's largest data miner. It turns out that DMC had been profiling virtually everyone in the United States, Europe and many other countries around the world. They have the world's fastest and most powerful computers with billions and billions of records from all sorts of services, including governments.*[151] *DMC had been processing all these records from different sources, including the latest ambient intelligence networks, and linking them together so that it was able to build up comprehensive profiles on every one of us.*[152]

*"Then, according to the FT, DMC discovered that someone had broken into its supercomputers and copied data on a lot of people. For a few weeks, DMC didn't say anything to anybody,*[153] *but then there was a big spike in the number of identity theft cases. People with credit cards were seeing all kinds of purchases on their monthly statements for stuff they hadn't bought. A lot more people and companies were reporting that they were being blackmailed with threats of releases of embarrassing information unless they paid up. The FT got wind of this big increase in credit card fraud and extortion, and was able to trace the source back to a theft of data from DMC.*

*"At first, DMC denied everything; then they said they wouldn't comment on it, because the theft was under police investigation. But by then, the DMC share price was plummeting on Wall Street and in London, and DMC had to call off plans for a listing on the Tokyo Stock Exchange. For a while, it looked like DMC was going bust, but the US government stepped in and propped up the company.*[154] *The President said that national security was involved, and they could not allow the company to go bust. People began badgering the Prime Minister about it. They had no idea just how pervasive ambient intelligence had become ..."*

*BBC presenter: "Personalised services are great, of course; they save us lots of time. And so are the improvements in our security, knowing when we are near known criminals or people disposed to terrorism, but isn't there a dark side?"*

*Miles: "Well, according to civil libertarians, yes, there is. And that's partly what's been coming out in the trial of DMC. Companies like DMC hold a lot of data*

---

[151] See Solove, p. 5: "Federal, state and local governments maintain public records spanning an individual's life from birth to death. These records contain a myriad of personal details. Until recently, public records were difficult to access. ... But with the Internet, public records are increasingly being posted online, where anybody anywhere can easily obtain and search them." In addition, those bent on identity theft can make use of freedom of information laws. See Solove, p. 150: "The vast majority of FOIA requests are made by businesses for commercial purposes."

[152] See O'Harrow, p. 49: " 'InfoBase Enhancement' enables Acxiom to take a single detail about a person and append, on behalf of its customers, a massive dossier. This generally happened without the individual ever knowing about it."

[153] See Krim, Jonathan, "Consumers Not Told Of Security Breaches, Data Brokers Admit," *The Washington Post*, 14 April 2005.

[154] See Safire, William, "Goodbye To Privacy", *The New York Times*, 10 April 2005: "Of all the companies in the security–industrial complex, none is more dominant or acquisitive than ChoicePoint of Alpharetta, Ga. This data giant collects, stores, analyses and sells literally billions of demographic, marketing and criminal records to police departments and government agencies that might otherwise be criticized (or de-funded) for building a national identity base to make American citizens prove they are who they say they are."

*about all of us. And we have to trust them that our data are safe, secure and accurate. But now we know that our data are not secure.*

*"Questions have also been raised about the accuracy of the data. People are entitled to see their records, but most people didn't even know about DMC, let alone the fact that they had built up such extensive records on every one of us.*[155] *So some consumer activist groups have banded together to sue DMC for negligence, for inadequate security of their records, for not complying with the Safe Harbour Agreement between Europe and the United States. It was one of the first class action suits in UK legal history. The European Commission has got involved too. They said that the Federal Trade Commission, which administers the Safe Harbour Agreement for the US, had not been ensuring proper compliance by American companies. The Commission has also said they were taking the US to the World Trade Organisation too, because a subsidy for DMC was against its rules. It's really turned into a big mess. After this six-month trial, and thousands of pages of testimony, the end looks to be in sight."*

*BBC presenter: "Thanks, Miles, for that recap. Weren't there some other issues that came out during the course of the trial?"*

*Miles: "There certainly were, Serena. It was discovered that not only has DMC failed to protect our data, but they've actually been selling large chunks of it to governments and to other companies who in turn were using the data to spam just about everybody in the United States and here in the UK too.*[156] *DMC claimed that they couldn't be held responsible for what their clients did with the data.*

*"We also heard about fraud arising from identity theft. Some of the prosecution's witnesses said that even though their credit card companies limited losses to the first £50, fraudulent use of their cards and other personal data had knock-on effects. Credit-reporting agencies raised red flags, not only about the cards, but also about the actual card-holders. Some witnesses said they had been trying to get wrong information cleaned from their records for almost two years, and have yet to succeed.*[157]

*"Most witnesses said they've suffered from the stress involved in trying to recover their identities and sorting out the mess they've been put in.*[158] *Some said*

---

[155] Schneier, Bruce, "The Future of Surveillance", *Crypto-Gram Newsletter*, 15 October 2003: "In the US, data about you is not owned by you. It is owned by the person or company that collected it."

[156] See O'Harrow, p. 135: "In 2002, the company [ChoicePoint] began allowing individuals to buy dossiers, including criminal checks, education records, and other personal details. ....Now everyone would soon be able to dig into the past of suspect acquaintances or employees."

[157] See Zeller, Tom Jr, "For Victims, Repairing ID Theft Can Be Grueling," *The New York Times*, 1 October 2005. The story reports cases where victims have been trying to overcome the consequences of identity theft for more than two years: "Victims are still left with the unsettling realization that the keys to their inner lives as consumers, as taxpayers, as patients, as drivers and as homeowners have been picked from their pockets and distributed among thieves."

[158] See Solove, p. 110: "Identity theft can be a harrowing experience. According to estimates, a victim typically spends over two years and close to 200 hours to repair the damage that identity theft causes." And p. 110: "Most identity thefts remain unsolved. Research firm Gartner Inc estimates that less than 1 in 700 instances of identity theft result in a conviction."

*they've been stigmatised. We heard also about DMC selling their services to companies who wanted to check on prospective employees. We heard that in many instances the information was wrong, that the data coming from so many different ambient technology networks were often in conflict or didn't make any sense. DMC countered that its proprietary software contains an algorithm for comparing data from different sources to maximise reliability and its predictive capability,[159] but under intense questioning from the prosecution, they admitted they could never eliminate unreliability nor could their predictions of who might be a terrorist or criminal be 100 per cent.*

*"We heard about one case involving a senior civil servant whose name was put on a suspect list when it shouldn't have been. As a result of a compromised fingerprint, he couldn't even get into his own office after the fingerprint template had been disabled without his knowing it. Because he couldn't deliver an urgent file to his Minister, he became so stressed that he had to be hospitalised. His case illustrated the problem arising from different technologies no longer trusting the readings they were getting from other technologies.*

*"As a result of the media interest in this case, many more people are now aware of how pervasive the new ambient intelligence technologies have become and how it's more important than ever that they check out what these big data aggregating companies have on them, the sources they draw on and what happens to their personal data after DMC and its competitors have processed it. If any good has come out of this case, that's surely been it."*

*BBC presenter: "And the DMC directors, what's going to happen to them?"*

*Miles: "We should find out after the jury comes back with the verdict. The DMC president, however, has already resigned, but she went out with a golden parachute – a severance package that included a cool $100 million – and now she's apparently living in Costa Rica."*

### 3.4.2  Analysis

### 3.4.3  The context

The scenario has two scenes, the first of which takes place in a corporate boardroom in the year 2017, the second outside a courtroom two years later. Hence, the scenario is in the business domain.

---

[159] See O'Harrow, p. 221: "CAPPS II, shorthand for the second-generation computer-assisted passenger screening program ... would piggyback on the data revolution of the 1990s, using mountains of demographic, public record, and consumer files to pluck out terrorists from the mass of people who posed no threat at all. It was to be a perpetually watchful network that would electronically absorb every passenger reservation, authenticate the identity of the travellers, and then create a profile of who they are. Then it would examine that profile, instantly and relentlessly, looking for anomalies in behaviour or lifestyle that might indicate ties to terrorist groups."

The scenario concerns the theft (copying) of personal information held by a data aggregator (Data Mining Corporation) by three rogue employees. Theft of identity occurs now, but the difference between such crimes today and in the future is the scale of the data involved.[160] In the future foreseen by this dark scenario, it will be possible to gather orders of magnitude more information about virtually every person in the United States, Europe and Japan. Our reliance on AmI will have grown immeasurably. The future is also marked by an increasing concentration in the control of personal data. Thus, the risks to individuals are much greater when something goes wrong. By the year 2017, there will have been significant technological advances, but this scenario posits that there will have been little evolution in business ethics, management practices and public awareness.

### 3.4.4  AmI technologies and devices

The scenario makes reference to several AmI or AmI-related technologies, including:

- Biometrics, including a fingerprint reader and iris scanner, which serve security purposes in admitting entrance to a restricted area (the boardroom) by only those authorised to enter.
- Networked sensors/actuators, which are linked to the fingerprint reader and iris scanner and which activate the lighting and air conditioning in the boardroom based on the known preferences of those entering the boardroom. To deal with several competing individual preferences, the actuators calculate the mid-points of those in the room.
- Wafer-thin displays which can switch from textual information (the corporate management committee's agenda) to visual imagery from surveillance cameras which, at the same time, display the reference person's location co-ordinates in real time.
- Voice-activated access to an intelligent environment as shown in the board room meeting.
- Surveillance technologies which management can use to monitor employees, both in the office and outside (e.g., in their homes or cars). Surveillance technologies include video cameras, key logging software, biometrics and other networked sensors, as well as location implants and location-reporting devices, which employees are obliged to bear or wear as a condition of employment.
- Machine-learning technologies which analyse past behaviour and preferences in order to predict needs and to personalise services.
- Networked RFIDs, sensors and actuators for gathering data about people and the products they have or services they use.
- Fourth-generation mobile phones, which combine today's PDA capabilities with third-generation mobile technology (and much else).

---

[160] See O'Brien, T.L., "Identity Theft Is Epidemic. Can It Be Stopped?", *The New York Times*, 24 October 2004.

### 3.4.5  AmI applications

The AmI technologies referenced in the scenario are used in various applications, including:

- Security – Biometrics are used for admission to restricted areas such as the corporate boardroom as well as the DMC headquarters building. Access control technologies (e.g., biometrics) are used to govern who can have access or make changes to DMC's databases.
- Surveillance – The president and his corporate colleagues are able to watch MacDonald in his office and on his way to the boardroom. References are made to surveillance of employees outside the office as well. Sensors in homes and cars are networked and provide information to DMC senior management as to whether an employee is at home or in his or her car.
- Immigration control – AmI technologies enable the building up of much more comprehensive profiles of individuals, so much so that prospective visitors or immigrants from countries without AmI networks may not in future be admitted to the developed countries because, in the absence of AmI networks in their own countries, there is not enough information to assess whether the candidate is trustworthy or a security risk.
- Personalisation of services – AmI is used for personalisation of services such as lighting and air conditioning set to one's preferences as well as services provided by products and services such as PDAs and mobile phones. Personalisation of services also leads to time-savings since AmI networks can, for example, monitor the status of one's consumables (such as food and drink) and place orders with the supermarket as necessary.
- Targeted marketing – With more detailed data on consumers, retailers, media conglomerates and others are able to engage in targeted marketing with greater precision.
- Improved profiling – Insurance companies and credit-reporting agencies are able to assess individuals against insurable risks and creditworthiness. While this is good for the insurance companies and credit-reporting agencies, it may not be so good for individuals who may find it harder to get insurance or credit.
- Counterterrorism and policing – With more detailed data on individuals, intelligence agencies and police forces are better able to assess and counter terrorist risks and combat crime.
- Critical infrastructure protection – Although protection of critical infrastructure is only mentioned in passing in the scenario, AmI provides the means to better protect critical infrastructure (including the AmI networks themselves) from intruders (but not necessarily insiders) bent on damaging or undermining those networks.
- Computer communications – Fourth-generation mobile phones combine today's PDA capabilities with third generation mobile technology (and much else) and are able to interoperate with heterogeneous networks.

While several positive, socially useful applications are alluded to, there are some negative applications too. Among them:

- Spamming – The huge increase in data about individuals facilitates more precision in spamming and targeted marketing.
- Fraud – Similarly, the opportunities for fraud are improved because more detailed information is available to criminals.
- Blackmail – With more detailed information, criminals are in a stronger position to blackmail those whose data they hold.
- Discrimination – With more detailed information, insurers are able to discriminate against some people who pose higher risks than others. Conversely, the lack of information on some people (e.g., those from developing countries) means that they too could suffer discrimination, i.e., if they do not have an adequate data trail, they may not be admitted to developed countries.
- Terrorism – Terrorists have more opportunities and better information to impersonate others when they have access to the detailed data on individuals provided through AmI networks.

## 3.4.6 Drivers

The scenario hinges on the theft of data from DMC and the consequences of that theft. The drivers at work here can largely be derived from the motives and needs of the principal characters or groups of characters.

DMC has aspired to be the leader in its market, something it has achieved. DMC's success can be attributed to at least two or three key factors. One is that it has been able to aggregate more data on individuals than any other company. A principal source of these data is the AmI networks that are able to generate far more information than ever before on individuals, their behaviours, habits, contacts, comings and goings, purchases, etc. A second success factor is that DMC has developed an algorithm for sifting through and processing all this data so that it is able to sell its products and services to a wide range of clients. A third factor could be the quality and vision of its management, without whose leadership (and their business plan) it would not have been able to achieve such success.

For the management, one could conclude that they are primarily driven by the profit motive and a desire for scale (i.e., to be the market leader and, presumably, to swallow or overwhelm competitors) and to create a situation where their clients are dependent on DMC services and products.

A second driver must be market demand, i.e., there are many companies and governmental agencies that want the processed data that DMC has been supplying.

A third driver, not so dissimilar from the first, is that the data thieves are also impelled by the profit motive. In their case, however, one could conclude that they see an opportunity to make more money more quickly by copying files from the DMC database and selling it to fraudsters. Before the spike in reported instances of identity theft, Perrier, DMC's vice president of security, speculates what the data thieves might do with the data, which points to drivers. He says the data thieves could sell the data to an insurance company or intelligence agency or to a terrorist organisation or blackmail DMC and/or the individuals whose data they have copied (i.e., the driver is to make money). MacDonald speculates that the data thieves might have committed their crime in the public interest – i.e., to make people aware of how much information DMC was collecting on them through the aggregation of data from AmI networks and to make people aware just how ill-protected and insecure their data are.

A fourth driver is respect for the law. This is indicated when DMC's general counsel expresses some disbelief at the suggestion that DMC should cover up the data theft from both the police and those whose files have been copied. As he makes only one intervention in scene 1, we might not want to attach too much importance to this driver. In scene 2, however, the court case indicates that respect for and redress through the law is a much stronger driver. The lawsuit against DMC is brought by consumer activists seeking restitution (= a fifth driver) for the aggravation caused to them through DMC's negligence.

Yet another driver can also be identified, i.e., the media's desire for a good story which has the benefit of raising public awareness about the pervasiveness of AmI and AmI's benefits (e.g., greater convenience through personalisation of services and improved security) as well as possible risks (encroachment on privacy, exploitation by terrorists, criminals, intelligence agencies, insurance companies, etc.).

### 3.4.7   Issues

The scenario raises several issues:

#### 3.4.7.1   Digital divide

The developed countries have AmI networks and the developing countries do not. There is a risk that this will lead to discrimination against developing countries because the intelligence agencies and immigration authorities may not admit visitors and emigrants from those countries because they do not have the detailed information on those individuals like they do on individuals from developed countries and, consequently, are not able to assess whether individuals from developing countries are a security risk.

On the other hand, DMC executives see an opportunity to set up AmI networks in developing countries which could overcome the concerns of the intelligence agencies and immigration authorities, but potentially leads to another form of discrimination whereby the data arising from the AmI networks are processed by DMC in the United States. A sop would be given to the developing countries, i.e., the raw data, but the real juice is in the processing and exploitation of the data. Switzer mentions the fears of developing countries that they would effectively be transferring their sovereignty to the developed countries (if not to DMC).

### 3.4.7.2 Concentration of power

DMC is the clear market leader in the aggregation and processing of AmI-generated data. Its clients include a wide range of powerful clients – the media, retailers, credit-reporting agencies, immigration authorities, intelligence agencies, etc. When there is a risk that DMC might collapse as a result of the fall-out from the theft, the US government steps in to prop up the company on the grounds that, for security reasons, it cannot permit the collapse. This in turn leads to a dispute between the United States and the European Union as the latter claims that a subsidy violates WTO rules.

### 3.4.7.3 Lack of public awareness

Despite the convenience of the increasing personalisation of services and the enhancements in security that AmI has made possible, most people have not comprehended just how pervasive AmI has become, nor of the scale and volume of data being generated about them by AmI networks. Everything produced will have an AmI-networked microchip.

Most people are willing to trade some of their privacy for better security. The scenario suggests that terrorism has become sufficiently serious that the intelligence agencies and immigration authorities are becoming unwilling to admit foreigners unless they have detailed information on each individual. Similarly, DMC employees seem willing to have location implants and surveillance equipment installed not only in their offices but also in their homes and cars. Probably, they see this as beneficial in security terms.

In the scenario, public awareness is increased as a result of the investigative reporting and media coverage of the theft of data from DMC, the resulting trial and the high-level political intervention. Identity theft is not, of course, a new crime, but what is new about the DMC case is just how extensive are the data from AmI networks compiled and processed by DMC.

### 3.4.7.4 The illusion of security

It is ironic that DMC and its directors face a class action lawsuit on the grounds that they were negligent in securing personal data. It would seem DMC has many security measures. They have installed surveillance equipment, biometrics, key-logging software and other access control measures to protect the data they hold. One of the vice presidents says it is hard to get into DMC headquarters. But the question is: have DMC executives done enough? Did they think their profiling of their own employees was sufficiently watertight so that they did not need to fear theft by insiders? Maybe. We are told that it was hard to get into DMC offices, but not hard to get out. Also, the president seems surprised by a breach in DMC security. Furthermore, they do not know which specific files have been copied, only that about 16 million were copied. DMC's security defences seem primarily aimed at keeping people out, from preventing breaches at its perimeter. The company seemed rather less focused on the enemy within, hence the three employees (who had authorised access to the data) were able to copy the files and exit the premises without having been challenged. Further, it seems relatively easy for them to have removed their location implants and to have disappeared without a trace.

### 3.4.7.5  Differences in legal regimes

In the first scene, MacDonald says he was questioned by a reporter about whether DMC was complying fully with the Safe Harbour Agreement. At this time (2007), there remains a difference between the privacy and data protection requirements in Europe and those in the United States. The Safe Harbour Agreement was supposed to ameliorate those differences, but questions have frequently been raised about its effectiveness and whether (some) companies are complying with the Agreement even if they say they are. The scenario suggests that DMC has largely ignored the Safe Harbour Agreement as it has sold data to a wide range of clients, including government agencies.

### 3.4.7.6  Honesty and trust

Given the lack of awareness of most people about the extensive records held by DMC, the issue of trust is not directly raised, but nevertheless it is an issue whenever a third party holds personal data, especially a lot of data as in the case of DMC. One would think that a data aggregator, processor and reseller like DMC would have some obligation to inform people whenever it sells data to others or takes over another company with personal data records. But this has not occurred. One could assume that some DMC clients such as the intelligence agencies and immigration authorities are content that individuals are *not* informed about what information DMC has on them.

In scene 1, we do not know the president's decision about whether to inform the police and individuals about the theft. Even so, MacDonald, the vice president in charge of media relations, does not hesitate in expressing the view that they should *not* inform the police or individuals. In any event, it seems DMC does not know (yet) whose records have been copied. In the United States, as mentioned in the footnote to Max Court's comment, California and a number of other states have strict laws requiring that companies *do* inform individuals when their data have been stolen or compromised – but that does not mean that they will. Compliance will depend as much on corporate culture and, especially, ethics as on legal deterrents. Senior managers must be seen to be fully compliant and to instil a culture of good corporate citizenship.

## 3.4.8  Legal synopsis

### 3.4.8.1  Global companies and local laws

DMC is active around the world. Which law will be applicable to which data collector and to which data processing? Is the Data Protection Directive 95/46 applicable outside the European Union? A second issue relates to the special provisions of the Directive concerning the transfer of personal data to third countries outside the European Union.

The first question is solved by Article 4 of the Data Protection Directive, which determines that the national law of the Member States will apply where the processing is carried out in the context of the activities of an establishment of the controller on the territory of that Member State. Such a requirement may often be fulfilled, even if we are not sure where the processing of data as such takes place. It may lead, however, to the application of many laws since most likely the data processor will be established in many states. Article 4 further stipulates that if the data controller is established on the territory of several Member States, he must ensure that each of those establishments complies with the obligations laid down by the laws applicable in each Member State. DMC has establishments in the United Kingdom, Japan and the United States. Article 4 (c) determines that if the controller is not established on Community territory, the national legislation of a Member State of the European Union will apply when the processor, for purposes of processing personal data, makes use of equipment, automated or otherwise, situated on the territory of the said Member State, unless such equipment is used only for purposes of transit through the territory of the Community. DMC could try to prove that the equipment in the United Kingdom is only used to transmit information to the United States or Japan, thus preventing the use of the Community legislation. However, the Article 29 Data Protection Working Party[161] interprets the term "equipment" broadly in the context of contemporary online services, covering, inter alia, personal computers which can be used for collecting data. Such interpretation broadens the application of the Data Protection Directive.

The personal data as well as the information and profiles deduced and extracted from the personal data are processed, transferred, licensed and otherwise traded on a worldwide level with hundreds of unknown clients. DMC grew through mergers and acquisitions and processes data (of European citizens) in many countries outside the European Union.

In regard to the second issue, Article 25 of the Data Protection Directive requires the third country to ensure an adequate level of protection of personal data before such data can be transferred to that country. The adequacy of the level of protection afforded by a third country shall be assessed in the light of all the circumstances surrounding a data transfer operation.[162] Where, according to the Commission, a third country does not ensure an adequate level of protection, Member States should prevent any transfer of data to that third country. The Commission, on the other hand, may find that a third country ensures an adequate level of protection by reason of its domestic law or of the international

---

[161] See Article 29 Data Protection Working Party, *Working document on determining the international application of EU data protection law to personal data processing on the Internet by non-EU based websites* (5035/01/EN/Final WP 56), 30 May 2002. http://ec.europa.eu/justice_home/fsj/privacy/docs/wpdocs/2002/wp56_en.pdf

[162] And, in particular, with regard to the nature of the data, the purpose and duration of the proposed processing operation or operations, the country of origin and country of final destination, the rules of law, both general and sectoral, in force in the third country in question and the professional rules and security measures complied with in that country.

commitments it has entered into, particularly upon conclusion of the negotiations, for the protection of the private lives and basic freedoms and rights of individuals.

In execution of this Article, the European Commission has concluded the "**Safe Harbour Agreement**" with the United States, which aims to ensure the protection of personal data transferred from European Member States. Organisations that wish to obtain and maintain recognition of the fact that they ensure an adequate level of protection must subscribe to the principles provided in the agreement, reveal their confidentiality rules and fall within the competence of the US Federal Trade Commission (or any other body fulfilling a similar mission). When DMC transfers data from the European Union to companies in the United States, it must thus ensure that these companies have subscribed to the Safe Harbour Agreement. The European Commission decided in Decision 2000/520/EC of 26 July 2000 that the "Safe Harbour Privacy Principles" ensure an adequate level of protection for personal data transferred to organisations in the United States.

The issue of enforcement is a major problem in international relations. There has been criticism of the Safe Harbour Agreement. The main criticism is that it relies on a self-regulatory system whereby companies merely promise not to violate their declared privacy practices.[163] Protection of personal data by the US administration was also tackled in relation to the processing and transfer of the passenger name records (PNRs) by airlines to the US Department of Homeland Security. Commission Decision 2004/535 EC of 14 May 2004, which stated that the US Bureau of Customs and Border Protection provides adequate protection of Passenger Name Record (PRN) data,[164] was annulled[165] by the Court of Justice. Following the Court judgment, negotiations began on a new PNR agreement, which the Council adopted.[166] However, both the European Data Protection Supervisor[167] and the Article 29 Working Party[168] expressed their lack of satisfaction with the new deal.

---

[163] http://www.privacyinternational.org/article.shtml?cmd[347] = x–347-82589& als[theme] = Privacy%20and %20Human%20Rights%202004#_Toc87939573

[164] Commission Decision 2004/535/EC of 14 May 2004 on the adequate protection of personal data contained in the Passenger Name Record of air passengers transferred to the United States' Bureau of Customs and Border Protection, *Official Journal* L 235, 6 July 2004, pp. 11–22.

[165] Joint cases C-317/04 and 318/04 *European Parliament* v. *Council* [2006]. See also Sturcke, James, and agencies, "US access to flight data unlawful," *The Guardian*, 30 May 2006.

[166] Council Decision 2007/551/CFSP/JHA of 23 July 2007 on the signing, on behalf of the European Union, of an Agreement between the European Union and the United States of America on the processing and transfer of Passenger Name Record (PNR) data by air carriers to the United States Department of Homeland Security (DHS) (2007 PNR Agreement) *Official Journal L 204/16, 4 august 2007*, pp. 16 , and Agreement between the European Union and the United States of America on the processing and transfer of Passenger Name Record (PNR) data by air carriers to the United States Department of Homeland Security (DHS) (2007 PNR Agreement), *Official Journal L 204/16, 4 august 2007*, pp. 18.

[167] Letter of the European Data Protection Supervisor, P. Hustinx, to Dr. W. Schauble, Minister of the Interior [of the EU presidency], dated 27 June 2007. http://www.epic.org/privacy/pdf/hustinx-letter.pdf

[168] Article 29 Data Protection Working Party, Opinion 5/2007 on the follow-up agreement between the European Union and the United States of America on the processing and transfer of passenger name record (PNR) data by air carriers to the United States Department of Homeland Security concluded in July 2007 (01646/07/EN-WP138). http://ec.europa.eu/justice_home/fsj/privacy/docs/wpdocs/2007/wp138_en.pdf

The Commission also decided that Argentina (Commission Decision C(2003) 1731), Canada (Commission Decision 2002/2/EC),[169] Switzerland (2000/518/EC), Guernsey (2003/821/EC) and Isle of Man (2004/411/EC) offer adequate protection. Only a limited number of countries have received such recognition. Transfer to African and other developing countries could pose problems, since they probably do not provide an adequate level of protection.

Article 26 provides for an exception: "A transfer or a set of transfers of personal data to a third country which does not ensure an adequate level of protection, may take place on condition that: (a) the data subject has given his consent unambiguously to the proposed transfer; or (b) the transfer is necessary for the performance of a contract between the data subject and the controller or the implementation of pre-contractual measures taken in response to the data subject's request; or (c) the transfer is necessary for the conclusion or performance of a contract concluded in the interest of the data subject between the controller and a third party; or (d) the transfer is necessary or legally required on important public interest grounds, or for the establishment, exercise or defence of legal claims; or (e) the transfer is necessary in order to protect the vital interests of the data subject; or (f) the transfer is made from a register which according to laws or regulations is intended to provide information to the public and which is open to consultation either by the public in general or by any person who can demonstrate legitimate interest, to the extent that the conditions laid down in law for consultation are fulfilled in the particular case." These conditions are clearly not fulfilled in this scenario. "A transfer or a set of transfers of personal data to a third country which does not ensure an adequate level of protection may also be authorized where the controller adduces adequate safeguards with respect to the protection of the privacy and fundamental rights and freedoms of individuals and as regards the exercise of the corresponding rights; such safeguards may in particular result from appropriate contractual clauses." In these last two cases, the Member State has to give permission, which DMC does not seem to have acquired.

### 3.4.8.2 Monitoring employees

The scenario shows that employees at the workplace are continuously monitored, with cameras installed everywhere and with location implants.

The issue of privacy in the context of professional activities has already been discussed.[170] People should not lose their privacy at the office or in a professional environment. Until now, the Court of Strasbourg has not decided a case of permanent monitoring at the workplace. Systems such as those using biolocation implants that allow a permanent monitoring, even when one is not working (e.g., to trace somebody who violates the security obligations), will likely be found incompatible with Article 8 ECHR, which not only protects the private life but also the family life and the home. Professional location implants that enable

---

[169] There are, however, questions whether Canada offers adequate protection.
[170] See section 3.2.8.1.

monitoring of an individual's behaviour at home and in one's private and family life will most probably be refused (mainly for being disproportionate).

Additional arguments for this reasoning can be drawn from the Data Protection Directive prohibiting excessive processing of data, and requiring the processing data to be "relevant" and processed for legitimate purposes (Article 6 of the Data Protection Directive). Indeed, it is difficult to imagine how permanent monitoring can be considered relevant, necessary for legitimate purposes and not excessive. The Directive also prohibits as a rule the processing of sensitive data. Permanent monitoring will reveal such data, e.g., the subject's going to certain hospitals or to locations such as churches or political meetings.

There seems to be no margin of negotiation if you want to be employed by DMC. Also, the so-called consent in an employment contract must be viewed in the light of Article 7 of the Data Protection Directive which provides that personal data may only be processed if the data subject has unambiguously given his consent. In this case, it could be argued that employees were forced to give their consent – i.e., if they wanted to work at DMC, they have to give their consent.

DMC needs to be sure that confidentiality is respected. Article 7 (f) provides that processing can be allowed when necessary for the purposes of legitimate interests pursued by the controller or by a third party or parties to whom the data are disclosed, except where such interests are overridden by the fundamental rights and freedoms of the data subject. There needs to be a balance between the legitimate interests of DMC and the fundamental rights and freedoms of the employees, including the right to privacy. Even if tough security measures are required (as in case of the critical infrastructures), one could still question whether such intrusive measures are necessary.

The data are collected for a specific purpose, to ensure the confidentiality and business interests of the company (Article 6 (b), though the legitimacy of such monitoring might still be questioned as less intrusive means can ensure confidentiality). The information obtained via the location implants could be used for totally different purposes. As a data mining company, DMC might use location implants to collect as much information as possible. This could happen without the consent of the employees or for purposes not previously agreed. There seems to be a problem with the principle of proportionality.

It should be added, as an example, that Belgium's Collective Labour Agreement no. 81 of 16 June 1998 explicitly prohibits permanent monitoring of employees. This Agreement was conceived as an additional tool to strengthen the existing Belgian data protection law of 1992, amended in 1998 to implement the Data Protection Directive. Harmonisation in this field is clearly needed.

The case of permanent monitoring will probably provoke a lot of reactions in the future. Although there is no general prohibition against it, we could assume that it will not become a general practice in the next decades, with the possible exception of certain groups.

### 3.4.8.3    Global interoperability

Most developing countries have no AmI or similar networks, thus building individual profiles is difficult, if not impossible. The immigration authorities of developed countries rely on such profiles, and threaten to refuse entry to people from countries without AmI or compatible networks.

Interoperability is of major importance within the EU countries, and globally too. The **Directive on technical standards and regulations**[171] provides a co-operation and information procedure in order to develop European standards. At an international level, similar standardisation initiatives have been and are being undertaken.[172]

The majority of those standards are created in the developed world and in many domains, it is expensive to comply with them. Developing countries, as mentioned in the scenario, may not be able to afford compatible technology. To ensure maximum interoperability, initiatives are needed beyond those aimed at the creation of common standards. Countries should be able to develop the necessary infrastructure to comply with them.

This is, however, only one aspect of the problem. A fully operational, interoperable AmI world would be a threat for a range of fundamental rights such as privacy, non-discrimination, free movement, the right to anonymity, sovereignty of developing countries, etc.

### 3.4.8.4    Trading of personal data and the role of the data subject

DMC has been trading data. Questions have been raised about the accuracy of the data, and people were unable to correct false information. In fact, most people did not even know about DMC, nor about the profiles the company had built. Data processed by DMC have not always come from legitimate sources.

Illegal acquisition of data refers to the issue of data laundering, which has already been discussed.[173] DMC sells data, which is often misused for spam and other types of fraud. All of this implies that DMC does not respect the fundamental data protection principles as expressed in the Data Protection Directive and the Privacy & Electronic Communications Directive.

Even at the first level of the collection of personal data (before DMC acquires and processes them into profiles), data controllers have an obligation under Article 10 of the Data Protection Directive to inform the data subjects of any processing of their data, about the purposes of the processing and transmission of

---

[171] Directive 98/34/EC of the European Parliament and of the Council of 22 June 1998 laying down a procedure for the provision of information in the field of technical standards and regulations, *Official Journal* L 204, 21 July 1998.

[172] Interoperability and standardisation have been discussed above in section 3.3.8.2.

[173] See section 3.2.8.8.

personal data to third parties.[174] Any further information such as the recipients or categories of recipients of the data, the existence of the right of access and the right to rectify their data is only required "in so far as such further information is necessary, having regard to the specific circumstances in which the data are collected to guarantee fair processing in respect of the data subject."

When personal data are disclosed to third parties, Article 11 ("Information where the data have not been obtained from the data subject") provides that the controller or his representative must, no later than at the time when the data are first disclosed, provide the data subject with at least the following information, except where he already has it: "(a) the identity of the controller and of his representative; (b) the purposes of the processing; (c) any further information such as the categories of data concerned, the recipients or categories of recipients, the existence of the right of access to and the right to rectify the data concerning him in so far as such further information is necessary, having regard to the specific circumstances in which the data are processed, to guarantee fair processing in respect of the data subject."

Let us assume the personal data are made anonymous before they were received by DMC (which is not the case in our scenario, as the data are used to screen visitors and immigrants from developing countries). In this case, the analysis is different, since data protection law does not apply to the processing of the anonymous data by DMC. Of course, the act of anonymising data is a processing that falls under the Data Protection Directive, but if other data controllers do the processing before DMC receives the anonymous data, DMC is not bound by the rules of the Data Protection Directive.

### 3.4.8.5   IPR and personal profiles

DMC owns all intellectual property rights to its databases and its profiles, built upon (anonymous or identifiable) personal data.

The databases owned by DMC and other companies are protected by intellectual property rights. The **Directive on legal protection of databases**[175] provides for double protection of databases: a copyright protection and a *sui generis* right for the database.

Databases are protected by copyright if they, by reason of the selection or arrangement of their contents, constitute the author's own intellectual creation.[176]

---

[174] The right to information is discussed in sections 3.2.8.4 and 3.2.8.7.

[175] Directive 96/9/EC of the European Parliament and of the Council of 11 March 1996 on the legal protection of databases, *Official Journal* L 077, 27 March 1996.

[176] As the author of the databases, DMC has the exclusive right to carry out or to authorise: "(a) temporary or permanent reproduction by any means and in any form, in whole or in part; (b) translation, adaptation, arrangement and any other alteration; (c) any form of distribution to the public of the database or of copies thereof. The first sale in the Community of a copy of the database by the right holder or with his consent shall exhaust the right to control resale of that copy within the Community; (d) any communication, display or performance to the public; (e) any reproduction, distribution, communication, display or performance to the public of the results of the acts referred to in (b)" (Article 5 of the Directive on the legal protection of databases).

Copyright protection does not apply to databases of which the contents are not selected or arranged through the author's *own intellectual* creation.

In an AmI world, service providers will use massive databases. They will not only use the content, but also the structure or selection or arrangement of the databases. AmI services will require the linking and integration of many databases. The protection offered is extensive and it is impossible to require a permission to reproduce, translate and/or communicate database content every time again. Article 6 provides for some exceptions to the exclusive rights of the author: "The performance by the lawful user of a database or of a copy thereof of any of the acts listed in Article 5 which is necessary for the purposes of access to the contents of the databases and normal use of the contents by the lawful user shall not require the authorization of the author of the database." It is unclear what must be understood by "lawful user". Depending on the interpretation, it could limit the scope of the exception to a greater or lesser extent. Article 6 also provides for optional exceptions to exclusive rights: "(a) reproduction for private purposes of a non-electronic database; (b) illustration for teaching or scientific research, as long as the source is indicated and to the extent justified by the non-commercial purpose to be achieved; (c) use for the purposes of public security or an administrative or judicial procedure; (d) other exceptions traditionally authorised under national law."

The database can also be protected by a *sui generis* right. In order to obtain this *sui generis* protection, the maker of the database has to show that "there has been qualitatively and/or quantitatively a substantial investment in either the obtaining, verification or presentation of the contents to prevent extraction and/or re-utilization of the whole or of a substantial part, evaluated qualitatively and/or quantitatively, of the contents of that database." The terms extraction and reutilisation are defined in a broad way (Article 7).[177]

Article 7 states that the *sui generis* protection shall apply irrespective of the eligibility of the contents of that database for protection by copyright and by other rights. This implies that the maker can obtain the *sui generis* protection even when the content consists of personal data. Although the user does not have a property right over his personal data, the maker of a personal database can obtain an exclusive right over the database containing such data. Article 8 gives the lawful users of a database the right, when the database is made available to the public in whatever manner, to extract and/or reutilise insubstantial (small) parts of its contents, evaluated qualitatively and/or quantitatively, for any purposes whatsoever. There are limits to this right: the user may not perform acts that conflict with normal exploitation of the database or unreasonably prejudice the legitimate interests of the maker of the database and may not cause prejudice to the holder of a copyright or related

---

[177] Article 7 (2) states: "(a) 'extraction' shall mean the permanent or temporary transfer of all or a substantial part of the contents of a database to another medium by any means or in any form; (b) 're-utilization' shall mean any form of making available to the public all or a substantial part of the contents of a database by the distribution of copies, by renting, by on-line or other forms of transmission. The first sale of a copy of a database within the Community by the right holder or with his consent shall exhaust the right to control resale of that copy within the Community; public lending is not an act of extraction or re-utilization."

right in respect of the works or subject matter contained in the database. Data protection will apply in cases where personal data are involved (which will not allow making such a database available to the public).

Article 9 provides for a number of optional exceptions, analogous to exceptions to the copyright protection of databases discussed above. Certain exceptions to the exclusive right of the maker of the database are thus provided, but they only apply to "lawful users" and, especially, to the lawful user of a database *made available to the public*. Consequently, for example, in the case of profiling, these exceptions are rather limited or even non-existing. The right to freely use publicly available databases might be in contradiction with the right to privacy which prohibits the owners of databases from making them public. In an AmI world where massive amounts of information and databases will be exchanged and traded, the protection of databases might thus turn out to be a burden.

Compared to the exclusive rights provided to the author or maker of the database, the exceptions are rather limited and do not provide a solution to the fact that service suppliers will not be able to ask the author of the database for permission every time. Databases containing addresses, locations, weather information, sports results, pollen information, medical data ... they all need to be coupled and need to co-operate to make AmI work. This is not possible in an intellectual property right system where copyright and database owners impose unreasonable prices, limit competition and make exclusive contracts with one company (excluding the other). Making databases available to the public may be difficult to reconcile with privacy and data protection law.

The **Copyright Directive**[178] is another instrument that has an impact on the intellectual property rights that are important for AmI. The Directive harmonises the three patrimonial rights that a copyright holder can enjoy, namely, the reproduction right, the right of communication to the public and the distribution right. It also reassesses the exceptions to the exclusive rights of the rights-holder in light of the new electronic environment. It provides for an exhaustive enumeration of exceptions and limitations to the reproduction right and the right of communication to the public (and to the distribution right).

The harmonisation is not absolute, since most exceptions and limitations provided are optional. The Member States are not allowed to provide exceptions other than those enumerated. An important exception for information technology concerns the exclusive right of reproduction: it allows certain acts of temporary reproduction, which are transient or incidental reproductions, forming an integral and essential part of a technological process and carried out for the sole purpose of enabling either efficient transmission in a network between third parties by an intermediary, or a lawful use of a work or other subject matter to be made. The acts of reproduction concerned should have no separate economic value of their own.

---

[178] Directive 2001/29/EC of the European Parliament and of the Council of 22 May 2001 on the harmonisation of certain aspects of copyright and related rights in the information society, *Official Journal* L 167, 22 June 2001. The anti-circumvention provision of this Directive and the Software Directive was discussed under 3.2.8.2.

#### 3.4.8.6 Data theft

Three DMC employees have illegally copied and made off with the personal data on a lot of people. For a few weeks, DMC didn't say anything to anybody.

The employees have possibly committed criminal offences as defined in the Cybercrime Convention, such as computer-related fraud; however, there is a lack of provisions in the Convention which would directly criminalise data theft. This act is most probably also punishable under the national criminal provision on theft. The Data Protection Directive, on the other hand, might also support a case regarding the liability of the data controller (who is obliged to ensure the security of processing).

The Cybercrime Convention and the Framework Decision 2005/222/JHA[179] both deal with the liability of legal persons, which could be invoked in the situation described in the scenario, as DMC could be accused of neglecting to take sufficient care to protect the databases from theft.

### 3.4.9 Conclusions

The principal conclusion we draw from this dark scenario and its analysis is that, although we can expect amazing advances in the development and deployment of ambient technologies, there is a risk that corporate ethics in the year 2017 will not be so different from those prevalent in the year 2007, which is to say that some companies will be good corporate citizens and some will not. Similarly, some companies will have rogue employees just as they do today who are capable of undermining the efficiency and credibility of new data-processing algorithms. A principal difference between today's world and that depicted in the year 2017 could be that security concerns about terrorism and antisocial behaviour will be such that unless individuals have really detailed profiles compiled from data from AmI networks, they may be barred from entering a developed country. Also, while people may welcome the convenience from personalisation of services and the ubiquity of surveillance technologies, they may be lulled into a false sense of security.

In view of the advances in surveillance technologies, biometrics and fourth-generation mobile systems, the AmI community, policy-makers and society must be alert to possible abuses of the technology. Consequently, it is important to build in safeguards that minimise the risks, even though it must be recognised that the risks can never be completely eliminated, no matter how strong and comprehensive the legislative and regulatory measures are.

---

[179] The Cybercrime Convention, offences defined by it and Framework Decision 2005/222/JHA are discussed above in sections 3.2.8.7, 3.2.8.10 and 3.3.8.1.

## 3.5   Scenario 4: An early morning TV programme reports on AmI

### 3.5.1   The scenario script

#### 3.5.1.1   Introduction

In the TV studios of an early morning news and variety show, a reporter/presenter is interviewing people who have made the news.

"Good morning ladies and gentlemen and thank you for joining us here on The Breakfast Show. Our guests today include a researcher in the Antarctic and the winner of last month's reality gardening show. We'll also have the latest traffic forecast across the city, which appears to be normal considering yesterday's chaos. The $CO_2$ pollution levels are below the threshold so all cars are allowed to enter the city centre. First though, we are pleased to welcome to the studio Markos, an MEP and one of the founding members of APPAG."

### Scene 1: The Anti-Personalised-Profiling Action Group (APPAG)

*Breakfast Show Presenter: "Markos, thank you for taking the time to join us today. Tell us about APPAG and how it came about."*

*"First off, Alexandra, I'd like to thank you for inviting me. APPAG is something I feel quite strongly about and I'm glad to have the opportunity to share it with your viewers. The initials stand for Anti-Personalised-Profiling Action Group. I would like to stress right from the beginning that we are not against aggregated profiling per se. In fact, I was an early adopter of the 'always-on' movement some 10 years ago during the broadband Internet/mobile convergence era. I am also used to being watched and surveyed at all times because of my position as an MEP. But I think a lot of people simply do not realise how much personal information they are constantly giving out.[180] APPAG wants to raise public awareness about this issue and wants to warn people that personalised profiling is simply too risky. I joined APPAG after some bad experiences."*

*"What kind of bad experiences?"*

*"First of all, during our last holiday, my wife and I discovered that we did not have access to the same information and services as other hotel guests. For example, there was a jazz concert in town during sunset but we did not get any information about it. We only found out the next day. I was really angry because my avatar knows I like such events. Also, the excursion to the old Roman ruins was already fully booked. We could only participate when paying a premium. This is so unfair. And do you know*

---

[180] Tuohey, Jasey, "Government Uses Color Laser Printer Technology to Track Documents. Practice embeds hidden, traceable data in every page printed", *PC World*, 22 November 2004. http://www.pcworld.com/news/article/0,aid,118664,00.asp. See also Jardin, Xeni, "Your Identity, Open to All", *Wired News*, 6 May 2005. http://www.wired.com/news/privacy/0,1848,67407,00. html

*why? Just because the company that has the profiling exclusivity on our family recently merged with another company. Because we did not opt in to their new travelling module, they ignored the travelling preferences of my avatar. And then suddenly, you realise how dependent you have become on these things."*

*"But is that solved now?"*

*"Yes, but ... it set me thinking. What happens if you decide not to do it? I began to make a point of switching off my AmI sensors in public places so that my preferences could not be revealed and monitored. I'll leave them on in the home where I control the environment, or at work where there are confidentiality clauses protecting us but the moment I step outside I switch them off. A cumbersome procedure, a real hassle, but it can be done. The downside is that I now find myself missing out on announcements – including the emergencies – or special promotions that I would have liked to take advantage of. Recently, I was in the airport where I actually found that I was banned from the frequent flyers' lounge because their sensors objected to my sensors opting out! Even though I showed them my card, they still wouldn't let me in. Can you believe that? Why should I be denied entry? Now I can see that if I have my AmI sensors off at the airport, there's a distinct risk that I'll be stopped and searched and maybe miss my flight."*

*"But why would you want to switch ...?"*

*"Because I value my privacy. I think a lot of people simply do not realise how much personal information they are constantly giving out. What I object to is the personal nature of this profiling. Personalised profiling leads to a lack of freedom in making a decision. Have you heard about the companies with plans to 'personalise' their self-service restaurants based on their customers' medical history? Imagine, you would like to have a steak but they give you a salad instead. ... And what if insurance companies get involved and start raising your premiums because they found out that you are not doing a lot of physical exercise?*

*"I understand companies collect anonymous information to better serve their clients or for particular marketing purposes although this also has caveats that one should look into. But it's the idea that you are being personally profiled wherever you go that really concerns me. It is the amount, quality and accuracy of data related to you that is generated and collected and archived for eternity that makes me shiver. How do you know the choice proposed by an avatar is a consequence of your preferences or simply the imposition of a commercial agreement?"*

*"What do you propose then?"*

*"Some believe that anonymity is the solution but I am not sure about that. The system needs your identity and you must give it in order to get access to the services. I think people should stop giving their data away for profiling purposes because once the system has them, the profile is built, improved, linked, added with other information. And you know what the worst thing is? Even if you refuse any profiling, and you want to act as if you are anonymous, you fall within a profiled category called 'the anonymous'. It is even one of the best profiled categories ...! You just can't escape it any more."*

*"You also say that we need to be careful when transferring human judgement and decision-making to computers."*

*"Yes, to give an example, a good friend was erroneously placed on a tourism black list. These lists are used by the major hotel chains to identify known trouble-makers, people with bad debt or whatever the case may be. If you present yourself at a hotel reception desk without an advance reservation, the big hotel chains will run a quick profile on you. The problem is that that it takes time to go through the massive amount of data. As a result, an early warning system is set up that already gives suggestions after only five per cent of the data has been processed. Experienced hotel staff know how to deal with such preliminary profiles but in this case the lady in question was refused a hotel room. The situation was not rectified until the following day. In the meantime, my friend had to spend the night in a hotel that was dirty, noisy, dangerous and twice as expensive but it was the only one that accepted her cash and did not require the result of the standard profiling applica-tion. On top of this, her suitcase was stolen there. Who do you think is liable for that? Moreover, there will probably always be a record of this somewhere, even if it was cleared up the next day, and you never know if something similar might happen again. Not a very nice prospect."*

*"Tell us about what APPAG proposes?"*

*"Well, one of the fundamental areas we want to work on is the legal framework. Though the data protection act covers personal data, we feel that there is a grey area about what really constitutes personal data and under what circumstances data col-lection is legal. I would argue that many of your preferences and lifestyle choices are, in fact, personal data. Furthermore, as I said earlier, we want to raise public awareness about these issues. Many people do not know what information is being collected and do not even know they have the right to opt out. This must change."*

### Scene 2: AmI divides

*"We now go live to New York where we are joined by Dr. Anthony Lazlo, a leading environmental scientist and pioneer of AmI for environmental protection who is very critical of current environmental protection programmes. Good morning, Anthony."*

*"Good morning, Alexandra, and thank you for the invitation to appear on your programme. I want to show you and your audience that our society is not making full use of the potential of environmental monitoring technologies but also that pol-icy-makers need to understand that intelligent devices and intelligent agents alone are not going to solve the problem. The future simulations we will project are based on the widespread use of AmI sensors throughout Antarctica which have been col-lecting all sorts of information during the last 10 years."*

*"Can you tell us more in detail what you mean, Anthony?"*

*"Of course, and I will show it to your audience. Have a look at these images live from Antarctica, which has one of the harshest climates on earth. Within the GCP – the Global Conservation Project – we have spread thousands of sensors in the environment to constantly monitor climate change.*[181] *That is because the costs of these tiny sensors – they are actually like smart dust*[182] *– have gone down drastically,*

---

[181] See Michahelles, F., et al., 2003.

[182] For details on the Smart Dust project, see http://robotics.eecs.berkeley.edu/~pister/SmartDust/

*although it is still very expensive to cover such a big landmass, especially under inhospitable conditions. But it is necessary, as rising sea levels have caused much destruction in the last few years. Look also at the projected graph with the information we receive on the water temperature, sea level, air pollution, etc. Similar smart monitoring projects in sensitive zones all over the world would help us a lot in combating environmental hazards and disasters, and could save many, many lives."*

*"So why are we not doing it then?"*

*"Because there is not enough money for it. I mean, there is little commercial interest in this, so it needs to come from public funding, but political and governmental priorities are elsewhere. Now look at these images from a very different place, the hot and dry Saharan desert. These images came from a film shot by a camera crew that travelled recently to the region. Here, too, we can see environmental destruction. But here we do not have the technology to enable us to act quickly and remotely. But let me be clear about this. I'm not just talking about environmental issues. AmI technologies could have life-saving potential – if we were able to monitor the spread of certain viruses, for example, we could target immunisation programmes more effectively and stand a better chance of eradicating diseases. Medics working in the field here do not even have the latest 4G terminals with language translation and direct connection to medical laboratories."*

*"So you're saying more public money is needed?"*

*"Yes, but not only that. We want to draw attention to the fact that although in some places we have been able to use this technology and harness its full capabilities, there are many other regions in the world that could greatly benefit but which do not have the funds to make the necessary investment. That is not fair. It should not be like that."*

*"Thanks, Anthony, for drawing our attention to this issue. Any last messages?"*

*"Yes. It is not only about money nor only about technology. You can invest lots of money in technology implementations but if no political action is taken or if people and companies are not willing to change certain behaviours, then we are going the wrong way. All the money in the world would not be able to change that nor the most fantastic technologies."*

*"Unfortunately, we have to leave it there, Anthony. We now go to Iris for the most recent traffic information."*

### Scene 3: Public life disrupted by virus attack

*"The traffic situation downtown is currently heavy but stable. The communication backbone seems to be coping today with the heavy traffic of all the machine-to-machine messages that maintain increased traffic throughput. Pollution levels are steady, the emergency response rate is up by a point, crime-monitoring is at alert level yellow, and the accident rate is close to zero. A distinct improvement compared to the situation at the same time yesterday. But let's talk to Peter, our correspondent at the city traffic office, for the latest news on yesterday's chaos."*

*"Good morning, Peter. Tell us what happened yesterday. Was it a virus attack?"*

*"Yes, it was. The city's intelligent traffic system went completely mad and the resulting traffic chaos was the worst we've seen in more than 15 years. Traffic lights kept on alternating every five seconds at random, for almost an hour. Cars were let*

*into the city centre without being automatically charged the congestion toll thus con-*
*tributing to the general chaos; road works were wrongly announced creating queues*
*of angry drivers complaining to technical staff and buses did not stop at (digital)*
*requests. According to a traffic official, the centre's main server was attacked by a*
*digital virus. Initially, the self-repairing anti-virus software was able to counter the*
*attack and in order to completely eradicate the hybrid virus (or multipartite virus),*
*the software had to search for, identify and download software updates. Unfortunately,*
*an unknown Trojan was able to briefly take control of the traffic management system.*
*Emergency back-up systems were able to restore control after 45 minutes, but the*
*impact on the city traffic lasted for many more hours."*

*"Peter, what did traffic administration say about it? It was obviously a serious*
*security breach."*

*"Well, during the crisis, it seems their primary goal was to restore the situation*
*back to normal as soon as possible. Once that was accomplished, they started ask-*
*ing questions about the attack. Who perpetrated it? What was their objective? Was*
*it a diversion for other types of attacks, such as crime, robbery, etc.? They are seri-*
*ously considering the possibility that this may have been a malicious terrorist*
*attack*[183] *and are trying to find the missing links. Their specialists looked into the*
*hybrid virus and the Trojan, and after analysis, they declared this morning that they*
*were not dealing with a new-generation virus. The consequences would have been*
*worse if this had been an attack using novel mutant type worms."*

*"Is there a longer term impact of the attack?"*

*"Well, city officials aren't saying anything officially, but there's a rumour that*
*the virus also caused partial loss of traffic data. That would mean that the traffic*
*system has lost its intelligence and that it has to learn again to optimise traffic*
*intervention measures. It could take up to two or three months, but again, this is an*
*unconfirmed report.*

*"Officially, the city traffic experts say only the obvious, that security is critical in AmI*
*environments like the traffic management system and that 'we' need to reduce the risks*
*relating to the upgrading, maintenance and interoperability of such systems. Is that*
*another way of saying they want more money? Who knows? Back to you, Iris."*

*Next, our events correspondent, Didi, is at the scene of yesterday's rock concert,*
*where security fears prompted the evacuation of almost 50,000 people. Fans are*
*now demanding their money back as it emerges mishaps with the technology used*
*by event organisers may have been to blame.*

### Scene 4: AmI system aided mass risk management

*"Here's Didi with our special report on the story." [Voiceover of report]*

*"Incidents in the past with big crowds led to the development of crowd manage-*
*ment strategies supported by AmI technologies.*[184] *AmI has proved to be effective in*

---

[183] Schneier, Bruce, "Identification and Security", *Crypto-Gram Newsletter*, 15 February 2004.
http://www.schneier.com/crypto–gram–back.html

[184] Hogan, Jenny, "Smart software linked to CCTV can spot dubious behaviour", NewScientist.
com, 11 July 2003. http://www.newscientist.com/article.ns?id=dn3918

*facilitating intelligent communication among infrastructural elements (AmI sensors), event organisers, security managers and members of the crowd. Through the use of Edibles, Personal Wrist Communicators (PWC) and Disposable Wrist Communicators (DWC), crowds and individual movements are monitored continuously so that any incidents are noticed immediately.*[185] *This time, however, the system did not function properly. The concert hall was evacuated completely because panic arose for no reason at all.*

*"Last night, not everyone made the switch to 'Concert' mode. Early generation devices, very popular among the teenagers, were not sold with pre-prepared profiles and users of these devices had to create the profile manually; some did not do so. Other users simply did not download the concert profile as it was sucking up resources of their personal AmI devices. Thus, their AmI devices did not function properly. On the other hand, people with implants, through their intelligent proxies, were able to effortlessly negotiate, check and download the appropriate concert profiles. Also, people who had bought their tickets from ticket touts, habitually labelled 'clones', tried to mask their identity and assume the name corresponding to the ticket.*

*"The concert began with a great performance from The Tumbling Rocks. Suddenly people say they heard a loud bang. Witnesses at the scene described hearing something that sounded like an explosion. Others assumed this was just a part of The Rocks' act. Those members of the audience with personal devices running the concert profile instantly received 'no-panic' messages; others were not notified at all. The security resources control centre received various messages from the audience as well as from the arena AmI sensors and the ground patrol who immediately approached the scene. The first priority of the ground patrol was to arrest all 'clones' as a matter of precaution. In addition, a special report was sent to all emergency services that were on stand-by including the status of the AmI sensors in the area and the list of who was in the audience and of their personal AmI devices. An in-depth identification analysis of all clones was also initiated.*

*"Parts of the audience started moving away from the affected spot despite the fact that there was no cause for concern. Crowd behaviour monitoring devices detected this panic movement and the AmI system automatically initiated the evacuation plan for this part of the arena without alarming others. Then, confusion occurred as some people took decisions in spite of AmI recommendations while others were unaware of any abnormal occurrence. It was finally decided to evacuate the whole arena and the appropriate plan was put in motion. Apart from a few people being lightly injured and some 'clones' being arrested, the evacuation plans were executed perfectly. Even so, everyone felt disappointed and cheated that the concert had to be abandoned. Naturally, people want their money back."*

*Back in the studio, Alexandra thanks Didi for the report and passes on to her next guest, the winner of last month's reality gardening show. Life goes on even in AmI space.*

---

[185] Upton, Mick, "Casual Rock Concert Events", June 2005. http://www.crowddynamics.com/Main/Concertrisks.htm

### 3.5.2   Analysis

### 3.5.3   The context

This scenario is intended to explore the implications of AmI technologies on a global scale and to consider risks for society as a whole. It highlights possible problems related to critical infrastructures, security and dependability. The scenario is composed of four interviews:

- The first deals with the application of personalised profiling in public spaces and voluntary exclusion from AmI services as a result of negative experiences (invasions of privacy, profiling, annoyance, etc.).
- The second tackles the issue of the digital divide.
- The third shows how AmI vulnerabilities and our dependence on critical infrastructure might affect public life.
- The last concerns application of AmI technologies for crowd management.

Scene 1

In this interview, a member of the Anti-Personalised-Profiling Action Group stresses the risks related to personalised profiling in public spaces as opposed to the milder risks as a result of aggregated profiling and underlines the lack of awareness of users and the lack of transparency on the part of service providers. Some critical situations are described:

- Being deprived of access to certain services or unable to get your leisure of choice
- Lack of freedom in decision-making
- Avoiding anonymity as it is a profiling category in itself
- The difficulty in recovering a "stable" (legitimate) situation as a consequence of transferring human judgement and decision-making to computers.

Scene 2

AmI technologies may contribute to improving the climate sciences,[186] by enhancing access to and integrating available information from sources such as electronic journals, satellite data, etc., including researchers in the global geoscience community and by enhancing virtual collaborations.

In addition, AmI technologies can help create a better understanding of climate change by enabling continuous monitoring and serving as an effective tool in reducing climate change impacts, such as natural disasters.[187] However, AmI

---

[186] Gettelman, A., "The Information Divide in the Climate Sciences", National Center for Atmospheric Research, May 2003. http://www.isse.ucar.edu/infodivide

[187] Müller, B., "Equity in Climate Change – The Great Divide", Executive summary, Oxford Institute for Energy Studies with the support of Shell Foundation. www.oxfordenergy.org/pdfs/great_divide_executive_summary.pdf

applications, installation and maintenance may have a prohibitive cost. The issue of digital divide at the global level is also addressed. The dark side has two manifestations: Not every country can benefit in the same way from AmI technologies, although the impacts are global. AmI technologies as such will not solve the digital divide problem. Effective distribution of organisational responsibilities and policy measures are needed as well.

Scene 3

This scene aims at raising awareness of our dependence on the infrastructure and the required level of security – a critical issue in AmI environments. Indeed, new technologies bring new vulnerabilities (as shown in the weakness of the self-repairing antivirus software). When they are exploited, the consequences (e.g., the traffic chaos caused by usurping control of the traffic management system) may be significant. A post-crisis analysis underlines the impacts and damages (e.g., loss of data) caused by this digital attack and the subsequent actions to be performed (e.g., application of learned lessons). With the complexity of the AmI environment and the increasing dependence on AmI-enabled services, security of systems becomes critical. They need to be protected from terrorists, common law criminals, hackers and software bugs.

Scene 4

The last interview recounts how continuous AmI monitoring of specific large public spaces such as a stadium and personalised communication to thousands of individuals may help risk management by establishing a direct channel of communication between people and event organisers in an emergency. The expected benefits are important, but the practice reveals some problems, such as inappropriate communication and confusion in the audience mainly due to lack of trust in the AmI suggestions. Even if the AmI system works as anticipated, the result might generate more inconvenience than benefit. In view of their ubiquity, AmI technologies and devices can help in risk management and crowd control, but challenges to their utility need to be pre-empted.

### 3.5.4   AmI technologies and devices

The scenario makes reference to several AmI or AmI-related technologies, including:

- Sensors
  - Tiny sensors (actually, smart dust) embedded in the environment with networking capabilities for monitoring climate change
  - Positioning
- Intelligent algorithms
  - Data mining (for providing personalised information such as about a jazz concert to hotel guests or for personalising self-service in a restaurant)

- Self-repairing algorithms, e.g., to optimise emergency intervention in traffic management
- Traffic-routing
- Language translation

- Wireless and wireline communications networks enabling interworking of heterogeneous devices, including networked sensors, computers and diverse personal devices.

## 3.5.5   Applications

The AmI technologies referenced in the scenario are used in various applications, including

- Personalisation of services – AmI profiling aims at providing well-being and helping users in their everyday life. Several examples can be found in this scenario, such as hotel-restaurant services and establishment of a specific channel for emergency use.
- Environmental monitoring – AmI applications will enable continuous monitoring, even under hostile conditions, and provide information/data in order to help solve global problems.
- Traffic, emergency and crowd management – Because AmI technologies can provide more detailed, individualised, real-time location data from networked sensors, intelligent systems can be implemented for crowd configuration, proactive and adaptive evacuation and incident notification. The key technologies or devices in such management applications include:

  - Profiling (personalised or for a group), which can improve the responsiveness of the AmI environment.
  - Avatars used to encapsulate user experiences, preferences and wants.
  - Disposable (e.g., edible) communication hardware.
  - 4G terminals enabling language translation among many other services.

- Self-repairing antivirus applications – AmI technology makes it is possible to design self-learning intelligent systems.
- Security measures – AmI has the capability to support effective decision-making.

Because new technologies bring new vulnerabilities, some negative applications may arise, including

- Propagation of viruses – Inherent in the implementation of any AmI environment is the interoperability of different technologies. That interoperability requires metadata, and we could expect such metadata to be exploited or attacked by a new generation of powerful viruses, mutant worms that can adapt to network and device heterogeneity to spread and disrupt different AmI devices including back-up systems.

- Fraudulent gathering of personal information and profiles.
- Exclusion of people by placing them on a black list based on automatically gathered information.

## 3.5.6 Drivers

The four scenes in this scenario are impelled by several drivers, of which the following are the most important.

### 3.5.6.1 Individual and social concerns about the deterioration of the environment

As a consequence of this prevalent concern, individuals, scientists, social groups and others have begun using AmI to monitor changes in the Antarctic environment. It is simply beneficial to all to facilitate the use of such advanced technology everywhere.

### 3.5.6.2 The desire to control others and the external world

This driver makes use of technologies enabling monitoring, profiling and tracing. These technologies are based on an intensive collection of several types of data (location data, personal data, etc.). Generally, users are not aware of the collection processes. Consequently, two subsequent issues rise: difficulty in protecting personal data and loss of control.

### 3.5.6.3 The belief in technological progress

This driver is associated with the willingness of individual citizens and consumers to use and adapt their behaviour to the technological possibilities of AmI. Acceptance of and demand for AmI products and services will drive the development and provision of applications. Consumer understanding of the benefits of AmI applications and the effectiveness of human–machine interfaces are relevant issues.

### 3.5.6.4 Costs

The drive towards cost saving could give a boost to the implementation of AmI but maintenance and updating could be more costly than expected. Therefore, costs may be the source of the digital divide between countries and categories of users.

### 3.5.6.5   The desire to live a private life

The right to privacy is an important driver as well as a key issue, particularly as it concerns the protection of personal data from exploitation (i.e., identity theft). Privacy is likely to play a key part in user acceptability of AmI applications and services. It will drive people to select (or not) products or services that offer privacy protection; it also forces manufacturers and service providers to build into their products and services privacy-enhancing technologies.[188]

## 3.5.7   Issues

### 3.5.7.1   Individual (personalised) profiling vs group profiling

The following remarks are based on a report from FIDIS, an FP6 Network of Excellence on the Future of Identity.[189] Individual and group profiling capacities have grown exponentially as a result of both the huge advances in technology and the increasing availability of readily processable data and traces. Today, an individual – consciously and unconsciously, voluntarily and involuntarily – leaves a vast number of electronic traces in his wake, which can be processed and correlated. The use of the Internet, mobile telephones, electronic financial systems, biometric systems, radio frequency identification tags, smart cards, ubiquitous computing, ambient intelligence and so forth, all participate in the spontaneous and automatic generation of data that can be correlated.

Profiling is a core application that operates by distilling usable information from a large amount of unstructured, raw information. Group profiling technologies build on sameness in the sense of similarity (categorisation); personalised profiling builds on sameness in the sense of unique identification or continuity with oneself. Group profiles are often used to identify persons or to attribute a certain lifestyle, health risks, learning capacity or customer preferences to a person. Even when a group profile does not necessarily apply to the individual members of the group, it may still be used based on the probability that part of the profile does apply. As a result, service providers, insurance companies, forensic agencies, fraud detection departments or agencies and even e-learning organisations use profiling technologies to identify and categorise their target populations. Individual profiles contain personalised knowledge about specific individuals, inferred from offline and online behaviour, registration of birth and/or biometric data.

---

[188] European Commission, Communication from the Commission to the European Parliament and the Council on Promoting Data Protection by Privacy Enhancing Technologies (PETs), COM (2007) 228 final, 2 May 2007.

[189] http://www.fidis.net.

The proliferation of automatically generated profiles could have a profound impact on a variety of decisions that influence the life of European citizens. At the same time, it seems unclear whether and how a person could trace back (identify or determine) the sources if and when decisions concerning her life are taken on the basis of such profiles.

### 3.5.7.2 Victimisation/democratic right not to be treated as a criminal

AmI technologies could jeopardise the presumption of innocence to the extent that decision-making is delegated to a computer or if a desire for anonymity is considered suspicious. In the interviews in scenes 1 and 4, we have two examples which illustrate this point: Anonymity profiling and arrest of the clones (one category of user).

### 3.5.7.3 Digital divide

The digital divide basically refers to the gap between those communities or groups that have access to the Internet, ICTs or any emerging new technologies and those that do not and to the disparities regarding the ability to use them or to learn how to use them. The digital divide is a societal, economic and political issue, all rolled into one. It raises several types of problems and difficulties involving costs, culture, organisation, education, acceptance, adaptation, geography and demographics.

AmI has the potential to bridge certain aspects of the current digital divide but at the same time, it can be assumed that in the future, other and new divides based on AmI technologies will emerge. Problems can be global (between different countries) or local (between different regions in the same country), as raised in scene 2. Not every nation or region benefits in the same way or to the same extent from technologies.

AmI may have the potential to exclude and/or include sections of society. Some concerns are raised about the potential of AmI to widen the digital gap between those with access to AmI and therefore to better services and improvements in standards of living in "smart homes" and those without such access ("digital hermits").[190]

AmI and related technologies could be used as a policy tool and specifically as a tool for innovative social welfare, to improve access to and provision of services for previously excluded or less included groups (e.g., the disabled, ill and elderly).

### 3.5.7.4 Dependency

Dependency grows when a technology is widely used. Users become dependent when they do not remain indifferent to the consequences of technology use. This

---

[190] FTC, "Future Threats and Crimes in an Ambient Intelligent Everyday Environment," supplied by Qinetiq and Transcrime for IPTS/JRC under contract 2215-2004-06-F7SC SEV GB, July 2005.

can be joyful when the technology works or frustrating when it does not. The consequences of dependency might affect users in an individual way as well as in an aggregated way. Interview one shows the frustration of a user when his avatar does not fulfil his expectations and in interview three, we see dependency on the system and the subsequent impact when something goes wrong (e.g., a traffic jam when a virus affects the system).

### 3.5.7.5 Loss of control

The feeling of a loss of control has two main sources: a misunderstanding of the context and a lack of training.

Misunderstandings can arise where there is lack of trust. Misunderstanding of context (prompted by either technical or human factors) can generate dark situations. Table 3.1 shows the different cases. Interview four illustrates the case of misunderstanding due to human factors when finally no problem has occurred.

Users often need training to master new devices and services, and this will also be true of AmI technologies because collectively they will create a technological revolution as a function of their ubiquity. Users lacking training lack awareness of the possibilities of the new technologies (services, preferences setting, etc.) and the associated risks. Without a minimum of training, users will likely encounter some problems in getting services that fulfil their expectations and/or they will be confronted with unwanted AmI behaviour. Consequently, frustration and a feeling of loss of control may arise. Interview one depicts situations of being deprived of access to certain services and being unable to get what one wants as leisure.

Another aspect of loss of control arises when trust is not established between the user and the technology. Trust reassures the user in his willingness to use the technology and in his acceptance of technological behaviour. Trust may be the result of a good knowledge of how the technology works acquired by training or directly as a result of a positive experience.

Loss of control appears when the interaction between the user and a technology is not optimised, transparent or easy (i.e., it is complex). Indeed, this interaction is

**Table 3.1** Different cases of misunderstanding

| Factors leading to misunderstanding | Context | |
|---|---|---|
| | Problem | No problem |
| Technical | AmI sensors are not able to detect the problem | AmI sensors detect a problem |
| Human | AmI sensors are able to detect the problem but the user misunderstands the alert messages | AmI sensors are able to confirm no problem exists but the users do not trust the AmI recommendations |

a crucial point for new emerging technologies. Optimal user interaction with technology entails three related challenges:

- User knowledge, i.e., the user should know how to manipulate the technology and take advantage of the available services.
- "Near zero" configuration, i.e., only minimal interaction should be necessary to perform a task.
- Trust, i.e., there should be minimal annoyance, minimal limitation on the data needed to use or share a service, adequate protection of user rights, privacy, reputation, etc.

#### 3.5.7.6 Function creep

"Function creep" is an important concern, i.e., that technology and processes introduced for one purpose will be extended to other purposes that were not discussed or agreed at the time of their implementation.

### 3.5.8 Legal synopsis

#### 3.5.8.1 Personal profiling

Service providers collect huge amounts of information and share it with other companies to offer more personalised services. This scenario raises concerns about personal profiling and the lack of public knowledge about this issue. Even an association has been created to fight against it.

Here again, the data protection rules apply, according to the **Data Protection Directive**. Personal data must be collected and processed for a specific purpose (Article 6 (c) of the Directive). When a profile is built upon personal data, the data protection law applies whether the profile is an individual profile (related to an identifiable person) or a group profile (related to a group of anonymous persons). Making the personal data anonymous is a processing that also falls under data protection laws. When an individual profile or a group profile (composed of anonymous data) is applied to an identifiable person, the application of a profile might also be subject to data protection law, obliging the controller to process the personal data on a legitimate basis.

If the personal data are collected and processed, the data subject has a right to be fully informed about the purpose, all phases and contexts of such processing.[191] If a purpose of processing includes the transmission of data to third parties, Article 11 of the Data Protection Directive obliges the third parties – the new controllers – to provide the data subject with the same information about the data processing.[192]

---

[191] The right to information was already discussed in sections 3.2.8.4, 3.2.8.7 and 3.4.8.4.

[192] For a discussion on Article 11, see section 3.4.8.4.

Such information rights are important since they indicate that profiles may be created. A health insurance company might seek to collect all possible data on a data subject's health from different sources. In this case, the user should be informed about this activity, the purpose for which the data are being collected and what is going to happen to the data.

AmI service providers will also be collecting sensitive data, defined by Article 8 of the Data Protection Directive as "personal data revealing racial or ethnic origin, political opinions, religious or philosophical beliefs, trade-union membership, and the processing of data concerning health or sex life". However, the processing of such sensitive data is in principle prohibited; nevertheless, the Data Protection Directive does allow the processing of sensitive personal data in some exceptional situations, as previously mentioned in section 3.3.8.4.[193]

On the basis of the data gathered, the insurance company may automatically decide to raise its premiums. But even if the personal data have been lawfully acquired, Article 15 of the Directive grants every person the right "not to be subject to a decision which produces legal effects concerning him or significantly affects him and which is based solely on automated processing of data intended to evaluate certain personal aspects relating to him, such as his performance at work, creditworthiness, reliability, conduct, etc." There is an exception, "if that decision is taken in the course of the entering into or performance of a contract, provided the request for the entering into or the performance of the contract, lodged by the data subject, has been satisfied or that there are suitable measures to safeguard his legitimate interests, such as arrangements allowing him to put his point of view".

On the basis of the information collected, the MEP in scene 1 receives personalised messages. Although some might be useful, the data subject should have the possibility to refuse some or all of these personalised messages. Such a right can be found in Article 14 of the Data Protection Directive.[194]

Personalised messages will often be commercial messages. There are issues regarding commercial communication, opt-in and opt-out rules, and the obligation imposed by law that requires commercial communication to be clearly identified as such. It might be very important to ensure the user understands the message and distinguishes between genuinely useful and manipulative information (as discussed in section 3.2.8.9).

The persons who collect, process and/or receive the personal data should guarantee that the data protection rules will be respected. Current solutions do not provide a proper balance between the risk arising from profiling, consent for data collection and workability of the system; it is probably not feasible to expect that consent can be obtained each time such data are to be collected. The obligation of the provider to act in accordance with the principle of proportionality may be

---

[193] On sensitive data, see also section 3.4.8.2

[194] "The data subject has a right to object, on request and free of charge, to the processing of personal data relating to him which the controller anticipates being processed for the purposes of direct marketing, or to be informed before personal data are disclosed for the first time to third parties or used on their behalf for the purposes of direct marketing, and to be expressly offered the right to object free of charge to such disclosures or uses."

relevant in resolving the issue. Similarly, the right of the data subject to refuse personal messages is, in fact, limited by putting on him the burden of un-subscription and the risk of losing the information or service in which he may be interested.

### 3.5.8.2   Service refusal and incomplete personal profiles

Concerns are raised in scene 4 about possible service refusal as a result of an inadequate profile check and the consequent harm suffered by the person confronted by such a situation.

When personal data are collected and processed, Article 6 (a), (c) and (d) of the Data Protection Directive provides that the personal data must be processed fairly and lawfully and that they must be adequate, relevant, accurate and, where necessary, kept up to date. Every reasonable step must be taken to ensure that inaccurate or incomplete data are erased or rectified. Article 12 of the Directive also provides for the right to access and rectify data. It says that every data subject has a right to obtain from the controller "without constraint at reasonable intervals and without excessive delay or expense: confirmation as to whether or not data relating to him are being processed and information at least as to the purposes of the processing, the categories of data concerned, and the recipients or categories of recipients to whom the data are disclosed; communication to him in an intelligible form of the data undergoing processing and of any available information as to their source; knowledge of the logic involved in any automatic processing of data concerning him at least in the case of the automated decisions". On the basis of Article 12 (b), the data subject has to obtain from the controller "as appropriate the rectification, erasure or blocking of data the processing of which does not comply with the provisions of this Directive, in particular because of the incomplete or inaccurate nature of the data". This makes it possible to correct an incorrect profile. Also, the data subject can ask on the basis of Article 12 (c) of the Data Protection Directive that any rectification, erasure or blocking carried out be notified to third parties to whom the data have been disclosed. Such guarantees do not, however, entirely protect the data subject against use of the incorrect profile, especially since enforcing such a right can be difficult for the average user, or he may not know that an incorrect profile is being processed before the damage occurs. However, Member States are obliged to determine the processing operations likely to present specific risks to the rights and freedoms of data subjects and check that these processing operations are examined prior to their start. The supervisory authority is also obliged to carry out prior checks following receipt of a notification from the controller or by the data protection official, who, in cases of doubt, must consult the supervisory authority.[195] Nevertheless, an ex-post guarantee of the data subject's rights is also necessary. In scene 1, the MEP recounts the story about a friend who was refused a room because the hotel had inaccurate data about her and did not respect several of the conditions described above. Unfortunately, it will be difficult

---

[195] Articles 18, 20 and 28 of the Data Protection Directive.

to hold the hotel liable for the incorrect profiling, not only because the profiling error arose from different data providers, but also because the causal link between the error and the damage will be difficult to establish. The difficulties are compounded by the fact that evidential issues (procedures) as well as tort rules and prerequisites (as causation) are regulated by national laws. It will also be difficult to meet the traditional tort law preconditions in such situations. The crucial question is: who should be held responsible or liable for the damage caused by the use of incorrect data? The error could have been caused by input of incorrect information. Or the hotel might have created a bad profile through misuse of correct information. According to Article 23 of the Data Protection Directive, however, any person who has suffered damage as a result of an unlawful processing operation or violation of national data protection law is entitled to receive compensation from the controller for the damage suffered. This is a strict liability, but the national law may exempt the controller from this strict liability if he proves that he is not responsible for the event giving rise to the damage. This means that a reversal of the onus of proof may be foreseen: the data controller may be allowed to prove that he is not responsible for the damage

The creation of wrong profiles on the basis of a request for the service and an automated decision based on the profiles must be examined against the antidiscrimination rules.[196] Profiles or decisions based on inadequate criteria (health data, nationality, income, etc.) may lead to discrimination. However, it is difficult to determine when it is objectively justified to use such data and criteria and when they are discriminatory. Further clarifications will be necessary as we enter the AmI world.

### 3.5.8.3   Digital virus damages public transport system

In scene 3, someone creates a virus that causes chaos and damages to the transport system. The person who did so committed several offences as defined in the Cybercrime Convention.[197] The majority of the criminal offences defined in the Cybercrime Convention require proof that the perpetrator had the intent to commit the specific crime. When a virus is created, however, it could be argued that a specific aim or intention does not exist. That is why in some situations the specific intention should not be a precondition of (criminal) liability. Even when there was no malicious intention, the creator could still be liable for the civil damage caused.

The creator of the virus might be untraceable. Thus, the focus shifts to the question of whether the providers of the different traffic services were protecting their system sufficiently against these attacks. Problems will arise when trying to prove which service provider was responsible for which part of the damage. The principles set out in the Directive on liability for defective products[198] could solve part of this problem if it were applicable to services and software.

---

[196] On non-discrimination, see section 3.3.8.4.

[197] On the Cybercrime Convention, see sections 3.2.8.7, 3.2.8.10 and 3.3.8.1.

[198] For our discussion of the Directive on liability for defective products, see sections 3.2.8.3, 3.3.8.1 and 3.3.8.3.

#### 3.5.8.4    Pseudonymous authentication

Temporary wireless pseudonymous authentication is possible thanks to new technology such as sensors and implants. In scene 4, implants were used for the crowd management application.

Only the issue of medical implants has been addressed in the European Union. The **Directive on the approximation of the laws of the Member States relating to active medical devices**[199] was intended to harmonise the level of safety by mandatory specifications relating both to the technical safety features and the inspection procedures for a number of medical devices, including active implantable medical devices. The Directive sets out strict rules. In an AmI world, however, implants might be used for non-medical purposes.

In scene 4, the concert organiser needs to ensure the safety and security of the people attending the concert. To this end, people carry chips that transmit an identity assigned to each person until the end of the concert. The chips enable concert-goers to remain anonymous and allow the concert organisers to check the behaviour of people at the concert. Thus, there is a balance between privacy and security, in keeping with Article 8 of the ECHR which protects the personal life of individuals. This protection implies the right to be anonymous. However, swallowing chips or using implants will not necessarily be regarded as a proportionate means to ensure safety. Less intrusive means (temporary chips in tickets or PDAs) could be envisaged, even if they might be less effective than intelligent implants[200] (as was the case in the scenario).

Even when technology seems to offer intelligent solutions to safety vs. privacy problems, the traditional logic of human rights law has to be applied, i.e., the principle of proportionality and necessity. The Luxembourg Court of Justice of the European Union has held in the Adidas case[201] that "It is apparent from both the abovementioned case-law and Directive 95/46 that protection for the sphere of private activity of natural and legal persons occupies an important place among the legal principles introduced by the Community legal order. However, that protection neither can nor should be absolute. The Court of Justice has held that restrictions may be imposed on fundamental rights provided that they in fact correspond to objectives of general public interest and do not constitute, with regard to the objectives pursued, a disproportionate and intolerable interference which infringes upon the very substance of the right protected."

The same spirit has inspired the authors of the Data Protection Directive. They did not consider the right to protection of privacy as absolute, which would mean a general prohibition on selecting and processing personal data. Rather than laying down an absolute prohibition, the Directive indicates the need to ensure a balance

---

[199] Council Directive 90/385/EEC on the approximation of the laws of the Member States relating to active medical devices, *Official Journal* L 323, 26 November 1997, p. 39.

[200] The scenario mentions the possibility of a lawsuit for damages caused by the improper functioning of the crowd management application. For our discussion on liability and possible damages, see sections 3.2.8.3, 3.3.8.1 and 3.3.8.3.

[201] Case C-223/88 Adidas AG [1999] ECR I-07081.

between the interests involved and having particular regard to the principle of pro-portionality. The processing of personal data must therefore be carried out with the consent of the person concerned "or be necessary for the conclusion or performance of a contract binding on the data subject, or as a legal requirement, or for the per-formance of a task carried out in the public interest or in the exercise of official authority, or in the legitimate interests of a natural or legal person." The processing must also relate to data that are "adequate, relevant and not excessive in relation to the purposes for which they are processed."

Not all concerts create safety problems. The concert organiser will need to ask the people attending a concert for their consent to use intrusive technologies. New technological developments such as those described in the scenario offer possible solutions to the problems of striking a balance between traditional privacy and security. Their use has to be carefully assessed within the framework of human rights law. In countries such as France, the data protection authorities play an active role in seeking this balance and have implemented a licence system obliging those who are responsible for the processing to declare their processing and to obtain permission in advance.

### 3.5.9 Conclusions

The risk society is the key theme of this scenario. The four scenes depict dark situ-ations, which stem from an inappropriate use, application or management of AmI technologies and which may generate a wide range of impacts on citizens, groups or even society. The four scenes raise private and public concerns, which have local and global scope. The scenes posit several problems related to the proliferation and protection of personal data, user acceptance, dependence, costs and enhancement or loss of trust. The scenario deals with issues including victimisation, digital divide, categorisation of users, dependency, loss of control and function creep.

All of these issues could lead to a major risk, that of an identity crisis. The risks at this level can be seen as a triptych:

- At an individual level, where you are unable to get what you want.
- At a social level, where you may be excluded because of the relatively high cost of new technologies.
- At a societal level, where one may be victimised through loss of social and legal recognition. This means:
  - One may become suspect by default, because acting anonymously may be considered as suspicious.
  - One may become an unrecognised person by law and may suffer impersonali-sation and/or misrepresentation. Indeed, in cases of fraudulent usage of personal data, it would be difficult to recover a normal situation or reputation in view of the AmI environment's voracious appetite for personal data, a difficulty compounded where the individual lacks adequate legal resources.

# Chapter 4
# Threats and vulnerabilities

In this chapter, we present a review of threats and vulnerabilities that could afflict society and individuals in the AmI world in the context of the key policy issues of privacy, identity, trust, security and digital divide.

We define a **threat** as the potential for one or more unwanted consequences caused by a circumstance, capability, action or event that could be harmful to a system or person. Threats can be caused naturally, accidentally or intentionally. In essence, a threat is a ubiquitous phenomenon. A **vulnerability** is a flaw or weakness in a system's design, its implementation, operation or management that could be exploited to violate the system and, consequently, cause a threat. Vulnerabilities may have different dimensions: technical, functional or behavioural.[1]

As will be apparent in the pages that follow, we foresee that many of the threats and vulnerabilities that afflict us now will also afflict the AmI world. Or, to put it differently, based on our research so far, we have discovered few threats and vulnerabilities that could be described as unique or new. To be clear about this, we mean *classes* or *types* of threats and vulnerabilities. In saying so, we do not in any way mean to assuage the AmI enthusiasts. It's been said that, if left unchecked, AmI could obliterate privacy,[2] but this is not a *new* threat. Our privacy has been eroding for a long time. By the time, a full-blown, all-singing, all-dancing AmI world is truly upon us, there may not be much left to obliterate. Similarly, it has been argued that AmI threatens the individual with a loss of control – if an intelligent environment surrounds us, we may cede much of our control over it to the intelligence embedded everywhere. But this loss-of-control phenomenon is not new either. We have already ceded a lot of control over our lives to the government and the corporate warlords who pillage consumer society today. What is different about AmI is the scale of the data that will be available, and the scale of technology control that is envisioned. When everything is embedded with intelligence, when AmI is pervasive, invisible,

---

[1] Xenakis, C., and S. Kontopoulou, "Risk Assessment, Security & Trust: Cross Layer Issues", Special Interest Group 2, 2006, p. 14.

[2] Brey, Philip, "Freedom and privacy in Ambient Intelligence", *Ethics and Information Technology*, Vol. 7, No. 3, 2005, p. 165.

D. Wright et al. (eds.), *Safeguards in a World of Ambient Intelligence.*
© Springer 2010

ubiquitous, when everything is connected[3] and linked, the threats and vulnerabilities that we know today will become even greater risks than they are now.

## 4.1 Privacy under attack

The notion of privacy is unstable, complex, difficult to fix. People's perception of privacy is context-dependent, in time and space. Our expectations of privacy may be different according to our age, gender, culture, location, family history, income, educational level and many other factors.[4] And governments' perception of what our privacy should be may be different from ours. It is no surprise that scholars understand privacy in different ways; some argue that autonomy and liberty are the values behind privacy, while others contend it is intimacy, confidentiality or the control over personal information.[5]

The threats to our privacy, however we define it, come from many different sources – from prurient neighbours, industry, government, Internet service providers, private detectives, hackers and even our friends or family, who might accidentally or on purpose reveal things that we had wished they did not.

In a world of ambient intelligence, the threats to our privacy multiply. In an AmI world, we can expect to be under surveillance ("transparent") wherever we go because the permanent and real-time registration and processing of our presence and behaviour is the precondition – the "code" – of ambient intelligence. The further development of an adaptive and intelligent environment of pervasive and ubiquitous computing is, in fact, dependent on intensive automatic processing of behavioural and thus personal data and, hence, of intensive registration and monitoring. Already, video cameras are mounted almost everywhere in London. It has been said that people in that city are recorded on camera more than 300 times a day.[6] With machine learning and intelligent software, our behaviour and preferences can be predicted. Like our credit cards, RFIDs can be used to monitor what we buy. Networking sensors can monitor what we are doing.[7] Mobile phone companies can monitor where we are. Amazon, Google, the credit card companies, the phone companies and

---

[3] See O'Harrow, Robert, *No Place to Hide*, Simon & Schuster, New York, 2005, p. 107: "We have created a unique identifier on everybody in the United States", said [Ole] Poulsen, the company's [Seisint Inc.] chief technology officer. "Data that belongs together is *already* linked together." [Italics added.]

[4] See Gutwirth, Serge, *Privacy and the Information Age*, Rowman & Littlefield, Lanham/Boulder/New York/Oxford, 2002, pp. 5–31 ("Privacy's complexities").

[5] See the discussions in Claes, Erik, Anthony Duff and S. Gutwirth (eds.), *Privacy and the criminal law*, Intersentia, Antwerp/Oxford, 2006.

[6] See Jordan, Mary, "Electronic Eye Grows Wider in Britain", *The Washington Post*, 7 January 2006: "People in Britain are already monitored by more than 4 million closed-circuit, or CCTV, cameras, making it the most-watched nation in the world, according to Liberty. The group said that a typical London resident is monitored 300 times a day."

[7] "Cybernetic systems that contextualise, learn and act autonomously present fascinating challenges," says the ARTEMIS Strategic Research Agenda, First Edition, March 2006, p. 8. http://www.artemis-office.org/DotNetNuke/PressCorner/tabid/89/Default.aspx

others know lots about us. And who can slow down the voracious appetite of government to know more about us than all of them put together?

ISTAG posed a challenge for researchers, which can be paraphrased as follows: How can we ensure that personal data can be shared to the extent the individual wishes and no more? It is not an easy question to answer. Some safeguards can be adopted, but the snag is that profiling and personalisation, as noted above, is inherent in AmI and operators and service providers invariably and inevitably will want to "personalise" their offerings as much as possible and as they do, the risks to personal information will grow. While there may be, to some extent, safeguards to help contain the risk (but the risk will never be eliminated), there are many unresolved issues. For example, in AmI networks, there are likely to be many operators and service providers, some of whom may be visible, some of whom will not be. Will consumers need to or even be able to negotiate their level of protection with each one? Will some services be on a "take-it-or-leave-it" basis? If you want a particular service, will you have no choice except to forego some of your privacy? Are the privacy policies of operators and service providers satisfactory from the consumer's point of view? Can they be trusted? Are the data protection safeguards put in place by the operator or service provider adequate? If new AmI networks have a profile-learning capability, will the "negotiated" privacy protection rules be relevant after a year or two of service? Will the network players be able to offer different levels of protection to different customers? Are new safeguards going to be effective or will they simply be closing the barn door after the horse has already bolted – i.e., is there already so much personal information about us "out there" that data miners can already find most of what they want?

## 4.2 Identity: Who goes there?

Identity, which potentially includes attributes as well as personal information, is distinctive to a given individual. For example, when a driver's licence is initially issued, an effort is made to bind the driver's licence number to an identity that is distinct enough to be linked, in theory, to the individual who requested the licence. Part of the identity comprises attributes such as eye and hair colour, height, weight, a photographic image of the individual, and so on.[8]

An **identifier** points to an individual. An identifier could be a name, a serial number or some other pointer to the entity being identified. Examples of personal identifiers include personal names, social security numbers, credit card numbers and employee identification numbers.

Identities have **attributes**. Examples of attributes include height, eye colour, employer and organisational role.

**Identification** is the process of using claimed or observed attributes of an individual to infer who the individual is. Identification can be regarded as a

---

[8] Kent, Stephen T., and Lynette I. Millett (eds.), *Who Goes There?: Authentication Through the Lens of Privacy*, Committee on Authentication Technologies and Their Privacy Implications, National Research Council, National Academies Press, Washington, DC, 2003, p. 131.

"one-to-many" check against multiple sets of data. **Verification (or authentication)** is the comparison of sets of data to establish the validity of a claimed identity. It is based on a "one-to-one" check. Neither identification, nor verification (authentication) *proves* that a particular person is who he or she claims to be; AmI technologies can only produce a certain level of confidence in the validity of that claim.

**Authorisation** is the process of deciding what an individual ought to be allowed to do.

Identity is associated with an individual as a convenient way to characterise that individual to others. The set of information and the identifier (name, label or sign) by which a person is known are also sometimes referred to as that person's "identity". The choice of information may be arbitrary, linked to the purpose of the identity verification (authentication) in any given context, or linked intrinsically to the person, as in the case of biometrics. For example, the information corresponding to an identity may contain facts (such as eye colour, age, address), capabilities (e.g., licensed to drive a car), medical history, financial activity and so forth. Generally, not all such information will be contained in the same identity, allowing a multiplicity of identities, each of which will contain information relevant to the purpose at hand.[9]

Computers have enabled us to digitise all sorts of information including that relating to our identity. Hence, a **digital identity** (or electronic identity, **eID**) is the electronic representation of an individual (or organisation). Digital identity mechanisms are not restricted to smart cards. An eID can potentially operate across different platforms, including, for example, mobile phone SIM cards. Whatever media are used, eID schemes need to be able to authenticate users and to support electronic transactions.

As we can be identified in many different ways, so the concept of **multiple identities** has arisen. We may have multiple identities, which serve different purposes in different contexts. Individuals usually have multiple identities – for family, for an employer or school, for neighbours, for friends, for business associates or professional colleagues, and so on. Thus, different sets of information are associated with an individual in different contexts. Multiple identities might be better termed as a collection of **partial identities**.

Multiple identities (i.e., multiple sets of information corresponding to a single individual) may allow individuals to control who has access to what kinds of information about them. The use of multiple identities can be a legitimate strategy for controlling personal privacy in an information society.[10]

In some instances, we can hide behind our cyber identity, that is, to minimise the disclosure of personal information. **Pseudonyms** can be used to mask identity or reveal parts of it for gaining specific benefits such as participation in a loyalty programme, establishing reputation or proving a legally valid identity in case of

---

[9] Kent, Stephen T., and Lynette I. Millett (eds.), *IDs – Not That Easy. Questions About Nationwide Identity Systems*, Committee on Authentication Technologies and Their Privacy Implications, National Research Council, National Academy Press, Washington, DC, 2002, pp. 18–20.

[10] Kent, Stephen T., and Lynette I. Millett (eds.), *IDs – Not That Easy. Questions About Nationwide Identity Systems*.

dealings with law enforcement. In other instances, this may not be so possible. For example, some service providers, like the government, may require personally identifiable information, so that if we want the service, we must provide the personal data demanded by the service provider.

For authentication of one of his multiple identities, the individual will need to have some means to choose the appropriate identity to use. In many cases, he will want to avoid linkages. Hence, he will need to be able to access some **identity management system** that will help him to choose the appropriate identity to use in the particular circumstances.

In AmI, a person can be identified directly, implicitly (without any effort) or explicitly. For example, biometrics use our body as an identification tool. People can be identified by their veins, fingerprints, iris scans, heart beat, typing behaviour, voice, gait, face and so on. In theory, this should enhance the comfort of users who do not need to actively identify themselves, thereby reducing ballast (identity papers) and time otherwise consumed by the identification or authentication process.

A person can also be identified indirectly, for example, by his or her accessories, which will be embedded with unique identifiers.

In an AmI world, we will need to identify ourselves or to use a partial identity in order to use an AmI service, most probably many times a day. In some instances, the identification or authentication process will be as a result of a conscious, deliberate decision on our part, in which case we may use our eID. In other instances, the identification process may happen automatically, by our mere presence in the AmI world, whether we agree to being identified or not.[11] Future technologies may pinpoint our identity, without our intervention, through some combination of embedded biometrics that identify us by the way we walk and/or our facial characteristics and/or our manner of speaking and/or how we respond to certain stimuli. Our identity could become an accumulation of not just our attributes and identifiers, as it is today, but an accumulation of where we have been, the services we have used, the things we have done, an accretion of our preferences and behavioural characteristics. Needless to say, this kind of identification process could give rise to a host of security, privacy and trust issues.

The future of identity is the focus of the FIDIS project, an EC-funded network of excellence. According to FIDIS,[12] the increasingly digital representation of personal

---

[11] Human beings leave a vast amount of processable and thus correlatable electronic traces, generated spontaneously by our presence and movement through the world. New technology enables collection, processing and correlation of this vast amount of data. These evolutions represent more than mere quantitative changes: they induce a significant qualitative shift that can be described by the notions of the "correlatable human" and/or "traceable or detectable human". See Gutwirth, S., and P. de Hert, *"Privacy and Data Protection in a Democratic Constitutional State"* in M. Hildebrandt and S. Gutwirth (eds.), *Profiling: Implications for Democracy and Rule of Law*, FIDIS deliverable 7.4, Brussels, 2005, p. 26. www.fidis.net. See also Hildebrandt, M., *"Profiling and the Identity of European Citizens"* in M. Hildebrandt and S. Gutwirth (eds.), *Profiling: Implications for Democracy and Rule of Law*, FIDIS deliverable 7.4, Brussels, 2005, p. 42. www.fidis.net

[12] See its website at www.fidis.net. FIDIS is focused on seven interrelated research themes: the "identity of identity", profiling, interoperability of IDs and ID management systems, forensic implications, de-identification, high-tech ID, and mobility and identity.

characteristics changes the ways of identifying individuals. Supplementary digital identities, so-called virtual identities, embodying concepts such as pseudonymity and anonymity, are being created for security, profit, convenience and even for fun. These new identities are feeding back into the world of social and business affairs, offering a mix of plural identities and challenging traditional notions of identity.

Third-party profiling could compromise our sense of identity in an AmI world. If our ambient intelligence environment assumes that, based on past activity and preferences, we can be expected to behave in a certain way in the future, we may be presented a course of action that might not have been our first choice. Worse, we may feel obliged to accept the AmI-presented course because it seems to be what is expected of us.[13] In this way, our sense of identity begins to erode. Such a situation could also be regarded as inimical not only to our personal freedom, but also to democracy itself. This is an instance of the chilling effect, which is more usually associated with one's recognition that one is under constant surveillance.

ISTAG posed the challenge: How should we manage the relationship between identification and anonymity, so that authentication can be achieved without compromising privacy? It's another tough question, but one that has focused the minds of researchers in several AmI-related projects. Virtually all of these projects agree that identity management and authentication should be easy for users and service providers to understand and use.[14]

Establishing one's identity and avoiding identify theft are important in many sectors. It particularly preoccupies the EC and Member States in their drive to put government online. Proof of citizen identity is a requisite for many e-government services, but so far no standard authentication system is accepted and widely used by citizens.

## 4.3   Can I trust you?

In engineering visions of ambient intelligence, technology is invisible in practice, functioning silently in the background – this entails the search for perceptual transparency in interaction – the tool itself should be invisible, non-focal, while the tasks and results are ready-to-hand.[15] This may lead to a conflict between the goals of

---

[13] This AmI phenomenon has been described as cognitive dissonance. See Brey, Philip, "Freedom and privacy in Ambient Intelligence", *Ethics and Information Technology*, Vol. 7, No. 3, 2005, p. 162. "Users may even start experiencing cognitive dissonance, when they believe they want one thing but a smart object tells them they want something else."

[14] PRIME (www.prime-project.eu.org) is one such notable project. It aims to develop models demonstrating innovative solutions for managing identities in real life situations, such as travel, location-based services, e-learning and e-health, and thereby bring privacy-enhancing technologies closer to the market.

[15] Weiser, M., and J.S. Brown, "The Coming Age of Calm Technology", in P.J. Denning and R.M. Metcalfe (eds.), *Beyond Calculation: The Next Fifty Years of Computing*, Copernicus, New York, 1997, pp. 75–85; Aarts, E., R. Harwig and M. Schuurmans, "Ambient Intelligence", in P. Denning, *The Invisible Future: The Seamless Integration of Technology in Everyday Life*, McGraw-Hill, New York, 2002, pp. 235–50; Streitz, N.A., and P. Nixon, "The Disappearing Computer", *Communications of the ACM*, Vol. 48, No. 3, 2005, pp. 32–35.

opacity and transparency/invisibility. Furthermore, the envisioned technologies are complex and can respond to users and to the environment in many ways, which might lead to users' perception of the new technologies as unpredictable. If AmI technologies are perceived as unpredictable and non-transparent at the same time, achieving trust in them will be much more difficult than achieving trust in current technologies which are not transparent either, but are sufficiently predictable. For example, most car drivers don't care about the technologies embedded in their cars because cars respond to human actions in a known way.

While technological transparency is thought to provide the ideal task-oriented situation, it also effectively black boxes the overall technological environment, makes it opaque and intangible, complicating trust based on a disclosure of intentions and qualifications. Not only does the background "presence-in-absence" status of such systems raise concerns about privacy and data access ("Who controls the data I give out? Who watches me now?"), but arguably they also complicate the giving out of trust because the object, the other or some index of presence is missing. The direction of trust, then, is free-floating, abstract and distributed, rather than localised, visible and embedded in present situations.

ISTAG posed the challenge: What measures are there, and what standards should there be for dependability, trustworthiness, privacy?

None of the projects that we reviewed specifically focuses on trust from the point of the individual AmI user, on how user trust can be earned or what measures must be taken in order to gain the confidence of the user and satisfy her concerns about particular technologies. The issue of trust from the user's perspective would seem to merit greater consideration and more detailed study than heretofore has been the case.

One of the most important inhibitors to public acceptance of the Internet for human interactions (commercial or otherwise) has been the lack of trust in the underlying cyber infrastructure and in other people whom we meet through that infrastructure. Incidents of massive identity theft from otherwise internationally trusted financial institutions, the never-ending resourcefulness of malicious hackers, intruders and spammers have increased the apprehension and uneasiness of the general public vis-à-vis the Internet and the Web – and there is strong evidence[16] that this will apply to an even greater extent to ambient intelligence services in the future.

It is a challenge to change this climate not only at the level of interactions among human agents (commercial or otherwise) through the use of the cyber infrastructure, but also among human and software agents. This is a grand challenge, since

---

[16] See, for example, Roussos, George, and Theano Moussouri, "Consumer Perceptions of Privacy, Security and Trust in Ubiquitous Commerce", *Personal and Ubiquitous Computing* 8, No. 6 (2004), pp. 416–429; Grabner-Kräuter, Sonja, and Ewald A. Kaluscha, "Empirical Research in on-Line Trust: A Review and Critical Assessment", *International Journal of Human-Computer Studies*, Vol. 58, No. 6 (2003), pp. 783–812; Spiekermann, Sarah, and Matthias Rothensee, "Soziale und psychologische Bestimmungsfaktoren des Ubiquitous Computing", Institut für Wirtschaftsinformatik, Humboldt-Universität zu Berlin, 2005. http://interval.hu-berlin.de/downloads/rfid/neuste%20forschungsergebnisse/SocioPsychofak.pdf

the "mechanics of trust" may vary drastically between different cultures. Moreover, there are trade-offs between trust and privacy, trust and security, and trust between commercial competitors that are not easily brought into a balance.

## 4.4 An insecure world

The traditional taxonomy of security threats distinguishes between three main domains in which threats may appear: confidentiality, integrity and availability.[17] Confidentiality implies protection of information from unauthorised use, integrity implies protection of information from unauthorised modification, and availability implies that the system is capable of providing a service when users expect it. The protection properties all rely on the distinction between authorised and unauthorised entities. Protecting confidentiality, integrity and availability is more difficult in a ubiquitous computing environment than in traditional networks for the following reasons:

- *Possible conflict of interests between communicating entities.* In the past, it has been relatively clear who needs to be protected against whom: for example, system owners and operators need to be protected against external attackers and misbehaving internal users, while protecting users against operators and service providers was not considered to be a major issue. Nowadays, it is clear that users may need to be protected against operators and service providers, and that different parties can have conflicting interests. An example is the typical conflict between the wish for privacy and the interest in service or co-operation. Thus, the concept of multilateral security has emerged. Multilateral security considers the security requirements of different parties and strives to balance these requirements.[18] It also regards all parties as possible attackers and takes into account possible conflicts of interest, negotiating them and enforcing the results of the negotiations.
- *Network convergence.* Wireless communication is envisioned to be seamless between different networks of devices, physical objects and smart dust, and between different communication technologies used. This implies that sensitive operations, such as banking, are frequently performed wirelessly and that during the banking session, the user device can switch several times between different wireless networks about which little is known beforehand.[19]

---

[17] Stajano, F., and R. Anderson, "The Resurrecting Duckling: Security Issues for Ubiquitous Computing", first Security & Privacy supplement to *IEEE Computer*, April 2002, pp. 22–26.

[18] Rannenberg, K., "Multilateral Security: A Concept and Examples for Balanced Security", ACM New Security Paradigms Workshop, September 2000, pp. 151–162.

[19] Stajano, F., and J. Crowcroft, "The Butt of the Iceberg: Hidden Security Problems of Ubiquitous Systems", in Basten et al. (eds.), *Ambient Intelligence: Impact on Embedded System Design*, Kluwer, Dordrecht, The Netherlands, 2003.

- *Large number of ad hoc communications.* In ad hoc communications (between nodes which encounter each other more or less unexpectedly), it is difficult to distinguish between normal and malicious devices, because little is known beforehand about the nodes in the environment. This implies that it is fairly easy to realise a denial-of-service (DoS) attack (to make the service unavailable) by adding ad hoc communicating devices that constantly send messages and ask for replies, thus disturbing normal operations.[20]
- *Small size and autonomous mode of operation of devices.* This makes it fairly easy to steal personal devices and smart dust nodes and to physically attack them (e.g., to destroy or modify the memory).[21]
- *Resource constraints of mobile devices.* Examples are limited battery life (making it easier to arrange DoS attacks by exhausting the battery due to unnecessary communications),[22] processing capabilities (which make it difficult to run sophisticated encryption or pattern recognition algorithms), limited communication range and limited broadband capabilities.

AmI will require security solutions very different from those of today's systems. ISTAG postulated what it called "a new security paradigm" characterised by "conformable" security in which the degree and nature of security associated with any particular type of action will change over time and circumstance.

ISTAG framed the challenge this way: How can we manage the security associated with the multiple personalities and roles we will adopt in a multiplicity of relationships? ISTAG adds that any security rules must be simple, user-understandable, user-friendly, intuitively usable, socially acceptable, based on co-operation.

Security threats and vulnerabilities fall into two major groups: malicious and unanticipated system behaviour.

Malicious threats and vulnerabilities stem from external attackers and insiders (authorised, but deceitful), who exploit internal system weaknesses. Malicious behaviour can be exhibited not only by criminals, but also by insurance or trading companies (e.g., in order to increase their profit, they might want to acquire information on drivers' driving behaviour or to modify user-defined filters in order to promote their own advertisements), by governmental organisations which fight against criminals by widespread surveillance, by employees and curious family members who want to benefit from or to satisfy their curiosity by spying.

---

[20] Creese, S., M. Goldsmith and I. Zakiuddin, "Authentication in Pervasive Computing", First International Conference on Security in Pervasive Computing, Boppard, Germany, 12–14 March 2003, pp. 116–129.

[21] Becher, A., Z. Benenson and M. Dornseif, "Tampering with Motes: Real-World Physical Attacks on Wireless Sensor Networks", Third International Conference on Security in Pervasive Computing, York, UK, April 2006, pp. 104–118.

[22] Stajano, F., and R. Anderson.

Malicious activity can be realised via viruses,[23] worms,[24] Trojans,[25] phishing,[26] denial of service attacks[27] or physical tampering.[28]

Among the causes of unanticipated system behaviour or failure are:

* Inadequate design and internal complexity, which are manifested in system use in circumstances not foreseen by the system designer; programming errors; insufficient reliability or resources of critical components; poor scalability or performance of chosen communication protocols; inadequate range of wireless transmissions.
* An increase in the number of personal computers and a lack of enthusiasm of their owners to invest in secure system use (which is understandable: security is not the primary goal of most computer systems).
* Lack of user-friendly security methods.
* Incompatibility of system hardware components or software versions after a system upgrade (the diversity of possible software configurations and limited testing time make thorough testing of all configurations literally impossible).
* Networking of personal devices and objects, including ad hoc networking.
* Economic reasons, such as uncertainty regarding costs of security holes.

These threats and vulnerabilities can have serious consequences, including:

* Disruption of the primary operation of the technical system or even its destruction
* Violation of the physical integrity of the victim's home and property
* Endangering one's health and life
* Assaults against personal dignity and general well-being.

## 4.5   The looming digital divide

Apart from the ISTAG scenarios, the digital divide issue has scarcely figured in any AmI-related projects, although the EC has initiated a significant eInclusion programme.

---

[23] A virus is hidden, self-replicating software that propagates by infecting – i.e., inserting a copy of itself into and becoming part of – another program. A virus cannot run by itself; it requires a host program to be activated.

[24] A worm is software that can run independently, can propagate a complete working version of itself onto other hosts in a network, and may consume computer resources destructively.

[25] A Trojan is software that appears to perform a useful or desirable function, but actually gains unauthorised access to system resources or tricks a user into executing other malicious logic.

[26] Phishing means tricking the user into providing identity or banking data by asking the user to confirm his personal data on a fake web site which pretends to be a legitimate site, and often looks exactly like a web page of, for example, a user's bank.

[27] Denial of service (DoS) is the prevention of authorised access to a system resource or the delaying of system operations and functions, e.g., the attacker sends a huge number of extra messages to a target service provider and in doing so denies access by others.

[28] Physical tampering means copying or changing data by physical manipulation of a device, e.g., replacing sensors in a sensor node so that they send wrong values.

The term "digital divide" was coined by Lloyd Morrisett, the former president of the Markle Foundation, in 1995 to denote the gap, the divide "between those with access to new technologies and those without"[29] or between the information "haves" and "have-nots".

At first glance, the digital divide concept encompasses two basic dimensions: the **global**, between developing and developed societies, and the **social**, which relates to the information haves and have-nots even within the same nation. Norris adds another dimension, that of the **democratic** divide, which signifies the difference between those who do, and do not, use digital resources to engage, mobilise and participate in public life.[30]

The advent of new technologies has enabled companies to collect a vast amount of personalised data from current and prospective customers, by purchasing information and/or conducting surveys. By using special data-mining techniques, companies are able to make investment and marketing decisions by targeting certain groups. This means that all organisations are increasingly able to exclude large numbers of people from access to basic services and opportunities by selecting more or less "valuable" customers and ignoring the rest. Profiling facilitates control of consumer behaviour as well as the construction of consumer identities; the latter inhibits social mobility and contributes to people's exclusion.[31]

Red-lining[32] has triggered a somewhat reverse concern from the one that has been contemplated until now. Information technology can be itself an engine of exclusion and people are not only excluded *from* information but *by* information as well.[33]

In the context of our information society or digital world, access to ICTs has become indispensable. Those who do not have access to the new technologies are highly disadvantaged or even excluded. In a world of ambient intelligence where technology is undoubtedly much more pervasive than today, access to and use of it become even more important: it will be part of our everyday life. In this

---

[29] National Telecommunications and Information Administration (NTIA), *Falling through the net: Towards Digital Inclusion. A Report on Americans' Access to Technology Tools*, US Department of Commerce, Economics and Statistics Administration, National Telecommunications and Information Administration, Washington, DC, 2000. http://search.ntia.doc.gov/pdf/fttn00.pdf

[30] Norris, Pippa, *Digital divide: Civic engagement, information poverty, and the Internet worldwide*, Cambridge University Press, Cambridge/New York, 2001.

[31] Kruger, Danny, *Access Denied? Preventing Information Exclusion*, Demos, London, 1998.

[32] The term "red-lining" refers to a system developed in the 19th century by drawing colour-coded maps of London showing the estimated affluence of the inhabitants in different boroughs and is used to describe the deliberate avoidance of certain large areas by the sellers of insurance (Kruger, 1998). The concept of the 21st century "digital red-lining" is not very far from the 19th century one.

[33] Perri 6 and Ben Jupp, *Divided by information? The "digital divide" and the implications of the new meritocracy*, Demos, London, 2001.

context, the digital divide is a crucial issue for societies and it is important to consider its trend: will AmI technologies contribute to the closing or further widening of the gaps?

In general, it seems that AmI will narrow some gaps, widen others and create new ones. Physical access to AmI equipment and infrastructure is likely to improve, since AmI applications will form an intrinsic part of our everyday lives and at least the basic infrastructure is bound to be available to the majority of people. Chances are high that the AmI infrastructure will become more affordable for larger segments of society (although it could also be argued that the network will be more complex, thus the cost higher for the providers). Furthermore, because of the envisioned user friendliness of AmI technology, the required skills and knowledge for its use will be less than those required today to use mobile phones, personal computers and the Internet, thus enabling more people to use its applications and receive the expected benefits. The majority of people are expected to be at least moderately computer literate, especially given the extent of use of technologies in everyday life.

On the other hand, there will still be a percentage of the population that will not have access to AmI applications and an even greater percentage that will have access only to basic infrastructure and not to more sophisticated technologies, thus excluding them from the full benefits of the AmI environment. It might happen, first, due to a lack of skills and knowledge. In a society with high levels of technology pervasiveness, people who do not possess the knowledge or the skills to use AmI to some extent will be more seriously excluded than today. Second, the digital divide in an AmI environment can arise from profiling: profiling is a prerequisite for many applications, which will provide more opportunities for companies and other organisations to target specific groups, while excluding and discriminating against other people on the basis of their profiles.

Digital divides will persist as a function of income, education and age[34] as well as gender and race/ethnicity. Should no measures be taken towards closing these divides, they will continue to exist more or less to the same degree as today. The gender gap, however, should be less pronounced than it is today, assuming that more women become confident enough to use new technologies.

The global dimension of the digital divide between developed and developing countries is likely to remain the same or even grow. As long as the gap between developing and developed nations in general does not close, the digital divide will also widen, especially as new technologies emerge to which the underdeveloped

[34] Bianchi, A., S. Barrios, M. Cabrera et al., *Revisiting eInclusion. From Vision to Action*, EC Directorate-General Joint Research Centre, Institute for Prospective Technological Studies (IPTS), Seville, 2006.

societies will not have access or will not be able to use. Some regions will most likely face an accumulation of divides, digital and otherwise.

## 4.6 Threats today and tomorrow too

Many of the threats to our privacy today will still be encountered in our AmI future. The same will be true of the threats to our identity and security as well as to our general willingness to trust other people, technologies and services. Among the principal threats that will afflict our AmI future are the following.

### 4.6.1 Hackers and malware

Today's networks, interconnected by the Internet, frequently are attacked by hackers who engage in spoofing, phishing, denial of service attacks via worms, Trojans, viruses and other assorted malware, including spyware, adware and spam. Malware has been an unfortunate feature of daily life on the Internet and, lately, with advanced mobile phones. Often, malware is aimed at uncovering and exploiting personal and confidential data.

Growing opportunities to make money via computers inevitably increases the number of attempts to acquire personal data. Such opportunities include, first, commercial structures: it helps to know an individual's personal financial situation and personal preferences in order to present him or her an attractive offer. Second, insurance companies might search for personal data in order to impose higher insurance fees on those users whose profiles suggest they are higher risks (e.g., users who often drive at night or who engage in dangerous sports such as skydiving). Both categories of interested organisations might provide financial support to developers of spyware.

AmI may provide new opportunities to commit a crime remotely, via networks, for example, by phishing or remote control of somebody else's personal belongings. Botnets do this on today's Internet. It has been estimated that 11 per cent of all computers connected to the Internet are infected by botnets. Indeed, the problem has become so serious that it is said to represent a fundamental threat to the viability of the commercial Internet.[35]

---

[35] Markoff, John, "Attack of the Zombie Computers Is Growing Threat", *New York Times*, 7 January 2007. Markoff adds, "botnets are being blamed for the huge spike in spam that bedeviled the Internet in recent months, as well as fraud and data theft ... botnets automate and amplify the effects of viruses and other malicious programs. What is new is the vastly escalating scale of the problem – and the precision with which some of the programs can scan computers for specific information, like corporate and personal data, to drain money from online bank accounts and stock brokerages." http://www.nytimes.com/2007/01/07/technology/07net.html?hp&ex=1168232400&en=60c6afb90ec2af68&ei=5094&partner=homepage

Malware will threaten personal privacy and security[36] – and consequently trust in AmI. AmI networks will supply data aggregators with massive amounts of data from new sources such as "smart dust" networks, RFIDs and the intelligent software driving the new 4G networks. As the scale of data aggregated expands exponentially, we can expect an increasing concentration and rationalisation in the data management industry as well as in the databases of governments intent on national ID schemes featuring biometrics including DNA data. The giants among the AmI data aggregators will undoubtedly present irresistible targets to hackers just as Microsoft does today.

A recent survey by the National Cyber Security Alliance and America Online found that four of five computers connected to the Web have some type of spyware or adware installed on them, with or without the owner's knowledge. A UK survey found in 2004 that computer viruses, misuse of systems, fraud and theft had risen sharply over the previous 2 years. Two thirds of companies (68 per cent) suffered at least one such incident in the previous year, up from 44 per cent in the 2002 survey and just 24 per cent in 2000. Three quarters of the 1,000 businesses polled – 94 per cent of the larger companies – had a security incident in the previous year. The average UK business now has roughly one security incident a month and larger ones around one a week. Security breaches frequently leave systems inoperable.[37] And the proliferation of malware continues to get worse: spyware reportedly trebled in 2005 over the previous year.[38]

Most computer users acquire spyware and adware simply by browsing certain websites, or agreeing to install games or software programmes that come bundled with spyware and adware. Computer users may or may not understand what they are consenting to when they click "OK" to the lengthy, legalistic disclosures that accompany games or videos. But those notices are legal contracts that essentially absolve the adware companies from any liability associated with the use or misuse of their programs.[39]

---

[36] Nowadays, even companies that provide security services have been exposed to breaches in their own security. Guidance Software – the leading provider of software used to diagnose hacker break-ins – has itself been hacked, resulting in the exposure of financial and personal data connected to thousands of law enforcement officials and network-security professionals. In December 2005, Guidance alerted its customers that hackers had broken into a company database and made off with approximately 3,800 customer credit card numbers. In March of that year, data aggregator LexisNexis acknowledged that hackers had illegally accessed information on more than 310,000 consumers, an attack that was later determined to have been launched after hackers broke into computers used by at least two separate police departments. Krebs, Brian, "Hackers Break Into Computer-Security Firm's Customer Database", *The Washington Post*, 19 December 2005.

[37] Leyden, John, "Hackers cost UK.biz billions", *The Register*, 28 April 2004. http://www.theregister.co.uk/2004/04/28/dti_security_survey/

[38] Kelly, Lisa, "Spyware attacks triple in 2005", *Computing*, 12 June 2006. http://www.vnunet.com/computing/news/2158112/spyware-attacks-triple-2005. See also Krebs, Brian, "Microsoft Releases Windows Malware Stats", *The Washington Post*, 12 June 2006. http://blog.washingtonpost.com/securityfix/2006/06/microsoft_releases_malware_sta.html

[39] Krebs, Brian, "Invasion of the Computer Snatchers", *The Washington Post*, 19 February 2006.

Since the amount of information, transmitted and stored in AmI networks will increase, and since taking care of security of personal devices is left to the owners of such devices, who may not have either the knowledge of or enthusiasm for security matters, hackers and malware present a serious threat to personal privacy, identity and security in an AmI world, as is already apparent in today's world.

### 4.6.2  Identity theft

Identity theft is one obvious example of why protection of personal data is needed. Identity theft (or identity-related crime) is one of the fastest-growing white-collar crimes. Typically, someone steals our financial details, most often our credit card details, to commit fraud. The identity thief can impersonate us financially, to take out loans, raid our bank accounts, purchase luxury items. The credit card companies may minimise our losses when purchases are made against our cards (or some facsimile thereof), but we may be liable for the other items. Identity theft can ruin our creditworthiness even if we are not culpable. It may take a long time, a lot of aggravation, to restore our creditworthiness and recover our financial identity.[40] As serious as identity theft is for us as individuals, the credit card companies feel no less aggrieved and, given the magnitude of identity theft, they have been devoting lots of resource and effort to deal with it. The recent replacement of our signature by chip and PIN cards is just one indication of their efforts to combat this form of fraud (and the new cards seem to have had a salutary effect in reducing fraud too, by some five per cent in the United Kingdom, according to reports[41]).

Identity fraud is costing the credit card sector billions of euros each year, and is a major source of privacy complaints.[42] Both MasterCard and Visa monitor web

---

[40] A survey conducted by Privacy Rights Clearinghouse and the California Public Interest Research Group found that the average victim of identity theft did not find out that he or she was a victim until 14 months after the identity theft occurred and that it took the victim an average of 175 hours to solve the problems that occurred as a result of the identity theft. Kent, Stephen T., and Lynette I. Millett (eds.), *Who Goes There?*, p. 99.

[41] However, researchers at Cambridge University have said they have found that the new cards can be exploited. They say they have devised a relatively easy way of capturing the cardholder's details, including his PIN. Jackson, Russell, "New fraud threat to chip-and-PIN cards", *The Scotsman*, 6 January 2007. http://news.scotsman.com/uk.cfm?id=26792007

[42] The FTC said identity theft again topped the number of consumer complaints it received in 2005, as it has in recent years. See FTC press release "FTC Releases Top 10 Consumer Fraud Complaint Categories", 25 January 2006. http://www.ftc.gov/opa/2006/01/topten.htm. See also Krim, Jonathan, "Data on 3,000 Consumers Stolen With Computer", *The Washington Post*, 9 November 2005. "Social Security numbers and other information about more than 3,000 consumers were stolen recently from TransUnion LLC, one of three US. companies that maintain credit histories on individuals, in the latest of many security breaches that have focused congressional attention on identity theft and fraud."

sites that broker stolen credit card numbers and other personal information; they have discovered that an identity is worth about US$10 on the Internet.[43]

Despite the prevalence of identity theft, prosecutions are rare, and police investigations – when they do happen – are time-consuming, costly and easily stymied. A 2003 study by Gartner, Inc. suggested that an identity thief had about a one in 700 chance of getting caught.[44]

It is an open question whether ambient intelligence will increase or decrease opportunities for identity theft and fraud. With orders of magnitude of more personal information generated in an AmI environment, one might not be too hopeful that the problem will go away. On the other hand, if some privacy-enhancing technologies, like those proposed in the PROGRESS Embedded Systems Roadmap or in the PISA and PRIME projects, are developed and become widely available, one might think the consumer will have better defences against at least some forms of identity theft.[45]

But technology can only help to some extent. Gullibility and carelessness, human traits, are less easily fixed.

### 4.6.3   Penetration of identity management systems

Identity management systems are subject to many of the attacks common to other Internet or computer-communications-based systems, such as hacking, spoofing, eavesdropping and denial of service.

There is no reason to think these sorts of attacks that plague us today are likely to go away in an AmI world.

### 4.6.4   Function creep

Function creep occurs whenever data are used for a purpose other than that for which they were originally collected. The economic logic behind such activity is

---

[43] O'Brien, Timothy L., "Identity Theft Is Epidemic. Can It Be Stopped?", *The New York Times*, 24 October 2004.

[44] Zeller, Tom, Jr., "For Victims, Repairing ID Theft Can Be Grueling", *The New York Times*, 1 October 2005.

[45] The term privacy-enhancing technologies (PETs) represents a spectrum of both new and well-known techniques to minimise the exposure of private data, for users of electronic services in the information society. Currently, no widely accepted definition of privacy-enhancing technologies has been established, but one can distinguish technologies for privacy protection (psydeunomiser, anonymiser and encryption tools, filters, tracks and evidence erasers) and for privacy management (informational and administrative tools). See, e.g., Koorn, R., H. van Gils, J. ter Hart, P. Overbeek, R. Tellegen and J. Borking, "Privacy-Enhancing Technologies: White Paper for Decision-Makers", The Hague, Ministry of the Interior and Kingdom Relations, 2004. http://www.dutch-dpa.nl/downloads_overig/PET_whitebook.pdf

obvious. It provides efficiencies and savings in cost and effort. Being able to reuse personal data presents a great temptation to industry and government. As AmI penetrates our environment and daily regimes, the amassed data will present new opportunities that were not even dreamed of. In some instances, the individual will benefit from greater personalisation of services and lower costs. In other instances, she will find some of the new services encroaching further upon her sense of privacy and the protection of her personal data.

AmI will give great impetus to function creep. It has been said that whatever can be linked together will be linked together, and therein lie the opportunities and temptations for function creep.

For example, function creep may occur due to penetration of identity management systems: some authentication systems make it possible to identify an individual without the individual's consent or even knowledge. Such systems deny the individual, and society, the opportunity to object to and to monitor the identification process. These technologies are particularly vulnerable to misuse because their use is hidden.[46]

The Data Protection Directive 95/46, which is not applicable in areas of criminal law and state security, defines an identity and any information related to an identified or identifiable *natural* person as personal data. Identification is a processing of personal data and therefore falls under the principles of data protection such as the principle of purpose specification and use limitation (use conforms only to the original purpose).

The growing awareness of identity theft has prompted many businesses to require customers to provide identification information, especially online and over the telephone. Identification information can come from passports or ID cards or drivers' licences as well as biographical data such as date of birth or mother's maiden name or from biometrics such as fingerprint or iris scans. In attempts to minimise the risk of identity theft and fraud, businesses may be increasing privacy risks.

Even if the decision is made to implement authentication systems only where people *today* attempt to discern identity, the creation of reliable, inexpensive systems will invite function creep – the use of authentication systems for other than their originally intended purposes – unless action is taken to prevent this from happening. Thus, the privacy consequences of both the intended design and deployment and the unintended, secondary uses of authentication systems must be taken into consideration by vendors, users, policy-makers and the general public.[47]

It is not hard to see signs of function creep when we travel from one country to another. The United States, the United Kingdom, Japan and other countries are introducing biometric requirements to supplement passport data. The United Kingdom has introduced iris scanning, supposedly to speed passengers through immigration controls. The scan is linked to their passport details. Now the government will have one more bit of data about United Kingdom and other citizens who choose to participate in the scheme. For its part, Japan, like the United States, has

---

[46] Kent, Stephen T., and Lynette I. Millett (eds.), *Who Goes There?*, pp. 30–31.
[47] Kent, Stephen T., and Lynette I. Millett (eds.), *Who Goes There?*, p. 29.

decided to fingerprint and photograph visitors. Gathering such biometric data is grist, not just for civil aviation authorities, but also for law enforcement, the intelligence agencies and immigration control. It is the same with loyalty cards that supermarkets foist on their customers. Such cards are purportedly to reward loyal customers when in reality they serve the market research and marketing departments. Such cards strip away the anonymity of cash-paying customers, enabling the supermarket chains to better target and spam customers.

As AmI becomes pervasive, at least in developed countries that can afford such networks, the opportunities for supplementing basic identifier data will surely grow and with it, function creep.

### 4.6.5 Exploitation of linkages by industry and government

An AmI world will be a highly networked world, with linkages between different networks. Hence, where today it is possible to have multiple partial identities that correspond to our different roles in society – as neighbour, employee, student, etc – AmI will facilitate linkages between these different partial identities leading to a great increase in their integration. Both government and industry, despite any protests to the contrary, will find it irresistible to facilitate such linkages for their own, sometimes nefarious, purposes. The more linkages that can be established, the more government and industry will know about us, our behaviour patterns, what we are doing, where we are at any given moment, our disposition towards particular products or services or activities some of which may be deemed as socially unacceptable. Using partial digital identities in communications with different organisations is not likely to help, because it is difficult to avoid usage of at least one attribute across those partial identities. Only one attribute shared by two partial identities is needed to establish a link between them and all the other attributes. It could be a telephone number, an e-mail address, a date of birth, almost anything will do. Even among those who understand the benefits of partial identities, it will be miraculous if they can avoid usage of at least one attribute across those partial identities.

From the individual's point of view, however, more linkages will raise more concerns about the security and protection of our personal data. It may also lead to an erosion of trust – how much trust are we likely to place in Big Brother and a host of "little brothers" when we feel they know almost as much about us as we do ourselves?

### 4.6.6 Surveillance

Surveillance is increasing in the streets, buses, underground, shops, workplace and on the motorways. Hence, it is now almost impossible to go outside your home without coming under surveillance.

Location-based services form a kind of surveillance. Mobile phone operators and industry have developed emergency service telephone numbers, which can be activated automatically and which will inform the network of the physical location of the user. New electronic services, such as those offered by uLocate and Wherify Wireless, provide the physical location of mobile phone users.[48]

One can imagine a day when almost everyone will have implantable devices, not only for monitoring their physiological condition, but also for tracking their whereabouts. At the same time, there may be considerable social pressure, perhaps even legal requirements, for individuals to bear such implants as a security measure. One could further foresee such implants interacting with the "intelligence"-embedded, networked environment too.

AmI devices such as implants or technologies that monitor our physiological condition and behaviour could well make our society more secure, particularly if they enable law enforcement authorities and intelligence agencies to take preventive measures. Preventive actions by the police are featured in the Steven Spielberg film *Minority Report*, but is this the kind of society we want? More control in order to prevent criminal acts, detect offenders and punish them may be counterproductive for society as a whole. In 1968, the philosopher Heinrich Popitz wrote a classic text on the "preventive effects of nescience" in which he argues that too much (precautionary) knowledge destabilises society, leads to a climate of distrust and finally to more instead of less crime. A world where every breach of the rule is detected and punished can only be hell.

Furthermore, law enforcement authorities and intelligence agencies' interest in surveillance in order to increase the security of society as a whole (on the assumption that total surveillance can help to decrease the number of terrorist acts) might hinder development of anti-spyware tools if they do not receive adequate financial support, or limit usage of such tools by the general public. The main problem with security is that security is not a primary goal of computer usage; and security measures are often neglected if they are not user-friendly. Thus, security of personal devices depends on how much governments support research, development and distribution of user-friendly security measures. Governments have the power to increase taxation of anti-spyware products and wiretapping detectors (or even to make them illegal) or to make them free of charge.

## 4.6.7   Profiling

As the AmI vision is geared towards a user-centric approach, one of the key means of meeting the users' individual needs is personalisation. In order to be able to

---

[48] See Harmon, Amy, "Lost? Hiding? Your Cellphone Is Keeping Tabs", *The New York Times*, 21 December 2003: "We are moving into a world where your location is going to be known at all times by some electronic device," said Larry Smarr, director of the California Institute for Telecommunications and Information Technology.

deliver customised services, user-specific profiles need to be created. Profiling in an AmI environment consists of constantly collecting and processing a broad range of data from numerous sources that are related to a user's identity, his/her activities, characteristics and preferences in specific environments. Based on constructed profiles, AmI systems are able to respond to the users' needs – or at least what is assumed to be their needs inferred from the interpretation of the collected information.

Problems of inadequate profiling can occur in two main situations: attribution conflicts involving numerous users and misinterpretation of user needs.

**Profiling can present threats to privacy**, because aggregated data can be used by governments and companies to support behavioural targeting and/or to implement dynamic pricing. A modern incarnation of price discrimination, dynamic pricing means that different prices are offered to customers based on their characteristics.[49]

Companies such as Amazon practise behavioural targeting: they keep track not only of their customers' purchases, but also their browsing, and with the accumulation of such data, they can build up increasingly accurate profiles of their customers in order to offer them other products in which they might be interested. Search engines keep a log file that associates every search made on their sites with the IP address of the searcher. Yahoo uses Web browsing information to sell advertising; car companies, for example, place display advertising shown only to people who have entered auto-related terms in Yahoo's search engine.[50] Companies such as Doubleclick specialise in building and analysing profiles by placing cookies on our personal computers and keeping track of our surfing behaviour across numerous affiliated web sites.

Customer-supplied data, data obtained from monitoring purchasing habits and surfing behaviour and data obtained from third parties may lead to a situation where people will only see choices presented to them on the basis of their profile. Their choices within these boundaries may lead to further refinements in their profile.[51]

---

[49] [PRIME] Hansen, Marit, and Henry Krasemann (eds.), Privacy and Identity Management for Europe – PRIME White Paper, Deliverable D 15.1.d, 18 July 2005, p. 10. http://www.prime-project.eu.org/public/prime_products/deliverables/

For a practical example of how mobile phone companies engage in differential pricing, see Richtel, Matt, "Suddenly, an Industry Is All Ears", *The New York Times*, 4 March 2006: "When a [Cingular call centre] representative answers the phone, an information page pops up that includes the caller's name and number, whether he or she has called in the last five days, and why that call was made. In the top right of the screen are two icons – one indicating whether the caller is a threat to quit service (largely a measure of whether the customer is still under contract), and the other showing how much money the caller spends each month (a measure of the customer's value). Before long, the screen indicates if the customer is profitable. If a customer is not very profitable, the company may be less likely to make concessions."

[50] Hansell, Saul, "Increasingly, Internet's Data Trail Leads to Court", *The New York Times*, 4 February 2006.

[51] [PRIME] Hansen, M., and H. Krasemann (eds.), Privacy and Identity Management for Europe – PRIME White Paper, p. 11.

**The fact that profiling cannot be perfect presents threats to security and trust**. Profiling may not seem like a security threat at first glance, at least not in the traditional understanding of security flaws as a malfunctioning of or as attacks on computers. However, nowadays the term "security" is often being used in a sense related to the safety of individuals, groups or societies. For the safety of users, inadequate profiling can present a threat if it forces users to attempt to fit into a particular profile or if it generates false positives. For example, if insurance companies impose higher fees on users whose lifestyle they consider "insecure" (e.g., if their food consumption, driving behaviour or recreational activity do not fit their standards), the users are left with the choice of paying more or changing their behaviour according to the wishes of the insurance companies; and this forced behaviour change might be dangerous for their health and life.

Security expert Bruce Schneier has pointed out flaws with profiling schemes. "Profiling has two very dangerous failure modes. The first one is ... the intent of profiling ... to divide people into two categories: people who may be evildoers ... and people who are less likely to be evildoers. ... But any such system will create a third, and very dangerous, category: evildoers who don't fit the profile. ... There's another, even more dangerous, failure mode for these systems: honest people who fit the evildoer profile. Because actual evildoers are so rare, almost everyone who fits the profile will turn out to be a false alarm. This not only wastes investigative resources that might be better spent elsewhere, but it causes grave harm to those innocents who fit the profile ... profiling harms society because it causes us all to live in fear...not from the evildoers, but from the police. ... Identification and profiling don't provide very good security, and they do so at an enormous cost."[52]

The PRIME project has echoed this sentiment: unbridled data collection and profiling by the State in the name of protecting (national) security may lead to unjust and ultimately unwarranted blacklists, however noble the intentions may be. This happens not only in totalitarian regimes, but also in free societies.[53]

**Profiling presents threats to identity** because choices, presented by AmI, can force people to behave in some way which they might not have chosen without AmI, if people feel obliged to accept the AmI-presented course because it seems to be what is expected of them.[54]

---

[52] Schneier, Bruce, "Identification and Security", *Crypto-Gram Newsletter*, 15 February 2004. http://www.schneier.com/crypto-gram-back.html. George Clooney provided us with a reminder of this in his recent film, *Good Night and Good Luck*, about Joe McCarthy, who professed that he was making America more secure by exposing Communists and their sympathisers, when in reality he was instilling fear and paranoia across society.

[53] [PRIME] Hansen, M., and H. Krasemann (eds.), Privacy and Identity Management for Europe – PRIME White Paper, p. 11.

[54] This AmI phenomenon has been described as cognitive dissonance. See Brey, Philip, "Freedom and privacy in Ambient Intelligence", *Ethics and Information Technology*, Vol. 7, No. 3, 2005, p. 162. "Users may even start experiencing cognitive dissonance, when they believe they want one thing but a smart object tells them they want something else."

**Profiling presents threats to trust** because it leads to misinterpretation of users' needs. The quality of a personal profile depends both on the scope and depth of the input data as well as on the adequacy of the data processing. However, even if service providers decide to invest sufficient resources into the continuous monitoring by numerous sensors and the development of "intelligent" software in order to improve the performance of an AmI system, the profiles developed from the collected data represent – at best – constructed approximations of the actual user preferences. Information collected by AmI sensors is mainly based on observed patterns of behaviour. Thus, just as in the case of empirical social research, profiling can merely capture a simplified extract of a complex reality; moreover, the data tend to be distorted by artefacts. In short, linking observable behaviour to an individual's intentions is highly problematic and prone to misleading interpretations – a challenge, of course, faced by every developer of an "intelligent" system.

The most common approach to ease the problem is to supplement the profiling process by requesting direct input from the user, which is at odds with one of the envisioned key characteristics of AmI – namely the disappearance of user interfaces. Predefined choices can either be very limited or, if the opposite strategy is implemented and a wide range of choices is offered, the user is burdened with time-consuming and perhaps annoying adjustment and programming procedures. Moreover, requesting direct input from the user may present other problems. One is that users are not always able to express their preferences adequately, for example, due to the unsuitability of the form in which they are required to express preferences (e.g., too small or too large a choice of actions or incompatible ontology). Another problem is that user preferences change over time, and asking users to update them can cause annoyance.

In the case of incorrect attribution, further complexity is added by multiuser situations (when two or more users are concurrently present in the same AmI environment). Since users' profiles, actions and preferences may not necessarily be congruent,[55] conflicts over shared services and resources might occur. If these conflicts are not resolved adequately, user acceptance is at stake. Finding a compromise between user profiles is not easy. Averaging out the disputed profile parameters is not likely to help in many areas of daily life – for example, where users have different musical preferences, such simple mathematical remedies are not feasible.

In addition, if individual preferences with regard to a specific application or situation tend to change frequently and dynamically, the expediency of profiling is significantly reduced.

Generally, most dimensions of human self-expression include implicit, intangible, subtle and fuzzy forms, making it – at least for the time being – impossible to reconstruct them adequately.

These considerations on profiling are not intended to support the conclusion that profiling is to be dismissed per se. Instead, a better understanding of the innate

---

[55] Schreurs, W., M. Hildebrandt, M. Gasson and K. Warwick, "Report on Actual and Possible Profiling Techniques in the Field of Ambient Intelligence", FIDIS Deliverable D7.3, 2005, p. 12.

limits to the construction of user profiles should entail a heightened awareness of the necessity to implement adequate provisions that help to reduce undesirable side effects. This could, for instance, be achieved by system designs that always enable users to easily overrule decisions made by an AmI system.[56]

**Profiling can facilitate the digital divide**, for example, if inadequate profiles provide an opportunity for denial of service or discrimination. Denial of services and incidents of discrimination may originate in procedural rules imposed by service providers – either in their own right or in compliance with regulations established by public authorities. In the first case, the individual preferences are the central point of reference for the AmI system; in the latter case, specified profile characteristics have to be met by the individual if he or she desires access to certain services or privileges. A user might not only be denied service because his profile does not match the required criteria (e.g., income, age, health record or other personal data). An individual's decision not to make available certain personal data may also result in exclusion. This raises questions about what degree of information disclosure is necessary and whether service providers should be barred from asking for or requiring some particular information.

Discriminatory refusals of services are characterised by asymmetric relationships in which one party is obliged to comply with standards set by the other party – though this will be hard to distinguish from the freedom of contract in individual cases. Two main realms of discriminatory practice due to allegedly inadequate profiles can be distinguished: concerns regarding civil security and practices driven by commercial interests.

- **Civil security:** Based on security concerns, users are requested to provide personal information as a prerequisite to obtain a service. In most cases, public authorities have established certain requirements, and private companies (e.g., transport services and airports) are obliged to implement these regulations. However, in cases of service denial, it is not necessarily clear to the user on which grounds the measure was imposed. Apart from the possibility of a technical error (e.g., faulty database), it is difficult to discern whether the refusal is based on public regulations or the service provider's own rationale – which draws attention to the second type of discriminatory practice. Other reasons for the refusal of services may stem from inadequate interoperability of information systems or, in the case of individuals from less developed regions, the absence of personal profile data.
- **Profit interests:** Apart from security motives, market and profit considerations can be at the heart of access rules. For instance, customers might be coerced into making available sensitive personal data if they wish to enjoy certain privileges or services (e.g., special insurance premiums and rebates). Moreover, if a customer decides not to comply for whatever reason, a service provider might

---

[56] Spiekermann, S., and F. Pallas, "Technology Paternalism – Wider Implications of Ubiquitous Computing", *Poiesis & Praxis*, Vol. 4, No. 1, 2006, pp. 6–18.

respond by limiting its own liability. Apart from any legal considerations, it seems obvious that users who have been deprived of real consumer choices will have little trust in the AmI application.

**Profiling can lead to victimisation.** An innocent individual might erroneously be identified as a criminal, a potential security threat or even a terrorist.[57] The likelihood of mistakes, of unfounded suspicion increases if security needs and privacy rights are not balanced adequately. Moreover, incomplete and/or decontextualised profile information may also contribute to the victimisation of citizens.

The misuse of profiling data by companies or other organisations may lead to discrimination of people according to their race, ethnicity or socio-economic status, thus exacerbating exclusion and widening the digital divide.

### 4.6.8   Authentication may intrude upon privacy

A US National Research Council report has warned that authentication technologies could intrude upon privacy in different ways. Authentication methods may require contact with or close proximity to the body, potentially raising concerns under the "bodily integrity" branch of privacy law. Authentication may introduce new opportunities to collect and reuse personal information, intruding on "information privacy". Authentication systems may be deployed in a manner that interferes with individuals' "decisional privacy" by creating opportunities for others to monitor and interfere with important expressive or other personal activities. Authentication methods may raise new opportunities to intercept or monitor a specific individual's communications, revealing the person's thoughts and the identities of the individuals with whom he or she communicates.[58]

Some authentication systems make it possible to identify an individual without the individual's consent or even knowledge. Such systems deny the individual, and society, the opportunity to object to and to monitor the identification process. These technologies are particularly vulnerable to misuse because their use is hidden.[59]

## 4.7   Lots of vulnerabilities

In addition to the threats highlighted above, privacy, identity management and security systems are subject to various vulnerabilities, among which are the following.

---

[57] Exactly this situation already occurs today. See, for example, Summers, Deborah, "Bureau admits innocents branded criminals", *The Herald* [Scotland], 22 May 2006: "The Home Office was plunged into yet more controversy yesterday as it emerged nearly 1500 innocent people had been branded criminals because of errors by its Criminal Records Bureau." http://www.theherald.co.uk/politics/62460.html

[58] Kent, Stephen T., and Lynette I. Millett (eds.), *Who Goes There?*, p. 63.

[59] Kent, Stephen T., and Lynette I. Millett (eds.), *Who Goes There?*, pp. 30–31.

## *4.7.1 System complexity, false positives and unpredictable failures*

The growing complexity of systems increases both the risk of unpredictable system behaviour and the risk of malicious attacks due to security holes caused by the interaction of components. Interactions between operational systems, anti-virus software and customer applications can hinder the functionality of antivirus software and increase the risk that virus attacks will succeed. They can also slow down customer applications. The complexity of customer applications can cause unpredictable behaviour if applications are used in situations or ways not predicted by their designers (and designers will not be able to predict everything). Further, the reliability and performance of critical components may be inadequate for the ways in which the components are ultimately used.

The primary operation of a technical system can be disrupted in many ways. For example, in a health care emergency, it may be necessary to connect a patient's personal device to the hospital network in order to acquire the patient's health care history. In order to interoperate with the hospital's emergency network, the patient's personal device may need to be reconfigured, which in turn could disrupt the operation of the personal device or of the emergency network. If the patient's personal device is contaminated with viruses, they may be transferred to the hospital's AmI system together with the patient's data or to another personal device.

Since more and more versions of hardware and software appear in the market, the problem of compatibility between different hardware components connected together and between different versions of software (running on the same device or during attempts to communicate between different devices) becomes critical. Moreover, that incompatibility can be invisible to the user in the sense that devices still function and communicate, but more slowly or with errors: e.g., incomplete compatibility in communication protocols can lead to distortion of transmitted data without the user's noticing it. Incompatibilities between new antivirus software and old operational systems can lead to security holes.

Security expert Bruce Schneier has said that it doesn't matter how well a system works, what matters is how it fails. No matter what their merits may be, if identity management, authentication and authorisation systems generate a large number of false positives, i.e., they authenticate or authorise someone to engage in some transaction when he should not be permitted to do so, they will be regarded as failures.

It may be assumed that biometrics will ultimately reduce the number of false positives in view of the supposedly unique nature of each set of fingerprints, irises and other physiological features, but false positives are still possible. Sometimes these false positives are generated not by the technology but by those who wield the technology, as happened when the FBI became convinced, wrongly, that they had identified an Oregon lawyer, a Muslim convert, as a participant in the terrorist attack on Madrid trains in March 2004, on the basis of a single fingerprint which was a near match to one found in Madrid.

Problems like this *could* be reduced if AmI networks generate so much data about the individual that the individual is virtually unmistakeable. But if we arrive at that situation, it may also mean that there is a significantly greater amount of personal information floating around, so that the capture and analysis of such information reduces the very protection of privacy that identity management systems are supposed to support.

If intelligence is embedded everywhere in an AmI world, there will be lots of people, companies, organisations collecting identity data. So questions will arise about their securing of our data. How well will supermarkets, or the corner grocery store, protect our identity data?

Governments and industry have been developing a multiplicity of identity management systems for various purposes, with the intent of putting more (or virtually all) of their services online or, in the instance of the rationale for national ID cards, for combating fraud and terrorism. Some systems, for example, the United Kingdom's Inland Revenue system that permits individuals to file their tax returns online, are becoming very big indeed with millions of files. Eventually the national ID card scheme will become even bigger. If common standards are agreed for national ID systems across the European Union, an EU ID card may not be long in coming. Inevitably, as the systems and their attendant databases become bigger, the complexity of the systems grows.

The multiplicity and complexity of such systems offers a possible foretaste of what identity management could become like in an AmI environment, when there will be many more systems, networks and services on offer. While there are some who believe that a single sign-on approach would reduce (somewhat) the complexity of interacting with a multiplicity of systems, others believe a decentralised approach reduces the risk that might arise from a massive failure or attack on a centralised system.

The snag with the growing complexity of computer communications systems, including those that will form the backbone of AmI networks, is that vulnerabilities increase with complexity. Experience has taught that systems – and, in particular, complex systems like networked information systems – can be secure, but only up to a point. There will always be residual vulnerabilities, always a degree of insecurity.[60]

The AmI vision promises a natural, intuitive and, therefore, unobtrusive way of human–technology interaction. If such a smooth co-operation cannot be attained, there is a risk that ambient intelligence will cause stress and distrust and, as a consequence, the technology will not generate the acceptance necessary to realise the (societal) benefits it promises.

Due to the technology's complexity or the different conception that programmers and users have of the proper use of information systems, users may conclude that they cannot rely on the AmI technology as expected.

---

[60] Committee on Information Systems Trustworthiness, *Trust in Cyberspace*, National Research Council, National Academies Press, Washington, DC, 1999, p. 119.

This is a problem especially for those users who are not familiar with information technology. These users often blame themselves if they do not attain the desired goal and are often too reluctant for a second try because they are afraid of damaging something. Only those groups that are always open-minded towards new technologies will adopt AmI and incorporate it into their daily life in the short term.

As the dependency on such systems increases, the potential harm, which could result from a misjudgement of system behaviour, also rises. Where more is at stake than the result of a few hours' work (as is the case with normal computer use today), the distrust of users will increase accordingly.

### 4.7.2 Lack of user-friendly security and configuration software

In days gone by, computers were not really personal: computers were owned by employers, and they took care of computer security, timely updates of hardware and antivirus software, compatibility of installed applications and so on. In today's world, computers have become personal; modern mobile phones themselves have become quite powerful personal computers. Consequently, the burden of taking care of the security of personal computers has shifted towards individual users.

Despite the fact that users must take care of their own security, the security of personal devices has not significantly improved compared to the early days of desktop computers: the main means of user authentication in mobile phones is still a PIN code, and user authentication happens only when the phone is switched on. Besides, proper configuration of security settings requires a certain knowledge (which most users do not have), while updates of software require significant explicit user effort. Even software updates on personal desktops are not user-friendly, and the need to restart the computer after every update is a hassle.

Consequently, it is safe to assume that many users will not keep their antivirus software up to date and will not authenticate themselves to their devices frequently enough.

### 4.7.3 Personal devices: networking with limited resources

The burden of taking care of the security of personal computers can be a hassle even for those who only have to care about the security of their own computers; the situation becomes worse in the case of mobile devices with limited capabilities. Mobile devices have already replaced desktops in many tasks, and this trend will increase in the AmI future. This increases threats to security because running sophisticated encryption algorithms and communication protocols and multitasking are difficult for mobile devices. Additionally, limited battery life carries a danger that the device becomes useless unexpectedly; the small screen size of mobile devices carries a danger that users will miss important information due to an unwillingness to scroll down, and so on.

In our AmI future, everything will be communicating with everything: objects, organisations and personal devices will constantly be exchanging messages. This endangers security significantly because one malicious network node can create problems for other nodes if it constantly broadcasts messages and requires replies. A malicious node can spread viruses or distribute false data. Even if other networking devices have good antivirus protection and do not get infected by this malicious node, and even if they are able to conclude that the received data are not trustworthy, part of their limited communication and computational capabilities and battery life are wasted anyway.

Additional security problem arise from the inflexible communication range of devices: radio signals from devices and objects located in one home or in one car can easily penetrate walls, so that thieves could detect whether a flat is empty or not, and break into one that is. Another problem is created by the sheer increase of radio communications, which can hinder device operation in some cases.

### 4.7.4  Lack of transparency

So many people and organisations hold personal data about us, it is virtually impossible to know who they are, let alone to keep track of what they are doing with our data, whether the data they hold are accurate, and how such data may change, be added to, deleted, amended or processed – even though, according to EU data protection legislation, data processors are supposed to notify national authorities of the categories of data processed, the purpose of processing, the retention period and the security and confidentiality measures taken and even though data controllers are expected to notify the individuals concerned so that they can access, amend or delete the data. Although these obligations exist, their efficacy has been undermined by the bad faith of some data controllers and because enforcement has not been rigorous.

We should not be surprised by comments made by executives of two major data brokers who acknowledged to a US Senate panel that their companies did not tell consumers about security breaches that exposed more than 400,000 people to possible identity theft.[61] Similarly, governments, notably the Bush administration, have been reticent about domestic surveillance before and even after *The New York Times* exposed the fact in December 2005 that the US National Security Agency had been spying, without warrants, on thousands of Americans.

As has been pointed out already, one of the key features of many existing and envisioned AmI applications is their ability to operate in the background, largely

---

[61] Krim, Jonathan, "Consumers Not Told Of Security Breaches, Data Brokers Admit", *The Washington Post*, 14 April 2005. See also Stout, David, "Data Theft at Nuclear Agency Went Unreported for 9 Months", *The New York Times*, 10 June 2006.

unnoticed by the user. While this defining characteristic doubtlessly has its merits in terms of usability, convenience and efficiency, it may have adverse effects on users' trust in and acceptance of AmI services. Because users know that AmI systems can operate invisibly, autonomously and unperceived, concerns about system control, the hidden agendas of some system operators, and secondary use of collected data may arise. System operators and service providers could reduce consumer distrust by effectively informing users about system procedures, purposes and responsibilities.

### 4.7.5   High update and maintenance costs

Security has a cost. As long as market requirements or legal regulations do not force manufacturers to provide products with user-friendly security included, and as long as costs of security problems caused by insecure products are somewhat indeterminate (the cost of manually deleting 100 spam e-mails, the time spent recovering from identity theft), the AmI world will face serious security problems. It is impossible to predict all possible configurations of components that users might install on or connect to their devices and how much it might cost them to recover from configurations that either fail or introduce insecurities. Similarly, competition forces companies producing software and hardware to get their products into the marketplace as quickly as possible with the result that they are not adequately testing their devices and software for potential vulnerabilities. When something goes wrong, the cost to the producers or service providers is possible to determine, but the cost to consumers who bear the consequences of failures is rather more difficult to estimate.

The drive towards cost-savings could give a boost to the implementation of AmI, but maintenance and updating could be much more costly than initially expected. High costs may lead to the widening of the digital divide *within* societies, where some people can bear the maintenance and some not, as well as *between* different societies.

### 4.7.6   Uncertainties about what to protect and the costs of protection

Just as privacy is an unstable notion, so it is almost impossible to know what to protect in all contexts, especially in view of the capabilities of data mining and powerful software that can detect linkages that might not otherwise be apparent.

With the emergence and deployment of AmI networks, the amount of data that can be captured from all sources will expand exponentially by many orders of magnitude. Hence, the cost of providing 100 per cent privacy protection may be prohibitive and unrealistic, even if there were some consensus about exactly what it is we wish to see protected.

There have been few studies aimed at analysing the value of privacy, either from a corporate point of view or that of the individual.[62] The cost of losing privacy is two-fold: On the one hand, one is confronted by the cost of becoming transparent; on the other, one is exposed to the cost of losing control. There is also the cost of new AmI-related crimes such as identity theft. The economic costs, therefore, are not only the design of the system, but also the consequence of the design in the long term.

Certainly, protecting personal data, through security measures, notably in compliance with the European Union's Data Protection Directive, carries a cost. The Directive requires data controllers and processors to protect personal data in proportion to "the risks represented by the processing and the nature of the data to be protected" (Article 17.1). Such costs might include the cost of encryption and establishing a range of protection measures, not least of which is training staff. The cost of implementing the information security measures detailed in ISO 17799 could be quite substantial. From a shareholder's point of view, these costs of protecting privacy can be identified, but the value of doing so might be more uncertain. Where's the payback, they might well ask.

There might be some payback in the context of the company's image, i.e., it could say that it complies with ISO 17799 and, accordingly, it might hope or have some expectation that doing so will engender more trust and loyalty on the part of its customers in the company's brand. Even so, doubts must remain as to whether that automatically translates into greater market share or additional profitability. If the company does gain greater market share or additional profitability, the cause might not be the fact that it has taken adequate measures to protect the personal data it holds, but some other factor. As a minimum, the company would need to do some careful market studies to determine what factors led to improvements in its market position.

Some indication of the economic value of privacy can be adduced from the costs borne by companies where there have been breaches of their databases resulting in the theft of personal data. In such cases, companies have had to bear the cost of informing users or subscribers of the breach, of compensating those whose personal data have been compromised, of establishing improved countermeasures, subjecting themselves to independent privacy audits and so on. Recently, ChoicePoint was subjected to a US$10 million federal fine over security breaches that exposed more than 160,000 people to possible identity theft. "The message to ChoicePoint and others should be clear: consumers' private data must be protected from thieves," FTC Chairman Deborah Platt Majoras said.[63] Such direct costs are only part of the overall cost equation, however. There are additional costs arising from, for example, damage to the company's image, reputation and name.

If companies have difficulty in assessing the value of their privacy protection measures, the individual is almost surely faced with even greater difficulties. If the individual is being spammed a lot, getting a lot of unwanted e-mail, how easy or

---

[62] But there have been some. For a list of articles on the economics of privacy, see http://www.heinz.cmu.edu/~acquisti/economics-privacy.htm

[63] Mohammed, Arshad, "Record Fine for Data Breach", *The Washington Post*, 27 January 2006.

difficult will it be to translate the nuisance it causes into cold hard cash? Is it simply the cost of the individual's time in deleting unwanted e-mail? Can a value be ascribed to the anguish the individual might feel in knowing that his contact details are on some spammer's e-mail list?

Those who have been victims of identity theft might have some pretty good ideas of the costs to them, in terms of lost time and perhaps direct financial loss, in trying to recover from the theft, but still there must be an open question about the stress and anguish caused by the theft and what is the monetary value of such stress and anguish.

Certainly there are social costs too arising from identity theft, but there appears to be no study analysing such social costs, even though the number of victims seem to be rather large. The US Federal Trade Commission has estimated the number of victims at around 10 per cent of the population, and the number of victims in the United Kingdom, if not the European Union as a whole, also has been estimated as increasing, if not yet to such levels.

While the costs of identity theft can be estimated, what is one to say about the costs of, for example, increased surveillance? How does the individual value the supposed increase in security versus the encroachment upon his privacy?

For the individual, the value of his personal data must be even more difficult to pin a figure to. For starters, the individual is highly unlikely to be aware of all those organisations that hold some of his data. And even if he were, he would most likely not be able to judge the cost to him of some threat to his privacy arising from the data mining operations and the linkages aimed at either providing him with more personalised services or establishing his culpability in the context of some supposed terrorist threat.

And what of the future? How easy will it be to place a value on what remains of our sense of privacy in 10 years, assuming encroachments continue, compared to the value that might be ascribed today? Is there a formula that can be devised to work out the net present value of privacy today compared with that in the AmI world a decade hence?

### 4.7.7  Misplaced trust in security mechanisms

Any technology, including single sign-on, that requires the user to relinquish control of his personal information should be regarded as a risk. Despite that risk, we may believe or we have been convinced that AmI privacy-enhancing technologies (PETs) will protect us. In doing so, we may be trusting security mechanisms that do not warrant our trust. In some cases, particularly where we are required by law and/or by law enforcement authorities, we may be forced to rely on (to trust) the adequacy of security mechanisms, of others' privacy policies.

This criticism has been levelled at national ID card schemes in the United Kingdom and elsewhere. Stella Rimington, a former director of MI5, has cast doubts on their efficacy as a security measure against terrorism. Security expert

Bruce Schneier has said, "The potential privacy encroachments of an ID card system are far from minor. And the interruptions and delays caused by incessant ID checks could easily proliferate into a persistent traffic jam in office lobbies and airports and hospital waiting rooms and shopping malls. It won't make us more secure. … No matter how unforgeable we make it, it will be forged. … And even if we could guarantee that everyone who issued national ID cards couldn't be bribed, initial cardholder identity would be determined by other identity documents … all of which would be easier to forge. … But the main problem with any ID system is that it requires the existence of a database. … Such a database would be a kludge of existing databases, databases that are incompatible, full of erroneous data, and unreliable. As computer scientists, we do not know how to keep a database of this magnitude secure, whether from outside hackers or the thousands of insiders authorized to access it. … A single national ID is an exceedingly valuable document, and accordingly there's greater incentive to forge it."[64]

In an AmI world, we may find an analogous situation, where identity management solutions are promoted by governments who expect us to take on trust that their solutions are inherently safe and secure. Many of us may accept their logic and blindly put our trust in the proposed solution until hard experience teaches us otherwise.

### 4.7.8 Lack of public awareness or concern about privacy rights

Many people are unaware of their rights and do not know what actually happens to their data. This is not surprising, given the opacity of the processes. Lack of public awareness is one thing, but lack of concern about one's rights or a willingness to trade off some of one's civil liberties for greater security is quite another. Recent public opinion polls in the United States suggest that a majority of the public is not really that concerned about encroachments on their privacy and civil liberties, that they are of a view that giving up some privacy or forsaking some of their civil liberties is the price of countering security threats, especially from terrorists.[65]

### 4.7.9 Lack of enforcement and erosion of rights

Most people are not even aware that data protection infringements are taking place. If they know or presume that infringement is taking place, they often just do not

[64] Schneier, Bruce, "National ID Cards", *Crypto-Gram Newsletter*, 15 April 2004. http://www.schneier.com/crypto-gram-back.html

[65] Drees, Caroline, "Civil liberties debate leaves much of America cold", Reuters, published in *The Washington Post*, 18 May 2006.

react, just as they regard spam as a nuisance but do not do anything about it. And even if they do react and want to enforce their rights, most EU legal systems require that damage must be proven.

Some of our personal data are held by the governments and organisations in our own countries, and some are held in other countries. Some countries may have legislation or regulation that affords relatively good protection of our privacy, while others may have regimes that offer no protection whatsoever.

No matter what the best of the legal regimes say, the complexity of the regulation, incomplete enforcement, and sometimes even conscious decisions by businesses and governments not to comply with the rules render legislation ineffective.[66]

The erosion of the right to privacy in the past century has been subtle, incremental, gradual and as relentless as technological advance. In today's surveillance society, where our personal data are not secure and are mined, monitored and captured, people have surrendered the right to be let alone in the interests of greater security (safety of society). For the most part, people have accepted the arguments of law enforcement and intelligence agencies that privacy has to be circumscribed so that they have the tools they need to apprehend criminals and terrorists and to combat the malicious code that floats around the Internet.

Perhaps most people view privacy as a right that can be sacrificed, at least to some extent, if it leads to greater security. But there are questions whether it *has* led to greater security, questions that are unlikely to be adequately answered before the widespread deployment of AmI networks in the near future.

Some have argued that privacy is fundamental to democracy, whether people recognise it or not. In addition to privacy, values such as autonomy (sovereignty), human dignity, physical and mental integrity and individuality are easily undermined by advanced methods of personal data collection, profiling and monitoring. Other fundamental rights – part of the European Charter of Fundamental Rights – may be under pressure in an AmI world, such as the freedom of thought (brain research shows that neural signals can be transformed into computer data and transmitted over networks), freedom of expression and information (the freedom to hold opinions and to receive and impart information and ideas without interference by public authorities and regardless of frontiers), freedom of assembly and association (location data can reveal assemblies, communication data can reveal associations), the right to education (computer education could become more valuable than traditional classroom education), non-discrimination (as a consequence of profiling), integration of persons with disabilities (who have less privacy as a (avoidable) consequence of system design) and so on.

After some years of experience of living in an AmI world, many people may care less about basic rights such as privacy than they do even today. But how much

---

[66] [PRIME] Hansen, M., and H. Krasemann (eds.), Privacy and Identity Management for Europe – PRIME White Paper, p. 12.

or how little they care will probably also be a direct function of how *their* privacy, *their* personal data, *their* communications are abused and/or to what extent they have ulterior motives for minimising their exposure to the authorities (i.e., they really may be criminals or terrorists). Press reports of abuse, of liberties taken with existing laws and constitutional rights may help to stimulate public demand for more protection of fundamental liberties.

### *4.7.10   People do not take adequate security precautions*

Since security mechanisms are not user-friendly, people often do not use them in a safe way. Today cyber citizens often use the same password or ID over different web sites and systems, which is a bit like writing down passwords on bits of yellow paper stuck on the side of computer screens: such actions undermine the point of having passwords. Similarly, use of the same identifier across multiple transactions can yield comprehensive profile information to the service provider on the usage, interests or behaviour of the user, by linking all available information, possibly from both the online and offline worlds.[67]

Unconsciously or not, most cyber citizens today do not take adequate care to protect their identity or identities. Some of the privacy-enhancing technology schemes that are being considered for today's cyber world and that of the AmI world may help reduce this problem, but it is unlikely to go away. Human nature, being what it is, means that some people just will not take even the most basic of steps towards protecting themselves. From this optic, identity theft may have a salutary effect of being a good learning experience, but this is a bit like saying that walking with your eyes closed across a busy street can be a good learning experience. In any event, once the theft has occurred, it may be as difficult or impossible to recover from it as from being run over by the number 9 bus.

### *4.7.11   Loss of control and technology paternalism*

As AmI networks manage more tasks in the future, some consumers may feel they exercise little or no control over the technologies that inhabit the space through which they move. The problems associated with loss of control can arise from (1) simple annoyances in day-to-day interactions with AmI, (2) uneasiness caused by the lack of transparency of systems operating in the background, (3) unpleasant or even frightening experiences if one is confronted with unexpected system behaviour, and (4) serious intimidations caused by malicious exploitation of technical

---

[67] [PRIME] Hansen, M., and H. Krasemann (eds.), Privacy and Identity Management for Europe – PRIME White Paper, p. 14.

vulnerabilities. In the first case, the system designer does not consider sufficient possibilities for users' control over the system. Failures of this kind originate in inadequate incorporation of user preferences and behavioural patterns in system design. Once more, the general problems with regard to adequate profiling establish natural limits to this remedy. In the second case, the very embeddedness and cloaked nature of many AmI services is accompanied by a lack of transparency. In the third case, the combination of technology dependency and a lack of understanding evoke stress and anger if the system does not behave as expected. And in the fourth case, security measures are circumvented.

One of the main rationales for creating and implementing AmI systems is to assist in the management of complex processes, which previously had to be accomplished by the user. AmI systems remove a certain burden – mostly standardised tasks with frequent repetitions – away from the individual in order to raise the level of convenience, security and/or efficiency. AmI systems will manage environmental parameters such as room temperature and lighting according to individual preferences, will manage communications according to predefined rules and/or based on machine-learning, and will implement security provisions that restrict certain behaviour or inform the user in case of a potential danger.

Another way of viewing loss of control is from the optic of technology paternalism,[68] which arises when machines make decisions autonomously on behalf of a user and supposedly in his best interest. Technology effectively infringes upon individual liberty if no easy-to-use and convenient override options are available and the user does not want to comply with the settings of an AmI system – for whatever reason. The possible drawbacks from technology paternalism can range from constant irritations to fundamental distrust in AmI, possibly leading to a decision to avoid AmI systems as far as possible.

## 4.7.12   Dependency

Two types of dependency can be identified: system and user dependency. **Technological dependency** refers to the fact that the proper functioning of a technology or a technological system such as AmI depends on the availability of other technologies of the same or even a previous generation. Due to the ubiquity of AmI, the likelihood of technological dependency will be amplified.

**User dependency** relates to a user's severe irritation, frustration or even panic if a certain technological function or service is temporarily not accessible, not available or does not function properly. In its extreme form, user dependency can display symptoms similar to those of psychological addictions or obsessions.

---

[68] For a detailed discussion of the concept, see Spiekermann, S., and F. Pallas, "Technology Paternalism – Wider Implications of Ubiquitous Computing", *Poiesis & Praxis*, Vol. 4, No. 1, 2006, pp. 6–18.

We have termed a negative aspect of user dependency as "AmI technosis", which refers to the disruption of social behaviour caused by a user's over-reliance and dependency on the new AmI technologies.

If the technology we have fully integrated into day-to-day routines is not accessible (even temporarily), we will not be able to perform in the usual way and that, in turn, will create additional stresses and strains on users and, possibly, society as a whole. Users may be uncertain whether it is possible to re-establish a previous functional state.

Another form of dependency is technological dependency and is manifested by insufficient interoperability. This vulnerability has two main aspects: spatial and temporal. The spatial aspect concerns the lack of interoperability between geographical entities. In order for AmI to function across borders, different regions and countries need to use technologies that interoperate. Further harmonisation of standards with varying degrees of geographical scope will be needed (e.g., EU, international). Some countries, however, will not be able to afford to fully comply with the standards created in developed countries. Solutions to overcome the potential divides based on insufficient interoperability need to be envisaged.

The temporal aspect refers to the lack of interoperability between different generations of tools and devices. This vulnerability may lead to the categorisation and, consequently, the discrimination of users based on socio-economic status or even because of conflicts of interests and preferences.

### 4.7.13   Unequal access and voluntary exclusion

The digital divide is often referred to as "information exclusion", where people are excluded from but also by information. In this sense, exclusion and discrimination regarding new technologies are two important aspects of the digital divide.

AmI technology has the potential – due to its foreseen user friendliness and intuitive aspects – to bridge some aspects of the current digital divide. On the other hand, AmI technology could also amplify other aspects of unequal access and use. This threat has technical as well as social and organisational dimensions. There are no guarantees that ambient intelligence services will become public utilities to the benefit of all. There will still be many people with limited or no access to more sophisticated AmI applications, and thus they will be unable to receive any of the envisioned value-added services and the expected benefits of the AmI environment. This is also the case between developing and developed countries.

It is likely that AmI, like any emerging technology, will be adopted gradually. Some people may refuse to adopt it, thus intentionally excluding or dividing themselves from others. Their rejection, a refusal to adopt new technologies, is basically caused by users' lack of trust in or sufficient awareness of new technologies and their implications; their resistance to change manifests an inertia of sorts displayed by a segment of society in response to the introduction of radical changes, which may in turn lead to unanticipated social disruptions.

# Chapter 5
# Safeguards

The multiplicity of threats and vulnerabilities associated with AmI will require a multiplicity of safeguards to respond to the risks and problems posed by the emerging technological systems and their applications. In some instances, a single safeguard might be sufficient to address a specified threat or vulnerability. More typically, however, a combination of safeguards will be necessary to address each threat and vulnerability. In still other instances, one safeguard might apply to numerous treats and vulnerabilities.

One could depict these combinations in a matrix or on a spreadsheet, but the spreadsheet would quickly become rather large and, perhaps, would be slightly misleading. Just as the AmI world will be dynamic, constantly changing, the applicability of safeguards should also be regarded as subject to a dynamic, i.e., different and new safeguards may need to be introduced in order to cope with changes in the threats and vulnerabilities.

For the purpose of this chapter, we have grouped safeguards into three main categories:

- Technological
- Socio-economic
- Legal and regulatory

## 5.1   Technological safeguards

The main privacy-protecting principles in network applications are:

- Anonymity (which is the possibility to use a resource or service without disclosure of user identity)
- Pseudonymity (the possibility to use a resource or service without disclosure of user identity, but to be still accountable for that use)
- Unlinkability (the possibility to use multiple resources or services without others being able to discover that these resources are being used by the same user)
- Unobservability (the possibility to use a resource or service without others being able to observe that the resource is being used).

D. Wright et al. (eds.), *Safeguards in a World of Ambient Intelligence.*
© Springer 2010

The main difference between existing network applications and emerging AmI applications is twofold: first, in the former case, the user has some understanding of which data about him are collected, and has some means to restrict data collection: e.g., to use a public computer anonymously to access certain Web pages; to switch off his mobile phone, to pay cash instead of using a Web service, etc. In the latter case, with the environment full of numerous invisible sensors (which might include video cameras), it is difficult (if not impossible) for users to understand and to control data collection and to achieve unobservability, anonymity and pseudonymity. Achieving anonymity is impossible if personal data are stored in a personal device (it is obvious that the data belong to the device owner) or in a video recording, as often suggested in AmI applications.

A second important difference between existing network applications and emerging AmI applications is that neither mobile devices nor Web usage penetrates through strong privacy-protecting borders such as walls (it is rarely 100 per cent certain who sends a request from a particular IP address or uses a mobile device) and the human body, while physiological, video and audio sensors, proposed for AmI applications, will have much stronger capabilities to identify a person, to reveal personal activities and feelings and to record them for future use (e.g., as in memory aid applications, which would allow a playback of events). Today, most of us are probably happy that some things are forgotten, but in an AmI world, everything may be remembered and nothing forgotten – if not in an individual memory then somewhere in the AmI system.

Furthermore, unlike most traditional computer applications, interactions in an AmI world are often envisioned to be initiated by technology (e.g., reminding a person to do something or opening an office door after verifying a user), which could be privacy-invasive in some situations, for example, if the AmI system reminds a user to pop his Prozac at a time when the user is in an important business meeting.

Future AmI applications in personal devices and smart environments will require stronger safeguards than today, many of which are not yet fully developed. Intelligent reasoning algorithms, limiting linkability and implementing strong access control to collected data, seem a promising way to protect privacy in AmI applications. However, if laws or poor access control allow the police, intelligence agencies or family members to search through personal data, AmI applications present potential privacy threats not only to the data subject, but also to other people who just happen to be in the background, just as today when we take a friend's photo in a busy street, other passers-by are also captured in the photo. The owner of an AmI memory aid might discover some interesting facts or faces in the background to which he had not paid any attention at the time he or she was concentrating on the main subject of conversation.

Current state-of-the art privacy protection is such that most efforts are concentrated on privacy protection in networked applications in the context of *current* technology, but even today current privacy protection mechanisms are far less mature than the technologies that can collect data. The distance between privacy-protecting technologies and data-capturing technologies is only like to grow. The

PRIME project, which studied the state of the art in privacy protection in network applications in 2005, pointed out many performance problems and security weaknesses.[1] The challenges in privacy-enhancing technologies for networked applications include developing methods for users to express their wishes regarding the processing of their data in machine-readable form ("privacy policies") and developing methods to ensure that the data are indeed processed according to users' wishes and legal regulations ("licensing languages" and "privacy audits": the former check the correctness of data processing during processing, while the latter check afterwards and should allow checking even after the data are deleted).

Privacy protection research is still new, and research on privacy protection in such emerging domains as personal devices, smart environments and smart cars is especially still in its infancy.[2] Privacy protection for personal mobile devices is particularly challenging due to the devices' limited capabilities and battery life. For these domains, only generic guidelines have been developed (see Lahlou et al.[3]). Langheinrich et al. show how difficult it might be to apply fair information practices (as contained in current data protection laws) to AmI applications.

Most of the research on privacy protection is concerned with dangers of information disclosure. Other privacy aspects have not received much attention from researchers. For example, the privacy aspect known as "the right to be let alone" is rarely discussed by technology researchers, despite its importance.

## 5.1.1   Research on overcoming the digital divide

Research is needed with regard to overcoming the digital divide in the context of AmI. The European Commission has already been sponsoring some research projects which form a foundation for needed future initiatives. Projects dealing with accessibility for all and e-Inclusion (such as COST219: "Accessibility for all to services and terminals for next generation mobile networks", ASK-IT: "Ambient intelligence system of agents for knowledge-based and integrated services for

---

[1] Camenisch, J. (ed.), First Annual Research Report, PRIME Deliverable D16.1, 2005. http://www.prime-project.eu.org/public/prime_products/deliverables/rsch/pub_del_D16.1.a_ec_wp16.1_V1_final.pdf

[2] Such research is, however, going on. An example is the EC-supported CONNECT project, which aims to implement a privacy management platform within pervasive mobile services, coupling research on semantic technologies and intelligent agents with wireless communications (including UMTS, WiFi and WiMAX) and context-sensitive paradigms and multimodal (voice/graphics) interfaces to provide a strong and secure framework to ensure that privacy is a feasible and desirable component of future ambient intelligence applications. The two-year project started in June 2006. http://cordis.europa.eu/search/index.cfm?fuseaction = proj.simpledocument&PJ_RCN = 8292795

[3] Lahlou, S., and F. Jegou, "European Disappearing Computer Privacy Design Guidelines V1", Ambient Agora Deliverable D15.4, Electricité de France, Clamart, 2003.

mobility impaired users") are concerned with standardisation, intuitive user interfaces, personalisation, interfaces to all everyday tools (e.g., domotics,[4] home health care, computer accessibility for people with disabilities and elderly people), adaptation of contents to the channel capacity and the user terminal and so on.

Standardisation in the field of information technology (including, e.g., biometrics) is important in order to achieve interoperability between different products. However, interoperability even in fairly old technologies (such as fingerprint-based identification) has not yet been achieved.

### 5.1.2   Minimal data collection, transmission and storage

Minimising personal data should be factored into all stages of collection, transmission and storage.[5] The goal of the minimal data transmission principle is that data should reveal little about the user even in the event of successful eavesdropping and decryption of transmitted data. Similarly, the principle of minimal data storage requires that thieves do not benefit from stolen databases and decryption of their data. Implementation of anonymity, pseudonymity and unobservability methods helps to minimise system knowledge about users at the stages of data transmission and storage in remote databases, but not in cases involving data collection by and storage in personal devices (which collect and store mainly the device owner's data) or storage of videos.

The main goals of privacy protection during data collection are, first, to prevent linkability between diverse types of data collected about the same user and, second, to prevent surveillance by means of spyware or plugging in additional pieces of hardware transmitting raw data (as occurs in wiretapping). These goals can be achieved by:

- Careful selection of hardware (so that data are collected and transmitted only in the minimally required quality and quantity to satisfy an application's goals, and there are no easy ways to spy on raw and processed data)
- An increase of software capabilities and intelligence (so that data can be processed in real time)
- Deleting data as soon as the application allows.

In practice, it is difficult to determine what "minimally needed application data" means. Moreover, those data can be acquired by different means. Thus, we suggest that data collection technologies less capable of violating personal privacy

---

[4] Domotics is the application of computer and robotic technologies to domestic appliances. Information and communication technologies are expected to provide for more comfort and convenience in and around the home. See www.domotics.com.

[5] Minimisation is a goal but has to be balanced against the need for data to provide services.

expectations be chosen over those more privacy-threatening technologies even if the accuracy of collected data decreases.

Software capabilities need to be maximised in order to minimise storage of raw data and avoid storage of data with absolute time and location stamps. We suggest this safeguard in order to prevent accidental logging of sensitive data, because correlation of different kinds of data by time stamps is fairly straightforward.

These safeguards are presented below in more detail:

- In our opinion, the most privacy-threatening technologies are physiological sensors and video cameras. Physiological sensors are privacy-threatening because they reveal what's going on in the human body and, accordingly, reveal health data and even feelings. Video cameras, especially those storing raw video data, are privacy-threatening because they violate people's expectations that "nobody can see me if I am hidden behind the wall" and because playback of video data can reveal more details than most people pay attention to in normal life. We suggest that usage of these two groups of devices should be restricted to safety applications until proper artificial intelligence safeguards (see below) are implemented.
- Instead of logging raw data, only data features (i.e., a limited set of pre-selected characteristics of data, e.g., frequency and amplitude of oscillations) should be logged. This can be achieved by using either hardware filters or real-time pre-processing of data or a combination of both.
- Time and location stamping of logged data should be limited by making it relative to other application-related information or by averaging and generalising the logged data.
- Data should be deleted after an application-dependent time, e.g., when a user buys clothes, all information about the textile, price, designer, etc., should be deleted from the clothes' RFID tag. For applications that require active RFID tags (such as for finding lost objects[6]), the RFID identifier tag should be changed, so that links between the shop database and the clothes are severed.
- Applications that do not require constant monitoring should switch off automatically after a certain period of user inactivity (e.g., video cameras should automatically switch off at the end of a game).
- Anonymous identities, partial identities and pseudonyms should be used wherever possible. Using different identities with the absolute minimum of personal data for each application helps to prevent discovery of links between user identity and personal data and between different actions by the same user.

---

[6]Orr, R.J., R. Raymond, J. Berman and F. Seay, "A System for Finding Frequently Lost Objects in the Home", *Technical Report* 99-24, Graphics, Visualization, and Usability Center, Georgia Tech, 1999.

### 5.1.3  Data and software security

Data and software protection from malicious actions should be implemented by intrusion prevention and by recovery from its consequences. Intrusion prevention can be active (such as antivirus software, which removes viruses) or passive (such as encryption, which makes it more difficult to understand the contents of stolen data).

At all stages of data collection, storage and transmission, malicious actions should be hindered by countermeasures such as the following:

- Cryptography
- Watermarking: a method to conceal a message in such a way that the very existence of the embedded message is undetectable
- Antivirus software and firewalls
- User-friendly updates of antivirus and firewall software
- Self-healing methods for personal devices, e.g., switching to redundant functionalities in the event of suspicious execution delays or spyware detection
- Detection of changes in hardware configuration
- Usage of trusted hardware modules
- Secure establishing of ad hoc communications.

### 5.1.4  Privacy protection in networking (transfer of identity and personal data)

Privacy protection in networking includes providing anonymity, pseudonymity and unobservability whenever possible. When data are transferred over long distances, anonymity, pseudonymity and unobservability can be provided by the following methods: first, methods to prove user authorisation locally and to transmit over the network only a confirmation of authorisation; second, methods of hiding relations between user identity and actions by, for example, distributing this knowledge over many network nodes. For providing anonymity, it is also necessary to use special communication protocols which do not use device IDs or which hide them. It is also necessary to implement authorisation for accessing the device ID: currently, most RFID tags and Bluetooth devices provide their IDs upon any request, no matter who actually asked for the ID. Another problem to solve is that devices can be distinguished by their analogue radio signals, and this can hinder achieving anonymity. Additionally, by analysing radio signals and communication protocols of a personal object, one can estimate the capabilities of embedded hardware and guess whether this is a new and expensive thing or old and inexpensive, which is an undesirable feature.

Unobservability can be implemented to some extent in smart spaces and personal area networks (PANs) by limiting the communication range so that signals do not penetrate the walls of a smart space or a car, unlike the current situation when two owners of Bluetooth-enabled phones are aware of each other's presence in neighbouring apartments.

Methods of privacy protection in network applications (mainly long-distance applications) include the following:

- Anonymous credentials (methods to hide user identity while proving the user's authorisation).
- A trusted third party: to preserve the relationships between the user's true identity and his or her pseudonym.
- Zero-knowledge techniques that allow one to prove the knowledge of something without actually providing the secret.
- Secret-sharing schemes: that allow any subset of participants to reconstruct the message provided that the subset size is larger than a predefined threshold.
- Special communication protocols and networks such as:
  - Onion routing: messages are sent from one node to another so that each node removes one encryption layer, gets the address of the next node and sends the message there. The next node does the same, and so on until some node decrypts the real user address.
  - Mix networks and crowds that hide the relationship between senders and receivers by having many intermediate nodes between them.
- Communication protocols that do not use permanent IDs of a personal device or object; instead, IDs are assigned only for the current communication session. Communication protocols that provide anonymity at the network layer, as stated in the PRIME deliverable,[7] are not suitable for large-scale applications: there is no evaluation on the desired security level, and performance is a hard problem.

## 5.1.5   Authentication and access control

Strong access control methods are needed in AmI applications. Physical access control is required in applications such as border control, airport check-ins and office access. Reliable user authentication is required for logging on to computers and personal devices as well as network applications such as mobile commerce, mobile voting and so on. Reliable authentication should have low error rates *and* strong anti-spoofing protection. Work on anti-spoofing protection of iris and fingerprint recognition is going on, but spoofing is still possible.

We suggest that really reliable authentication should be unobtrusive, continuous (i.e., several times during an application-dependent time period) and multimodal. So far, there has been limited research on continuous multimodal access control systems.

Authentication methods include the following:

---

[7] Camenish, 2005.

### 5.1.5.1 Biometrics

Some experts don't believe that biometrics should be the focus of the security approach in an AmI world, since the identification and authentication of individuals by biometrics will always be approximate, is like publishing passwords, can be spoofed and cannot be revoked after an incident.[8]

### 5.1.5.2 Tokens

Tokens are portable physical devices given to users who keep them in their possession.

### 5.1.5.3 Implants

Implants are small physical devices, embedded into a human body (nowadays they are inserted with a syringe under the skin). Implants are used for identification by unique ID number, and some research aims to add a GPS positioning module in order to detect the user's location at any time.

### 5.1.5.4 Multimodal fusion

With multimodal fusion, identification or authentication is performed by information from several sources, which usually helps to improve recognition rates and anti-spoofing capabilities. Multimodal identification and/or authentication can also be performed by combining biometric and non-biometric data.

Methods for reliable, unobtrusive authentication (especially for privacy-safe, unobtrusive authentication) should be developed. Unobtrusive authentication should enable greater security because it is more user-friendly. People are not willing to use explicit authentication frequently, which reduces the overall security level, while unobtrusive authentication can be used frequently.

Methods for context-dependent user authentication, which would allow user control over the strength and method of authentication, should be developed, unlike the current annoying situation when users have to go through the same authentication procedure for viewing weather forecasts and for viewing personal calendar data.

---

[8] See, for example, Engberg, Stephan, "Empowerment and Context Security as the route to Growth and Security", and Pfitzmann, Andreas, "Anonymity, unobservability, pseudonymity and identity management requirements for an AmI world". Both papers were presented at the SWAMI Final Conference, Brussels, 21–22 March 2006.

#### 5.1.5.5 User-configured applications settings

Recently, the meaning of the term "access control" has broadened to include checking which software is accessing personal data and how the personal data are processed.

Access control to software (data processing methods) is needed for enforcing legal privacy requirements and personal privacy preferences.

User-friendly interfaces are needed for providing awareness and configuring privacy policies. Maintaining privacy is not at the user's focus, so privacy information should not be a burden for a user. However, the user should easily be able to know and configure the following important settings:

- Purpose of the application (e.g., recording a meeting and storing the record for several years)
- How much autonomy the application has
- Information flow *from* the user
- Information flow *to* the user (e.g., when and how the application initiates interactions with the user).

Additionally, user-friendly methods are needed for fast and easy control over the environment, which would allow a person (e.g., a home owner but not a thief) to override previous settings, and especially those settings learned by AmI technologies.

Standard concise methods of initial warnings should be used to indicate whether privacy-violating technologies (such as those that record video and audio data, log personal identity data and physiological and health data) are used by ambient applications.

Licensing languages or ways to express legal requirements and user-defined privacy policies should be attached to personal data for the lifetime of their transmission, storage and processing. These would describe what can be done with the data in different contexts (e.g., in cases involving the merging of databases), and ensure that the data are really treated according to the attached licence. These methods should also facilitate privacy audits (checking that data processing has been carried out correctly and according to prescribed policies), including instances when the data are already deleted. These methods should be tamper-resistant, similar to watermarking.

### 5.1.6 Generic architecture-related solutions

High-level application design to provide an appropriate level of safeguards for the estimated level of threats can be achieved by data protection methods such as encryption and by avoiding usage of inexpensive RFID tags that do not have access control to their ID and by minimising the need for active data protection on the part of the user.

High-level application design should also consider what level of technology control is acceptable and should provide easy ways to override automatic actions. When communication capabilities move closer to the human body (e.g., embedded in clothes, jewellery or watches), and battery life is longer, it will be much more difficult to avoid being captured by ubiquitous sensors. It is an open question how society will adapt to such increasing transparency, but it would be beneficial if the individual were able to make a graceful exit from AmI technologies at his or her discretion.

To summarise, the main points to consider in system design are:

- Data filtering on personal devices is preferred to data filtering in an untrustworthy environment. Services (e.g., location-based services) should be designed so that personal devices do not have to send queries; instead, services could simply broadcast all available information to devices within a certain range. Such an implementation can require more bandwidth and computing resources, but is safer because it is unknown how many devices are present in a given location. Thus, it is more difficult for terrorists to plan an attack in a location where people have gathered.

- Authorisation should be required for accessing not only personal data stored in the device, but also for accessing device ID and other characteristics.

- Good design should enable detection of problems with hardware (e.g., checking whether the replacement of certain components was made by an authorised person or not). Currently, mobile devices and smart dust nodes do not check anything if the battery is removed, and do not check whether hardware changes were made by an authorised person, which makes copying data from external memory and replacement of external memory or sensors relatively easy, which is certainly inappropriate in some applications, such as those involved in health monitoring.

- Personal data should be stored not only encrypted, but also split according to application requirements in such a way that different data parts are not accessible at the same time.

- An increase in the capabilities of personal devices is needed to allow some redundancy (consequently, higher reliability) in implementation and to allow powerful multitasking: simultaneous encryption of new data and detection of unusual patterns of device behaviour (e.g., delays due to virus activity). An increase in processing power should also allow more real-time processing of data and reduce the need to store data in raw form.

- Software should be tested by trusted third parties. Currently, there are many kinds of platforms for mobile devices, and business requires rapid software development, which inhibits thorough testing of security and the privacy-protecting capabilities of personal devices. Moreover, privacy protection requires extra resources and costs.

- Good design should provide the user with easy ways to override any automatic action, and to return to a stable initial state. For example, if a personalisation application has learned (by coincidence) that the user buys beer every week, and includes beer on every shopping list, it should be easy to return to a previous state in which system did not know that the user likes beer. Another way to solve this problem might be to wait until the system learns that the user does not like beer. However, this would take longer and be more annoying.

- Good design should avoid implementations with high control levels in applications such as recording audio and images as well as physiological data unless it is strictly necessary for security reasons.
- Means of disconnecting should be provided in such a way that it is not taken as a desire by the user to hide.

## 5.1.7 Artificial intelligence safeguards

To some extent, all software algorithms are examples of artificial intelligence (AI) methods. Machine-learning and data-mining are traditionally considered to belong to this field. However, safeguarding against AmI threats requires AI methods with very advanced reasoning capabilities. Currently, AI safeguards are not mature, but the results of current research may change that assessment.

Many privacy threats arise because the reasoning capabilities and intelligence of software have not been growing as fast as hardware capabilities (storage and transmission capabilities). Consequently, the development of AI safeguards should be supported as much as possible, especially because they are expected to help protect people from accidental, unintentional privacy violation, such as disturbing a person when he does not want to be, or from recording some private activity. For example, a memory aid application could automatically record some background scene revealing personal secrets or a health monitor could accidentally send data to "data hunters" if there are no advanced reasoning and anti-spyware algorithms running on the user's device. Advanced AI safeguards could also serve as access control and antivirus protection by catching unusual patterns of data copying or delays in program execution.

We recommend that AmI applications, especially if they have a high control level, should be intelligent enough to:

- Detect sensitive data in order to avoid recording or publishing such data
- Adapt to a person's ethics
- Adapt to common sense
- Adapt to different cultures and etiquettes for understanding privacy-protecting requirements
- Summarise records intelligently in real time
- Interpret intelligently user commands with natural interfaces
- Provide language translation tools capable of translating ambiguous expressions
- Detect unusual patterns of copying and processing of personal data
- Provide an automatic privacy audit, checking traces of data processing, data- or code-altering, etc.

These requirements are not easy to fulfil in full scale in the near future; however, we suggest that it is important to fulfil these requirements as far as possible and as soon as possible.

## 5.1.8   Recovery means

Data losses and identity theft will continue into the future. However, losses of personal data will be more noticeable in the future because of the growing dependence on AmI applications. Thus, methods must be developed to inform all concerned people and organisations about data losses and to advise and/or help them to replace compromised data quickly (e.g., if somebody's fingerprint data are compromised, a switch should be made to another authentication method in all places where the compromised fingerprint was used).

Another problem, which should be solved by technology means, is recovery from loss of or damage to a personal device. If a device is lost, personal data contained in it can be protected from strangers by diverse security measures, such as data encryption and strict access control. However, it is important that the user does not need to spend time customising and training a new device (so that denial of service does not happen). Instead, the new device should itself load user preferences, contacts, favourite music, etc, from some back-up service, like a home server. We suggest that ways be developed to synchronise data in personal devices with a back-up server in a way that is secure and requires minimal effort by the user.

## 5.1.9   Conclusions and recommendations

We suggest that the most important, but not yet mature technological safeguards are the following:

- Communication protocols that either do not require a unique device identifier at all or that require authorisation for accessing the device identifier
- Network configurations that can hide the links between senders and receivers of data
- Improving access control methods by multimodal fusion, context-aware authentication and unobtrusive biometric modalities (especially behavioural biometrics, because they pose a smaller risk of identity theft) and by aliveness detection in biometric sensors
- Enforcing legal requirements and personal privacy policies by representing them in machine-readable form and attaching these special expressions to personal data, so that they specify how data processing should be performed, allow a privacy audit and prevent any other way of processing
- Developing fast and intuitive means of detecting privacy threats, informing the user and configuring privacy policies
- Increasing hardware and software capabilities for real-time data processing in order to minimise the lifetime and amount of raw data in a system
- Developing user-friendly means to override any automatic settings in a fast and intuitive way

- Providing ways of disconnecting in such a way that nobody can be sure why a user is not connected
- Increasing security by making software updates easier (automatically or semi-automatically, and at a convenient time for the user), detection of unusual patterns, improved encryption
- Increasing software intelligence by developing methods to detect and to hide sensitive data; to understand the ethics and etiquette of different cultures; to speak different languages and to understand and translate human speech in many languages, including a capability to communicate with the blind and deaf
- Developing user-friendly means for recovery when security or privacy has been compromised.

The technological safeguards require actions by industry. We recommend that industry undertake such technological safeguards. Industry may resist doing so because it will increase development costs, but safer, more secure technology should be seen as a good investment in future market growth and protection against possible liabilities. It is obvious that consumers will be more inclined to use technology if they believe it is secure and will shield, not erode their privacy.

We recommend that industry undertake such safeguards voluntarily. It is better to do so than to be forced by bad publicity that might arise in the media or from action by policy-makers and regulators.

Security guru Bruce Schneier got it right when he said that "The problem is ... bad design, poorly implemented features, inadequate testing and security vulnerabilities from software bugs. ... The only way to fix this problem is for vendors to fix their software, and they won't do it until it's in their financial best interests to do so. ... Liability law is a way to make it in those organizations' best interests."[9] If development costs go up, industry will, of course, pass on those costs to consumers, but since consumers already pay, in one way or another, the only difference is who they pay.

Admittedly, this is not a simple problem because hardware manufacturers, software vendors and network operators all face competition and raising the cost of development and lengthening the duration of the design phase could have competitive implications, but if all industry players face the same exacting liability standards, then the competitive implications may not be so severe as some might fear.

## 5.2   Socio-economic safeguards

Co-operation between producers and users of AmI technology in all phases from R&D to deployment is essential to address some of the threats and vulnerabilities posed by AmI. The integration of or at least striking a fair balance between the

---

[9] Schneier, Bruce, "Information security: How liable should vendors be?", *Computerworld*, 28 October 2004. http://www.schneier.com/essay-073.html

interests of the public and private sectors will ensure more equity, interoperability and efficiency. Governments, industry associations, civil rights groups and other civil society organisations can play an important role in balancing these interests for the benefit of all affected groups.

### 5.2.1  Standards

Standards form an important safeguard in many domains, not least of which are those relating to privacy and information security. Organisations should be expected to comply with standards, and standards-setting initiatives are generally worthy of support.

While there have been many definitions and analyses of the dimensions of privacy, few of them have become officially accepted at the international level, especially by the International Organization for Standardization. The ISO has at least achieved consensus on four components of privacy, i.e., anonymity, pseudonymity, unlinkability and unobservability.[10] (See section 5.1, p. 179, above for the definitions.)

Among the ISO standards relevant to privacy and, in particular, information security are ISO/IEC 15408 on evaluation criteria for IT security and ISO 17799, the Code of practice for information security management.

The ISO has also established a Privacy Technology Study Group (PTSG) under Joint Technical Committee 1 (JTC1) to examine the need for developing a privacy technology standard. This is an important initiative and merits support. Its work and progress should be tracked closely by the EC, Member States, industry and so on.

The ISO published its standard ISO 17799 in 2000, which was updated in July 2005. Since then, an increasing number of organisations worldwide formulate their security management systems according to this standard. It provides a set of recommendations for information security management, focusing on the protection of information as an asset. It adopts a broad perspective that covers most aspects of information systems security.[11]

Among its recommendations for organisational security, ISO 17999 states that "the use of personal or privately owned information processing facilities ... for processing business information, may introduce new vulnerabilities and necessary controls should be identified and implemented."[12] By implementing such controls,

---

[10] ISO/IEC 15408, *Information technology – Security techniques – Evaluation criteria for IT security*, First edition, International Organization for Standardization, Geneva, 1999. The standard is also known as the Common Criteria.

[11] Similar standards and guidelines have also been published by other EU Member States: The British standard BS7799 was the basis for the ISO standard. Another prominent example is the German IT Security Handbook (BSI, 1992).

[12] ISO/IEC 17799:2005(E), *Information Technology – Security techniques – Code of Practice for Information Security Management*, International Organization for Standardization, Geneva, 2005, p. 11.

organisations can, at the same time, achieve a measure of both organisational security and personal data protection.

ISO 17799 acknowledges the importance of legislative requirements, such as legislation on data protection and privacy of personal information and on intellectual property rights, for providing a "good starting point for implementing information security".[13]

ISO 17799 is an important standard, but it could be described more as a framework than a standard addressing specificities of appropriate technologies or how those technologies should function or be used. Also, ISO 17799 was constructed against the backdrop of today's technologies, rather than with AmI in mind. Hence, the adequacy of this standard in an AmI world needs to be considered. Nevertheless, organisations should state to what extent they are compliant with ISO 17799 and/or how they have implemented the standard.

## 5.2.2  Audits

Audit logs may not protect privacy since they are aimed at determining whether a security breach has occurred and, if so, who might have been responsible or, at least, what went wrong. Audit logs could have a deterrent value in protecting privacy and certainly they could be useful in prosecuting those who break into systems without authorisation.

In the highly networked environment of our AmI future, maintaining audit logs will be a much bigger task than now where discrete systems can be audited. Nevertheless, those designing AmI networks should ensure that the networks have features that enable effective audits.

## 5.2.3  Open standards

Apart from the positive effects of open innovations as such, we would support the development of protection software (against viruses, spam, spyware, etc.) under the open source development model. Though open source is no panacea for security problems, there is evidence that open source software can lead to robust and reliable products.

Promoting open systems and open standards at a European level could help to build a more trustworthy system, to mediate between public and private control over networked systems and, therefore, to contribute to security and privacy in AmI.[14]

---

[13] ISO/IEC 17799:2005, p. ix.

[14] Kravitz, D.W., K.-E. Yeoh and N. So, "Secure Open Systems for Protecting Privacy and Digital Services", in T. Sander (ed.), *Security and Privacy in Digital Rights Management*, ACM CCS-8 Workshop DRM 2001, Philadelphia, 5 November 2001, Revised Papers, Springer, Berlin, 2002, pp. 106–25; Gehring, R. A., "Software Development, Intellectual Property, and IT Security", *The Journal of Information, Law and Technology*, 1/2003. http://elj.warwick.ac.uk/jilt/03-1/gehring.html

### 5.2.4 Codes of practice

The OECD has been working on privacy and security issues for many years. It produced its first guidelines more than 25 years ago. Its Guidelines on the Protection of Privacy and Transborder Flows of Personal Data[15] were (are) intended to harmonise national privacy legislation. The guidelines were produced in the form of a Recommendation by the Council of the OECD and became applicable in September 1980. The guidelines are still relevant today and may be relevant in an AmI world too, although it has been argued that they may no longer be feasible in an AmI world.[16]

The OECD's more recent Guidelines for the Security of Information Systems and Networks are also an important reference in the context of developing privacy and security safeguards. These guidelines were adopted as a Recommendation of the OECD Council (in July 2002). In December 2005, the OECD published a report on "The Promotion of a Culture of Security for Information Systems and Networks", which it describes as a major information resource on governments' effective efforts to date to foster a shift in culture as called for in the aforementioned Guidelines for the Security of Information Systems and Networks.

In November 2003, the OECD published a 392-page volume entitled *Privacy Online: OECD Guidance on Policy and Practice*, which contains specific policy and practical guidance to assist governments, businesses and individuals in promoting privacy protection online at national and international levels.

In addition to these, the OECD has produced reports on other privacy-related issues including RFIDs, biometrics, spam and authentication.[17]

Sensible advice can also be found in a report published by the US National Academies Press in 2003, which said that to best protect privacy, identifiable information should be collected only when critical to the relationship or transaction that is being authenticated. The individual should consent to the collection, and the minimum amount of identifiable information should be collected and retained. The relevance, accuracy and timeliness of the identifier should be maintained and, when necessary, updated. Restrictions on secondary uses of the identifier are important in order to safeguard the privacy of the individual and to preserve the security of the authentication system. The individual should have clear rights to access information about how data are protected and used by the authentication system and the individual should have the right to challenge, correct and amend any information related to the identifier or its uses.[18]

---

[15] http://www.oecd.org/document/18/0,2340,en_2649_34255_1815186_1_1_1_1,00.html

[16] See Čas, Johann, "Privacy in Pervasive Computing Environments – A Contradiction in Terms?", *Technology and Society Magazine*, IEEE, Vol. 24, No. 1, Spring 2005, pp. 24–33.

[17] http://www.oecd.org/department/0,2688,en_2649_34255_1_1_1_1_1,00.html

[18] Kent, Stephen T., and Lynette I. Millett (eds.), *Who Goes There?*, Chapter 3.

Among privacy projects, PRIME has identified a set of privacy principles in the design of identity management architecture:

Principle 1:  Design must start from maximum privacy.
Principle 2:  Explicit privacy rules govern system usage.
Principle 3:  Privacy rules must be enforced, not just stated.
Principle 4:  Privacy enforcement must be trustworthy.
Principle 5:  Users need easy and intuitive abstractions of privacy.
Principle 6:  Privacy needs an integrated approach.
Principle 7:  Privacy must be integrated with applications.[19]

## 5.2.5  Trust marks and trust seals

Trust marks and trust seals can also be useful safeguards because the creation of public credibility is a good way for organisations to alert consumers and other individuals to an organisation's practices and procedures through participation in a programme that has an easy-to-recognise symbol or seal.

Trust marks and seals are a form of guarantee provided by an independent organisation that maintains a list of trustworthy companies that have been audited and certified for compliance with some industry-wide accepted or standardised best practice in collecting personal or sensitive data. Once these conditions are met, they are allowed to display a trust seal logo or label that customers can easily recognise.[20]

A trust mark must be supported by mechanisms necessary to maintain objectivity and build legitimacy with consumers. Trust seals and trust marks are, however, voluntary efforts that are not legally binding and an effective enforcement needs carefully designed procedures and the backing of an independent and powerful organisation that has the confidence of all affected parties.

Trust seals and trust marks are often promoted by industry, as opposed to consumer-interest groups. As a result, concerns exist that consumers' desires for stringent privacy protections may be compromised in the interest of industry's desire for the new currency of information. Moreover, empirical evidence indicates that even some eight years after the introduction of the first trust marks and trust seals in Internet commerce, citizens know little about them and none of the existing seals has reached a high degree of familiarity among customers.[21] Though

---

[19] For more details about each principle, see Sommer, Dieter, Architecture Version 0, PRIME Deliverable D14.2.a, 13 October 2004, pp. 35–36 and pp. 57–58. www.prime-project.eu.org

[20] Pennington, R., H.D. Wilcox and V. Grover, "The Role of System Trust in Business-to-Consumer Transactions", *Journal of Management Information System*, Vol. 20, No. 3, 2004, pp. 197–226; Subirana, B., and M. Bain, *Legal Programming: Designing Legally Compliant RFID and Software Agent Architectures for Retail Processes and Beyond*, Springer, New York, 2005.

[21] Moores, T., "Do Consumers Understand the Role of Privacy Seals in E-Commerce?" *Communications of the ACM*, Vol. 48, No. 3, 2005, pp. 86–91.

this does not necessarily mean that trust marks are not an adequate safeguard for improving security and privacy in the ambient intelligence world, it suggests that voluntary activities like self-regulation have – apart from being well designed – to be complemented by other legally enforceable measures.[22]

### 5.2.6  *Reputation systems and trust-enhancing mechanisms*

In addition to the general influence of cultural factors and socialisation, trust results from context-specific interaction experiences. As is well documented, computer-mediated interactions are different from conventional face-to-face exchanges due to anonymity, lack of social and cultural clues, "thin" information, and the uncertainty about the credibility and reliability of the provided information that commonly characterise mediated relationships.[23]

In an attempt to reduce some of the uncertainties associated with online commerce, many websites acting as intermediaries between transaction partners are operating so-called reputation systems. These institutionalised feedback mechanisms are usually based on the disclosure of past transactions rated by the respective partners involved.[24] Giving participants the opportunity to rank their counterparts creates an incentive for rule-abiding behaviour. Thus, reputation systems seek to imitate some of the real-life trust-building and social constraint mechanisms in the context of mediated interactions.

So far, reputation systems have not been developed for AmI services. And it seems clear that institutionalised feedback mechanisms will only be applicable to a subset of future AmI services and systems. Implementing reputation systems only makes sense in those cases in which users have real choices between different suppliers (for instance, with regard to AmI-assisted commercial transactions or information brokers). AmI infrastructures that normally cannot be avoided if one wants to take advantage of a service need to be safeguarded by other means, such as trust seals, ISO guidelines and regulatory action.

Despite quite encouraging experiences in numerous online arenas, reputation systems are far from perfect. Many reputation systems tend to shift the burden of quality control and assessment from professionals to the – not necessarily entirely

---

[22] Prins, J.E.J., and M.H.M. Schellekens, "Fighting Untrustworthy Internet Content: In Search of Regulatory Scenarios", *Information Polity*, Vol. 10, 2005, pp. 129–139.

[23] For an overview of the vast literature on the topic, see Burnett, R., and P.D. Marshall, *Web Theory: An Introduction*, Routledge, London 2002, pp. 45–80.

[24] Resnick, P., and R. Zeckhauser, "Trust Among Strangers in Internet Transactions: Empirical Analysis of eBay's Reputation System", in Michael R. Baye (ed.), *The Economics of the Internet and E-Commerce*, Vol. 11 of Advances in Applied Microeconomics, JAI Press, Amsterdam, 2002, pp. 127–157; Vishwanath, A., "Manifestations of Interpersonal Trust in Online Interaction", *New Media and Society*, Vol. 6, No. 2, 2004, pp. 224 et seq.

informed – individual user. In consequence, particularly sensitive services should not exclusively be controlled by voluntary and market-style feedbacks from customers. Furthermore, reputation systems are vulnerable to manipulation. Pseudonyms can be changed, effectively erasing previous feedback. And the feedback itself need not necessarily be sincere, either due to co-ordinated accumulation of positive feedback, due to negotiations between parties prior to the actual feedback process, because of blackmailing or the fear of retaliation.[25] Last but not least, reputation systems can become the target of malicious attacks, just like any net-based system.

An alternative to peer-rating systems are credibility-rating systems based on the assessment of trusted and independent institutions, such as library associations, consumer groups or other professional associations with widely acknowledged expertise within their respective domains. Ratings would be based on systematic assessments along clearly defined quality standards. In effect, these variants of reputation- and credibility-enhancing systems are quite similar to trust marks and trust seals. The main difference is that professional rating systems enjoy a greater degree of independence from vested interests. And, other than in the case of peer-rating systems which operate literally for free, the independent professional organisations need to be equipped with adequate resources.

On balance, reputation systems can contribute to trust-building between strangers in mediated short-term relations or between users and suppliers, but they should not be viewed as a universal remedy for the ubiquitous problem of uncertainty and the lack of trust.

## 5.2.7   Service contracts

A possible safeguard is a contract between the service provider and the user that has provisions about privacy rights and the protection of personal data and notification of the user of any processing or transfer of such data to third parties. While this is a possible safeguard, there must be some serious doubt about the negotiating position of the user. It's quite possible the service provider would simply say here are the terms under which I'm willing to provide the service, take it or leave it. Also, from the service provider's point of view, it is unlikely that he would want to conclude separate contracts with every single user.

In a world of ambient intelligence, such a prospect becomes even more unlikely in view of the fact that the "user", the consumer-citizen will be moving through

---

[25] Resnick, P., R. Zeckhauser, E. Friedman and K. Kuwabara, "Reputation Systems: Facilitating Trust in Internet Interactions", *Communications of the ACM*, 43 (12), 2000, pp. 45–48. http://www.si.umich.edu/~presnick/papers/cacm00/reputations.pdf.

different spaces where there is likely to be a multiplicity of different service providers. It may be that the consumer-citizen would have a digital assistant that would inform him of the terms, including the privacy implications, of using a particular service in a particular environment. If the consumer-citizen did not like the terms, he would not have to use the service.

Consumer associations and other civil society organisations (CSOs) could, however, play a useful role as a mediator between service providers and individual consumers and, more particularly, in forcing the development of service contracts (whether real or implicit) between the service provider and the individual consumer. Consumer organisations could leverage their negotiating position through the use of the media or other means of communication with their members. CSOs could position themselves closer to the industry vanguard represented in platforms such as ARTEMIS by becoming members of such platforms themselves. Within these platforms, CSOs could encourage industry to develop "best practices" in terms of provision of services to consumers.

### 5.2.8   Guidelines for ICT research

Government support for new technologies should be linked more closely to an assessment of technological consequences. On the basis of the far-reaching social effects that ambient intelligence is supposed to have and the high dynamics of the development, there is a clear deficit in this area.[26] Research and development (at least publicly supported R&D) must highlight future opportunities and possible risks to society and introduce them into public discourse. Every research project should commit itself to explore possible risks in terms of privacy, security and trust, develop a strategy to cover problematic issues and involve users in this process as early as possible.

A template for "design guidelines" that are specifically addressing issues of privacy has been developed by the "Ambient Agora" project[27] which has taken into account the fundamental rules by the OECD, notably its *Guidelines on the Protection of Privacy and Transborder Flows of Personal Data*, adopted on 23

---

[26] Langheinrich, M., "The DC-Privacy Troubadour – Assessing Privacy Implications of DC-Projects", Paper presented at the Designing for Privacy Workshop, DC Tales Conference, Santorini, Greece, 2003.

[27] Lahlou, S., and F. Jegou, "European Disappearing Computer Privacy Design Guidelines V1", Ambient Agora Deliverable D15.4, Electricité de France, Clamart, 2003. http://www.ambient-agoras.org/downloads/D15[1].4_-_Privacy_Design_Guidelines.pdf. The guidelines were subsequently and slightly modified and can be found at http://www.rufae.org/privacy. See also Langheinrich, M., "Privacy by Design – Principles of Privacy-Aware Ubiquitous Systems", in G.D. Abowd, B. Brumitt and S.A. Shafer (eds.), *Proceedings of the Third International Conference on Ubiquitous Computing* (Ubicomp 2001), Springer-Verlag, Berlin, 2001, pp. 273–291.

September 1980, and the more recent *Guidelines for the Security of Information Systems and Networks.*[28]

## 5.2.9 Public procurement

If the state acts as a buyer of strategically important innovative products and services, it contributes to the creation of the critical demand that enables suppliers to reduce their business risk and realise spillover effects. Thus, public procurement programmes can be used to support the demand for and use of improved products and services in terms of security and privacy or identity protection.

In the procurement of ICT products, emphasis should therefore be given to critical issues such as security and trustworthiness. As in other advanced fields, it will be a major challenge to develop a sustainable procurement policy that can cope with ever-decreasing innovation cycles. The focus should not be on the characteristics of an individual product or component, but on the systems into which components are integrated.

Moreover, it is important to pay attention to the secondary and tertiary impacts resulting from deployment of large technical systems such as ambient intelligence. An evaluation of the indirect impacts is especially recommended for larger (infrastructure) investments and public services.

While public procurement of products and services that are compliant with the EU legal framework and other important guidelines for security, privacy and identity protection is no safeguard on its own, it can be an effective means for the establishment and deployment of standards and improved technological solutions.[29]

## 5.2.10 Accessibility and social inclusion

Accessibility is a key concept in helping to promote the social inclusion of all citizens in the information society embedded with AmI technologies. Accessibility is needed to ensure user control, acceptance, enforceability of policy in a user-friendly manner and the provision of citizens with equal rights and opportunities in a world of ambient intelligence.

---

[28] *OECD Guidelines on the Protection of Privacy and Transborder Flows of Personal Data,* Organisation for Economic Co-operation and Development, Paris, 2001; *OECD Guidelines for the Security of Information Systems and Networks: Towards a Culture of Security,* Organisation for Economic Co-operation and Development, Paris, 2002.

[29] See for instance Edler, J. (ed.), "Politikbenchmarking Nachfrageorientierte Innovationspolitik", Progress report No. 99, Office for Technology Assessment at the German Parliament, Berlin, 2006; Molas-Gallart, J., "Government Policies and Complex Product Systems: The Case of Defence Standards and Procurement", *International Journal of Aerospace Management,* Vol. 1, No. 3, 2001, pp. 268–280.

Accessibility depends on four safeguards (or principles) relating to:

- Equal rights and opportunities
- Usability (vs complexity)
- Training
- Dependability.

### 5.2.10.1  Equal rights and opportunities

All citizens should have equal rights to benefit from the new opportunities that AmI technologies will offer. This principle promotes the removal of direct and indirect discrimination, fosters access to services and encourages targeted actions in favour of under-represented groups.

### 5.2.10.2  Usability (vs complexity of use)

This principle promotes system design according to a user-centric approach (i.e., the concept of "design for all"). The design-for-all concept enables all to use applications (speech technology for the blind, pictures for the deaf). It means designing in a way to make sure applications are user-friendly and can be used intuitively. In short, industry has to make an effort to simplify the usage of ICTs, rather than forcing prospective users to learn how to use otherwise complex ICTs.

Better usability will then support easy learning (i.e., learning by observation), user control and efficiency, thus increasing satisfaction and, consequently, user acceptance.

This principle aims to overcome user dependency and more particularly user isolation and stress due to the complexity of new technology, which leads to loss of control.

### 5.2.10.3  Training

Education programmes on how to use new technologies will increase user awareness about the different possibilities and choices offered by AmI technologies and devices. Training and education help to overcome user dependency and social disruptions. User awareness is important to reduce the voluntary exclusion caused by a misunderstanding on how the technology works.

### 5.2.10.4  Dependability

This safeguard is essential in order to prevent almost all facets of dependency, system dependency as well as user dependency.

## 5.2.11 Raising public awareness

Consumers need to be educated about the privacy ramifications arising from virtually any transaction in which they are engaged. An education campaign should be targeted at different segments of the population. School-age children should be included in any such campaign.

Any networked device, particularly those used by consumer-citizens, should come with a privacy warning much like the warnings on tobacco products.

When the UK Department of Trade and Industry (DTI) released its 2004 information security review, the UK e-commerce minister emphasised that everyone has a role to play in protecting information: "Risks are not well managed. We need to dispel the illusion the information security issues are somebody else's problem. It's time to roll up our sleeves."[30]

The OECD shares this point of view. It has said that "all participants in the new information society ... need ... a greater awareness and understanding of security issues and the need to develop a 'culture of security'."[31] The OECD uses the word "participants", which equates to "stakeholders", and virtually everyone is a participant or stakeholder – governments, businesses, other organisations and individual users. OECD guidelines are aimed at promoting a culture of security, raising awareness and fostering greater confidence (i.e., trust) among all participants.

There are various ways of raising awareness, and one of those ways would be to have some contest or competition for the best security or privacy-enhancing product or service of the year. The US government's Department of Homeland Security is sponsoring such competitions,[32] and Europe could usefully draw on their experience to hold similar competitions in Europe.

## 5.2.12 Education

In the same way as the principle that "not everything that you read in the newspapers is true" has long been part of general education, in the ICT age, awareness should generally be raised by organisations that are trustworthy and as close to the citizen as possible (i.e., on the local or regional level. Questions of privacy, identity

---

[30] Leyden, John, "Hackers cost UK.biz billions", *The Register*, 28 April 2004. http://www.theregister.co.uk/2004/04/28/dti_security_survey/

[31] *OECD Guidelines for the Security of Information Systems and Networks: Towards a culture of security*, OECD, Paris, 2002, p. 7.

[32] Lemos, Robert, "Cybersecurity contests go national", *The Register*, 5 June 2006. http://www.theregister.co.uk/2006/06/05/security_contests/. This article originally appeared at *Security Focus*. http://www.securityfocus.com/news/11394

and security are, or should be, an integral part of the professional education of computer scientists.

We agree with and support the Commission's "invitation" to Member States to "stimulate the development of network and information security programmes as part of higher education curricula".[33]


### 5.2.13   Media attention, bad publicity and public opinion

Perhaps one of the best safeguards is public opinion, stoked by stories in the press and the consequent bad publicity given to perceived invasions of privacy by industry and government.

New technologies often raise policy issues, and this is certainly true of ambient intelligence. AmI offers great benefits, but the risk of not adequately addressing public concerns could mean delays in implementing the technologies, a lack of public support for taxpayer-funded research and vociferous protests by privacy protection advocates.


### 5.2.14   Cultural safeguards

Cultural artefacts, such as films and novels, may serve as safeguards against the threats and vulnerabilities posed by advanced technologies, including ambient intelligence. Science fiction in particular often presents a dystopian view of the future where technology is used to manipulate or control people, thus, in so doing, such artefacts raise our awareness and serve as warnings against the abuse of technology. A *New York Times* film critic put it this way: "It has long been axiomatic that speculative science-fiction visions of the future must reflect the anxieties of the present: fears of technology gone awry, of repressive political authority and of the erosion of individuality and human freedom."[34]

An example of a cultural artefact is Steven Spielberg's 2002 film, *Minority Report*, which depicts a future embedded with ambient intelligence, which serves

---

[33] European Commission, *A strategy for a Secure Information Society – "Dialogue, partnership and empowerment"*, Communication from the Commission to the Council, the European Parliament, the European Economic and Social Committee and the Committee of the Regions, Brussels, COM(2006) 251, Brussels, 31 May 2006, p. 9 (section 3.3.1). http://ec.europa.eu/information_society/doc/com2006251.pdf

[34] Scott, A.O., "A Future More Nasty, Because It's So Near", Film review of "Code 46", *The New York Times*, 6 August 2004.

to convey messages or warnings from the director to his audience.[35] *Minority Report* is by no means unique as a cultural artefact warning about how future technologies are like a double-edged knife that cuts both ways.

### 5.2.15  Conclusion and recommendation

To implement socio-economic safeguards will require action by many different players. Unfortunately, the very pervasiveness of AmI means that no single action by itself will be sufficient as a safeguard. A wide variety of socio-economic safeguards, probably even wider than those we have highlighted in the preceding sections, will be necessary.

As implementation of AmI has already begun (with RFIDs, surveillance systems, biometrics, etc.), it is clearly not too soon to begin implementation of safeguards. We recommend, therefore, that all stakeholders, including the public, contribute to this effort.

## 5.3  Legal and regulatory safeguards

### 5.3.1  Introduction

The fast emergence of information and communication technologies and the growth of online communication, e-commerce and electronic services that go beyond the territorial borders of the Member States have led the European Union to adopt numerous legal instruments such as directives, regulations and conventions on e-commerce, consumer protection, electronic signature, cyber crime, liability, data protection, privacy and electronic communication ... and many others. Even the European Charter of Fundamental Rights will play an important role in relation to the networked information society.

Our analysis of the dark scenarios shows that we may encounter serious legal problems when applying the existing legal framework to address the intricacies of an AmI environment.

Our proposed legal safeguards should be considered as general policy options, aimed at stimulating discussion between stakeholders and, especially, policy-makers.

---

[35] Wright, David, "Alternative futures: AmI scenarios and *Minority Report*", *Futures*, Vol. 40:5, June 2008.

## 5.3.2   *General recommendations*

### 5.3.2.1   Law and architecture go together (Recommendation 1)

Law is only one of the available sets of tools for regulating behaviour, next to social norms, market rules, "code"[36] – the architecture of the technology (e.g., of cyberspace, wireless and wired networks, security design, encryption levels, rights management systems, mobile telephony systems, user interfaces, biometric features, handheld devices and accessibility criteria) and many other tools.

The regulator of ambient intelligence can, for instance, achieve certain aims directly by imposing laws, but also indirectly by, for example, influencing the rules of the market. Regulatory effect can also be achieved by influencing the architecture of a certain environment. The architecture of AmI might well make certain legal rules difficult to enforce (for example, the enforcement of data protection obligations on the Internet or the enforcement of copyright in peer-to-peer networks), and might cause new problems, particularly related to the new environment (spam, dataveillance[37]). On the other hand, the "code" has the potential to regulate by enabling or disabling certain behaviour, while law regulates via the threat of sanction. In other words, software and hardware constituting the "code", and architecture of the digital world, causing particular problems, can be at the same time the instrument to solve them. Regulating through code may have some specific advantages: Law traditionally regulates ex post, by imposing a sanction on those who did not comply with its rules (e.g., in the form of civil damages or criminal prosecution). Architecture regulates by putting conditions on one's behaviour, allowing or disallowing something, not allowing the possibility to disobey. It regulates ex ante.

Ambient intelligence is particularly built on software code. This code influences how ambient intelligence works, e.g., how the data are processed, but this code itself can be influenced and accompanied by regulation.[38] Thus, the architecture can be a tool of law. This finding is more than elementary. It shows that there is a choice: should the law change because of the "code"? Or should the law change "code" and thus ensure that certain values are protected?

---

[36] Lessig, Lawrence, "The Law of the Horse: What Cyberlaw Might Teach", *Harvard Law Review*, Vol. 113, 1999, pp. 501–546. See also Brownsword, Roger, "Code, control, and choice. Why East is East and West is West", *Legal Studies*, Vol. 25, No. 1, March 2005, pp. 1–21.

[37] "Dataveillance means the systematic monitoring of people's actions or communications through the application of information technology." See M. Hansen and H. Krasemann (eds.), *Privacy and Identity Management for Europe – PRIME White Paper – Deliverable 15.1.d.*, 18 July 2005, p. 11 (35 p.), with a reference to Clarke, R., "Information Technology and Dataveillance", *Communications of the ACM*, 31(5), May 1988, pp. 498–512, and re-published in C. Dunlop and R. Kling (eds.), *Controversies in Computing*, Academic Press, 1991, available at http://www.anu.edu/people/Roger.Clarke/DV/CACM88.html

[38] Contrary to the long-lasting paradigm, as Lessig writes. See Lessig, L., *Code and Other Laws of Cyberspace*, Basic Books, New York, 1999, and "The Law of the Horse: What Cyberlaw Might Teach", pp. 501–546.

The development of technology represents an enormous challenge for privacy, enabling increasing surveillance and invisible collection of data. A technology that threatens privacy may be balanced by the use of a privacy-enhancing technology: the "code", as Lessig claims,[39] can be the privacy saviour. Other technologies aim to limit the amount of data actually collected to the necessary minimum. However, most of the current technologies simply ignore the privacy implications and collect personal data when there is no such need. A shift of the paradigm to privacy-by-design is necessary to effectively protect privacy. Indeed, technology can facilitate privacy-friendly verification of individuals via, for example, anonymous and pseudonymous credentials. Leenes and Koops recognise the potential of these privacy-enhancing technologies (PETs) to enforce data protection law and privacy rules.[40] But they also point at problems regarding the use of such technologies, which are often troublesome in installation and use for most consumers. Moreover, industry is not really interested in implementing privacy-enhancing technology. They see no (economic) reason to do it.

The analysis of Leenes and Koops shows that neither useful technology, nor law is sufficient in itself. Equally important is raising stakeholder awareness, social norms and market rules. All regulatory means should be used and have to be used to respond to problems of the new environment to tackle it effectively. *For the full effectiveness of any regulation, one should always look for the optimal mixture of all accessible means.*[41]

### 5.3.2.2  Precaution or caution through opacity? (Recommendation 2)

As the impact and effects of the large-scale introduction of AmI in societies spawn a lot of uncertainties, the careful demarche implied by the precautionary principle, with its information, consultation and participation constraints, might be appropriate. The application of this principle might inspire us in devising legal policy options when, as regards AmI, fundamental choices between opacity tools and transparency tools must be made.[42] **Opacity tools** proscribe the interference by powerful actors into the individual's autonomy, while **transparency tools** accept such interfering practices, though under certain conditions which guarantee the control, transparency and accountability of the interfering activity and actors.

---

[39] Lessig, L., *Code and Other Laws of Cyberspace*, op. cit.

[40] Leenes, R., and B.J. Koops, " 'Code': Privacy's Death or Saviour?", *International Review of Law, Computers & Technology*, Vol. 19, No. 3, 2005.

[41] Lessig, L., "The Law of the Horse: What Cyberlaw Might Teach", op. cit., pp. 501–546.

[42] De Hert, Paul, and Serge Gutwirth, "Privacy, data protection and law enforcement. Opacity of the individual and transparency of power" in Erik Claes, Anthony Duff and Serge Gutwirth (eds.), *Privacy and the Criminal Law*, Antwerp/Oxford, Intersentia, 2006, pp. 61–104.

*In our opinion, most of the challenges arising in the new AmI environment should be addressed by transparency tools (such as data protection and security measures). Transparency should be the default position, although some prohibitions referring to political balances, ethical reasons or core legal concepts should be considered too.*

Legal scholars do not discuss law in general terms. Their way of thinking always involves an application of the law in concrete or exemplified situations. The legislator will compare concrete examples and situations with the law and will not try to formulate general positions or policies. Thus, the proposed legal framework will not deal with the AmI problems in a general way, but focus on concrete issues, and apply opacity and transparency solutions accordingly.

### 5.3.2.3 Central lawmaking for AmI is not recommended (Recommendation 3)

Another particularity of legal regulation in cyberspace is the absence of a central legislator. Though our legal analysis is based mostly on European law, we emphasise that not everything is regulated at a European level. Regulation of (electronic) identity cards, for instance, concerns a crucial element in the construction of an AmI environment, but is within the powers of the individual Member States.

Both at European and national level, some decision-making competences have been delegated to independent advisory organs (children's rights commissioners, data protection authorities). Hence, there exist many, what we can call, "little legislators" that adjust in some way the often executive power origin of legislation: The Article 29 Data Protection Working Party, national children's rights commissioners and international standardisation bodies can and do, for example, draft codes of conduct that constitute often (but not always) the basis for new legislation.

*We do not suggest the centralisation of the law-making process. On the contrary, we recommend respect for the diversity and plurality of lawmakers. The solutions produced by the different actors should be taken into consideration and be actively involved in policy discussions. Development of case law should also be closely observed. Consulting concerned citizens and those who represent citizens (including legislators) at the stage of development would increase the legitimacy of new technologies.*

## 5.3.3 Preserving the core of privacy and other human rights

### 5.3.3.1 Recommendations regarding privacy

Privacy aims to ensure no interference in private and individual matters. It offers an instrument to safeguard the opacity of the individual and puts limits to the interference by powerful actors into the individual's autonomy. Normative in nature, regulatory opacity tools should be distinct from regulatory transparency tools, of which the goal is to control the exercise of power rather than to restrict power.[43]

We observe today that the reasonable expectation of privacy is eroding due to emerging new technologies and possibilities for surveillance: it develops into an expectation of being monitored. Should this, however, lead to diminishing the right to privacy? Ambient intelligence may seriously threaten this value, but the need for privacy (e.g., the right to be let alone) will probably remain, be it in another form adapted to new infrastructures (e.g., the right to be left offline).

The right to privacy in a networked environment could be enforced by any means of protecting the individual against any form of dataveillance. Such means are in line with the data minimisation principle of data protection law, which is a complementary tool to privacy. However, in ambient intelligence where collecting and processing personal data is almost a prerequisite, new tools of opacity such as the right to be left offline (in time, e.g., during certain minutes at work, or in space, e.g., in public bathrooms) could be recognised.

Several instruments of opacity can be identified. We list several examples, and there may be others. Additional opacity recommendations are made in subsequent sections, for example, with regard to biometrics. We observe that there is not necessarily an internal coherence between the examples listed below. The list should be understood as a wish list or a list with suggestions to be consulted freely.

---

[43] Opacity designates a zone of non-interference which should not be confused with a zone of invisibility: privacy, for instance, does not imply secrecy; it implies the possibility of being oneself openly without interference. Another word might have been "impermeability" which is too strong and does not contrast so nicely with "transparency" as "opacity" does. See Hildebrandt, M., and S. Gutwirth (eds.), *Implications of profiling on democracy and the rule of law*, FIDIS (Future of Identity in the Information Society), Deliverable D7.4, September 2005. http://www.fidis.net. See also De Hert, P., and S. Gutwirth, "Privacy, data protection and law enforcement. Opacity of the individual and transparency of power" in E. Claes, A. Duff and S. Gutwirth (eds.), *Privacy and the Criminal Law*, Antwerp/Oxford, Intersentia, 2005, pp. 61–104; De Hert, P. and S. Gutwirth, "Making sense of privacy and data protection. A prospective overview in the light of the future of identity, location based services and the virtual residence" in *Security and Privacy for the Citizen in the Post-September 11 Digital Age: A prospective overview*, Report to the European Parliament Committee on Citizens' Freedoms and Rights, Justice and Home Affairs (LIBE), Institute for Prospective Technological Studies – Joint Research Centre, Seville, July 2003, pp. 111–162 (ftp://ftp.jrc.es/pub/EURdoc/eur20823en.pdf); and Gutwirth, S., "De polyfonie van de democratische rechtsstaat" [The polyphony of the democratic constitutional state] in M. Elchardus (ed.), *Wantrouwen en onbehagen* [Distrust and uneasiness], Balans 14, VUB Press, Brussels, 1998, pp. 137–193.

### 5.3.3.2   Recommendation regarding digital territories

The concept of a digital territory represents a vision that introduces the notions of space and borders in future digitised everyday life. It could be visualised as a bubble, the boundaries and transparency of which depend on the will of its owner. The notion of a digital territory aims for a "better clarification of all kinds of interactions in the future information society. Without digital boundaries, the fundamental notion of privacy or the feeling of *being at home* will not take place in the future information society."[44] The concept of digital territories encompasses the notion of a virtual residence, which can be seen as a virtual representation of the smart home.

The concept of digital territories could provide the individual with a possibility to access – and stay in – a private digital territory of his own at (any) chosen time and place. This private, digital space could be considered as an extension of the private home. Today, already, people store their personal pictures on distant servers, read their private correspondences online, provide content providers with their viewing and consuming behaviour for the purpose of digital rights management, communicate with friends and relatives through instant messengers and Internet telephony services. The "prognosis is that the physical home will evolve to 'node' in the network society, implying that it will become intimately interconnected to the virtual world."[45]

The law guarantees neither the establishment nor the protection of an online private space in the same way as the private space in the physical world is protected. Currently, adequate protection is lacking.[46] For example, the new data retention law requires that telecommunication service providers keep communication data at the disposal of law enforcement agencies. The retention of communication data relates to mobile and fixed phone data, Internet access, e-mail and e-telephony. Data to be retained includes the place, time, duration and destination of communications. What are the conditions for accessing such data? Is the individual informed when such data are accessed? Does he have the right to be present when such data are examined? Does the inviolability of the home extend to the data that are stored on a distant server? Another example of inadequate protection concerns the increasing access to home activities from a distance, for example, as a result of the communication data generated by domestic

---

[44] Beslay, L., and H. Hakala, "Digital Territory: Bubbles", in P. T. Kidd (ed.), *European Visions for the Knowledge Age: A Quest for New Horizons in the Information Society*, Cheshire Henbury, Macclesfield, UK, 2007, p. 1.
http://cybersecurity.jrc.es/docs/DigitalTerritoryBubbles.pdf

[45] De Hert, P., and S. Gutwirth, "Making sense of privacy and data protection. A prospective overview in the light of the future of identity, location based services and the virtual residence", p. 159.

[46] Idem. See also Beslay, L., and Y. Punie, "The Virtual Residence: Identity, Privacy and Security", *Security and Privacy for the Citizen in the Post-September 11 Digital Age: a Prospective Overview*, p. 67.

applications that are connected to the Internet. In both examples, there is no physical entrance in the private place.[47]

*To ensure that these virtual private territories become a private domain for the individual, a regulatory framework could be established to prevent unwanted and unnoticed interventions similar to that which currently applies to the inviolability of the home.*

*A set of rules needs to be envisaged to guarantee such protection, amongst them, the procedural safeguards similar to those currently applicable to the protection of our homes against state intervention (e.g., requiring a search warrant). Technical solutions aimed at defending private digital territories against intrusion should be encouraged and, if possible, legally enforced.[48] The individual should be empowered with the means to freely decide what kinds of information he or she is willing to disclose, and that aspect should be included in the digital territory concept. Similarly, vulnerable home networks should be granted privacy protection. Such protection could be extended to the digital movement of the person, that is, just as the privacy protection afforded the home has been or can be extended to the individual's car, so the protection could be extended to home networks, which might contact external networks.[49]*

### 5.3.3.3 Recommendation regarding spy-free territories for workers and children

Privacy at the workplace has already been extensively discussed.[50] Most of the legal challenges, we believe, that may arise can be answered with legal transparency rules. More drastic, prohibitive measures may be necessary in certain situations involving too far-reaching or unnecessary surveillance, which a society considers as infringing upon the dignity of the employee. *One of the ways to grant the individual a possibility to escape such disproportional surveillance at the workplace is obliging organisations to create physical spaces at work without surveillance technology, e.g., in social areas where the individual can take a short break and in bathrooms. The idea of cyber territories, accessible to the individual when he is in*

---

[47] See Koops, B.J., and M.M. Prinsen, "Glazen woning, transparant lichaam. Een toekomstblik op huisrecht en lichamelijke integriteit" ["Glass house, transparent body. A future view on home law and body integrity"], *Nederland Juristenblad*, 12 March 2005, pp. 624–630.

[48] De Hert, P., and S. Gutwirth, "Making sense of privacy and data protection: A prospective overview in the light of the future of identity, location-based services and virtual residence", p. 159.

[49] Beslay, L., and Y. Punie, "The Virtual Residence: Identity, Privacy and Security", p. 67.

[50] See Chapter 3, section 3.2.8.1. See also Article 29 Data Protection Working Party, *Working document on the surveillance of electronic communications in the workplace* (5401/01/EN/Final – WP 55), adopted on 29 May 2002. http://ec.europa.eu/justice_home/fsj/privacy/

*the workplace, would grant him the possibility of being alone in his private digital or cyber activities.*[51]

In addition, transparency rules are needed to regulate other, less intrusive problems. We recall here the specific role of law-making institutions in the area of labour law. Companies must discuss their surveillance system and its usage in collective negotiations with labour organisations and organisations representing employees before its implementation in a company or a sector, taking into account the specific needs and risks involved (e.g., workers in a bank vs. workers in public administration). *All employees should always be clearly and a priori informed about the employee surveillance policy of the employer (when and where surveillance is taking place, what is the finality, what information is collected, how long it will be stored, what are the (procedural) rights of the employees when personal data are to be used as evidence, etc.).*[52]

Specific cyber territories for children have to be devised along the same lines. The United Nations Convention on the Rights of the Child (1990) contains a specific privacy right for children, and sets up monitoring instruments such as National Children's Rights Commissioners. Opinions of such advisory bodies should be carefully taken into account in policy discussion. National Children's Rights Commissioners could take up problems relating to the permanent digital monitoring of children.

### 5.3.3.4    Recommendation regarding restrictions on use of illegally obtained evidence

As concluded in the legal analysis of the dark scenarios above, courts are willing to protect one's privacy but, at the same time, they tend to admit evidence obtained through a violation of privacy or data protection.[53] There is a lack of clarity and uniformity regarding the consequence of privacy violations.

The European Court of Human Rights is unwilling to recognise a right to have evidence obtained through privacy violations rejected.[54] This line of reasoning is

---

[51] A similar recommendation has been proposed by the Article 29 Data Protection Working Party in *Working Document on the Processing of Personal Data by means of Video Surveillance* (11750/02/EN–WP67), adopted on 25 November 2002. http://ec.europa.eu/justice_home/fsj/privacy/

[52] Article 29 Data Protection Working Party, *Working document on the surveillance of electronic communications in the workplace*, op. cit.

[53] See Chapter 3, section 3.2.8.1.

[54] In the case of *Khan* v. *United Kingdom*, judgment of 12 May 2000, the European Court of Human Rights rejected the exclusionary rule. In that case, the evidence was secured by the police in a manner incompatible with the requirements of Article 8 of the European Convention on Human Rights (ECHR). The court accepted that the admission of evidence obtained in breach of the privacy right is not necessarily a breach of the required fairness under Article 6 of ECHR (the right to a fair trial), since the process taken as a whole was fair in the sense of Article 6. The evidence against the accused was admitted and led to his conviction. The Khan doctrine (followed in cases such as *Doerga* v. *The Netherlands* and *P.G. and J.H.* v. *The United*

followed by at least some national courts.[55] The fact that there is no general acceptance of an exclusionary rule creates legal uncertainty. Its general acceptance is,
however, necessary to protect the opacity of the individual in a more effective
way.

*The departure from such position by the courts (namely "no inclusion of evi-
dence obtained through privacy and/or data protection law infringements") could
be considered and legislative prohibition of the admissibility (or general acceptance of the exclusionary rule) of such obtained evidence envisaged.*[56]

### 5.3.3.5 Recommendations regarding implants

In ambient intelligence, the use of implants can no longer be considered as a kind of
futuristic or extraordinary exception. Whereas it is clear that people may not be
forced to use such implants, people may easily become willing to equip themselves
with such implants on a (quasi) voluntary basis, be it, for example, to enhance their
bodily functions or to obtain a feeling of security through always-on connections to
anticipate possible emergencies. Such a trend requires a careful assessment of the
opacity and transparency principles at a national, European and international level.

Currently, in Europe, the issue of medical implants has already been addressed.[57]
In AmI, however, implants might be used for non-medical purposes. One of our
dark scenarios suggests that organisations could force people to have an implant so
they could be located anywhere at any time.

*Now, the law provides for strict safety rules for medical implants. The highest
standards of safety should be observed in AmI. The European Group on Ethics in
Science and New Technologies also recommends applying the precautionary
principle as a legal and ethical principle when it considers the use of implantable
technologies. It also reminds us that the principles of data minimisation, purpose
specification, proportionality and relevance are in particular applicable to
implants. It means, inter alia, that implants should only be used when the aim*

---

*Kingdom*) is discussed in De Hert, P., "De soevereiniteit van de mensenrechten: aantasting door
de uitlevering en het bewijsrecht" [Sovereignty of human rights: threats created by the law of
extradition and by the law of evidence], Panopticon, *Tijdschrift voor strafrecht, criminologie en
forensisch welzijnswerk*, Vol. 25, No. 3, 2004, pp. 229–238 and in De Hert, P., and F.P. Ölcer, "Het
onschadelijk gemaakte Europees privacybegrip. Implicaties voor de Nederlandse strafrechtspleging" [The notion of privacy made innocent. Implications for criminal procedure], *Strafblad. Het
nieuwe tijdschrift voor strafrecht*, Vol. 2, No. 2, 2004, pp. 115–134. See also De Hert, P.,
*Biometrics: legal issues and implications*, Background paper for the Institute of Prospective
Technological Studies, DG JRC, European Commission, Seville, January 2005, p. 33.

[55] Cour de Cassation (Belgium) 2 March 2005. http://www.juridat.be

[56] Although such a finding seems to contradict current case law (such as the *Khan* judgment), which
has refused to apply the principle that evidence obtained in violation of privacy be rejected.

[57] Council Directive 90/385/EEC on the approximation of the laws of the Member States relating
to active medical devices, *Official Journal* L 323, 26 November 1997, p. 39.

*cannot be achieved by less body-intrusive means. Informed consent is necessary to legitimise the use of implants. We agree with those findings.*

The European Group on Ethics in Science and New Technologies goes further, stating that non-medical (profit-related) applications of implants constitute a potential threat to human dignity. Applications of implantable surveillance technologies are only permitted when there is an urgent and justified necessity in a democratic society, and must be specified in legislation.[58] We agree that such applications should be diligently scrutinised.

*We propose that the appropriate authorities (e.g., the Data Protection Officer) control and authorise applications of implants after the assessment of the particular circumstances in each case. When an implant enables tracking of people, people should have the possibility to disconnect the implant at any given moment and they should have the possibility to be informed when a (distant) communication (e.g., through RFID) is taking place.*

*We agree with the European Group on Ethics in Science and New Technologies that irreversible ICT implants should not be used, except for medical purposes. Further research on the long-term impact of ICT implants is also recommended.[59]*

### 5.3.3.6  Recommendations regarding anonymity, pseudonymity, credentials and trusted third parties

Another safeguard to guarantee the opacity of the individual is the possibility to act under anonymity (or at least under pseudonymity or "revocable anonymity").

The Article 29 Working Party has considered anonymity as an important safeguard for the right to privacy. We repeat here its recommendations:

(a) The ability to choose to remain anonymous is essential if individuals are to preserve the same protection for their privacy online as they currently enjoy offline.
(b) Anonymity is not appropriate in all circumstances.
(c) Legal restrictions which may be imposed by governments on the right to remain anonymous, or on the technical means of doing so (e.g., availability of encryption products) should always be proportionate and limited to what is necessary to protect a specific public interest in a democratic society.
(d) The sending of e-mail, the passive browsing of World Wide Web sites, and the purchase of most goods and services over the Internet should all be possible anonymously.

---

[58] European Group on Ethics in Science and New Technologies, "Ethical Aspects of ICT Implants in the Human Body", Opinion to the Commission, 16 March 2005. http://europa.eu/comm/european_group_ethics/docs/avis20en.pdf

[59] Ibid.

(e) Some controls over individuals contributing content to online public fora are needed, but a requirement for individuals to identify themselves is in many cases disproportionate and impractical. Other solutions are to be preferred.

(f) Anonymous means to access the Internet (e.g., public Internet kiosks, prepaid access cards) and anonymous means of payment are two essential elements for true online anonymity.[60]

According to the Common Criteria for Information Technology Security Evaluation Document (ISO 15408),[61] anonymity is only one of the requirements for the protection of privacy, next to pseudonymity, unlinkability, unobservability, user control/information management and security protection. All these criteria should be considered as safeguards for privacy.

The e-signature Directive promotes the use of pseudonyms and, at the same time, aims to provide security for transactions. *The probative value of digital signatures is regulated differently under the national laws of Member States.[62] More clarity as to the legal value of electronic signatures would be desirable, so that its admissibility as evidence in legal proceedings is fully recognised.[63] The status of pseudonymity under the law needs further clarification. A pseudonym prevents disclosure of the real identity of a user, while still enabling him to be held responsible to the other party if necessary. It may provide a privacy tool, and remedy against profiling. Using different pseudonyms also prevents the merging of profiles from different domains. However, the legal status of pseudonyms is unclear, i.e., whether they should be regarded as anonymous data or as personal data falling under the data protection regime. Clarification of the issue is desirable.[64]*

---

[60] Article 29 Data Protection Working Party, *Recommendation 3/97: Anonymity on the Internet* (WP 6), adopted on 3 December 1997. http://ec.europa.eu/justice_home/fsj/privacy/

[61] ISO/IEC 15408, *Information technology – Security techniques – Evaluation criteria for IT security*, First edition, International Organization for Standardization, Geneva, 1999.

[62] The German example was described in Gasson, M., M. Meints and K. Warwick (eds.), *A study on PKI and Biometrics*, FIDIS (Future of Identity in the Information Society) Deliverable D3.2, July 2005, p. 29. http://www.fidis.net

[63] Currently, the Directive on electronic signatures states that only advanced electronic signatures (those based on a qualified certificate and created by a secure signature-creation device) satisfy the legal requirements of a signature in relation to data in electronic form in the same manner as a handwritten signature satisfies those requirements in relation to paper-based data and are admissible as evidence in legal proceedings. Member States must ensure that an electronic signature (advanced or not) is not denied legal effectiveness and admissibility as evidence in legal proceedings solely on the grounds that it is: (a) in electronic form, (b) not based upon a qualified certificate, (c) not based upon a qualified certificate issued by an accredited certification service-provider, or (d) not created by a secure signature-creation device.

[64] Olsen T., T. Mahler et al., "Privacy – Identity Management, Data Protection Issues in Relation to Networked Organisations Utilizing Identity Management Systems", *LEGAL Issues for the Advancement of Information Society Technologies*, LEGAL IST Deliverable D11, 2005. See the LEGAL IST web site http://193.72.209.176/default.asp?P = 369&obj = P1076

In ambient intelligence, the concept of *unlinkability* can become as important as the concept of anonymity or pseudonymity. Unlinkability "ensures that a user may make multiple uses of resources or services without others being able to link these uses together. ... Unlinkability requires that users and/or subjects are unable to determine whether the same user caused certain specific operations in the system."[65] When people act pseudonymously or anonymously, their behaviour in different times and places in the ambient intelligence network could still be linked and consequently be subject to control, profiling and automated decision-making: linking data relating to the same *non-identifiable* person may result in similar privacy threats as linking data that relate to an identified or identifiable person.

*Thus, in addition to and in line with the right to remain anonymous goes the use of anonymous and pseudonymous credentials, accompanied with unlinkability in certain situations (e.g., e-commerce), reconciling thus the privacy requirements with the accountability requirements of, e.g., e-commerce. In fact, such mechanisms should always be foreseen when disclosing someone's identity or when linking the information is not necessary. Such necessity should not be easily assumed, and in every circumstance more privacy-friendly technological solutions should be sought.[66] However, the use of anonymity should be well balanced. To avoid its misuse, digital anonymity could be further legally regulated, especially stating when it is not appropriate.[67]*

### 5.3.3.7   Recommendation regarding criminal liability rules

Provisions on criminal liability are necessary to prevent cybercrime. The criminal law is a basic means to fight hackers, attackers and others tending to abuse the possibilities of communication. Moreover, *effective* criminal provisions have a general deterrent effect, thus stopping people from undertaking criminal activities.

Cybercrime has cross-border dimensions and global implications. The restrictive interpretation of criminal laws ("nulla poena sine crimen") requires international consensus on the definition of the different crimes. This issue has been addressed

---

[65] ISO99 ISO IS 15408, 1999. http://www.commoncriteria.org/. See also Pfizmann, A., and M. Hansen, *Anonymity, Unlinkability, Unobservability, Pseudonymity, and Identity Management – A Consolidated Proposal for Terminology*, Version v0.27, 20 February 2006. http://dud.inf.tu-dresden.de/Anon_Terminology.shtml. Pfizmann and Hansen define unlinkability as follows: "*Unlinkability* of two or more items (e.g., subjects, messages, events, actions, ...) means that within the system (comprising these and possibly other items), from the attacker's perspective, these items are no more and no less related than they are related concerning his a-priori knowledge."

[66] Leenes, Ronald, and Bert-Jan Koops, "'Code': Privacy's Death or Saviour?", *International Review of Law, Computers &Technology*, Vol. 19, No. 3, 2005, p. 37.

[67] Compare Gasson, M., M. Meints and K. Warwick (eds.), "A study on PKI and biometrics", FIDIS (Future of Identity in the Information Society) Deliverable D3.2, July 2005, pp. 35–36. http://www.fidis.net

by the Cybercrime Convention,[68] which provides a definition for several criminal offences related to cybercrime and for general principles concerning international co-operation. The Cybercrime Convention, however, allows for different standards of protection. The Convention obliges its signatories to criminalise certain offences under national law, but Member States are free to narrow the scope of the definitions. The most important weakness of this Convention is the slow progress in its ratification by signatory states.

Council Framework Decision 2005/222/JHA[69] also provides for criminal sanctions against cybercrimes. The Framework decision is limited, however, both in scope and territory, since it only defines a limited number of crimes and is only applicable to the Member States of the European Union.

*It is highly recommended that governments ensure a proper ratification of the Cybercrime Convention. A "revision" mechanism would desirable so that signatories could negotiate and include in the Convention definitions of new, emerging cybercrimes. Specific provisions criminalising identity theft and (some forms of) unsolicited communication could be included within the scope of the Convention.*

International co-operation in preventing, combating and prosecuting criminals is needed and may be facilitated by a wide range of technological means, but these new technological possibilities should not erode the privacy of innocent citizens who are deemed to be not guilty until proven otherwise. Cybercrime prosecution, and more importantly crime prevention, might be facilitated by a wide range of technological means, among them, those that provide for the security of computer systems and data against attacks.[70]

## 5.3.4 Specific recommendations regarding data protection

### 5.3.4.1 Introduction

Almost all human activity in AmI can be reduced to personal data processing: opening doors, sleeping, walking, eating, putting lights on, shopping, walking in a street, driving a car, purchasing, watching television and even breathing. In short, all physical actions become digital information that relates to an identified or identifiable individual.

Often, the ambient intelligence environment will need to adapt to individuals and will therefore use profiles applicable to particular individuals or to individuals

---

[68] Council of Europe, Cybercrime Convention of 23 November 2001.

[69] Council Framework Decision 2005/222/JHA of 24 February 2005 on attacks against information systems, *Official Journal* L 069, 16 March 2005.

[70] Pfitzmann, A., and M. Kohntopp, "Striking a Balance between Cyber-Crime and Privacy", *IPTS Report* 57, EC-JRC, Seville, September 2001. http://www.jrc.es/home/report/english/articles/vol57/welcome.htm

within a group profile.[71] AmI will change not only the amount, but also the quality of data collected so that we can be increasingly supported in our daily life (a goal of ambient intelligence). AmI will collect data not only about what we are doing, when we do it and where we are, but also data on how we have experienced things.[72] One can assume that the accuracy of the profiles, on which the personalisation of services depends, will improve as the amount of data collected grows. But as others hold more of our data, so grow the privacy risks. Thus arises the fundamental question: Do we want to minimise personal data collection?

Instead of focusing on reducing the amount of data collected alone, should we admit that they are indispensable for the operation of AmI, and focus rather on empowering the user with a means to control such processing of personal data?

Data protection is a tool for empowering the individual in relation to the collection and processing of his or her personal data. The European Data Protection Directive imposes obligations on the data controller and supports the rights of the data subject with regard to the transparency and control over the collection and processing of data. It does not provide for prohibitive rules on data processing (except for the processing of sensitive data and the transfer of personal data to third countries that do not ensure an adequate level of protection). Instead, the EU data protection law focuses on a regulatory approach and on channelling, controlling and organising the processing of personal data. As the title of Directive 95/46/EC indicates, the Directive concerns both the protection of the individual with regard to the processing of personal data *and* the free movement of such data. The combination of these two goals in Directive 95/46/EC reflects the difficulties we encounter in the relations between ambient intelligence and data protection law.

There is no doubt that some checks and balances in using data should be put in place in the overall architecture of the AmI environment. Civil movements and organisations dealing with human rights, privacy or consumer rights, observing and reacting to the acts of states and undertakings might provide such guarantees. It is also important to provide incentives for all actors to adhere to legal rules. Education, media attention, development of good practices and codes of conducts are of crucial importance. Liability rules and rules aimed at enforcement of data protection obligations will become increasingly important.

---

[71] See Hildebrandt, M., and J. Backhouse (eds.), *Descriptive analysis and inventory of profiling practices*, FIDIS (Future of Identity in the Information Society) Deliverable D7.2; Schreurs, W., M. Hildebrandt, M. Gasson and K. Warwick (eds.), *Report on Actual and Possible Profiling Techniques in the Field of Ambient Intelligence*, FIDIS Deliverable D7.3. Chapter 7 of this deliverable deals with legal issues on profiling. See also Hildebrandt, M., and S. Gutwirth (eds.), *Implications of profiling on democracy and the rule of law*, FIDIS Deliverable D7.4, September 2005. http://www.fidis.net

[72] Lahlou, Saadi, Marc Langheinrich and Carsten Rocker, "Privacy and trust issues with invisible computers", *Communications of the ACM*, Vol. 48, No. 3, March 2005, pp. 59–60.

### 5.3.4.2 The right to be informed

Data protection law provides for the right to information on data processing, access to or rectification of data, which constitute important guarantees of individual rights. However, its practical application in an AmI era could easily lead to an administrative nightmare, as information overload would make it unworkable. We should try to remedy such a situation in a way that does not diminish this right.

The individual's right to information is a prerequisite to protect his interests. Such a right corresponds to a decentralised system of identity (data) management, but it seems useful to tackle it separately to emphasise the importance of the individual's having access to information about the processing of his data. Because of the large amounts of data to be processed in an AmI world, the help of or support by intelligent agents to manage such information streams seems indispensable.

*The obligation to inform the data subject about when and which data are collected, by whom and for what purpose gives the data subject the possibility to react to mistakes (and thus to exercise his right to rectification of data) or abuses, and enables him to enforce his right in case of damage. It would be desirable to provide the individual not only with information about what data relating to him are processed, but also what knowledge has been derived from the data.*

Information about what knowledge has been derived from the data could help the individual in proving causality in case of damage. Further research on how to reconcile access to the knowledge in profiles (which might be construed as a trade secret in some circumstances) with intellectual property rights would be desirable.

### 5.3.4.3 Information notices

The right to be informed could be facilitated by providing information in a machine-readable language, enabling the data subject to manage the information flow through or with the help of (semi-) autonomous intelligent agents. Of course, this will be more difficult in situations of passive authentication, where no active involvement of the user takes place (e.g., through biometrics and RFIDs).

Thus, information on the identity of the data controller and the purposes of processing could exist both in human-readable and machine-readable language. The way such information is presented to the user is of crucial importance – i.e., it must be presented in an easily comprehensible, user-friendly way.

In that respect, the Article 29 Working Party has provided useful guidelines and proposed multilayer EU information notices[73] essentially consisting of three layers:

---

[73] Article 29 Data Protection Working Party, *Opinion on More Harmonised Information Provisions* (11987/04/EN – WP 100), adopted on 25 November 2004. http://ec.europa.eu/justice_home/fsj/privacy/. The Article 29 WP provides examples of such notices (appendixes to the opinion on More Harmonised Information Provisions). See also Meints, M., "AmI – The European Perspective on Data Protection Legislation and Privacy Policies", presentation at the SWAMI International Conference on Safeguards in a World of Ambient Intelligence, 21 March 2006.

**Layer 1 – The short notice** contains core information required under Article 10 of the Data Protection Directive (identity of the controller, purpose of processing, or any additional information which, in the view of the particular circumstances of the case, must be provided to ensure fair processing). A clear indication must be given as to how the individual can access additional information.

**Layer 2 – The condensed notice** contains all relevant information required under the Data Protection Directive. This includes the name of the company, the purpose of the data processing, the recipients or categories of recipients of the data, whether replies to the questions are obligatory or voluntary, as well as the possible consequences of failure to reply, the possibility of transfer to third parties, the right to access, to rectify and oppose choices available to the individual. In addition, a point of contact must be given for questions and information on redress mechanisms either within the company itself or details of the nearest data protection agency.

**Layer 3 – The full notice** includes all national legal requirements and specificities. It could contain a full privacy statement with possible additional links to national contact information.

*We recommend that industry and law enforcement agencies consider an approach for AmI environments similar to that recommended by the Article 29 Working Party. Electronic versions of such notices should be sufficient in most of circumstances.*

### 5.3.4.4   Data laundering obligations

Our dark scenarios indicate a new kind of practice that has emerged in recent years in the sector of personal data trading: while some companies collect personal data in an illegal way (not informing the data subjects, transfer of data to third parties without prior consent, usage for different purposes, installing spyware, etc.), these personal data are shared, sold and otherwise transferred throughout a chain of existing and disappearing companies to the extent that the origin of the data and the original data collector cannot be traced back. This practice has been described as "data laundering", with analogy to money laundering: it refers to a set of activities aiming to cover the illegitimate origin of data. In our AmI future, we should assume the value of personal data and therefore the (illegal) trading in these data will only grow.

*A means to prevent data laundering could be to oblige those who buy or otherwise acquire databases, profiles and vast amounts of personal data to check diligently the legal origin of the data. Without checking the origin and/or legality of the databases and profiles, one could consider the buyer equal to a receiver of stolen goods and thus held liable for illegal data processing. They could be obliged to notify the national data protection officers when personal data(bases) are acquired. Those involved or assisting in data laundering could be subject to criminal sanctions.*

### 5.3.4.5  Restricted interoperability

AmI requires efficient, faultless exchanges of relevant data and information throughout the AmI network. The need for efficiency requires interoperable data formats and interoperable hardware and software for data processing. Dark scenario 2 (about the bus accident) has shown the need for interoperability in ambient intelligence, but it must be recognised that, at the same time, interoperable data and data processing technologies in all sectors and all applications could threaten trust, privacy, anonymity and security. Full interoperability and free flow of personal data are not always desirable, and should not be considered as unquestionable.

Interoperability can entail an unlimited availability of personal data for any purpose. Interoperability may infringe upon the finality and purpose specification principles and erode the rights and guarantees offered by privacy and data protection law. Moreover, the purposes for which the data are available are often too broadly described (What is "state security", "terrorism", "a serious crime"?). Data can become available afterwards for *any* purpose. Interoperability of data and data processing mechanisms facilitates possible *function creep* (use of data for purposes other than originally envisaged).

Interoperability could contribute to the criminal use of ambient intelligence, for example, by sending viruses to objects in the network (interoperability opens the door for fast transmission and reproduction of a virus) or abusing data (interoperable data formats make data practical for any usage). Interoperability is thus not only a technological issue.

Awareness – already today – of the possible negative sides of interoperability should bring about a serious assessment of both law and technology *before* the market comes up with tools for interoperability. Legal initiatives in France (e.g., requiring interoperability of the iTunes music platform) and sanctions imposed by the European Commission (imposing interoperability of the Microsoft work group server operating system) indicate clearly that the need for interoperability is desired on a political and societal level.

In the Communication from the Commission to the Council and the European Parliament on improved effectiveness, enhanced interoperability and synergies among European databases in the area of Justice and Home Affairs of 2005,[74] interoperability is defined as the "ability of IT systems and of the business processes they support to exchange data and to enable the sharing of information and knowledge". This is, however, a more technological definition: It "explicitly disconnects the technical and the legal/political dimensions from interoperability, assuming that the former are neutral and the latter can come into play later or elsewhere. ... Indeed, technological developments are not inevitable or neutral, which is *mutatis*

---

[74] Commission of the European Communities, Communication to the Council and the European Parliament on improved effectiveness, enhanced interoperability and synergies among European databases in the area of Justice and Home Affairs, COM (2005) 597 final, Brussels, 24 November 2005.

*mutandis* also the case for technical interoperability. The sociology of sciences has shown that any technological artefact has gone through many small and major decisions that have moulded it and given it its actual form. Hence, the development of information technology is the result of micro politics in action. Technologies are thus interwoven with organisation, cultural values, institutions, legal regulation, social imagination, decisions and controversies, and, of course, also the other way round. Any denial of this hybrid nature of technology and society blocks the road toward a serious political, democratic, collective and legal assessment of technology. This means that technologies cannot be considered as *faits accomplis* or extra-political matters of fact."[75]

This way of proceeding has also been criticised by the European Data Protection Supervisor, according to whom this leads to justifying the ends by the means.[76]

*Taking into account the need for interoperability, restrictions in the use and implementation of interoperability are required based on the purpose specification and proportionality principles. To this extent, a distinction between the processing of data for public (enforcement) and private (support) purposes may be absolutely necessary. Access to the databases by state enforcement agencies may be granted only on a case-by-case basis. Hereby, interoperability should not only be seen as a technical issue (solved by technical means) but also as a political, legal and economic issue (solved by political, legal and economic means). In addition, interoperability of the ambient intelligence system with third country systems that do not offer an adequate level of protection is very questionable.*[77]

To achieve certain purposes, for which access to data has been granted, access to the *medium* carrying the information (e.g., a chip) may be sufficient, for example, when verifying one's identity. There should always be clarity as to what authorities are being granted access. In the case of deployment of centralised databases, a list of authorities that have access to the data should be promulgated in an adequate,

---

[75] De Hert, P., and S. Gutwirth, "Interoperability of police databases: an accountable political choice", *International Review of Law Computers & Technology*, Vol. 20, Nos. 1 and 2, March–July 2006; De Hert, P., "What are the risks and what guarantees need to be put in place in a view of interoperability of the databases?", *Standard Briefing Note 'JHA & Data Protection'*, No. 1, 2006. www.vub.ac.be/LSTS/pub/Dehert/006.pdf

[76] European Data Protection Supervisor (EDPS), *Opinion on the Proposal for a Council Framework Decision on the exchange of information under the principle of availability (COM(2005) 490 final)*, Brussels, 28 February 2006. http://www.edps.eu.int/legislation/ Opinions_A/06-02-28_Opinion_availability_EN.pdf

[77] European Data Protection Supervisor (EDPS), *Opinion on the Proposal for a Regulation of the European Parliament and of the Council concerning the Visa Information System (VIS) and the exchange of data between Member States on short stay-visas (COM (2004)835 final)*, *Official Journal* C 181/27, 23 July 2005, pp. 13–29, sub 3.13. See also De Hert, P., "What are the risks and what guarantees need to be put in place in a view of interoperability of the databases?", *Standard Briefing Note 'JHA & Data Protection'*, No. 1. www.vub.ac.be/LSTS/pub/Dehert/006.pdf

official, freely and easily accessible publication.[78] Such clarity and transparency would contribute to security and trust, and protect against abuses in the use of databases.

### 5.3.4.6 Proportionality and purpose limitation principle

The proportionality and purpose limitation principles are already binding under existing data protection laws. The collection and exchange of data (including inter-operability) should be proportional to the goals for which the data have been collected. It will not be easy to elaborate the principles of proportionality and purpose limitation in ambient intelligence; previously collected data may serve for later developed applications or discovered purposes. Creation and utilisation of databases may offer additional benefits (which are thus additional purposes), e.g., in the case of profiling. Those other (derived) purposes should, as has been indicated in the opinion of the European Data Protection Supervisor, be treated as independent purposes for which all legal requirements must be fulfilled.[79]

Technical aspects of system operation can have a great impact on the way a system works, and how the proportionality principles and purpose limitation principles are implemented since they can determine, for example, if access to the central database is necessary, or whether access to the chip or part of the data is possible and sufficient.

### 5.3.4.7 Biometrics

Biometric technology can be a useful tool for authentication and verification, and may even be a privacy-enhancing technology. However, it can also constitute a threat to fundamental rights and freedoms. Thus, specific safeguards should be put in place. Biometric safeguards have already been subject of reflection by European data protection authorities: the Article 29 Working Party has stated that biometric data are in most cases personal data, so that data protection principles apply to processing of such data.[80]

---

[78] European Data Protection Supervisor, *Opinion on the Proposal for a Regulation of the European Parliament and of the Council concerning the Visa Information System (VIS) and the exchange of data between Member States on short stay-visas, (COM (2004) 835 final), Official Journal* C 181/27, 23 July 2005, pp. 13–29, sub 3.7.

[79] Ibid., sub 3.2.

[80] See Article 29 Data Protection Working Party, *Working document on biometrics* (12168/02/EN – WP 80), adopted on 1 August 2003. http://ec.europa.eu/justice_home/fsj/privacy/. See also Gasson, M., M. Meints and K. Warwick (eds.), *A study on PKI and biometrics*, FIDIS (Future of Identity in the Information Society) Deliverable D3.2, July 2005, available through http://www.fidis.net [deliverables]

On the principle of proportionality, the Article 29 Working Party points out that it is not necessary (for the sake of authentication or verification) to store biometric data in central databases, but in the medium (e.g., a card) remaining in the control of the user.[81]

*The creation and use of centralised databases should always be carefully assessed before their deployment, including prior checking by data protection authorities. In any case, all appropriate security measures should be put in place.*

Framing biometrics is more than just deciding between central or local storage. Even storage of biometric data on a smart card should be accompanied by other regulatory measures that take the form of rights for the card-holders (to know what data and functions are on the card; to exclude certain data or information from being written onto the card; to reveal at discretion all or some data from the card; to remove specific data or information from the card).[82]

Biometric data should not be used as unique identifiers, mainly because biometric data still do not have sufficient accuracy.[83] Of course, this might be remedied in the progress of science and technological development. There remains, however, a second objection: using biometrics as the primary key will offer the possibility of merging different databases, which can open the doors for abuses (function creep).

European advisory bodies have considered biometric data as a unique identifier. Generally speaking, since the raw data might contain more information than actually needed for certain finalities (including information not known at the moment of the collection, but revealed afterwards due to progress in science, e.g., health information related to biometric data), it should not be stored.[84] Other examples of opacity rules applied to biometrics might be prohibitions on possible use of

---

[81] See also De Hert, P., *Biometrics: legal issues and implications*, Background paper for the Institute of Prospective Technological Studies, EC – JRC, Seville, January 2005, p. 13. http://cybersecurity.jrc.es/docs/LIBE%20Biometrics%20March%2005/LegalImplications_Paul_de_Hert.pdf

[82] Neuwrit, K., *Report on the protection of personal data with regard to the use of smart cards*, Report of Council of Europe (2001), accessible through http://www.coe.int/T/E/Legal_affairs/Legal_co-operation/Data_protection/Documents, quoted by De Hert, P., *Biometrics: legal issues and implications*, p. 26.

[83] Institute for Prospective Technological Studies (IPTS), *Biometrics at the frontiers: assessing the impact on Society*, Study commissioned by the LIBE committee of the European Parliament, EC – DG Joint Research Centre, Seville, February 2005. http://ec.europa.eu/justice_home/doc_centre/freetravel/doc/biometrics_eur21585_en.pdf

[84] European Data Protection Supervisor (EDPS), *Comments on the Communication of the Commission on interoperability of European databases*, 10 March 2006. http://www.edps.eu.int/legislation/Comments/06-03-10_Comments_interoperability_EN.pdf

"strong" multimodal biometrics (unless for high security applications)[85] for every-day activities. Codes of conduct can be appropriate tools to further regulate the use of technology in particular sectors.[86]

### 5.3.4.8  RFIDs

AmI will depend on profiling as well as authentication and identification technolo-gies. To enable ubiquitous communication between a person and his or her environ-ment, both things and people will have to be traced and tracked. RFID seems to offer the technological means to implement such tracking. Like biometrics, RFID is an enabling technology for real-time monitoring and decision making. Like biometrics, RFIDs can advance the development of AmI and provide many advan-tages for users, companies and consumers.[87]

No legislative action seems needed to support this developing technology. Market mechanisms are handling this. There is, however, a risk to the privacy inter-ests of the individual and for a violation of the data protection principles, as CASPIAN and other privacy groups have stated.[88]

RFID use should be in accordance with privacy and data protection regulations. The Article 29 Working Party has already given some guidelines on the application of the principles of EU data protection legislation to RFIDs.[89] It stresses that the data protection principles (purpose limitation principle, data quality principle, conservation

---

[85] Biometrics, and especially multimodal biometrics, may increase the security of an application, and thus privacy as well. In its technical safeguards, the SWAMI consortium proposes use of mul-timodal fusion of several less privacy-intrusive biometrics (e.g., fat, weight, height, gait, behavioural patterns) for everyday activities such as user-friendly authentication in mobile phones or authenti-cation of car drivers. Such biometrics have low accuracy now, but such emerging technology will most likely become more accurate in due course and represent a lower threat to privacy than "strong" biometrics. For high-security applications, we recommend a combination of strong mul-timodal biometrics with continuous unobtrusive authentication by less strong biometrics, provided that all modalities of the strong biometrics have good anti-spoofing capabilities. Use of biometrics should always be accompanied by adequate PETs.

[86] Article 29 Data Protection Working Party, *Working document on biometrics*.

[87] A description of RFID technologies and of usages can be found in Hildebrandt, M., and J. Backhouse (eds.), *Descriptive analysis and inventory of profiling practices*, FIDIS (Future of Identity in the Information Society), Deliverable D7.2, June 2005. http://www.fidis.net

[88] See e.g. Günther, Oliver, and Sarah Spiekermann, "RFID and the Perception of Control: The Consumer's View", *Communications of the ACM*, Vol. 48, No. 9, 2005, pp. 73–76.

[89] Article 29 Data Protection Working Party, *Working document on data protection issues related to RFID technology* (10107/05/EN – WP 105), 19 January 2005. http://ec.europa.eu/justice_home/fsj/privacy/

principle, etc.) must always be complied with when the RFID technology leads to processing of personal data in the sense of the Data Protection Directive.[90]

As the Article 29 Working Party points out, the consumer should always be informed about the presence of both RFID tags and readers, as well as of the responsible controller, the purpose of the processing, whether data are stored and the means to access and rectify data. Here, techniques of (visual) indication of activation would be necessary. The data subject would have to give his consent for using and gathering information for any specific purpose. The data subject should also be informed about what type of data is gathered and whether the data will be used by the third parties.

*In AmI, such rights may create a great burden, both on the data subject, on the responsible data controller and on all data processors. Though adequate, simplified notices about the data processors' policy would be welcome (e.g., using adequate pictograms or similar means). In our opinion, such information should always be provided to consumers when RFID technology is used, even if the tag does not contain personal data in itself.*[91] The data subject should also be informed how to discard, disable or remove the tag. The right to disable the tag can relate to the consent principle of data protection, since the individual should always have the possibility to withdraw his consent.

*Disabling the tag should at least be possible when the consent of the data subject is the sole legal basis for processing the data. Disabling the tag should not lead to any discrimination of the consumer (e.g., in terms of the guarantee conditions).*

Technological and organisational measures (e.g., the design of RFID systems) are of crucial importance in ensuring that the data protection obligations are respected (privacy by design, e.g., by technologically blocking unauthorised access to the data). Thus, availability and compliance with privacy standards are of particular importance.[92]

---

[90] The concept of "personal data" in the context of RFID technology is contested. WP 29 states: In assessing whether the collection of personal data through a specific application of RFID is covered by the Data Protection Directive, we must determine: (a) the extent to which the data processed relates to an individual, and (b) whether such data concerns an individual who is identifiable or identified. Data relates to an individual if it refers to the identity, characteristics or behaviour of an individual or if such information is used to determine or influence the way in which that person is treated or evaluated. In assessing whether information concerns an identifiable person, one must apply Recital 26 of the Data Protection Directive which establishes that "account should be taken of all the means likely reasonably to be used either by the controller or by any other person to identify the said person." And further: "Finally, the use of RFID technology to track individual movements which, given the massive data aggregation and computer memory and processing capacity, are if not identified, identifiable, also triggers the application of the data protection Directive." Article 29 Data Protection Working Party, *Working document on data protection issues related to RFID technology*, 10107/05/EN WP 105, 19 January 2005, point 4.1.

[91] Still, such information on a tag can be a unique identifier enabling the profiling activities. See Kardasiadou, Z., and Z. Talidou, *Report on Legal Issues of RFID Technology*, LEGAL IST (Legal Issues for the Advancement of Information Society Technologies) Deliverable D15, 2006, p. 16.

[92] Some standards have already been adopted in the RFID domain. The International Organization for Standardization has developed sector-specific standards, as well as more generic standards. EPCglobal Ltd. (www.epcglobal.org), an industry-driven organisation, has also developed some standards on connecting servers containing information relating to items identified by EPC (Electronic Product Code) numbers.

*Data protection concerns should be reflected in initiatives leading to standardisation of technical specifications. Privacy assessment of each particular RFID application could be a legally binding obligation.*[93]

*Further research on the RFID technology and its privacy implications is recommended.*[94] This research should also aim at determining whether any legislative action is needed to address the specific privacy concerns of RFID technology. Further development of codes of conducts and good practices is also recommended.[95]

### 5.3.4.9 Data protection and profiling: a natural pair

Profiling is as old as life, because it is a kind of knowledge that unconsciously or consciously supports the behaviour of living beings, humans not excluded. It might well be that the insight that humans often "intuitively know" something before they "understand" it can be explained by the role profiling spontaneously plays in our minds.

Thus, there is no reason to prohibit automated profiling and data mining concerning individuals with opacity rules. Profiling activities should in principle be ruled by transparency tools. In other words, the processing of personal data – collection, registration and processing in the strict sense – is not prohibited but submitted to a number of conditions guaranteeing the visibility, controllability and accountability of the data controller and the participation of the data subjects.

Data protection rules apply to profiling techniques (at least in principle).[96] The collection and processing of traces surrounding the individual must be considered as processing of personal data in the sense of existing data protection legislation.

---

[93] Borking, J., "RFID Security, Data Protection & Privacy, Health and Safety Issues", presentation made during European Commission Consultation on RFID, Brussels, 17 May 2006.

[94] Such research is now carried out in the framework of the FIDIS programme. See FIDIS Deliverable 7 on AmI, profiling and RFID.

[95] An example of such (emerging) initiatives is the EPCglobal Ltd. guidelines regarding privacy in RFID technology, http://www.epcglobal.org/public_policy/public_policy_guidelines.html, and the CDT (Centre for democracy and technology) Working Group on RFID: Privacy Best Practices for Deployment of RFID Technology, Interim Draft, 1 May 2006. http://www.cdt.org/privacy/20060501rfid-best-practices.php. Though these are good examples of the involvement of stakeholders in the discussion, the results are not fully satisfactory. As a compromise between the different actors, the guidelines do not go far enough in protecting the interests of consumers. The ambiguous wording of some guidelines (e.g., whether practicable) may give flexibility to industry to interpret the scope of their obligations.

[96] We add "at least in principle" because we are well aware of the huge practical difficulties of effectively enforcing and implementing data protection, more particularly in the field of profiling. See Schreurs, W., M. Hildebrandt, M. Gasson and K. Warwick (eds.), *Report on Actual and Possible Profiling Techniques in the Field of Ambient Intelligence*, FIDIS (Future of Identity in the Information Society) Deliverable D7.3, August 2005. http://www.fidis.net. See also Schreurs, W., M. Hildebrandt, E. Kindt and M. Vanfleteren, *"Cogitas, ergo sum.* The role of data protection law and non-discrimination law in group profiling in the private sector", to be published in M. Hildebrandt and S. Gutwirth (eds.), *Profiling the European citizen*, Springer, Dordrecht, 2008 (forthcoming). See also the discussion on RFID above.

Both individual and group profiling are dependent on such collection and on the processing of data generated by the activities of individuals. And that is precisely why, in legal terms, no profiling is thinkable outside data protection.

There is an ongoing debate in contemporary legal literature about the applicability of data protection to processing practices with data that are considered anonymous, i.e., they do not allow the identification of a specific individual.[97] Some contend that data protection rules do not allow processing practices that bring together data on certain individuals without trying to identify the said individual (in terms of physical location or name). Some contend that data protection rules do not apply to profiling practices that process data relating to non-identifiable persons (in the sense of the Data Protection Directive). We hold that it is possible to interpret the European data protection rules in a broad manner covering *all* profiling practices,[98] but the courts have not spoken on this yet.

*Data protection should apply to all profiling practices. When there is confusion in the application and interpretation of the legal instruments, they should be adapted so that they do apply to all profiling practices. Profiling practices and the consequent personalisation of the ambient intelligence environment lead to an accumulation of power in the hands of those who control the profiles and should therefore be made transparent.*

The principles of data protection are an appropriate starting point to cope with profiling in a democratic constitutional state as they do impose good practices. Nevertheless, while the default position of data protection is transparency ("Yes, you can process, but ..."), it does not exclude opacity rules ("No, you cannot process, unless ..."). In relation to profiling, two examples of such rules are relevant. On the one hand, of course, there is the explicit prohibition against taking decisions affecting individuals solely on the basis of the automated application of a profile without human intervention (see Article 15 of the Data Protection Directive).[99] This seems obvious because in such a situation, probabilistic knowledge is applied to a real

---

[97] We recall that *personal data* in the EU Data Protection Directive refers to "any information relating to an identified or identifiable natural person" (Article 1).

[98] De Hert, P., "European Data Protection and E-Commerce: Trust Enhancing?", in J.E.J. Prins, P.M.A. Ribbers, H.C.A. Van Tilborg, A.F.L. Veth and J.G.L. Van Der Wees (eds.), *Trust in Electronic Commerce*, Kluwer Law International, The Hague, 2002, pp. 190–199. See also Schreurs, W., M. Hildebrandt, E. Kindt and M. Vanfleteren, "*Cogitas, ergo sum*. The role of data protection law and non-discrimination law in group profiling in the private sector."

[99] Article 15 on automated individual decisions states: "1. Member States shall grant the right to every person not to be subject to a decision which produces legal effects concerning him or significantly affects him and which is based solely on automated processing of data intended to evaluate certain personal aspects relating to him, such as his performance at work, creditworthiness, reliability, conduct, etc. 2. Subject to the other Articles of this Directive, Member States shall provide that a person may be subjected to a decision of the kind referred to in paragraph 1 if that decision: (a) is taken in the course of the entering into or performance of a contract, provided the request for the entering into or the performance of the contract, lodged by the data subject, has been satisfied or that there are suitable measures to safeguard his legitimate interests, such as arrangements allowing him to put his point of view; or (b) is authorized by a law which also lays down measures to safeguard the data subject's legitimate interests."

person. On the other hand, there is the (quintessential) purpose specification principle, which provides that the processing of personal data must meet specified, explicit
and legitimate purposes. As a result, the competence to process is limited to well-
defined goals, which implies that the processing of the same data for other incompatible aims is prohibited. This, of course, substantially restricts the possibility to link
different processing and databases for profiling or data mining objectives. The purpose specification principle is definitely at odds with the logic of interoperability and
availability of personal data: the latter would imply that all databases can be used
jointly for profiling purposes.[100] In other words, the fact that the legal regime applicable to profiling and data mining is data protection does not give a *carte blanche* to
mine and compare personal data that were not meant to be connected.[101]

The European Data Protection Supervisor indicated in his Annual Report 2005 a
number of processing operations that are likely to encompass specific risks to the
rights and freedoms of data subjects, even if the processing does not occur upon
sensitive data. This list relates to processing operations (a) of data relating to health
and to suspected offences, offences, criminal convictions or security measures, (b)
intended to evaluate personal aspects relating to the data subject, including his or her
ability, efficiency and conduct, (c) allowing linkages, not provided for pursuant to
national or Community legislation, between data processed for different purposes,
and (d) for the purpose of excluding individuals from a right, benefit or contract.[102]

### 5.3.5 *Specific recommendations regarding security*

Software can be the tool for regulating one's behaviour by simply allowing or not
allowing certain acts. Thus, technology constituting the "software code" can affect
the architecture of the Internet (and thus potentially of AmI) and can provide effective means for enforcing the privacy of the individual. For example, cryptology
might give many benefits: it could be used for pseudonymisation (e.g., encrypting
IP addresses) and ensuring confidentiality of communication or commerce.[103]

*Privacy-enhancing technologies can have an important role to play, but they
need an adequate legal framework.*

---

[100] De Hert, P., "What are the risks and what guarantees need to be put in place in view of interoperability of police databases?", Standard Briefing Note 'JHA & Data Protection', No. 1, produced
in January 2006 on behalf of the European Parliament. http://www.vub.ac.be/LSTS/

[101] Gutwirth, S., and P. De Hert, "Regulating profiling in a democratic constitutional state", to be
published in M. Hildebrandt and S. Gutwirth (eds.), *Profiling the European citizen*, Springer,
Dordrecht, 2008 (forthcoming).

[102] European Data Protection Supervisor (EDPS), *Annual Report 2005*, pp. 22–23. http://www.
edps.eu.int/publications/annual_report_en.htm

[103] Leenes, Ronald, and Bert-Jan Koops, "'Code': Privacy's Death or Saviour?", *International
Review of Law, Computers &Technology*, Vol. 19, No. 3, 2005, pp. 331–332.

The Directive on the legal protection of software[104] obliges Member States to provide appropriate remedies against a person committing any act of putting into circulation, or the possession for commercial purposes of, any means the sole intended purpose of which is to facilitate the unauthorised removal or circumvention of any technical devices which may have been applied to protect a computer program. This mechanism aims to protect programmes enforcing the intellectual property rights against circumvention.

*Similar legal protection against circumvention of privacy-enhancing technologies could be legally foreseen.*

Technology might go beyond what the law permits (e.g., DRM prevents intellectual property infringements but at the same time might limit the rights of the lawful user). Negative side effects of such technologies should be eliminated. More generally, when introducing new technology on the market, manufacturers together with relevant stakeholders should undertake a privacy impact assessment. *Development of a participatory impact assessment procedure would allow stakeholders to quickly identify and react to any negative features of technology* (see also section 5.3.10).

### 5.3.5.1  Empowering the individual

The European Data Protection Directive imposes obligations on the data controller and gives rights to the data subject. It aims to give the individual control over the collection and processing of his data. Many provisions in the Data Protection Directive have several weaknesses in an AmI environment. Principles of proportionality and fairness are relative and may lead to different assessments in similar situations; obtaining consent might not be feasible in the constant need for the collection and exchange of data; obtaining consent can be simply imposed by the stronger party. Individuals might not be able to exercise the right to consent, right to information, access or rectification of data due to the overflow of information. Thus, those rules might simply become unworkable in an AmI environment. And even if workable (e.g., thanks to the help of the digital assistants), are they enough? Should we not try to look for an approach granting the individual even more control?

### 5.3.5.2  Decentralised identity (data) management

Several European projects are involved in research on identity management. They focus on a decentralised approach, where a user controls how much and what kind of information he or she wants to disclose. Identity management systems, while operating on a need-to-know basis, offer the user the possibility of acting under pseudonyms, under unlinkability or anonymously, if possible and desirable.

---

[104] Council Directive 91/250/EEC of 14 May 1991 on the legal protection of computer programs, *Official Journal* L 122, 17 May 1991, pp. 0042–0046.

Among the other examples of such systems,[105] there are projects that base their logic on the assumption that the individual has property over his data, and then could use licensing schemes when a transfer of data occurs. Granting him property over the data[106] is seen as giving him control over the information and its usage in a "distribution chain". However, it is doubtful if granting him property over the data will really empower the individual and give him a higher level of protection and control over his data. The property model also assumes that the data are disseminated under a contract. Thus, the question might arise whether the Data Protection Directive should serve as a minimum standard and thus limit the freedom of contracts.[107] But as our dark scenarios show, there exist many cases in which the individual will not be able to *freely* enter into a contract. Another question arises since *our* data are not always collected and used for commercial purposes. In most situations, the processing of personal data is a necessary condition for entering into a contractual relation (whereas the Data Protection Directive states in Article 7 that data processing without the individual's consent to use of his personal data is legitimate when such processing is necessary for the performance of a contract). The most obvious example is the collection of data by police, social insurance and other public institutions. The individual will not always be free to give or not give his data away. The property model will not address these issues. It will also not stop the availability of the data via public means.[108]

A weakness of the property model is that it might lead to treating data only as economic assets, subject to the rules of the market. But the model's aim is different: the aim is to protect personal data, without making their processing and transfer impossible. Regarding data as property also does not address the issue of the profile knowledge derived from personal data. This knowledge is still the property of the owner or the licenser of the profile. The data-as-property option also ignores the new and increasingly invisible means of data collection, such as RFIDs, cameras or online data collection methods.

Discussing the issue of whether personal data should become the individual's property does not solve the core problem. On the one hand, treating data as property may lead to a too high level of protection of personal information, which would conflict with the

---

[105] An overview of the existing identity management systems has been given by Bauer, M., M. Meints and M. Hansen (eds.), *Structured Overview on Prototypes and Concepts of Identity Management Systems*, FIDIS (Future of Identity in the Information Society) Deliverable D3.1, September 2005, and Hildebrandt, M., and J. Backhouse (eds.), *Descriptive analysis and inventory of profiling practices*, FIDIS Deliverable D7.2, June 2005, and Müller, G., and S. Wohlgemuth (eds.), *Study on Mobile Identity Management*, FIDIS Deliverable D3.3, May 2005. http://www.fidis.net

[106] See Lessig, L., *Code and other law of cyberspace*, Basic Books, New York, 1999, and Leenes, Ronald, and Bert-Jan Koops, " 'Code': Privacy's Death or Saviour?", *International Review of Law, Computers & Technology*, Vol. 19, No. 3, 2005, p. 329. See also Samuelson, P., "Privacy As Intellectual Property?", *Stanford Law Review*, Vol. 52, 2000.

[107] However, currently this is not the case. The weaker party in the contract is now protected by the general principles of law. Prins, J.E.J., "The Propertization of Personal Data and Identities", *Electronic Journal of Comparative Law*, Vol. 8.3, October 2004. http://www.ejcl.org/

[108] Ibid.

extensive processing needs of AmI. On the other hand, it would, by default, turn personal data into a freely negotiable asset, no longer ruled by data protection, but left to market mechanisms and consent of the data subjects (more often than not to the detriment of the latter). Finally, the data-as-property option loses its relevance in the light of a focus upon anonymisation and pseudonymisation of data processed in AmI applications.

The PRIME consortium proposes identity management systems controlled by data subjects.[109] It aims to enable individuals to negotiate with service providers the disclosure of personal data according to the conditions defined. Such agreement would constitute a contract.[110] An intelligent agent could undertake the management on the user side. This solution is based on the data minimisation principle and on the current state of legislation. It proposes the enforcement of (some) current data protection and privacy laws. It seems to be designed more for the needs of the world today than for a future AmI world. The user could still be forced to disclose more information than he or she wishes, because he or she is the weaker party in the negotiation; he or she needs the service.

The FIDIS consortium has also proposed a decentralised identity management, the vision of which seems to go a bit further than the PRIME proposal. It foresees that the user profiles are stored on the user's device, and preferences relevant for a particular service are (temporarily) communicated to the service provider for the purpose of a single service. The communication of the profile does not have to imply disclosure of one's identity. If there is information extracted from the behaviour of the user, it is transferred by the ambient intelligent device back to the user, thus updating his profile.[111] Thus, some level of exchange of knowledge is foreseen in this model, which can be very important for the data subject's right to information.

*A legal framework for such sharing of knowledge from an AmI-generated profile needs to be developed, as well as legal protection of the technical solution enabling such information management. Such schemes rely on automated protocols for the policy negotiations. The automated schemes imply that the consent of the data subject is also organised by automatic means. We need a legal framework to deal with the situation wherein the explicit consent of the data subject for each collection of data is replaced by a "consent" given by an intelligent agent.*

In such automated models, one could envisage privacy policies following the data. Such "sticky" policies, attached to personal data, would provide for clear information and indicate to data processors and controllers which privacy policy applies to the data concerned.[112] Sticky policies could facilitate the auditing and

---

[109] Hansen, M., and H. Krasemann (eds.), *Privacy and Identity Management for Europe*, PRIME White Paper, Deliverable D 15.1.d, 18 July 2005. http://www.prime-project.eu.org/

[110] Ibid., p. 7.

[111] Schreurs, W., M. Hildebrandt, M. Gasson and K. Warwick (eds.), *Report on Actual and Possible Profiling Techniques in the Field of Ambient Intelligence*, FIDIS (Future of Identity in the Information Society) Deliverable D7.3, August 2005, p. 32. http://www.fidis.net

[112] Meints, M., "AmI – The European Perspective on Data Protection Legislation and Privacy Policies", Presentation at the SWAMI Final Conference on Safeguards in a World of Ambient Intelligence, 21 March 2006.

self-auditing of the lawfulness of the data processing by data controllers.[113] *In any event, research in this direction is desirable.*

*Since AmI is also a mobile environment, there is a need to develop identity management systems addressing the special requirements of mobile networks.* The FIDIS consortium has prepared a technical survey of mobile identity management. It has identified some special challenges and threats to privacy in the case of mobile networks and made certain recommendations:

- Location information and device characteristics both should be protected.
- Ease of use of the mobile identity management tools and simplified languages and interfaces for non-experts should be enhanced.
- A verifiable link between the user and his digital identity has to be ensured. Accordingly, privacy should also be protected in peer-to-peer relationships.[114]

### 5.3.6 Specific recommendations regarding consumer protection law

The importance of consumer protection will grow in ambient intelligence, because of the likelihood that consumers will become more dependent on online products and services, and because product and service providers will strengthen their bargaining position through an increasing information asymmetry. Without the constraints of law, ambient intelligence service providers could easily dictate the conditions of participation in new environments. Consumer protection should find the proper balance in AmI.

Consumer protection law defines the obligations of the producers and the rights of consumer and consists of a set of rules limiting the freedom to contract, for the benefit of the consumer. Consumer protection law plays a role of its own, but can support the protection of privacy and data protection rights.[115]

The basis for the European framework for consumer protection rules can be found in Article 153 of the EC Treaty: "In order to promote the interests of consumers and to ensure a high level of consumer protection, the Community shall contribute to protecting the health, safety and economic interests of consumers, as well as

---

[113] For example, such an approach was adopted by the PAW project (Privacy in an Ambient World), which has developed the language enabling the distribution of data in a decentralised architecture, with the usage policies attached to the data that would provide information on what kind of usage has been licensed to the particular actor (licensee). Enforcement relies on auditing. http://www.cs.ru.nl/paw/results.html

[114] Müller, G., and S. Wohlgemuth (eds.), *Study on Mobile Identity Management*, FIDIS Deliverable D3.3, May 2005. http://www.fidis.net

[115] Although our focus here is on services, in an AmI environment, it can be difficult to distinguish between a product and a service. It is often difficult to draw the line between the two, and different legal regimes apply. Product liability issues are discussed below under section 5.3.8.4.

to promoting their right to information, education and to organise themselves in order to safeguard their interests."

Consumer protection at European level is provided by (amongst others) Directive 93/13 on unfair terms in consumer contracts,[116] Directive 97/7 on consumer protection in respect of distance contracts[117] and the Directive on liability for defective products (discussed below). Directive 93/13 and Directive 97/7 were both already discussed (in Chapter 3, sections 3.2.8.6 and 3.3.8.3). In many respects, their rules are not fitted to AmI and they need to be re-adapted. This especially relates to extending the scope of protection of those directives, thereby making sure that all services and electronic means of communications and trading are covered (including those services on the World Wide Web not currently covered by the Distance Contract Directive).[118]

### 5.3.6.1  Contracts could be concluded by intelligent agents

*Due to the increasing complexity of online services, and due to the possibility of information overflow, it seems necessary to find legal ways to assess and recognise contracts made through the intervention of intelligent agents. Is the legal system flexible enough to endorse this? Moreover, the same should apply to the privacy policies and to the consent of individuals for the collection of data (because, in identity management systems, intelligent agents will decide what data are to be disclosed to whom).*

Here is a challenge: how to technologically implement negotiability of contracts and the framework of binding law in electronic, machine-readable form?

### 5.3.6.2  Unfair privacy policies

*Suppliers should not be allowed to set up privacy conditions which are manifestly not in compliance with the generally applicable privacy rules and which disadvantage the customer.*

Data protection legislation and consumer protection law could constitute the minimum (or default) privacy protection level. Similar rules as those currently applicable under the consumer protection of Directive 93/13 on unfair terms in consumer contracts could apply. Mandatory rules of consumer protection require, *inter alia*, that contracts be drafted in plain, intelligible language, that the consumer

---

[116] Council Directive 93/13/EEC of 5 April 1993 on unfair terms in consumer contracts, *Official Journal* L 095, 21 April 1993, pp. 29–34.

[117] Directive 97/7/EC of the European Parliament and of the Council of 20 May 1997 on the protection of consumers in respect of distance contracts, *Official Journal* L 144, 04 June 1997, pp. 0019–0027.

[118] Henderson, K., and A. Poulter, "The Distance Selling Directive: Points for Further Revision", *International Review for Law Computers & Technology*, Vol. 16, No. 3, 2002, pp. 289–300.

be given an opportunity to examine all terms, that – in cases of doubt – the interpretation most favourable to the consumer prevail.

*Suppliers should not be allowed to unfairly limit their liability for security problems in the service they provide to the consumer.*

In this respect, more attention could be given to a judgment of the Court of First Instance of Nanterre (France) in 2004 in which the online subscriber contract of AOL France was declared illegal in that it contained not less than 31 abusive clauses in its standard contractual terms (many of which infringed consumer protection law).[119]

### 5.3.6.3 Information to the consumer

The Directive on unfair terms in consumer contracts and the Directive on consumer protection in respect of distance contracts provide a broad right to information for the consumer. *It should be sufficient to dispense such information in electronic form,*[120] in view of the large amount of information directed towards consumers that would have to be managed by intelligent agents.

*An increasing number of service providers will be involved in AmI services and it cannot be feasible to provide the required information about all of them. The solution may be to provide such information only about the service provider whom the consumer directly pays and who is responsible towards the consumer. Joint liability would apply (for liability issues, see below).*

### 5.3.6.4 Right to withdrawal

The right to withdrawal, foreseen by the Directive 97/7 on consumer protection with respect to distance contracts, may not apply (unless otherwise agreed) to contracts in which (a) the provision of services has begun with the consumer's agreement before the end of the seven-working-day period and (b) goods have been made to the consumer's specifications or clearly personalised or which, by their nature, cannot be returned or are liable to deteriorate or expire rapidly.

*In an AmI world, services will be provided instantly and will be increasingly personalised. This implies that the right of withdrawal will become inapplicable in many cases. New solutions should be developed to address this problem.*

---

[119] Tribunal de grande instance de Nanterre, 2 June 2004 (*UFC Que Choisir* v. *AOL Bertelsmann Online France*). http://www.legalis.net/jurisprudence-decision.php3?id_article = 1211. For an English analysis, see Naylor, David, and Cyril Ritter, "B2C in Europe and Avoiding Contractual Liability: Why Businesses with European Operations Should Review their Customer Contracts Now", 15 September 2004. http://www.droit-technologie.org

[120] Currently, insofar as it is not received on a permanent medium, consumers must also receive written notice in good time of the information necessary for proper performance of the contract.

### 5.3.6.5   Temporary accounts

In AmI, payments will often occur automatically, at the moment of ordering or even offering the service.

*Temporary accounts, administered by trusted third parties, could temporarily store money paid by a consumer to a product or service provider. This can support consumer protection and enforcement, in particular with respect to fraud and for effectively exercising the right of withdrawal.* This would be welcome for services that are offered to consumers in the European Union by service providers located in third countries, as enforcement of consumer protection rights is likely to be less effective in such situations.

### 5.3.6.6   Group litigation and consumer claims

The possibility of group consumer litigation[121] can increase the level of law enforcement and, especially, enforcement of consumer protection law. Often an individual claim does not represent an important economic value, thus, individuals are discouraged from making efforts to enforce their rights.

*Launching collective claims or similar actions would increase the effective power against service providers. A similar solution is now available at European level in the case of injunctions.*

Bodies or organisations with a legitimate interest in ensuring that the collective interests of consumers are protected *can* institute proceedings before courts or competent administrative authorities and seek termination of any behaviour adversely affecting consumer protection and defined by law as illegal.[122] However, as far as actions for damages are concerned, issues such as the form and availability of group litigation are regulated by the national laws of the Member States as part of procedural law. The possibility to bring such a claim is restricted to a small number of states.[123]

---

[121] Group litigation is a broad term which captures collective claims (single claims brought on behalf of a group of identified or identifiable individuals), representative actions (single claims brought on behalf of a group of identified individuals by, e.g., a consumer interest association), class action (one party or group of parties may sue as representatives of a larger class of unidentified individuals), among others. These definitions as well as the procedural shape of such claims vary in different Member States. Waelbroeck D., D. Slater and G. Even-Shoshan G [Ashurst], *Study on the conditions of claims for damages in case of infringement of EC Competition rules*, commissioned by European Commission DG Competition, 2004, p. 44. http://ec.europa.eu/comm/competition/antitrust/others/actions_for_damages/study.html. The SWAMI consortium abstains from designating one of these forms as adequate, which points to the controversial character of class actions on European grounds and thus proposes to focus on other possible forms. Instead, we recommend that the appropriate authority study the issue further.

[122] Directive 98/27/EC of the European Parliament and of the Council of 19 May 1998 On injunctions for the protection of consumers' interests, *Official Journal* L 166, 11 June 1998, pp. 51–55.

[123] Belgian law provides that in certain circumstances associations can bring collective damage action or action for several individual damages. Waelbroeck D., D. Slater and G. Even-Shoshan [Ashurst], *Study on the conditions of claims for damages in case of infringement of EC Competition rules*, commissioned by European Commission DG Competition, 2004, pp. 44–47. http://ec.europa.eu/comm/competition/antitrust/others/actions_for_damages/study.html

## 5.3.7    Specific recommendations regarding electronic commerce

### 5.3.7.1    The scope of the Directive on electronic commerce

The Directive on electronic commerce[124] aims to provide a common framework for information society services in the EU Member States. An important feature of the Directive is that it also applies to legal persons. Similar to the consumer protection legislation, the Directive contains an obligation to provide certain information to customers. In view of the increasing number of service providers, it may not be feasible to provide information about all of them. *Providing information about the service provider whom the customer pays directly and who is responsible towards him could be a solution to the problem of the proliferating number of service providers (joint liability may also apply here). The Directive should also be updated to include the possibility of concluding contracts by electronic means (including reference to intelligent agents) and to facilitate the usage of pseudonyms, trusted third parties and credentials in electronic commerce.*

### 5.3.7.2    Unsolicited communication (spam)

Unsolicited commercial communication is an undesirable phenomenon in cyberspace. It constitutes a large portion of traffic on the Internet, using its resources (bandwidth and storage capacity) and forcing Internet providers and users to adopt organisational measures to fight it (by filtering and blocking spam). Spam can also constitute a security threat.[125] The dark scenarios show that spam may become an even more serious problem than it is today.[126] An increase in the volume of spam can be expected because of the emergence of new means of electronic communication. Zero-cost models for e-mail services encourage these practices, and similar problems may be expected when mobile services pick up a zero-cost or flat-fee model.

As we become increasingly dependent on electronic communication – ambient intelligence presupposes that we are almost constantly online – we become more vulnerable to spam. In the example from the first dark scenario, spamming may cause irritation and make the individual reluctant to use ambient intelligence.

---

[124] Directive 2000/31/EC of the European Parliament and of the Council of 8 June 2000 on certain legal aspects of information society services, in particular electronic commerce, in the Internal Market ("Directive on electronic commerce"), *Official Journal* L 178, 17 July 2000, pp. 0001–0016.

[125] Sorkin, David E., "Technical and Legal Approaches to Unsolicited Electronic Mail", *University of San Francisco Law Review*, Vol. 35, 2001, p. 336 ff.

[126] See Chapter 3, Scenario 1, situation 2.

Fighting spam may well demand even more resources than it does today as new methods of spamming – such as highly personalised and location-based advertising – emerge.

Currently, many legal acts throughout the world penalise unsolicited communication, but without much success. The Privacy & Electronic Communication Directive[127] provides for an opt-in regime, applicable in the instance of commercial communication, thus inherently prohibiting unsolicited marketing.[128] Electronic communications are, however, defined as "any information exchanged or conveyed between a finite number of parties by means of a publicly available electronic communications service. This does not include any information conveyed as part of a broadcasting service to the public over an electronic communications network except to the extent that the information can be related to the identifiable subscriber or user receiving the information."[129] The communications need to have a commercial content in order to fall under the opt-in regulation of the Privacy & Electronic Communication Directive.[130]

Consequently, this Directive may not cover unsolicited, location-based advertisements with a commercial content that are broadcast to a group of people ("the public"). The impact of this exception cannot be addressed yet since location-based services are still in their infancy.

*A broad interpretation of electronic communications is necessary (the Directive is technology-neutral). Considering any unsolicited electronic communication as spam, regardless of the content and regardless of the technological means, would offer protection that is adequate in ambient intelligence environments in which digital communications between people (and service providers) will exceed physical conversations and communications.[131]*

---

[127] Directive 2002/58/EC of the European Parliament and of the Council of 12 July 2002 concerning the processing of personal data and the protection of privacy in the electronic communications sector (Privacy & Electronic Communications Directive), *Official Journal* L 201, 31 July 2002, pp. 37–47.

[128] Andrews, S., *Privacy and human rights 2002*, produced by the Electronic Privacy Information Center (EPIC), Washington, DC, and *Privacy International*, London, 2002, p. 12. http://www.privacyinternational.org/survey/phr2002/

[129] Article 2 (d) of Directive 2002/58/EC.

[130] Recital 40 states, "Safeguards should be provided for subscribers against intrusion of their privacy by unsolicited communications for direct marketing purposes in particular by means of automated calling machines, telefaxes, and e-mails, including SMS messages. These forms of unsolicited commercial communications may on the one hand be relatively easy and cheap to send and on the other may impose a burden and/or cost on the recipient."

[131] Schreurs, W., M. Hildebrandt, E. Kindt and M. Vanfleteren, "*Cogitas, ergo sum*. The role of data protection law and non-discrimination law in group profiling in the private sector", *op. cit*; Schreurs, W., "Spam en electronische reclame [Spam and electronic communication]", *Nieuw Juridisch Weekblad*, 2003-48, pp. 1174–1185.

## 5.3.8 *Specific recommendation regarding liability law*

### 5.3.8.1 General

Civil damages address a harm already done, and compensate for damages sustained. Effective civil liability rules might actually form one of the biggest incentives for all actors involved to adhere to the obligations envisaged by law. One could establish liability for breach of contract, or on the basis of general tort rules. To succeed in court, one has to prove the damage, the causal link and the fault. Liability can be established for any damages sustained, as far as the conditions of liability are proven and so long as liability is not excluded (as in the case of some situations in which intermediary service providers are involved[132]). However, in AmI, to establish such proof can be extremely difficult.

As we have seen in the dark scenarios, each action is very complex, with a multiplicity of actors involved, and intelligent agents acting for service providers often undertake the action or decision causing the damage. Who is then to blame? How easy will it be to establish causation in a case where the system itself generates the information and undertakes the actions? How will the individual deal with such problems? The individual who is able to obtain damages addressing his harm in an efficient and quick way will have the incentive to take an action against the infringer, thus raising the level of overall enforcement of the law. Such an effect would be desirable, especially since no state or any enforcement agency is actually capable of providing a sufficient level of control and/or enforcement of the legal rules.

The liability provisions of the Directive on electronic commerce can become problematic. The scope of the liability exceptions under the Directive is not clear. The Directive requires ISPs to take down the content if they obtain knowledge on the infringing character of the content (notice-and-take-down procedure). However, the lack of a "put-back" procedure (allowing content providers whose content has been wrongfully alleged as illegal, to re-publish it on the Internet) or the verification of take-down notices by third parties is said to possibly infringe freedom of speech.[133]

*It is recommended that the liability rules be strengthened and that consideration be given to means that can facilitate their effectiveness.*

---

[132] Articles 12 to 15 of the Directive 2000/31/EC of the European Parliament and of the Council of 8 June 2000 on certain legal aspects of information society services, in particular electronic commerce, in the Internal Market ("Directive on electronic commerce"), *Official Journal* L 178, 17 July 2000, pp. 1–16. The Directive provides for exceptions to the liability of intermediary service providers (ISPs) under certain conditions. In the case of hosting, for example, a service provider is not liable for the information stored at the request of a recipient of the service, on condition that (a) the provider does not have actual knowledge of illegal activity or information and, as regards claims for damages, is not aware of facts or circumstances from which the illegal activity or information is apparent or (b) the provider, upon obtaining such knowledge or awareness, acts expeditiously to remove or to disable access to the information. See also section 3.3.8.

[133] See Sutter, Gavin, "'Don't Shoot the Messenger?' The UK and Online Intermediary Liability", *International Review of Law Computers & Technology*, Vol. 17, No. 1, 2003, pp. 73–84; Julia-Barcelo, R., and K.J. Koelman, "Intermediary Liability in the E-commerce Directive: So far so Good, But It's not Enough", *Computer Law and Security Report*, Vol. 16, No. 4, 2000, pp. 231–239.

### 5.3.8.2   Liability for infringement of privacy law

In addition to the general considerations regarding liability presented in this section, we also draw attention to the specific problems of liability for infringement of privacy, including security infringements. Currently, the right to remedy in such circumstances is based on the general liability (tort) rules. The Data Protection Directive refers explicitly to liability issues stating that an immediate compensation mechanism shall be developed in case of liability for an automated decision based on inadequate profiles and refusal of access. However, it is not clear whether it could be understood as a departure from general rules and a strengthening of the liability regime. Determining the scope of liability for privacy breach and security infringements might also be problematic. In any case, the proof of the elements of a claim and meeting the general tort law preconditions (damage, causality and fault) can be very difficult.

*Opacity instruments, as discussed above, aiming to prohibit the interference into one's privacy can help to provide some clarity as to the scope of the liability. In addition, guidelines and interpretations on liability would be generally welcome, as would standards for safety measures, to provide for greater clarity and thus greater legal certainty for both users and undertakings.*

### 5.3.8.3   Joint and several liability

As already mentioned, it can be difficult for a user to identify the party actually responsible for damages, especially if he or she does not know which parties were actually involved in the service and/or software creation and delivery.

*The user should be able to request compensation from the service provider with whom he or she had direct contact in the process of the service. Joint and several liability (with the right to redress) should be the default rule in the case of providers of AmI services, software, hardware or other products. The complexity of the actions and multiplicity of actors justify such a position.*[134] Moreover, this recommendation should be supplemented by the consumer protection recommendation requiring the provision of consumer information by the service or product provider having the closest connection with the consumer, as well as the provision of information about individual privacy rights (see above) in a way that would enable the individual to detect a privacy infringement and have a better chance to prove it in court. There is a need to consider the liability regime with other provisions of law.

---

[134] The Directive on liability for defective products makes provision for joint and several liability. See also sections 3.2.8.3 and 5.3.8.4.

### 5.3.8.4  Strict liability

The Directive on liability for defective products[135] provides for a liability with-out fault (strict liability).[136] As a recital to the Directive states, strict liability shall be seen as "the sole means of adequately solving the problem, peculiar to our age of increasing technicality, of a fair apportionment of the risks inherent in modern technological production." We should keep this reasoning in mind since it seems even more adequate when thinking about the liability issues in AmI.

Most of the "products" offered in the AmI environment will consist of software-based, highly personalised services. We should then think about adjusting the liabil-ity rules to such an environment. If it is difficult to distinguish between hardware and software from a technological perspective, why should we draw such a distinc-tion from a legal perspective?[137] *An explicit provision providing for strict liability for software can be considered.*[138] Nevertheless, such a proposal is controversial as it is said to threaten industry. Since software is never defect-free, strict liability would expose software producers unfairly to claims against damages. Thus, the degree of required safety of the programmes is a policy decision.[139] Strict liability could also impede innovation, especially the innovation of experimental and life-saving applications.[140] Others argue that strict liability might increase software quality by making producers more diligent, especially, in properly testing their products.[141]

Despite these policy considerations, there are some legal questions about the applicability of strict liability to software. The first question is whether the software can be regarded as "goods" or "products" and whether they fall under the strict

---

[135] Council Directive 85/374/EEC of 25 July 1985 on the approximation of the laws, regulations and administrative provisions of the Member States concerning liability for defective products, *Official Journal* L 210, 07 August 1985, pp. 29–33.

[136] A strict product liability regime based on the Directive is the basis of the claims under the gen-eral tort regime. See Giensen, I., and M.B.M. Loos, "Liability for Defective Products and Services: The Netherlands", *Netherlands Comparative Law Association*, 2002, pp. 75–79. http://www.ejcl.org/64/art64-6.html

[137] Hilty, Lorenz, et al., *The Precautionary Principle in the Information Society, Effects of Pervasive Computing on Health and Environment*, Report of the Centre for Technology Assessment, February 2005, p. 269.

[138] In such a case, the intelligent software agent's failure and the PET's failure might be covered by the strict liability regime. Special derogation for PETs could be envisaged.

[139] Alheit, K., "The applicability of the EU Product Liability Directive to Software", *The Comparative and International Law Journal of South Africa*, Vol. 3, No. 2, 2001, p. 204.

[140] Singsangob, A., *Computer Software and Information Licensing in Emerging Markets, The Need for a Viable Legal Framework*, Aspen Publishers, 2003, p. 113.

[141] Desai, M.S., J. Oghen and T.C. Richards, "Information Technology Litigation and Software Failure", *The Journal of Information, Law & Technology*, 2002 (2). http://www2.warwick.ac.uk/fac/soc/law/elj/jilt/2002_2/desai/

liability regime.[142] In fact, the answer depends on national laws and how the Directive has been implemented. The Directive applies to products defined as movables,[143] which might suggest that it refers to tangible goods. Software not incorporated into a tangible medium (available online) will not satisfy such a definition. There are a growing number of devices (products) with embedded software (e.g., washing machines, microwaves, possibly RFIDs), which fall under the Directive's regime.[144] This trend will continue; the software will be increasingly crucial for the proper functioning of the products themselves, services and whole environments (smart car, smart home). Should the distinction between the two regimes remain?

Strict liability is limited to death or personal injury, or damage to property intended for private use.[145] The damage relating to the product itself, to the product used in the course of business and the economic loss will not be remedied under the Directive.[146] Currently, defective software is most likely to cause financial loss only, thus the injured party would not be able to rely on provisions of the Directive in seeking redress. However, even now in some life-saving applications, personal injury dangers can emerge. Such will also be the case in the AmI world (see, e.g., the first and second dark scenarios in which software failures cause accidents, property damage and personal injury) so the importance and applicability of the Directive on liability for defective products will grow. The increasing dependence on software applications in everyday life, the increasing danger of sustaining personal injury due to a software failure and, thus, the growing concerns of consumers justify strengthening the software liability regime.

However, the Directive allows for a state-of-the-art defence. Under this defence, a producer is not liable if the state of scientific and technical knowledge at the time the product was put into circulation was not such that the existence of the defect would be discovered. It has been argued that the availability of such a defence (Member States have the discretion whether to retain it in national laws[147]) will always be possible since, due to the complexity of "code", software will never be defect-free.[148]

These policy and legal arguments indicate the difficulty in broadening the scope of the Directive on liability for defective products to include software. Reversal of the burden of proof might be a more adequate alternative solution, one that policymakers should investigate.

---

[142] Similar discussion takes place in the United States. It seems that, despite the fact that the issue is not clearly stated, there is a tendency to regard software as a good, especially if the parties to the contract intended to treat it as such (as opposed to an information service). See Singsangob A., *Computer Software and Information Licensing in Emerging Markets, The Need for a Viable Legal Framework*, Aspen Publishers, 2003, p. 113.

[143] Article 2 of the Directive.

[144] Reed, Ch., and A. Welterveden, "Liability", in Ch. Reed and J. Angel (eds.), *ComputerLaw*, London, 2000, p. 99.

[145] Article 9 of the Directive on liability for defective products.

[146] Giensen, I., and M.B.M. Loos, "Liability for Defective Products and Services: The Netherlands", *Netherlands Comparative Law Association*, 2002, p. 82. http://www.ejcl.org/64/art64-6.html

[147] Article 15 (1)(b) of the Directive on liability for defective products.

[148] Alheit, K., p. 204.

It is often difficult to distinguish software from hardware because both are necessary and interdependent to provide a certain functionality. Similarly, it may be
difficult to draw the line between software and services. Transfer of information via
electronic signals (e.g., downloaded software) could be regarded as a service.[149]
Some courts might also be willing to distinguish between mass-market software
and software produced as an individual product (on demand). AmI is a highly personalised environment where software-based services will surround the individual,
thus the tendency to regard software as a service could increase.

Strict liability currently does not apply to services. Service liability is regulated
by national laws.[150] Extending such provision to services may have far-reaching
consequences, not only in the ICT field. The AmI environment will need the innovation and creativity of service providers; therefore, one should refrain from creating a framework discouraging them from taking risks. However, some procedural
rules could help consumers without upsetting an equitable balance. The consumer,
usually the weaker party in a conflict with the provider, often has difficulty proving
damages. Reversing the burden of proof might facilitate such proof. Most national
laws seem to provide a similar solution.[151]

*Since national law regulates the issue of service liability, differences between
national regulations might lead to differences in the level of protection. The lack of a
coherent legal framework for service liability in Europe is regrettable. Learning from
the differences and similarities between the different national legal regimes, as indicated in the* Analysis of National Liability Systems for Remedying Damage Caused
by Defective Consumer Services,[152] *is the first step in remedying such a situation.*


### 5.3.8.5   Reversing the burden of proof

Reversing the burden of proof is less invasive than the strict liability rules where the
issue of fault is simply not taken into consideration. Such a solution has been
adopted in the field of the non-discrimination and intellectual property laws, as well
as in national tort regimes.[153] An exception to the general liability regime is also

---

[149] The OECD has treated software downloads as a service for the VAT and custom duties purposes.
See Henderson, K., and A. Poulter, "The Distance Selling Directive: points for further revision",
*International Review for Law Computers & Technology*, Vol. 16, No. 3, 2002, pp. 289–300.

[150] As a basis for liability, the contractual liability or the fault-based tort liability applies. See Giensen,
I., and M.B.M. Loos, op. cit., as well as Magnus, U., and H.W. Micklitz, *Comparative Analysis of
National Liability Systems for Remedying Damage Caused by Defective Consumer Services*: A study
commissioned by the European Commission, Final Report, Part D: The Comparative Part, April 2004,
p. 62. http://europa.eu.int/comm/consumers/cons_safe/serv_safe/liability/reportd_en.pdf

[151] Magnus, U., and H.W. Micklitz, p. 8.

[152] Magnus, U., and H.W. Micklitz. http://europa.eu.int/comm/consumers/cons_safe/serv_safe/lia-
bility/reportabc_en.pdf and http://europa.eu.int/comm/consumers/cons_safe/serv_safe/liability/
reportd_en.pdf

[153] Magnus, U., and H.W. Micklitz.

provided in Directive 1999/93/EC on the community framework for electronic signatures.[154] In that Directive, the certification service provider is liable for damage caused by non-compliance with obligations imposed by the Directive[155] unless he proves he did not act negligently.[156]

Technology could potentially remedy the information asymmetry between users and AmI service suppliers or data processors. The latter could have an obligation to inform consumers what data are processed, how and when and what is the aim of such activities (thus actually fulfilling their obligations under the Data Protection Directive). This information could be stored and managed by an intelligent agent on behalf of the user, who is not able to deal with such information flow. However, the user would have the possibility to use such information to enforce his rights (e.g., to prove causation). Other technological solutions (e.g., watermarking) could also help the user prove his case in court.

### 5.3.8.6  Consumer claims and fixed damages

In many cases, the damage sustained by the individual will be difficult to assess in terms of the economic value or too small to actually provide an incentive to bring an action to court. However, acts causing such damage can have overall negative effects. Spam is a good example. *Fixed damages, similar to the ones used in the United States, or punitive damages could remedy such problems (some US state laws provide for fixed damages such as US$200 for each unsolicited communication without the victim needing to prove such damage). They would also provide clarity as to the sanctions or damages expected and could possibly have a deterrent effect.* The national laws of each Member State currently regulate availability of punitive damages; a few countries provide for punitive and exemplary damages in their tort systems.[157]

---

[154] On issues relating to digital signatures, see Gasson, M., M. Meints and K. Warwick (eds.), *A study on PKI and biometrics*, FIDIS (Future of Identity in the Information Society) Deliverable D3.2, July 2005. http://www.fidis.net. See also Directive 1999/93/EC of the European Parliament and of the Council of 13 December 1999 on a Community framework for electronic signatures, *Official Journal* L 013, 19 January 2000, pp. 0012–002. See also section 3.2.8.6.

[155] For example, the service provider is liable for the inaccuracy or incompleteness of the information contained in the certificate at the time the certificate was issued.

[156] The liability rules described above seem sufficient as a legal framework for qualified digital signatures. The general tort rules apply in relation to liability in all other cases (other than qualified signatures).

[157] There are not enough sources to state if they would apply in anti-spam cases. "Available sources" refers here to antitrust claims. Waelbroeck D., D. Slater and G. Even-Shoshan [Ashurst], *Study on the conditions of claims for damages in case of infringement of EC Competition rules*, commissioned by European Commission DG Competition, 2004, pp. 44–47. http://ec.europa.eu/comm/competition/antitrust/others/actions_for_damages/study.htm

Actions allowing consolidation of the small claims of individuals could be also examined (i.e., group consumer actions).

## 5.3.9 Specific recommendation regarding equality law

### 5.3.9.1 What is non-discrimination law?

Non-discrimination law can regulate and forbid the unlawful usage of processed data, for example, in making decisions or undertaking other actions on the basis of certain characteristics of the data subjects. This makes non-discrimination law of increasing importance for AmI. The *creation* of profiles does not fall under non-discrimination law[158] (potential use), but decisions based on profiling (including group profiling based on anonymous data) that affect the individual might provide the grounds for application of the non-discrimination rules. They apply in the case of identifiable individuals as well as to anonymous members of the group.[159]

Profiles or decisions based on certain criteria (health data, nationality, income, etc.) may lead to discrimination against individuals. It is difficult to determine when it is objectively justified to use such data and criteria, and when they are discriminatory (e.g., the processing of health-related data by insurance companies leading to decisions to raise premiums). Further legislative clarity would be desirable.

However, certain negative dimensions of profiling still escape the regime of non-discrimination law (e.g., manipulation of individuals' behaviour by targeted advertising). Here no remedies have been identified.

The non-discrimination rules should be read in conjunction with the fairness principle of data protection law. The application of the two may have similar aims and effects; they might also be complementary: Can the limitations of non-discrimination law be justified if they are regarded as not fair, as in the example of insurance companies raising premiums after processing health data? They can address a range of actions undertaken in AmI, such as dynamic pricing or refusal to provide services (e.g., a refusal of service on the grounds that no information (profile) is available could be regarded as discriminatory).

*Non-discrimination rules should be taken into consideration at the design stage of technology and service development.*

---

[158] However, such issues might be addressed by the data protection legislation. In the opinion of Gutwirth and De Hert, principles of data protection are appropriate to cope with profiling. Hildebrandt, M., and S. Gutwirth (eds.), *Implications of profiling practices on democracy and rule of law*, FIDIS Deliverable D7.4, September 2005. http://www.fidis.net/fidis_del.html

[159] Custers, B., *The Power of Knowledge, Ethical, Legal and Technological Aspects of Data Mining and Group Profiling in Epidemiology*, Wolf Legal Publishers, Nijmegen, 2004, pp. 164–165.

### 5.3.9.2  Universal service

The Universal Service Directive[160] provides for a minimum of telecommunication services for all at an affordable price as determined by each Member State. Prices for universal services may depart from those resulting from market conditions.[161] Such provisions aim at overcoming a digital divide and allowing all to enjoy a certain minimum of electronic services. The Directive is definitely a good start in shaping the Information Society and the AmI environment. The development of new technologies and services generates costs, both on individuals and society. Many high-added-value AmI services will be designed for people who will be able to pay for them. Thus, AmI could reinforce the inequalities between the poor and rich. Everyone should be able to enjoy the benefits of AmI, at least at a minimum level. *The Commission should consider whether new emerging AmI services should be provided to all. Some services (e.g., emergency services) could even be regarded as public and provided free of charge or as part of social security schemes.*

## 5.3.10  Specific recommendations regarding interoperability and IPR

### 5.3.10.1  General

As shown in Scenario 2, AmI might cause major problems for current intellectual property protection, because AmI requires interoperability of devices, software, data and information, for example, for crucial information systems such as health monitoring systems used by travelling seniors. There is also a growing need to create means of intellectual property protection that respect privacy and allow for anonymous content viewing. Intellectual property rights give exclusive rights over databases consisting of personal data and profiles, while the data subjects do not have a property right over their own information collected. We discuss these issues below.

### 5.3.10.2  Protection of databases and profiling

The Directive on the legal protection of databases[162] provides for a copyright protection of databases, if they constitute the author's own intellectual creation by

---

[160] Directive 2002/22/EC of the European Parliament and of the Council of 7 March 2002 on universal service and users' rights relating to electronic communications networks and services (Universal Service Directive), *Official Journal* L 108, 24 April 2002, pp. 0051–0077.

[161] For more on the Directive, see section 3.3.8.2.

[162] Directive 96/9/EC of the European Parliament and of the Council of 11 March 1996 on the legal protection of databases, *Official Journal* L 077, 27 March 1996, pp. 0020–0028.

virtue of his selection or arrangement of their content. The Directive also foresees a *sui generis* protection if there has been a qualitatively and/or quantitatively substantial investment in either the acquisition, verification or presentation of the content. *Sui generis* protection "prevents the extraction and/or the re-utilization of the whole or of a substantial part, evaluated qualitatively and/or quantitatively, of the contents of that database".[163] This implies that the database maker can obtain a *sui generis* protection of a database even when its content consists of personal data. Although the user does not have a property right over his personal data, the maker of a database can obtain an exclusive right over this type of data. Hence, a profile built on the personal data of a data subject might constitute somebody else's intellectual property.

*The right to information about what knowledge has been derived from one's data could, to some extent, provide a safeguard against profiling. We recommend that further research be undertaken on how to reconcile this with intellectual property rights.*[164]

### 5.3.10.3 DRMs

The Copyright Directive[165] provides for the protection of digital rights management (DRMs) used to manage the licence rights of works that are accessed after identification or authentication of a user.[166] But DRMs can violate privacy, because they can be used for processing of personal data and constructing (group) profiles, which might conflict with data protection law.

*Less invasive ways of reconciling intellectual property rights with privacy should be considered.*

This not only relates to technologies but also to an estimation of the factual economic position of the customer. For example, the general terms and conditions for subscribing to an interactive television service – often a service offered by just a few players – should not impose on customers a condition that personal data relating to their viewing behaviour can be processed and used for direct marketing or for transfer to "affiliated" third parties.

As the Article 29 Working Party advises, greater attention should be devoted to the use of PETs within DRM systems.[167] In particular, it advises that tools be used to

---

[163] Article 7 (1) of Directive 96/9/EC of the European Parliament and of the Council of 11 March 1996 on the legal protection of databases. http://europa.eu.int/ISPO/infosoc/legreg/docs/969ec.html

[164] See section 5.3.4 on the right to information.

[165] Directive 2001/29/EC of the European Parliament and of the Council of 22 May 2001 on the harmonisation of certain aspects of copyright and related rights in the information society, *Official Journal* L 167, 22 June 2001, pp. 0010–0019.

[166] See also section 5.3.5, Specific recommendation regarding security.

[167] Article 29 Data Protection Working Party, *Working document on data protection issues related to intellectual property rights* (WP/ 104), adopted on 18 January 2005. http://ec.europa.eu/justice_home/fsj/privacy

preserve the anonymity of users and it recommends the limited use of unique identifiers. Use of unique identifiers allows profiling and tagging of a document linked to
an individual, enabling tracking for copyright abuses. Such tagging should not be
used unless necessary for performance of the service or unless with the informed
consent of individual. All relevant information required under data protection legislation should be provided to users, including categories of collected information, the
purpose of collecting and information about the rights of the data subject.[168]

The Directive on the legal protection of software[169] obliges Member States to
provide appropriate remedies against a person's committing any act of putting into
circulation or the possession for commercial purposes of any means the sole
intended purpose of which is to facilitate the unauthorised removal or circumvention
of any technical device which may have been applied to protect a computer program.
*The Software Directive only protects against the putting into circulation of such
devices and not against the act of circumventing as such. It would be advisable to
have a uniform solution in that respect. DRMs can also violate consumer rights, by
preventing the lawful enjoyment of the purchased product. The anti-circumvention
provisions should be then coupled with better enforcement of consumer protection
provisions regarding information disclosure to the consumer.[170] The consumer
should always be aware of any technological measures used to protect the content
he wishes to purchase, and restrictions in use of such content as a consequence of
technological protection (he should also be informed about technological consequences of DRMs for his devices, if any, e.g., about installing the software on his
computer).[171] Product warnings and consumer notifications should always be in
place and should aim to raise general consumer awareness about the DRMs.*

### 5.3.10.4 Decompilation right

*As interoperability is a precondition for AmI, AmI would have to lead to limitations
on exclusive intellectual property rights. One could argue that software packages
should be developed so that they are interoperable with each other. That implies
creating standards. ICT global standards are desirable for interoperability and*

---

[168] Ibid.

[169] Council Directive 91/250/EEC of 14 May 1991 on the legal protection of computer programs,
*Official Journal* L 122, 17 May 1991, pp. 0042–0046.

[170] See also OECD, *Report on Disclosure Issues Related to the Use of Copy Control and Digital
Rights Management Technologies*, DSTI/CP(2005)15/FINAL, 2006. https://www.oecd.org/datao-
ecd/47/31/36546422.pdf. For comments on consumer needs re DRM, see also INDICARE
Project, "Content Providers' Guide to Digital Rights Management: Any side effects in using
DRM?". www.indicare.org

[171] Those restrictions might, inter alia, prevent the user from making backups or private copies,
downloading music to portable devices, playing music on certain devices, or constitute the geographical restrictions such as regional coding of DVDs.

*privacy protection. A broader scope of the decompilation right under software protection would be desirable.*

The EC's battle with Microsoft was in part an attempt to strengthen the decompilation right with the support of competition law.

## 5.3.11 Specific recommendations regarding international co-operation

### 5.3.11.1 Jurisdiction in criminal matters

Currently, there is no international or European framework determining jurisdiction in criminal matters, thus, national rules are applicable. The main characteristics of the legal provisions in this matter have already been discussed in Chapter 3, section 3.3.8.1; however, it seems useful to refer here to some of our earlier conclusions. The analysis of the connecting factors for forum selection (where a case is to be heard) shows that it is almost always possible for a judge to declare himself competent to hear a case. Certain guidelines have already been developed, both in the context of the Cybercrime Convention[172] as well as the 2005 EU Framework Decision on attacks against information systems[173] on how to resolve the issue of concurrent competences. According to the Cybercrime Convention, "The Parties involved shall, where appropriate, consult with a view to determining the most appropriate jurisdiction for prosecution."[174]

The 2005 EU Framework Decision on attacks against information systems states, "Where an offence falls within the jurisdiction of more than one Member State and when any of the States concerned can validly prosecute on the basis of the same facts, the Member States concerned shall co-operate in order to decide which of them will prosecute the offenders with the aim, if possible, of centralizing proceedings in a single Member State."[175]

*Legal experts and academics should follow any future developments in application of those rules that might indicate whether more straightforward rules are needed. The discussion on the Green Paper on double jeopardy should also be closely followed.*[176]

---

[172] Council of Europe, Cybercrime Convention of 23 November 2001.

[173] Council Framework Decision 2005/222/JHA of 24 February 2005 on attacks against information systems, *Official Journal* L 069, 16 March 2005, pp. 67–71.

[174] Article 22 paragraph 5 of the Cybercrime Convention.

[175] Article 10 paragraph 5 of the 2005 EU Framework Decision on attacks against information systems raises the possibility of invoking any institutional mechanism to facilitate such co-operation, and factors that should be taken into account when considering an appropriate forum.

[176] European Commission, Green Paper on Conflicts of Jurisdiction and the Principle of *ne bis in idem* in Criminal Proceedings, COM(2005) 696, December 2005.http://ec.europa.eu/comm/off/green/index_en.htm

### 5.3.11.2  Private international law

Scenario 2 ("A crash in AmI space") turns on an accident involving German tourists in Italy, while travelling with a tourist company established in a third country.[177] It raises questions about how AmI might fit into a legal framework based on territorial concepts. Clear rules determining the law applicable between the parties are an important guarantee of legal certainty.

Private international law issues are dealt at the European level by the Rome Convention on the law applicable to contractual obligations[178] as well as the Rome II Regulation on the law applicable to non-contractual obligations,[179] the Brussels Regulation on jurisdiction and enforcement of judgments.[180]

### 5.3.11.3  Jurisdiction in civil matters

The Regulation on jurisdiction and enforcement of judgments in civil and commercial matters covers both contractual and non-contractual matters. It also contains specific provisions for jurisdiction over consumer contracts, which aim to protect the consumer in case of court disputes.[181] These provisions should be satisfactory and workable in an AmI environment.

However, provisions of this Regulation will not determine the forum if the defendant is domiciled outside the European Union.[182] Also, the provisions on the jurisdiction for consumer contracts apply only when both parties are domiciled in EU Member States. Although the Regulation provides for a forum if the dispute arises from an operation of a branch, agency or other establishment of the defendant in a Member State, a substantial number of businesses offering services to EU

---

[177] See also Chapter 3 section 3.3.1 (the scenario script) and section 3.3.8.1 on the legal analysis of private international law aspects of the scenario.

[178] Convention of Rome on the law applicable to contractual obligations opened for signature in Rome on 19 June 1980 (80/934/EEC), *Official Journal L* 266, 9 October 1980, pp. 0001–0019 (Consolidated version CF498Y0126(03)).

[179] Regulation (EC) No 864/2007 of the European Parliament and of the Council of 11 July 2007 on the law applicable to non-contractual obligations (Rome II). *Official Journal L* 199, 31 July 2007, pp. 40–49.

[180] Council Regulation (EC) No 44/2001 of 22 December 2000 on jurisdiction and the recognition and enforcement of judgments in civil and commercial matters, *Official Journal L* 012, 16 January 2001, pp. 0001–0023.

[181] Consumer contracts are regulated by Articles 15–17 of the Brussels Regulation. The consumer may bring a case in the court of the company domicile or in his own domicile. On the other hand, consumers may be sued only in a court of their own domicile. Such rules aim to protect the consumer who is the weaker party in a contractual relationship.

[182] Article 4 of the Brussels Regulation states: 1. If the defendant is not domiciled in a Member State, the jurisdiction of the courts of each Member State shall, subject to Articles 22 and 23, be determined by the law of that Member State; 2. Any person domiciled in a Member State may, whatever his nationality, avail himself of the rules of jurisdiction in force in that State, and in particular those specified in Annex I, in the same way as the nationals of that State.

consumers will still be outside the reach of this Regulation. *This emphasises again the need for a more global approach*[183] *beyond the territory of the Member States.*

*Clarification and simplification of forum selection for non-consumers would also be desirable. The complexity of the business environment, service and product creation and delivery would justify such approach. It would be of special importance for SMEs.*

### 5.3.11.4 Applicable law

Currently, the applicable law for contractual obligations is determined by the 1980 Rome Convention.[184] Efforts have been undertaken to modernise the Rome Convention and replace it with a Community instrument. Recently, the Commission has presented a proposal for a Regulation of the European Parliament and the Council on the law applicable to contractual obligations.[185]

The provisions of the Rome Convention refer to contractual issues only. Recently, the so-called Rome II Regulation[186] has been adopted, which provides for rules applicable to non-contractual obligations.

The Rome Convention on law applicable to contractual obligations relies heavily on the territorial criterion. It refers to the habitual residence, the central administration or place of business as the key factors determining the national law most relevant to the case.[187] But IT services can be supplied at a distance by electronic means. The AmI service supplier could have his habitual residence or central administration anywhere in the world and he could choose his place of residence (central administration) according to how beneficial is the national law of a given country. The habitual residence factor has been kept and strengthened in the Commission's proposal for a new regulation replacing the Rome Convention (Rome I proposal, Article 4).[188]

---

[183] Ofcom, the UK regulator for communications, has made a similar point: "The global reach and open nature of the internet gives rise to some well-known problems, which cannot be addressed by a translation of existing powers and structures." *Online protection: A survey of consumer, industry and regulatory mechanisms and systems*, 21 June 2006, p. 1. http://www.ofcom.org.uk/research/technology/onlineprotection/report.pdf

[184] Convention of Rome on the law applicable to contractual obligations opened for signature in Rome on 19 June 1980 (80/934/EEC), *Official Journal* L 266, 9 October 1980, pp. 0001–0019.

[185] The Commission has presented the proposal for a regulation of the European Parliament and the Council on the law applicable to contractual obligations (Rome I), COM (2005) 650 final, 2005/0261 (COD).

[186] Regulation (EC) No 864/2007

[187] According to Article 4, "the contract shall be governed by the law of the country with which it is most closely connected." Article 4 further reads: "It shall be presumed that the contract is most closely connected with the country where the party who is to effect the performance which is characteristic of the contract has, at the time of conclusion of the contract, his habitual residence, or, in the case of a body corporate or unincorporated, its central administration. However, if the contract is entered into in the course of that party's trade or profession, that country shall be the country in which the principal place of business is situated or, where under the terms of the contract the performance is to be effected through a place of business other than the principal place of business, the country in which that other place of business is situated."

[188] The new proposal does not use the presumption that the country of habitual residence is the most closely connected with the case, as it is under the Rome Convention. In the proposal, the relevant factor of the habitual residence of, inter alia, the seller or service provider is the fixed rule.

The new proposal for the Rome I Regulation amends the consumer protection provisions.[189] It still relies on the *habitual residence* of the consumer, but it brings the consumer choice of contract law in line with the equivalent provisions of the Brussels Regulation, and broadens the scope of the application of its provisions. The Commission proposal for the Regulation on the law applicable to contractual obligations is a good step forward.

The Rome II Regulation on law applicable to non-contractual obligations applies to the tort or delict, including claims arising out of strict liability. The basic rule under the Regulation is that a law applicable should be determined on the basis of where the direct damage occurred (*lex loci damni*). However, some "escape clauses" are foreseen and provide for a more adequate solution if more appropriate in the case at hand. This allows for flexibility in choosing the best solution. Special rules are also foreseen in the case of some specific torts or delicts.

Uniform rules on applicable law at the European level are an important factor for improving the predictability of litigation, and thus legal certainty. In that respect, the new Regulation should be welcomed. The Regulation will apply from January 2009.

Some other legislative acts also contain rules on applicable law. Most important are provisions in the Data Protection Directive. This Directive also chooses the territorial criterion to determine the national law applicable to the processing of data, which is the law of the place where the processing is carried out in the context of an establishment of the data controller. Such a criterion, however, might be problematic: more than one national law might be applicable.[190] Moreover, in times of globalisation of economic activity, it is easy for an undertaking to choose the place of establishment, which offers the most liberal regime, beyond the reach of European data protection law. In situations when a non-EU state is involved, the Directive points out a different relevant factor, the location of the equipment used,[191] thus enabling broader application of the EU Data Protection Directive.[192]

---

[189] As recital 10 of the proposal states, these amendments aim to take into account the developments in distance selling, thus including ICT developments.

[190] Article 4 (1) of the Directive stipulates: Each Member State shall apply the national provisions it adopts pursuant to this Directive to the processing of personal data where: (a) the processing is carried out in the context of the activities of an establishment of the controller on the territory of the Member State; when the same controller is established on the territory of several Member States, he must take the necessary measures to ensure that each of these establishments complies with the obligations laid down by the national law applicable.

[191] The Directive stipulates in article 4 (1) that the national law of a given Member State will apply when the controller is not established on Community territory and, for purposes of processing personal data, makes use of equipment, automated or otherwise, situated on the territory of the said Member State, unless such equipment is used only for purposes of transit through the territory of the Community.

[192] The Article 29 Data Protection Working Party interprets the term "equipment" as referring to all kinds of tools or devices, including personal computers, which can be used for many kinds of processing operations. The definition could be extended to all devices with a capacity to collect data, including sensors, implants and maybe RFIDs. (Active RFID chips can also *collect* information. They are expensive compared to passive RFID chips but they are already part of the real world.) See Article 29 Data Protection Working Party, *Working document on determining the international application of EU data protection law to personal data processing on the Internet by non-EU based websites* (5035/01/EN/Final WP 56), 30 May 2002. http://ec.europa.eu/justice_home/ fsj/privacy/ docs/wpdocs/2002/wp56_en.pdf

As we see, in all these cases, the territorial criterion (establishment) prevails. *We should consider moving towards a more personal criterion, especially since personal data are linked with an identity and a state of the data subject (issues which are regulated by the national law of the person). Such a criterion could be more easily reconciled with the AmI world of high mobility and without physical borders.* The data subject will also be able to remain under the protection of his/her national law, and the data controller/service provider will not have the possibility of selecting a place of establishment granting him the most liberal treatment of law.[193]

### 5.3.11.5   Data transfer

Data transfer is another issue highlighting the need for international co-operation in the creation of a common playing field for AmI at the global level. What is the sense of protecting data in one country if they are transferred to a country not affording comparable (or any) safeguards? Also, the globalisation of economic and other activities brings the necessity of exchanging personal data between the countries. The Data Protection Directive provides a set of rules on data transfer to third countries.[194] Data can be transferred only to countries offering an adequate level of protection. The Commission can conclude agreements (e.g., the Safe Harbour Agreement) with third countries which could help ensure an adequate level of protection. The Commission can also issue a decision in that respect. However, the major problem is enforcement of such rules, especially in view of the fact that some "safeguards" rely on self-regulatory systems whereby companies merely promise not to violate their declared privacy policies (as is the case with the Safe Harbour Agreement). *Attention by the media and consumer organisations can help in the enforcement of agreed rules. The problem of weak enforcement also emphasises the need to strengthen international co-operation with the aim of developing new enforcement mechanisms. Providing assistance in good practices in countries with less experience than the European Union would also be useful.*

---

[193] Such a solution has the advantage of covering, with the protection of EU legislation, third country residents whose data are processed via equipment in the EU. A broad interpretation of the term "equipment" would help guarantee the relatively broad application of such a rule (see above). As a result, in most cases, application of the domicile/nationality rule or the place of the equipment used as the relevant factor would have the same result. However, we can envisage the processing of data not using such equipment, for example, when the data are already posted online. Then the EU law could not be applicable.

[194] See chapter 3, section 3.4.8.1.

# Chapter 6
# Recommendations for stakeholders

Chapter 5 identified safeguards against the threats and vulnerabilities affecting privacy, identity, trust, security and the digital divide in an AmI world. In this chapter, we offer to particular stakeholders several specific recommendations some of which flow from the safeguards identified above.

## 6.1 Adopting a risk assessment/risk management approach to AmI

Since their creation, the Internet and the World Wide Web have become a critical infrastructure, arguably *the* critical infrastructure in virtually all countries and all societies. The Internet's interconnectedness and the dependency of other critical infrastructures (banking, transport, telecoms, electricity, water, etc.) upon it have made it indispensable to the functioning of our societies and economies. Further, many people now use the Internet more everyday than they watch TV. As exponential as has been its growth and as pervasive as it has become, the Internet is just a stepping stone on the way to an even more pervasive network and set of technologies that will provide us with ambient intelligence.

Yet the development and implementation of ambient intelligence is taking place with little involvement of the wide range of stakeholders in an assessment of the risks (especially to security) that it poses. And, it is important to recall, risks are not static. Risks are growing as things become more interconnected.[1] No one has yet called for the rigour of a formalised risk assessment/risk management process for

---

[1] "As a result of increasing interconnectivity, information systems and networks are now exposed to a growing number and a wider variety of threats and vulnerabilities." OECD *Guidelines for the Security of Information Systems and Networks: Towards a culture of security*, OECD, Paris, 2002, p. 7. The OECD has made the point in other of its reports too. See, for example, *Emerging Systemic Risks in the 21st Century*, 2003, p. 13: "The openness and connectedness of systems and ... technology and information increase the number of potential interactions that can generate or influence a hazard. Risks become more complex."

D. Wright et al. (eds.), *Safeguards in a World of Ambient Intelligence.*
© Springer 2010

deployment of AmI even though it will have far-ranging impacts on our way of life. AmI offers great benefits, but poses great risks too.

Of course, no such process was followed when the Internet was constructed, but that is no reason to forsake such a process for AmI. Also, most people in the early 1990s were unaware of the coming of the Internet and the WWW, nor of how quickly they would take root. Such is not the case with AmI. Many people know AmI is coming and many experts have already starting raising yellow flags of caution.

Some people undoubtedly, and perhaps even justifiably, might argue that the development of ambient intelligence per se does not require a formalised risk assessment/risk management process. But ambient intelligence, as wonderful as it may seem, despite its many benefits, will not be risk free; it poses serious risks, not only to our privacy (and, as a consequence, to our democratic values), but also to our security (societal safety).

What is especially new or different about an AmI world compared to today's world (or, even better, compared to the pre-Internet world) is the *scale* of data generated, the omnipresence and pervasiveness of the new technologies and, consequently, the scale of the risks that arise from (theoretically) connecting everything and everybody.

Given the magnitude of risks, not just to privacy, but also to security, it seems eminently reasonable to us that a formalised risk assessment/risk management process should be initiated to consider the risks posed by AmI and the optimum way of treating them. Risk can never be eliminated, but some ways of treating risks are better than others. The key is involving stakeholders in the process in order to determine what ways of treating risks are the most socially acceptable, that have the most consensus of stakeholders.

We think all stakeholders should have the opportunity to participate in the process of assessing and managing the risks posed by AmI.

We are not alone in thinking so. In its guidelines towards a culture of security, the OECD has emphasised that "all participants are responsible for the security of information systems and networks" and that "participants should conduct risk assessments". Further, it has been said that "security management should be based on risk assessment and should be dynamic, encompassing all levels of participants' activities and all aspects of their operations. It should include forward-looking responses to emerging threats."[2]

We would not expect the outcome of any risk assessment/risk management process to call a halt to the deployment of AmI. Even if that were desirable, it is not practicable, nor feasible. In any event, deployment of AmI technologies has already begun.

We recommend that the Commission should initiate a consultation process. It could proceed by announcing the initiation of such a process and invite comments,

---

[2] OECD *Guidelines for the Security of Information Systems and Networks: Towards a culture of security*, OECD, Paris, 2002, pp. 10–12.

as the UK House of Lords has done on the issue of personal Internet security or it could prepare an initial consultation document on AmI, outlining its benefits, threats and vulnerabilities, identify stakeholder groups and solicit their views with regard to those threats and vulnerabilities and the best ways of managing the risks.

We think that a formalised risk assessment/risk management process would, if nothing else, help to raise awareness of AmI and the risks it poses. Consulting concerned citizens and those who represent citizens (including legislators) at the stage of development would increase the legitimacy of new technologies, how they should be deployed and used.

The Commission has invited the private sector to "Involve the insurance sector in developing appropriate risk management tools and methods to tackle ICT-related risks and foster a culture of risk management in organisations and business (in particular in SMEs)".[3] We agree with and support this encouragement from the Commission, particularly, because "risk management tools and methods" have not much of a history in being applied to high-tech social and security risks such as ambient intelligence. A Commission staff paper has also suggested that one option to improve the security of communication networks is to implement and maintain adequate risk management systems based on recognised international standards.[4] However, while it is good that the Commission recognises the value of applying risk management tools and methods to ICT-related risks, we do not think that this Commission suggestion goes far enough, particularly in involving all stakeholders, as we recommend.[5] Furthermore, the aforementioned option would involve EU legislation imposing detailed technical and organisational obligations for providers of electronic communications networks and/or services, whereas we recommend that the Commission initiate the risk management process described above. We agree with the Commission when it says, "Identifying and meeting security challenges in

---

[3] European Commission, *A strategy for a Secure Information Society – "Dialogue, partnership and empowerment"*, Communication from the Commission to the Council, the European Parliament, the European Economic and Social Committee and the Committee of the Regions, COM(2006) 251, Brussels, 31 May 2006, p. 9 (section 3.3.2). http://ec.europa.eu/information_society/doc/com2006251.pdf

[4] Impact Assessment: Commission Staff Working Document, Communication from the Commission to the Council, the European Parliament, the European Economic and Social Committee and the Committee of the Regions on the Review of the EU Regulatory Framework for electronic communications networks and services, SEC(2006) 817, Brussels, 28 June 2006, p. 27. http://ec.europa.eu/information_society/policy/ecomm/doc/info_centre/public_consult/review/impactassessment_final.pdf

[5] In this context, it is useful to note that the UK House of Lords Select Committee on Science and Technology initiated an investigation into personal Internet security and opened its consultation to all, including the public, by inviting comments and inputs by the end of October 2006. It issued its report in the summer of 2007. See House of Lords Science and Technology Select Committee, *Personal Internet Security*, 10 August 2007. http://www.parliament.uk/hlscience.

relation to information systems and networks in the EU requires the full commitment of all stakeholders,"[6] but getting that commitment, aye, there's the rub. In
order to get that commitment, stakeholders must be given and encouraged to play
a meaningful role from the outset of the risk management process, rather than simply leaving it up to the private sector and the insurance industry to devise some
appropriate tools.

## 6.2   Recommendations for the European Commission

### 6.2.1   Research and development

The development of AmI safeguards should be supported as much as possible,
especially because they are the main means expected to help protect people from
accidental as well as intentional privacy violations.

Further harmonisation of standards with varying degrees of geographical scope
will be needed (e.g., EU, international). Some countries, however, will not be able
to afford to fully comply with the standards created in developed countries.
Solutions to overcome the potential divides based on insufficient interoperability
need to be envisaged.

The Commission should ensure that privacy, identity, trust, security and digital
divide issues are taken into account in any project it supports. As has been demon-
strated, it is crucial to integrate privacy and security aspects from the very beginning
in any development process. Once certain technical platforms, standards or system
designs are established, it is often too late or the additional costs become unreasonably
high to adequately include appropriate safeguards.

Research on technologies that could help protect our privacy and strengthen the
security of networks and devices (against attackers and other vulnerabilities), and
that could help to minimise the digital divide should be increased. Certain problems cannot be solved by other than technology means: if there are no human–
technology interfaces for all categories of possible users (including disabled users
or people capable of speaking only one language), then the digital divide will continue to exist. If no user-friendly security exists, security recommendations will
not be followed.

Hence concrete, step-by-step initiatives such as the EC-initiated consultation on
RFIDs in March 2006[7] are to be welcomed. Further research on the RFID technology
and its privacy implications is recommended. This research should also aim at
determining whether any legislative action is needed to address the specific privacy

---

[6] COM(2006) 251, section 4.

[7] http://www.rfidconsultation.eu/

concerns of RFID technology. We also recommend further development of codes of conducts and good practices with regard to the use of RFIDs.

Similar consultations with regard to other relevant technologies and concepts, e.g., biometrics and interoperability, could be considered. The implications for privacy caused by other technologies, such as location-tracking systems, physiological sensors, video and audio sensors should be evaluated, and good practices in use of these technologies should be developed and widely promulgated.

## 6.2.2 Internal market and consumer protection

### 6.2.2.1 Prevent discriminatory service refusal

Effective safeguards to reduce the possibility of ill-founded service refusals mainly apply to the regulatory sphere.

- Regulations and user-friendly tools (which present all relevant information in concise and impressive form, perhaps with examples of possible negative consequences) need to provide for sufficient transparency. This would contribute to strengthening the customers' position and serve as a limitation to the exploitation of asymmetric power relations.
- AmI applications should be implemented preferably on the basis of an opt-in option (the user explicitly chooses to accept the application). In cases when applications are built in such a way that they are constantly attentive to all people around (e.g., to all visitors in a smart space), an option to opt-out needs to be incorporated, confining disadvantages as far as possible.
- Alternative procedures need to be available at reasonable cost in case of technical failures or if individuals request access without having the ability to meet the technical standards.
- Users should have the option to switch off different functionalities of personal devices independently of each other, unlike the current situation when many types (although not all) of mobile phones keep the wireless connection always on when the phone is switched on, so that it is impossible to use, for example, the calendar application without your service provider's being aware of your current location.

By the same token, individuals should have the option to switch off their personal AmI devices (either completely or selected functionalities, e.g., to switch off wireless communication) so that even if they are being captured by surveillance cameras, their own devices are not contributing to their being tracked. Effective, free, informed and specific consent should be the basis of the EU policy regarding the internal market and consumer protection.

#### 6.2.2.2   Prevent victimisation

As in the case of service refusals, in order to reduce the adverse side effects of victimisation based, for instance, on faulty profiling, secondary back-up procedures
need to be in place, incorporating additional contextual information which enable
authorities to take informed decisions without being entirely dependent upon a
technical system.

#### 6.2.2.3   Electronic commerce and consumer protection

The Directive on electronic commerce should be updated to include the possibility
of concluding contracts by electronic means (including reference to intelligent
agents). In any updating of the Directive, there is also a need to facilitate the usage
of pseudonyms, trusted third parties and credentials in electronic commerce.
Intelligent agents could also assist consumers in the management of (electronic)
information to which, under the law, they are entitled.

An increasing number of service providers will be involved in AmI services
and it may not be feasible for all of them to provide the required information
about their data processing activities to consumers. One solution may be a
requirement to provide such information about only the service provider whom
the consumer directly pays and who is responsible to the consumer (joint liability
would apply).

In an AmI world, services will be provided instantly and will be increasingly
personalised. In many cases, the right of the consumer to withdraw from the service
may not be applicable, feasible or practicable. New solutions should be developed
to address this problem.

### 6.2.3   Privacy and security policy framework

On 31 May 2006, the Commission issued a communication in which it proposed
a strategy for a secure Information Society.[8] We agree with and support the measures set out in the communication, however, we do not think that it goes far
enough. The strategy proposes measures that the Commission itself, Member
States, the private sector and individuals can take to combat the bad guys who are
responsible for attacking our network and information security. There is an
implicit assumption that the bad guys who are "increasingly motivated by profit
rather than by the desire to create disruption for its own sake" are someone else.

---

[8] European Commission, *A strategy for a Secure Information Society.*

However, we are reminded of the famous line from Pogo, the American cartoon strip from the 1960s: "We have met the enemy and he is us." We have, we trust, cited a sufficient number of press reports in this book to indicate that the bad guys are not just rogue individuals from rogue states, but also governments and the private sector here at home.

The Commission "proposes a dynamic and integrated approach that involves all stakeholders", but is rather thin on specific initiatives with regard to involving users and civil society organisations. It mentions a "structured multi-stakeholder debate" and cites the "i2010 – Towards a Ubiquitous European Information Society" conference in September 2006,[9] as a contribution to this debate. It also proposes "a seminar reflecting on ways to raise security awareness and strengthen the trust of end-users in the use of electronic networks and information systems". However, given the seriousness and pervasiveness of the risks to security and privacy posed by AmI, we think such initiatives are a good start, but do not go far enough.

Security should be valued as a collective asset. It is a collective good that should in principle be open to everyone. Governments should not leave choices regarding security to the market alone, but impose high standards and invest the necessary means. To claim security rights with such a strong collective basis, associations of all kinds are far better placed than individuals. If privacy and security have a future, associations should be allowed to defend them in court.

### 6.2.4   Correcting the lacunae that exist in legislation, regulation

We recommend that most of the challenges of new AmI environments be met by legal instruments that do not prohibit new technologies but channel them (transparency tools). In practice, this means data protection and security measures, rather than criminal law prohibitions and heavy administrative burdens. Transparency

---

[9] The conference, held in Finland on 27–28 September 2006 during Finland's Presidency of the EU, was arranged by the Finnish Ministry of Transport and Communications, the European Commission and the European Network and Information Security Agency (ENISA). The conference examined the opportunities and challenges of the new information technology and the impacts on data security, e-services and communication networks. See http://eu2006.mintc.fi/communications/i2010. For the Finnish Presidency's conclusions from the conference, see http://europa.eu.int/information_society/eeurope/i2010/index_en.htm. Among the conclusions were that "The development of the ubiquitous information society requires the participation of all the relevant stakeholders, including civil society, national governments, industry and academia." The concept of the Ubiquitous Information Society ("U-society") refers to the next overall phase of the information society, in which people's ways of life and work will be based on their having ICT services that are available at all times and in all places.

should be the default position, although some prohibitions based on political balances, ethical reasons and core legal concepts should also be considered in policy debates.

We recommend respect for the diversity and plurality of law-makers within Europe. Without underestimating the role of the EU institutions, it would not be beneficial to single out these institutions as solely responsible for the AmI environment. The proposals produced by different stakeholders should be taken into consideration and they should be actively involved in policy discussions. Development of case law should also be closely observed.

In initiatives leading to standardisation of technical specifications for RFIDs, as well as any other similar technology, data protection concerns should be reflected. Privacy assessment of each particular RFID application could be a legally binding obligation.

Development of participatory impact assessment procedures would allow stakeholders to quickly identify and react to any negative features of technology.

A legal framework for sharing knowledge from AmI-generated profiles should be developed, as well as legal protection of technical solutions enabling such information management. A legal framework is needed to cover automated protocols for policy negotiations as well as automated schemes that imply the consent of the data subject. The legal framework should cover situations wherein the explicit consent of the data subject for each collection of data is expanded to include a "consent" given by an intelligent agent.

It is necessary to consider development of legal rules with regard to issues that are specific to AmI. In that respect, we propose that legal schemes be developed for digital territories as an important safeguard of privacy in the digital world of AmI. Especially, we propose to protect such territories against unlawful and unnecessary interference. The specific legal schemes would also be necessary to address the use of software agents and PETs.

The consumer should always be aware of any technological measures embedded in any product he purchases, and restrictions in use of such products as a consequence of technological protection. Product warnings and consumer notifications should always be in place, and should serve to raise consumer awareness about DRMs, RFIDs and any other technologies having similar impacts.

The right to information (manageable by intelligent agents) is not only a safeguard of consumer rights, but also a privacy safeguard. Thus, we think the individual should have access to information, in both human and machine-readable form, possibly facilitated by use of user-friendly information notices.

Effective liability rules, facilitating proof and empowering individuals (e.g., via representative actions, reversing the burden of proof and strict liability rules), can have a big impact in enforcement of legal provisions. Further examination of such issues is merited.

With regard to jurisdiction and the applicable law, more clarity and legal certainty are desirable. The Commission should consider a departure from the territorial criterion currently used in private international law towards a personal criterion, especially since personal data are linked with an identity and a state of a data subject (issues which are regulated by the national law of the person).

The biggest weakness in enforcement of rights is the limitation of any European rules to Member States only or to countries that have signed international conventions such as the Cybercrime Convention. Clearly, IT and AmI have global dimensions. International co-operation in developing and enforcing the legal framework is necessary. Therefore, the development of a more comprehensive international co-operation framework that would take AmI technologies and capabilities into account is urgent.[10]

## 6.2.5   Socio-economic measures

The Commission should consider whether new emerging AmI services or at least a basic set of such services should be provided to all in the context of an updated Universal Service Directive. Some services (e.g., emergency services) could be provided free of charge or as part of social security schemes.

## 6.3   Recommendations for the Member States

In the procurement of ICT products, Member States should give emphasis to critical issues such as security and trustworthiness.

Member States should consider introducing legislative prohibitions on the admissibility (or general acceptance of the exclusionary rule) of evidence obtained through infringements of privacy and/or data protection law.

Appropriate authorities (e.g., the Data Protection Officer) should control and authorise applications of implants after the assessment of the particular circumstances in each case. When an implant enables tracking of people, people should have the possibility to disconnect the implant and to be informed when a (distant) communication (e.g., through an RFID) is taking place.

We agree with the European Group on Ethics in Science and New Technologies that irreversible ICT implants should not be used, except for medical purposes. Further research on the long-term impact of ICT implants is recommended.[11]

---

[10] Ofcom, the UK communications regulator, echoes our conclusion with regard to today's Internet: "Effective consumer protection on the internet requires more significant levels of international co-operation than currently exist." Ofcom, *Online protection: A survey of consumer, industry and regulatory mechanisms and systems*, Office of Communications, London, 21 June 2006, p. 4. http://www.ofcom.org.uk/research/technology/onlineprotection/report.pdf

[11] European Group on Ethics in Science and New Technologies, "Ethical Aspects of ICT Implants in the Human Body", Opinion to the Commission, 16 March 2005. http://europa.eu/comm/european_group_ethics/docs/avis20en.pdf

In addition to and in line with the right to remain anonymous goes the use of anonymous and pseudonymous credentials, accompanied by unlinkability in certain situations (e.g., e-commerce). Some reconciliation may be necessary between privacy requirements and accountability requirements, for example, in e-commerce. In fact, such mechanisms should always be foreseen when disclosing someone's identity or when linking information is not necessary. Such necessity should not be easily assumed, and in every circumstance more privacy-friendly technological solutions should be sought.[12] However, the use of anonymity should be well balanced. To avoid its misuse, digital anonymity could be further legally regulated, especially stating when it is not appropriate.[13]

Governments that have not yet done so should ratify the Cybercrime Convention. A "revision" mechanism would be desirable so that signatories could negotiate and include in the Convention definitions of new, emerging cybercrimes. Specific provisions criminalising identity theft and (some forms of) unsolicited communication could be included within the scope of the Convention.

An obligation to prevent data laundering should be imposed on those who buy or otherwise acquire databases, profiles and vast amounts of personal data and to check diligently the legal origin of the data. If the buyer does not check the origin and/or the legality of the databases and profiles, he could be considered a receiver of stolen goods and thus held liable for illegal data processing. An obligation could also be created which would require buyers to notify the national data protection officers when personal data(bases) are acquired. Persons or companies involved or assisting in data laundering could be made subject to criminal sanctions.

Governments could fundamentally contribute to the development of good standards by increasing technical regulations, by financing and co-operating in research that leads to standards and by imposing taxes on non-standardised goods and services.

Improving awareness and education should be the responsibility of Member States and/or regional or local authorities (following the subsidiarity principle).

## 6.4   Recommendations for industry

An approach to alleviate concerns about latent operations and data misuse, thus reducing distrust, is to enhance transparency by effectively informing users about system procedures, purposes and responsibilities. Any networked device, particularly

---

[12] Leenes, Ronald, and Bert-Jan Koops, "'Code': Privacy's Death or Saviour?", *International Review of Law, Computers &Technology*, Vol. 19, No. 3, 2005, p. 37.

[13] See Gasson, M., M. Meints and K. Warwick (eds.), *A study on PKI and biometrics*, FIDIS (Future of Identity in the Information Society), Deliverable D3.2, July 2005, pp. 35–36. http://www.fidis.net

those used by consumer-citizens should come with a privacy warning much like the warnings on tobacco products.

All employees should always be clearly informed about their employer's surveillance policy (when and where surveillance is taking place, what use is made of surveillance data, what information is collected, how long it is stored, what are the (procedural) rights of the employees when personal data are to be used as evidence, etc.).

The International Organization for Standardization (ISO) has developed helpful standards and evaluation criteria relevant for IT privacy and security including, most notably, the ISO 15408 and ISO 17799 standards. Industrial organisations and leaders should highlight the value of ISO certification processes and established codes of practice.

Organisations that compile databases with personal data (even if such compilation is incidental to their primary lines of business) should state on their websites and on product information to what extent they are compliant with ISO 17799 and/ or how they have implemented the standard. An organisation could also mention to what extent they follow other guidelines dealing with privacy and security, such as those produced by the OECD.

Those designing AmI networks should ensure that the networks have features that enable effective audits.

Industry should expend less effort on fighting new regulations and more effort on involving stakeholders in the assessment and management of risks to privacy, identity, trust, security and inclusiveness. Involving stakeholders at an early stage will minimise downstream risks.

With regard to use of key AmI technologies (such as networking of devices and objects, location tracking, authentication, etc.), manufacturers, suppliers and network operators must do their utmost to avoid negative impacts and the bad publicity that follows as a consequence. This will best be done by involving privacy advocates and public interest groups at an early stage in the development of new technologies, especially in actively seeking their views about possible impacts and how such impacts are best addressed.

Engineers and others should not regard technology as "neutral". New technologies often raise policy issues, and this is certainly true of ambient intelligence. AmI offers great benefits, but the risk of not adequately addressing public concerns could mean delays in implementing the technologies, a lack of public support for taxpayer-funded research and vociferous protests by privacy protection advocates.

As interoperability is a precondition for AmI, programmes should be developed so that they are interoperable with each other. That implies a need for new standards applicable to AmI. It also implies that AmI may need limitations on exclusive intellectual property rights. Broader scope of the decompilation right would be desirable.

Achieving worldwide interoperability based on standards could also lead to a narrowing of the digital divide. Assistance to the countries and societies that cannot afford to comply with standards developed by the rich and technologically advanced countries is desirable and may be necessary.

## 6.5   Recommendations for civil society organisations

An alternative to peer-rating systems are credibility-rating systems based on the assessment of trusted and independent institutions, such as library associations, consumer groups or other professional associations with widely acknowledged expertise within their respective domains. Ratings should be based on systematic assessments against clearly defined quality standards.

Consumer associations and other civil society organisations (CSOs) could play a useful role as a mediator between service providers and individual consumers and, more particularly, in forcing the development of service contracts (whether real or implicit) between the service provider and the individual consumer. Consumer organisations could leverage their negotiating position through the use of the media or other means of communication with their members. CSOs could position themselves closer to the industry vanguard as represented in platforms such as ARTEMIS by becoming members of such platforms themselves. Within these platforms, CSOs could encourage industry to develop "best practices" in terms of provision of services to consumers.

## 6.6   Recommendations for academia

Institutes of higher education should ensure that courses in ICT-relevant disciplines include content such as the following:

- Impacts of ICTs on society
- Knowledge from technology assessment or from "impact and design research", which has come into being in the field of computing
- Promotion of awareness of health and environmental considerations in the development of new technologies.

Such content should, where possible, be integrated into existing school courses. The focus should be on longer-term principles, and shorter-lived phenomena should be included only where they provide a clear example of a general principle. Incorporation of these issues into revised curricula will require additional training for teaching staff.

Consumers need to be educated about the privacy ramifications arising from virtually any transaction in which they are engaged. An education campaign should be targeted at different segments of the population. Targeting school-age children should be included in any such campaign.

Universities should (continue to) participate in the development of technological safeguards, such as privacy and security protection in networks (including mobile, ad-hoc and sensor networks, as well as personal area networks), in personal devices and in smart spaces, in identity management systems and in developing technological means to minimise the digital divide (such as user interfaces for all, language translation tools and e-learning methods).

## 6.7   Recommendations for individuals

Users cannot be innocent bystanders and expect others to look after their interests with regard to privacy and security aspects of the emerging AmI world. We concur with the OECD when it says "Participants [including individual users] should be aware of the need for security of information systems and networks and what they can do to enhance security. ... Participants should be aware of the ... good practices that they can implement to enhance security, and the needs of other participants."[14] At the same time, we recognise that such good advice cannot be taken onboard by all users, such as children, the disabled and the elderly. Hence, provision needs to be made for disadvantaged segments of the population.

---

[14] OECD *Guidelines for the Security of Information Systems and Networks: Towards a Culture of Security*, OECD, Paris, 2002, p. 10.

# Chapter 7
# Conclusions

## 7.1 User control and enforceability

Some say that an increase in security does not necessarily mean a further encroachment on privacy – indeed, security is necessary to protect personal data and our privacy. Networks must be secure, our personal devices, reliable, dependable and trustworthy. But security is a multifaceted term, with many dimensions.

We are of the view that an increase in security most likely *will* encroach upon our privacy in an ambient intelligence world. Surveillance cameras will continue to proliferate. We assume that, whatever the law is, whatever privacy protections government and business *say* they honour, our telecommunications, e-mails and Internet usage will be monitored to an increasing degree. The same will be true of our interfaces with the world of ambient intelligence. The products we buy and use will be linked to us. Personal data will be mined, linked and processed, traded, shared and sold. Many such practices will be unjustified and will violate our rights and civil liberties. We assume or should assume that those encroaching upon our rights and civil liberties will be not only criminals, but (supposedly) legitimate businesses and governments. Even so, the majority of the population may be willing to accept such encroachments because they are genuinely concerned about their own security, that of their family and fellow citizens. The so-called war on terror has undoubtedly provided fertile ground for acceptance of new security measures.[1]

In an AmI world, we can expect to see a direct trade-off between privacy and security, where the latter refers to the safety of the individual and/or especially the community or society in which he or she lives. We can assume that gains in security

---

[1] "Since the 2001 terror attacks, a slim majority of the American public has favoured protecting security over preserving civil liberties, according to opinion pollsters." Mohammed, Arshad, and Sara Kehaulani Goo, "Government Increasingly Turning to Data Mining", *The Washington Post*, 15 June 2006. http://www.washingtonpost.com/wp-dyn/content/article/2006/06/14/AR2006061402063.html

D. Wright et al. (eds.), *Safeguards in a World of Ambient Intelligence.*
© Springer 2010                                                                267

will be made at the expense of losses in privacy.[2] We do not see an easy solution to this problem: indeed, there may not be any. Perhaps the most we can hope for is that unjustified encroachments, abuses and violations will come to light and that offenders will be prosecuted. Coupled with this unhappy prospect is the need for users to be aware, to be vigilant at all times when and where their privacy is put at risk or might be at risk and what they can do, individually and collectively, to mini-mise those risks. We trust that the safeguards we have suggested in this report go some distance towards minimising those risks.

We also see a problem in the trade-off between restricting the availability of personal data and personalisation of services. Many of the benefits of AmI lie in the availability of such data in order to personalise services. The greater the restrictions on such data, the greater is the risk that we will not enjoy the full benefits offered by AmI.[3] The restrictions on such data may be imposed by law or by the individual or even by model corporate citizens. Government and, especially, corporate service providers will inevitably want as much personal data as they can get in order to personalise services as much as possible. However, the law may set some limits on how much they can get, and users with their personal devices and privacy-enhancing technologies may also set some limits. Where these limits are set partly depends on how much confidence or trust we (individually and collectively) have in AmI net-works (or any network for that matter). If we were confident in the security of the networks and our devices and the software that drives them, then we might be will-ing to extend those limits and accordingly enjoy greater benefits from AmI. But breaches in networks and software are a daily occurrence today and as networks become increasingly interconnected and complex, we can (should) assume that breaches will continue to plague us for the foreseeable future. Theoretically, it might be possible to solve or at least greatly reduce the risk of breaches in security, but then we run up against the human dimension. Even if it is possible to build totally secure networks and services, how much trust are we willing to extend to governments and businesses or anyone that they will respect our privacy and not abuse it? Unfortunately, even if technology could be made reliable and secure, the prospect of changing human behaviour is less promising.

Given the problems, the best prospect for ensuring user control and enforceabil-ity of policy in an accessible manner is to involve the user in the process of formu-lating policy, to achieve so far as possible consensus on a policy development to which the user has contributed. The user should be encouraged to express his or her

---

[2] Security expert Bruce Schneier has commented, "We're not trading privacy for security; we're giving up privacy and getting no security in return." Schneier, Bruce, "Why Data Mining Won't Stop Terror", *Wired News*, 9 March 2005. http://www.schneier.com/essay-108.html

[3] The point is made in Cas, Johann, "Privacy in Pervasive Computing Environments – A Contradiction in Terms?", *IEEE Technology and Society Magazine*, Vol. 24, Issue 1, Spring 2005, pp. 24–33. http://www-personal.si.umich.edu/~rfrost/courses/SI110/paper_support/Cas,%20Privacy%20and%20Ubiquity.pdf

views, to provide information that might be helpful to other stakeholders. The views of all stakeholders (including users) should be carefully considered and they should be informed to what extent they have been taken into account or, if they have not been, then why not.

Needless to say, user control and enforceability of policy will work best in a transparent decision-making process, and we commend, as stated above, a formalised risk assessment/risk management process to that end.

In addition, we think industry initiatives, notably that of the ARTEMIS platform, would be more successful if user concerns were recognised and taken into account through the participation of civil society organisations. Issues of privacy, identity management and digital divide should be considered by all working groups in academia and industry. Industry participants should not see regulatory concerns as barriers to be overcome, but as opportunities to ensure user acceptance of AmI. As the Commission has generally been promoting platforms as a means of strengthening European success in key areas, so the Commission could take the initiative to encourage ARTEMIS to establish a working group devoted to the policy issues that have been the focus of this book. This recommendation could also be applicable to other EC-inspired platforms.

## 7.2 The top six

This book has identified many threats and vulnerabilities and many safeguards for dealing with them. Perhaps we have identified too many safeguards or made too many recommendations, at least, in the sense that so many may seem daunting. Hence, we have prioritised them and selected the following as our top six recommendations.

1. The Commission, together with Member States, perhaps under the auspices of ENISA, should initiate a formalised risk assessment/risk management process with regard to the risks posed by AmI to security and privacy. We recommend that the assessment and decision-making process be open, transparent and inclusive, that stakeholder groups be identified and contacted and encouraged to take part in the process. Individuals should also be given an opportunity to express their views. Such a process could be initiated by means of a green paper on the risks to security and privacy in an AmI world. Whatever the outcome of the process, we recommend that the risk assessment be undertaken again (and again) in the future with some regularity, the periodicity of which might depend on the rapidity with which AmI is deployed (bearing in mind that the technologies for AmI are already being developed and deployed).

   We also recommend that the precautionary approach be taken into account when developing and deploying new technologies. Such an exercise might be considered as a legal obligation.

2. The Commission and Member States should invest in an awareness campaign specifically focused on AmI, the purpose of which would be to explain to all stakeholders, but especially the public, that AmI is on its way, that it offers great benefits, but also raises security and privacy issues. There are many ways of raising awareness (through education, the media, etc.), but to give this recommendation some specific focus, we recommend that Member States hold annual national contests which would offer some form of recognition to the best product or service offering privacy and security protection. We recommend a run-off at European level. This could be a counterpoint to the bad publicity that RFIDs has received in recent years.[4]

   Any such campaign aimed at informing the public about ambient intelligence services and at inspiring trust should involve *all* stakeholders and any such competition should be judged by independent evaluators.

3. The Commission and Member States should review carefully the inadequacies and lacunae noted in this book in the existing legal and regulatory framework with respect to AmI. Law is only one of the available tools for regulating behaviour; others include social norms, market rules and the "code", i.e., the architecture of the technology (e.g., cyberspace, ambient intelligence and mobile telephony). The law can be a regulator on its own, but it can also regulate via influencing the "code" and other modalities of regulation. In order to tackle the identified problems effectively, it is necessary to consider different approaches simultaneously.

4. Most of the challenges of new AmI environments should be met by legal instruments that do not prohibit new technological developments, but channel them (such as by data protection and security measures). Transparency should be the default position, although some prohibitions based on political balances, ethical reasons and core legal concepts should also be considered in policy discussions. Focusing on concrete technologies rather than trying to produce general solutions seems to be more appropriate for AmI, an environment that adapts and responds to changes in context. Privacy and other legal issues are also context dependent.

5. The biggest weakness in enforcement of rights is the limitation of any European rule to Member States only, or to countries that have signed international conventions such as the Cybercrime Convention. Clearly, ICTs and AmI have global dimensions. International co-operation in developing and enforcing the legal framework is necessary. Therefore, the Commission and Member States should be proactive in the development of a more comprehensive international co-operation framework that would take AmI technologies and capabilities into account as a matter of urgency.

---

[4] RFID technologies and their promoters have received Big Brother Awards in various countries worldwide. See, e.g., *http://bigbrotherawards.de/2003/.cop/*; *http://www.edri.org/edrigram/number4.3/frenchbba?PHPSESSID=a08c4d85ac916daab3d8660a1d377dd8*; *http://www.privacyinternational.org/article.shtml?cmd%5B347%5D=x-347-187899*; http://www.bigbrotherawards.cz/en/winners_2005.html

6. The European Commission should ensure that projects that it funds take questions of privacy, security and trust into account. Research programmes should contain a project line of accompanying measures covering the societal impact. Currently, EC calls say that project participants must conform to relevant EU legislation, inter alia, the Data Protection Directive. It is, of course, necessary that project participants (or any third party funded by the EC) conform to EU legislation, but we think the Commission should be more demanding – i.e., it should require those it funds to specifically speculate what privacy or security impacts might arise from their projects and what measures should be taken to address those. In other words, simply conforming to legislation is not enough. Project participants must be asked to foresee or even to speculate what privacy or security implications their projects *might* have. By the same token, the EC proposal and tender evaluators should also be asked to evaluate project proposals and tenders from the same optic. We recommend that Member States adopt a similar approach. We would like to especially emphasise the importance of funding research on technological safeguards for protecting privacy, enhancing security and minimising the digital divide. If technology does not provide solutions for human–technology interfaces for all, or for user-friendly security, other safeguards will not be able to solve the problem. We suggest that among technological safeguards, research on intelligent algorithms is especially important.

As a final, parting comment, we believe that, sooner or later, we will live in a world of ambient intelligence. For ambient intelligence to be a success story, in human terms, according to democratic principles, and not to be an Orwellian world, all stakeholders must be cognisant of the threats and vulnerabilities and work together to ensure that adequate safeguards exist. Certainly, industry should become more active in creating applications that are secure and privacy enhancing since this is the best way to create consumer trust and make ambient intelligence fruitful to *all* participants. Industry should not view privacy, security, identity, trust and inclusion issues as regulatory barriers to be overcome. Rather, they should regard such measures as necessary, justified and, in the end, crucial to ensuring that their fellow citizens will use ambient intelligence technologies and services. In the meantime, we encourage all stakeholders to be vigilant.

# References

Aarts, E.H.L., and J.L. Encarnação (eds.), *True Visions: The Emergence of Ambient Intelligence*, Springer, Berlin/Heidelberg, 2006.

Aarts, E., R. Harwig and M. Schuurmans, "Ambient Intelligence", in P. Denning, *The Invisible Future: The Seamless Integration of Technology in Everyday Life*, McGraw-Hill, New York, 2002.

Aarts, E., and S. Marzano (eds.), *The New Everyday: Views on Ambient Intelligence*, Uitgeverij 010 Publishers, Rotterdam, 2003.

Åkesson, K.-P., J. Humble, A. Crabtree and A. Bullock, *Usage and Development Scenarios for the Tangible Toolbox*, ACCORD Deliverable D1.3, Swedish Institute of Computer Science, Kista, 2001.

Alahuhta, P., M. Jurvansuu and H. Pentikäinen, "Roadmap for network technologies and service", *Tekes Technology Review* 162/2004, Tekes, Helsinki, 2004.

Albrecht, K., "Supermarket Cards: The Tip of the Retail Surveillance Iceberg", *Denver University Law Review*, No. 79, 2002, pp. 534–539, 558–565.

Alheit, K., "The applicability of the EU Product Liability Directive to Software", *The Comparative and International Law Journal of South Africa*, Vol. 3, No. 2, 2001.

Andrews, S., *Privacy and Human Rights 2002*, produced by the Electronic Privacy Information Center (EPIC), Washington, DC, and *Privacy International*, London, 2002. http://www.privacyinternational.org/survey/phr2002/

*ARTEMIS Strategic Research Agenda*, First Edition, March 2006. http://www.artemis-office.org/DotNetNuke/PressCorner/tabid/89/Default.aspx

Article 29 Data Protection Working Party, *Recommendation 3/97: anonymity on the Internet* (WP 6), adopted on 3 December 1997, available through http://ec.europa.eu/justice_home/fsj/privacy/

Article 29 Data Protection Working Party, *Opinion on more harmonised information provisions* (11987/04/EN – WP 100), adopted on 25 November 2004, available through http://ec.europa.eu/justice_home/fsj/privacy/

Article 29 Data Protection Working Party, *Working document on the surveillance of electronic communications in the workplace* (5401/01/EN/Final – WP 55), adopted 29 May 2002, available through http://ec.europa.eu/justice_home/fsj/privacy/

Article 29 Data Protection Working Party, *Working document on determining the international application of EU data protection law to personal data processing on the Internet by non-EU based web sites* (5035/01/EN/Final WP 56), 30 May 2002. http://ec.europa.eu/justice_home/fsj/privacy/docs/wpdocs/2002/wp56_en.pdf

Article 29 Data Protection Working Party in *Working document on the processing of personal data by means of video surveillance* (11750/02/EN – WP 67), adopted 25 November 2002, available through http://ec.europa.eu/justice_home/fsj/privacy/

Article 29 Data Protection Working Party, *Working document on biometrics* (12168/02/EN – WP 80), adopted on 1 August 2003, available through http://ec.europa.eu/justice_home/fsj/privacy/

Article 29 Data Protection Working Party, *Working document on data protection issues related to intellectual property rights* (WP 104), adopted on 18 January 2005. http://ec.europa.eu/justice_home/fsj/privacy/

Article 29 Data Protection Working Party, *Working document on data protection issues related to RFID technology* (10107/05/EN – WP 105), 19 January 2005. http://ec.europa.eu/justice_home/fsj/privacy/

Article 29 Working Party, Opinion 4/2005 on the Proposal for a Directive on the retention of Data processed in connection with the Provision of Public Electronic Communications Services and Amending Directive 2002/58/EC. http://ec.europa.eu/justice_home/fsj/privacy/workinggroup/index_en.htm

Article 29 Data Protection Working Party, Opinion 5/2007 on the follow-up agreement between the European Union and the United States of America on the processing and transfer of passenger name record (PNR) data by air carriers to the United States Department of Homeland Security concluded in July 2007 (01646/07/EN-WP138). http://ec.europa.eu/justice_home/fsj/privacy/docs/wp138_en.pdf

Aschmoneit, P., and M. Höbig, *Context-Aware Collaborative Environments for Next Generation Business Networks: Scenario Document*, COCONET deliverable D 2.2, Telematica Institute, Enschede, 2002. http://www.mosaic-network.org/library/scenarios.html

Bauer, M., M. Meints and M. Hansen (eds.), *Structured Overview on Prototypes and Concepts of Identity Management Systems*, FIDIS (Future of Identity in the Information Society) Deliverable D3.1, September 2005.

Becher, A., Z. Benenson and M. Dornseif, "Tampering with Motes: Real-World Physical Attacks on Wireless Sensor Networks", Third International Conference on Security in Pervasive Computing, York, UK, April 2006, pp. 104–118.

Beslay, L., and H. Hakala, "Digital Territory: Bubbles", in P.T. Kidd (ed.), *European Visions for the Knowledge Age: A Quest for New Horizons in the Information Society*, Cheshire Henbury, Macclesfield, UK, 2007. http://cybersecurity.jrc.es/docs/DigitalTerritoryBubbles.pdf

Beslay, L., and Y. Punie, "The Virtual Residence: Identity, Privacy and Security", *Security and Privacy for the Citizen in the Post-September 11 Digital Age: a Prospective Overview*, IPTS Report to the European Parliament Committee on Citizens' Freedoms and Rights, Justice and Home Affairs (LIBE), July 2003. http://www.jrc.es/pages/iptsreport/vol67/english/IPT3E676.html

Bianchi, A., S. Barrios, M. Cabrera et al., *Revisiting eInclusion: from Vision to Action*, EC Directorate-General Joint Research Centre, Institute for Prospective Technological Studies (IPTS), Seville, 2006.

Biever, Celeste, "RFID chips watch Grandma brush teeth", Newscientist.com news service, 17 March 2004.

Björk, S., "Designing Mobile Ad Hoc Collaborative Applications: Scenario Experiences with Smart-Its", www.smart-its.org

Bolle, R.M., J.H. Connell, S. Pankanti, N.K. Ratha and A.W. Senior, *Guide to Biometrics*, Springer, New York, 2004.

Börjeson, L., M. Höjer, K.-H. Dreborg, T. Ekvall and G. Finnveden, "Towards a user's guide to scenarios – a report on scenario types and scenario techniques", Version 1.1b, Department of Urban Studies,Royal Institute of Technology, Stockholm, 2005. http://www.infra.kth.se/fms/pdf/Scenario RapportVer1_1b.pdf

Borking, J., "RFID Security, Data Protection & Privacy, Health and Safety Issues", presentation made during European Commission Consultation on RFID, Brussels, 17 May 2006.

Brey, P., "Freedom and privacy in Ambient Intelligence", *Ethics and Information Technology*, Vol. 7, No. 3, 2005.

Brownsword, R., "Code, Control, and Choice: Why East is East and West is West", *Legal Studies*, Vol. 25, No. 1, March 2005, pp. 1–21.

BSI, IT-Sicherheitshandbuch: Handbuch für die sichere Anwendung der Informationstechnik, Version 1.0, BSI 7105, Bundesamt für Sicherheit in der Informationstechnik [Federal Office for Information Security], Bonn, März 1992.

Burnett, R., and P.D. Marshall, *Web Theory: An Introduction*, Routledge, London, 2002.

Cabrera Giráldez, M., and C. Rodríguez Casal, "The role of Ambient Intelligence in the Social Integration of the Elderly" in G. Riva, F. Vatalaro et al. (eds.), *Ambient Intelligence: The Evolution of Technology, Communication and Cognition Towards the Future of Human-Computer Interaction*, IOS Press (Studies in New Technologies and Practices in Communication, 6), Amsterdam, 2005, pp. 265–280.

Camenisch, J. (ed.), *First Annual Research Report*, PRIME Deliverable D16.1, 2005. http://www.prime-project.eu.org/public/prime_products/deliverables/rsch/pub_del_D16.1.a_ec_wp16.1_V1_final.pdf

Carr, S., "Wireless Tagging in Hospitals is 'Inevitable': Prepare to be chipped …", silicon.com, 7 December 2004. http://hardware.silicon.com/storage/0,39024649,39126387,00.htm

Čas, J., "Privacy in Pervasive Computing Environments – A Contradiction in Terms?", *Technology and Society Magazine*, IEEE, Vol. 24, Issue 1, Spring 2005, pp. 24–33.

CDT (Centre for democracy and technology) Working Group on RFID: Privacy Best Practices for Deployment of RFID Technology, Interim Draft, 1 May 2006, http://www.cdt.org/privacy/20060501rfid-best-practices.php

Claes, E., A. Duff and S. Gutwirth (eds.), *Privacy and the Criminal Law*, Intersentia, Antwerp/Oxford, 2006.

Clarke, R., "Information Technology and Dataveillance", *Communications of the ACM*, Vol. 31, No. 5, May 1988, pp. 498–512.

Creese, S., M. Goldsmith and I. Zakiuddin, "Authentication in Pervasive Computing", First International Conference on Security in Pervasive Computing, Boppard, Germany, 12–14 March 2003, pp. 116–129.

Custers, B., *The Power of Knowledge, Ethical, Legal and Technological Aspects of Data Mining and Group Profiling in Epidemiology*, Wolf Legal Publishers, Nijmegen, 2004.

Da Costa, O., M. Boden, Y. Punie and M. Zappacosta, "Science and Technology Roadmapping from Industry to Public Policy", in *The IPTS Report*, 73, 2003.

Daugman, J., "Iris Recognition: Anti-spoofing Liveness Testing, Stable Biometric Keys, and Further Research Directions", BioSecure 1st Residential Workshop, Paris, August 2005.

De Hert, P., "European Data Protection and E-Commerce: Trust Enhancing?", in J.E.J. Prins, P. M.A. Ribbers, H.C.A. Van Tilborg, A.F.L. Veth and J.G.L. Van Der Wees (eds.), *Trust in Electronic Commerce*, Kluwer Law International, The Hague, 2002, pp. 190–199.

De Hert, P., "De soevereiniteit van de mensenrechten: aantasting door de uitlevering en het bewijsrecht" [Sovereignty of human rights: threats created by the law of extradition and by the law of evidence], *Panopticon, Tijdschrift voor strafrecht, criminologie en forensisch welzijnswerk*, Vol. 25, No. 3, 2004, pp. 229–238.

De Hert, P., *Biometrics: Legal Issues and Implications*, Background paper for the Institute of Prospective Technological Studies, EC – JRC, Seville, January 2005. http://cybersecurity.jrc.es/docs/LIBE%20Biometrics%20March%2005/LegalImplications_Paul_de_Hert.pdf

De Hert, P., "What are the risks and what guarantees need to be put in place in a view of interoperability of the databases?", *Standard Briefing Note "JHA & Data Protection"*, No. 1. January 2006, http://www.vub.ac.be/LSTS/pub/Dehert/006.pdf

De Hert, P., and S. Gutwirth, "Making sense of privacy and data protection. A prospective overview in the light of the future of identity, location based services and the virtual residence" in *Security and Privacy for the Citizen in the Post-September 11 Digital Age: A Prospective Overview*, Report to the European Parliament Committee on Citizens' Freedoms and Rights, Justice and Home Affairs (LIBE), Institute for Prospective Technological Studies – Joint Research Centre, Seville, July 2003, pp. 111–162. ftp://ftp.jrc.es/pub/EURdoc/eur20823en.pdf

De Hert, P., and S. Gutwirth, "Interoperability of police databases: an accountable political choice", *International Review of Law Computers & Technology*, Vol. 20/no. 1–2, 2006, pp. 21–35.

De Hert, P., and S. Gutwirth, "Privacy, data protection and law enforcement. Opacity of the individual and transparency of power" in E. Claes, A. Duff and S. Gutwirth (eds.), *Privacy and the Criminal Law*, Intersentia, Antwerp/Oxford, 2006, pp. 61–104.

De Hert, P., and M. Loncke, "Camera Surveillance and Workplace Privacy in Belgium", in S. Nouwt, B.R. de Vries and C. Prins (eds.), *Reasonable Expectations of Privacy? Eleven Country Reports on Camera Surveillance and Workplace Privacy*, TMC Asser Press, The Netherlands, 2005.

De Hert, P., and F.P. Ölcer, "Het onschadelijk gemaakte Europees privacybegrip. Implicaties voor de Nederlandse strafrechtspleging" [The notion of privacy made innocent. Implications for criminal procedure], *Strafblad. Het nieuwe tijdschrift voor strafrecht*, Vol. 2, No. 2, 2004, pp. 115–134.

Desai, M.S., J. Oghen and T.C. Richards, "Information Technology Litigation and Software Failure", *The Journal of Information, Law & Technology*, Vol. 2, 2002. http://www2.warwick. ac.uk/fac/soc/law/elj/jilt/2002_2/desai/

Dey, A., and J. Mankoff, "Designing Mediation for Context-Aware Applications", *ACM Transactions on Computer-Human Interaction*, Special issue on Sensing-Based Interactions, Vol. 12, Issue 1, March 2005, pp. 53–80.

Drees, C., "Civil liberties debate leaves much of America cold", Reuters, published in *The Washington Post*, 18 May 2006.

Ducot, C., and G.J. Lubben, "A Typology for Scenarios", *Futures*, Vol. 12, February 1980.

Edler, J. (ed.), "Politikbenchmarking Nachfrageorientierte Innovationspolitik", Progress report No. 99, Office for Technology Assessment at the German Parliament, Berlin, 2006.

Eggermont, L.D.J., *Embedded Systems Roadmap 2002*: Vision on technology for the future of PROGRESS, STW Technology Foundation/PROGRESS, Utrecht, 2002. http://www.stw.nl/ progress/ESroadmap/index.html

Emiliani, P.L., and C. Stephanidis, "Universal access to ambient intelligence environments: opportunities and challenges for people with disabilities", *IBM Systems Journal*, Vol. 44, No. 3, 2005, pp. 605–619.

Engberg, S., "Empowerment and Context Security as the route to Growth and Security", SWAMI Final Conference, Brussels, 21–22 March 2006.

Eriksen, E.O., J.E. Fossum and A.J. Menéndez (eds.), *The Chartering of Europe: The European Charter of Fundamental Rights and its Constitutional Implications*, Nomos Verlag, Baden-Baden, 2003.

Espiner, T., "Philips unfurls prototype flexible display", ZDNet UK. http://news.zdnet.co.uk/ hardware/emergingtech/0,39020357,39216111,00.htm

Espiner, T., "Viruses cause most security breaches", ZDNet UK, 28 February 2006. http://news. zdnet.co.uk/0,39020330,39254929,00.htm

Espiner, T., "Philips unfurls prototype flexible display", ZDNet UK, 2 September 2005. http:// news.zdnet.co.uk/hardware/emergingtech/0,39020357,39216111,00.htm

Estrin, D. (ed.), *Embedded, Everywhere*: A Research Agenda for Networked Systems of Embedded Computers, National Academy Press, Washington, DC, 2001.

European Commission, eEurope 2002: An Information Society For All, Action Plan prepared by the Council and the European Commission for the Feira European Council, 19–20 June 2000. http://ec.europa.eu/information_society/eeurope/2002/action_plan/pdf/actionplan_en.pdf

European Commission, *Technology Platforms: from Definition to Implementation of a Common Research Agenda*: Report compiled by a Commission Inter-Service Group on Technology Platforms, Office for Official Publications of the European Communities, Luxembourg, 2004. http://www.eurogif.org/wimages/Technology_Platforms_21_September_2004.pdf

European Commission, *Science and Technology, the Key to Europe's Future – Guidelines for Future European Union Policy to Support Research*, COM(2004) 353 final, Brussels, 2004. ftp://ftp.cordis.lu/pub/era/docs/com2004_353_en.pdf

European Commission, Communication from the Commission to the Council and the European Parliament. The Hague Programme – Ten priorities for the next five years. The Partnership for European renewal in the field of Freedom, Security and Justice, COM(2005) 184 final.

European Commission, Communication from the Commission to the Council, the European Parliament, the European Economic and Social Committee and the Committee of the Regions, eEurope 2005: An information society for all. http://europa.eu.int/information_society/eEurope/2002/news_library/documents/eeurope2005/eeurope2005_en.pdf

European Commission, *Report on European Technology Platforms and Joint Technology Initiatives*: Fostering Public-Private R&D Partnerships to Boost Europe's Industrial Competitiveness, Commission Staff Working Document, SEC(2005) 800, Brussels, 2005.

European Commission, Communication to the Council and the European Parliament on improved effectiveness, enhanced interoperability and synergies among European databases in the area of Justice and Home Affairs, COM (2005) 597 final, Brussels, 24 November 2005.

European Commission, Green Paper on Conflicts of Jurisdiction and the Principle of *ne bis in idem* in Criminal Proceedings, COM(2005) 696, December 2005. http://ec.europa.eu/comm/off/green/index_en.htm

European Commission, *European Technology Platforms: Moving to Implementation*, Second Status Report, Office for Official Publications of the European Communities, Luxembourg, May 2006. ftp://ftp.cordis.europa.eu/pub/technology-platforms/docs/ki7305429ecd.pdf

European Commission, A strategy for a Secure Information Society – "Dialogue, Partnership and Empowerment", Communication from the Commission to the Council, the European Parliament, the European Economic and Social Committee and the Committee of the Regions, Brussels, COM(2006) 251, Brussels, 31 May 2006. http://ec.europa.eu/information_society/doc/com2006251.pdf

European Commission, Impact Assessment: Commission Staff Working Document, Communication from the Commission to the Council, the European Parliament, the European Economic and Social Committee and the Committee of the Regions on the Review of the EU Regulatory Framework for electronic communications networks and services, SEC(2006) 817, Brussels, 28 June 2006. http://ec.europa.eu/information_society/policy/ecomm/doc/info_centre/public_consult/review/impactassessment_final.pdf

European Commission, Communication from the Commission to the European Parliament and the Council on Promoting Data Protection by Privacy Enhancing Technologies (PETs), COM (2007) 228 final, Brussels, 2 May 2007.

European Data Protection Supervisor (EDPS), *Opinion on the Proposal for a Regulation of the European Parliament and of the Council Concerning the Visa Information System (VIS) and the Exchange of Data between Member States on Short Stay-visas*, COM (2004) 835 final, *Official Journal* C 181/27, 23 July 2005.

European Data Protection Supervisor (EDPS), *Annual Report 2005*. http://www.edps.eu.int/publications/annual_report_en.htm

European Data Protection Supervisor (EDPS), *Comments on the Communication of the Commission on Interoperability of European Databases*, 10 March 2006. http://www.edps.eu.int/legislation/Comments/06-03-10_Comments_interoperability_EN.pdf

European Data Protection Supervisor (EDPS), *Opinion on the Proposal for a Council Framework Decision on the Exchange of Information under the Principle of Availability (COM (2005) 490 final)*, Brussels, 28 February 2006. http://www.edps.eu.int/legislation/Opinions_A/06-02-28_Opinion_availability_EN.pdf

European Group on Ethics in Science and New Technologies, "Ethical Aspects of ICT Implants in the Human Body", Opinion to the Commission, 16 March 2005. http://europa.eu/comm/european_group_ethics/docs/avis20en.pdf

Friedewald, M., R. Lindner and D. Wright (eds.), *Threats, Vulnerabilities and Safeguards in Ambient Intelligence*, Deliverable D3, A report of the SWAMI consortium to the European Commission, 3 July 2006.

Friedewald, M., E. Vildjiounaite, Y. Punie and D. Wright, "The Brave New World of Ambient Intelligence: An Analysis of Scenarios Regarding Privacy, Identity and Security Issues", in J. A. Clark et al. (eds.), *Security in Pervasive Computing*: Proceedings of the Third International Conference, SPC 18–21 April 2006, York, UK, Springer, Berlin, 2006.

Friedewald, M., and D. Wright (eds.), *Report on the Final Conference*, Brussels, 21–22 March 2006, SWAMI Deliverable D5, 2006.

Friedewald, M., E. Vildjiounaite and D. Wright, *The Brave New World of Ambient Intelligence*, Deliverable D1, A report of the SWAMI consortium to the European Commission under contract 006507, June 2005.

FTC, "Future Threats and Crimes in an Ambient Intelligent Everyday Environment" supplied by Qinetiq and Transcrime for IPTS/JRC under contract 22152-2004-06-F7SC SEV GB, July 2005.

Fujawa, J.M., "Privacy Made Public: Will National Security Be the End of Individualism?" *Computers and Society*, Vol. 35, No. 2, 2005.

Fule, P., and J.F. Roddick, "Detecting Privacy and Ethical Sensitivity in Data Mining Results" in V. Estivill-Castro (ed.), *Computer Science 2004*, Twenty-Seventh Australasian Computer Science Conference (ACSC2004), Dunedin, New Zealand, January 2004, Australian Computer Society (CRPIT, 26), 2004, pp. 159–166.

Garate, A., I. Lucas, N. Herrasti and A. Lopez, "Ambient Intelligence Technologies for Home Automation and Entertainment", in EUSAI 2004, Workshop "Ambient Intelligence Technologies for Well-Being at Home", 2004.

García, R.A., "The General Provisions of the Charter of Fundamental Rights of the European Union", Jean Monnet Working Paper 4/02. http://www.jeanmonnetprogram.org

Garlan, D., D. Siewiorek, A. Smailagic and P. Steenkiste, "Project Aura: Toward Distraction-Free Pervasive Computing" in *IEEE Pervasive Computing*, Vol. 21, No. 2, 2002.

Gasson, M., M. Meints and K. Warwick (eds.), *A study on PKI and Biometrics*, FIDIS (Future of Identity in the Information Society) Deliverable D3.2, July 2005. http://www.fidis.net

Gavigan, J.P., F. Scapolo, M. Keenan, I. Miles, F. Farhi, D. Lecoq, M. Capriati, T. Di Bartolomeo (eds.), "A practical guide to Regional Foresight", EUR 20128 EN, IPTS, Seville, December 2001.

Gehring, R.A., "Software Development, Intellectual Property, and IT Security", *The Journal of Information, Law and Technology*, 1/2003. http://elj.warwick.ac.uk/jilt/03-1/gehring.html

Gettelman, A., "The Information Divide in the Climate Sciences", National Center for Atmospheric Research, May 2003. http://www.isse.ucar.edu/infodivide/

Giensen, I., and M.B.M. Loos, "Liability for Defective Products and Services: The Netherlands", *Netherlands Comparative Law Association*, 2002, pp. 75–79. http://www.ejcl.org/64/art64-6.html

Godet, M., "The art of scenario and strategic planning: tools and pitfalls", *Technological Forecasting and Social Change*, Vol. 65, 2000, pp. 3–22.

Goldman, J., "Privacy and individual empowerment in the interactive age" in Y. Poullet, C. De Terwangne and P. Turner (eds.), *Privacy: New Risk and Opportunities*, Story-Scientia, Diegem, 1997.

Grabner-Kräuter, S., and E.A. Kaluscha, "Empirical Research in on-Line Trust: A Review and Critical Assessment", *International Journal of Human-Computer Studies*, Vol. 58, No. 6, 2003, pp. 783–812.

Günther, O., and S. Spiekermann, "RFID and the Perception of Control: The Consumer's View", *Communications of the ACM*, Vol. 48, No. 9, 2005.

Gutwirth, S., "De polyfonie van de democratische rechtsstaat" [The polyphony of the democratic constitutional state] in M. Elchardus (ed.), *Wantrouwen en onbehagen* [Distrust and uneasiness], Balans 14, VUBPress, Brussels, 1998, pp. 137–193.

Gutwirth, S., *Privacy and the Information Age*, Rowman & Littlefield, Lanham/Boulder/New York/Oxford, 2002, pp. 5–20.

Gutwirth, S., and P. de Hert, "Privacy and Data Protection in a Democratic Constitutional State" in M. Hildebrandt and S. Gutwirth (eds.), *Profiling: Implications for Democracy and Rule of Law*, FIDIS deliverable 7.4, Brussels, 2005. www.fidis.net

Gutwirth, S., and P. De Hert, "Regulating profiling in a democratic constitutional state", to be published in M. Hildebrandt and S. Gutwirth (eds.), *Profiling the European Citizen*, Springer, Dordrecht, 2008 (forthcoming).

Hansell, S., "Increasingly, Internet's Data Trail Leads to Court", *The New York Times*, 4 February 2006.

Hansen, M., and H. Krasemann (eds.), *Privacy and Identity Management for Europe* – PRIME White Paper, Deliverable D 15.1.d, 18 July 2005. http://www.prime-project.eu.org/public/prime_products/deliverables/

Harmon, Amy, "Lost? Hiding? Your Cellphone Is Keeping Tabs", *The New York Times*, 21 December 2003.

Henderson, K., and A. Poulter, "The Distance Selling Directive: Points for Further Revision", *International Review for Law Computers & Technology*, Vol. 16, No. 3, 2002, pp. 289–300.

Heusel, W. (ed.), *Grundrechtecharta und Verfassungsentwicklung in der EU*, Bundesanzeiger (Shriftenreihe der Europäischen Rechtsakademie Trier, Vol. 35), Köln, 2002.

Hildebrandt, M., "Profiling and the Identity of European Citizens" in M. Hildebrandt and S. Gutwirth (eds.), *Profiling: Implications for Democracy and Rule of Law*, FIDIS deliverable 7.4, Brussels, 2005. www.fidis.net

Hildebrandt, M., and J. Backhouse (eds.), *Descriptive Analysis and Inventory of Profiling Practices*, FIDIS (Future of Identity in the Information Society) Deliverable D7.2. http://www.fidis.net

Hildebrandt, M., and S. Gutwirth (eds.), *Implications of Profiling on Democracy and the Rule of Law*, FIDIS (Future of Identity in the Information Society), Deliverable D7.4, September 2005. http://www.fidis.net

Hilty, L., et al., *The Precautionary Principle in the Information Society, Effects of Pervasive Computing on Health and Environment*, Report of the Centre for Technology Assessment, February 2005.

Hogan, J., "Smart software linked to CCTV can spot dubious behaviour", New Scientist.com, 11 July 2003. http://www.newscientist.com/article.ns?id=dn3918

Hustinx, P., Letter of the European Data Protection Supervisor (EDPS) to Dr W. Schauble, 27 June 2007. http://www.epic.org/privacy/pdf/hustinx-letter.pdf

Inayatullah, S., "Alternative Futures for the Islamic Ummah", Metafuture.org (undated). http://www.metafuture.org/Articles/AltFuturesUmmah.htm

INDICARE Project, "Content Providers' Guide to Digital Rights Management: Any side effects in using DRM?". http://www.indicare.org

ISO/IEC 15408, *Information Technology – Security Techniques – Evaluation Criteria for IT Security*, First edition, International Organization for Standardization, Geneva, 1999.

ISO/IEC 17799:2005(E), *Information Technology – Security Techniques – Code of Practice for Information Security Management*, International Organization for Standardization, Geneva, 2005.

IST Advisory Group, *Ambient Intelligence: From Vision to Reality*. For participation – in society and business, Office for Official Publications of the European Communities, Luxembourg, 2003. http://www.cordis.lu/ist/istag-reports.html

IST Advisory Group, *Trust, Dependability, Security and Privacy for IST in FP6*, Office for Official Publications of the European Communities, Luxembourg, 2002. http://www.cordis.lu/ist/istag-reports.html

IST Advisory Group, K. Ducatel, M. Bogdanowicz et al., *Scenarios for Ambient Intelligence in 2010*, EUR 19763 EN, EC-JRC, Institute for Prospective Technological Studies (IPTS), Seville, 2001. http://www.cordis.lu/ist/istag-reports.html

ITEA *Technology Roadmap for Software-Intensive Systems*, 2nd edition, Information Technology for European Advancement (ITEA) Office Association, Eindhoven, 2004. www.itea-office.org

Ito, M., A. Iwaya, M. Saito et al., "Smart Furniture: Improvising Ubiquitous Hot-spot Environment" in *Proceedings of the 23rd International Conference on Distributed Computing Systems Workshops* (ICDCSW'03), Providence, RI, 19–22 May 2003, IEEE Press, 2003, pp. 48–53.

Jackson, R., "New fraud threat to chip-and-PIN cards", *The Scotsman*, 6 January 2007. http://news.scotsman.com/uk.cfm?id=26792007

Jardin, X., "Your Identity, Open to All", *Wired News*, 6 May 2005. http://www.wired.com/news/privacy/0,1848,67407,00.html

Jordan, M., "Electronic Eye Grows Wider in Britain", *The Washington Post*, 7 January 2006.

Juels, A., D. Molnar and D. Wagner, "Security and Privacy Issues in E-passports", ePrint Archive Cryptology Report 2005/095. http://eprint.iacr.org/

Julia-Barcelo, R., and K.J. Koelman, "Intermediary Liability in the E- commerce Directive: So far so Good, But It's not Enough", *Computer Law and Security Report*, Vol. 16, No. 4, 2000, pp. 231–239.

Kaasinen, E., K. Rentto, V. Ikonen and P. Välkkynen, *MIMOSA Initial Usage Scenarios*, MIMOSA Deliverable D1.1, version 1.0, 2004. http://www.mimosa-fp6.com/cgi-bin/WebObjects/MIMOSA.woa/1/wo/g6hDj8CHIFBQDjTQXuNVGM/8.0.5.11.

Kardasiadou, Z., and Z. Talidou, *Report on Legal Issues of RFID Technology*, LEGAL IST (Legal Issues for the Advancement of Information Society Technologies) Deliverable D15, 2006.

Kato, U., T. Hayashi, N. Umeda et al. (eds.), *Flying Carpet: Towards the 4th Generation Mobile Communications Systems*, Ver. 2.00, 4th Generation Mobile Communications Committee, 2004. http://www.mitf.org/public_e/archives/index.html

Kawahara, Y., M. Minami, S. Saruwatari et al., "Challenges and Lessons Learned in Building a Practical Smart Space", in *The First Annual International Conference on Mobile and Ubiquitous Systems: Networking and Services*, Boston, MA, 22–26 August 2004, pp. 213–222.

Kelly, L., "Spyware attacks triple in 2005", *Computing*, 12 June 2006. http://www.vnunet.com/computing/news/2158112/spyware-attacks-triple-2005

Kent, S.T., and L.I. Millett (eds.), *Who Goes There? Authentication Through the Lens of Privacy*. National Academies Press, Washington, DC, 2003.

Kent, S.T., and L.I. Millett (eds.), *IDs – Not That Easy. Questions About Nationwide Identity Systems*, Committee on Authentication Technologies and Their Privacy Implications, National Research Council, National Academy Press, Washington, DC, 2002.

Knospe, H., and H. Pohl, "RFID Security", in *Information Security Technical Report*, Vol. 9, No. 4, 2004, S. 30–41.

Koops, B.J., and M.M. Prinsen, "Glazen woning, transparant lichaam. Een toekomstblik op huisrecht en lichamelijke integriteit" ["Glass house, transparent body. A future view on home law and body integrity"], *Nederland Juristenblad*, 12 March 2005, pp. 624–630.

Koorn, R., H. van Gils, J. ter Hart, P. Overbeek, R. Tellegen and J. Borking, "Privacy-Enhancing Technologies. White Paper for Decision-Makers", Ministry of the Interior and Kingdom Relations, The Hague, 2004. http://www.dutchdpa.nl/downloads_overig/PET_whitebook.pdf

Korhonen, I., P. Aavilainen and A. Särelä, "Application of ubiquitous computing technologies for support of independent living of the elderly in real life settings" in *UbiHealth 2003: The 2nd International Workshop on Ubiquitous Computing for Pervasive Healthcare Applications*, Seattle, 8 October 2003.

Kravitz, D.W., K.-E. Yeoh and N. So, "Secure Open Systems for Protecting Privacy and Digital Services", in T. Sander (ed.), *Security and Privacy in Digital Rights Management*, ACM CCS-8 Workshop DRM 2001, Philadelphia, 5 November 2001, Revised Papers, Springer, Berlin, 2002, pp. 106–125.

Krebs, B., "Hackers Break Into Computer-Security Firm's Customer Database", *The Washington Post*, 19 December 2005.

Krebs, B., "Microsoft Releases Windows Malware Stats", *The Washington Post*, 12 June 2006. http://blog.washingtonpost.com/securityfix/2006/06/microsoft_releases_malware_sta.html

Krebs, B., "Invasion of the Computer Snatchers", *The Washington Post*, 19 February 2006.

Krebs, B., "Hacked Home PCs Fueling Rapid Growth in Online Fraud", *The Washington Post*, 19 September 2005. http://www.washingtonpost.com/wp-dyn/content/article/2005/09/19/AR2005091900026.html

Krim, J., "Consumers Not Told Of Security Breaches, Data Brokers Admit", *The Washington Post*, 14 April 2005.

Krim, J., "Data on 3,000 Consumers Stolen With Computer", *The Washington Post*, 9 November 2005.

Krikke, J., "T-Engine: Japan's Ubiquitous Computing Architecture Is Ready for Prime Time", in *Pervasive Computing*, Vol. 4, No. 2, 2005, pp. 4–9.

Kruger, D., *Access Denied? Preventing Information Exclusion*, Demos, London, 1998.

Lahlou, S., and F. Jegou, "European Disappearing Computer Privacy Design Guidelines V1", Ambient Agora Deliverable D15.4, Electricité de France, Clamart, 2003. http://www.ambient-agoras.org/downloads/D15[1].4_-_Privacy_Design_Guidelines.pdf

Lahlou, S., M. Langheinrich and C. Rocker, "Privacy and Trust Issues with Invisible Computers", *Communications of the ACM*, Vol. 48, No. 3, March 2005.

Langheinrich, M., "Privacy by Design – Principles of Privacy-Aware Ubiquitous Systems", in G.D. Abowd, B. Brumitt and S.A. Shafer (eds.), *Proceedings of the Third International Conference on Ubiquitous Computing* (Ubicomp 2001), Springer, Berlin, 2001, pp. 273–91.

Langheinrich, M., "The DC-Privacy Troubadour – Assessing Privacy Implications of DC-Projects", Paper presented at the Designing for Privacy Workshop, DC Tales Conference, Santorini, Greece, 2003.

Leenes, R., and B.J. Koops, "'Code': Privacy's Death or Saviour?" *International Review of Law, Computers & Technology*, Vol. 19, No. 3, 2005.

Lemos, R., "Cybersecurity contests go national", *The Register*, 5 June 2006. http://www.theregister.co.uk/2006/06/05/security_contests/. This article originally appeared at *SecurityFocus*. http://www.securityfocus.com/news/11394

Lessig, L., "The Law of the Horse: What Cyberlaw Might Teach", *Harvard Law Review*, Vol. 133, 1999, pp. 501–546.

Lessig, L., *Code and Other Laws of Cyberspace*, Basic Books, New York, 1999.

Lewis, Paul, "Court victory hailed as spam stopper", *The Guardian*, 28 December 2005. http://www.guardian.co.uk/uk_news/story/0,,1674316,00.html

Leyden, J., "Hackers cost UK.biz billions", *The Register*, 28 April 2004. http://www.theregister.co.uk/2004/04/28/dti_security_survey/

Maghiros, I. (ed.), *Security and Privacy for the Citizen in the Post-September 11 Digital Age: A Prospective Overview*, Report to the European Parliament Committee on Citizens' Freedoms and Rights, Justice and Home Affairs (LIBE), IPTS Technical Report, Institute for Prospective Technological Studies, Seville, 2003. ftp://ftp.jrc.es/pub/EURdoc/eur20823en.pdf

Maghiros, I., Y. Punie, S. Delaitre et al., *Biometrics at the Frontiers: Assessing the Impact on Society*, Study commissioned by the LIBE committee of the European Parliament, EC – DG Joint Research Centre, EUR 21585 EN, Institute for Prospective Technological Studies (IPTS), Seville, 2005. http://www.jrc.es/home/pages/detail.cfm?prs=1235.

Magnus, U., and H.W. Micklitz, *Comparative Analysis of National Liability Systems for Remedying Damage Caused by Defective Consumer Services*: A study commissioned by the European Commission, Final Report, April 2004. http://europa.eu.int/comm/consumers/cons_safe/serv_safe/liability/reportabc_en.pdf; http://europa.eu.int/comm/consumers/ cons_safe/serv_safe/liability/reportd_en.pdf

Markoff, J., "Attack of the Zombie Computers Is Growing Threat", *New York Times*, 7 January 2007. http://www.nytimes.com/2007/01/07/technology/07net.html?hp&ex=1168232400&en=60c6afb90ec2af68&ei=5094&partner=homepage

Masera, M., and R. Bloomfeld, *A Dependability Roadmap for the Information Society in Europe*, AMSD Delilverable D1.1, 2003. https://rami.jrc.it/roadmaps/amsd

Massini, E.H., and J.M. Vasquez, "Scenarios as seen from a human and social perspective", *Technological Forecasting and Social Change*, Vol. 65, 2000, pp. 49–66.

Meints, M., "AmI – The European Perspective on Data Protection Legislation and Privacy Policies", presentation at the SWAMI International Conference on Safeguards in a World of Ambient Intelligence, 21 March 2006.

Michahelles, F., P. Matter, A. Schmidt, B. Schiele, "Applying Wearable Sensors to Avalanche Rescue: First Experiences with a Novel Avalanche Beacon" in *Computers and Graphics*, Vol. 27, No. 6, 2003, pp. 839–847.

Mietzner, D., and G. Reger, "Scenario Approaches – History, Differences, Advantages, and Disadvantages", in F. Scapolo and E. Cahill, *New Horizons and Challenges for Future-Oriented Technology Analysis*: Proceedings of the EU-US Scientific Seminar: New Technology

Foresight, Forecasting and Assessment Methods, 13–14 May 2004, European Commission DG JRC-IPTS, Seville, 2004. http://www.jrc.es/projects/fta/

Miles, I., M. Keenan and J. Kaivo-Oja, "Handbook of Knowledge Society Foresight", European Foundation for the Improvement of Living and Working Conditions, Dublin, 2003. This handbook is available in electronic format only: http://www.eurofound.eu.int

Mohammed, A., "Record Fine for Data Breach", *The Washington Post*, 27 January 2006.

Mohammed, A., and S. Kehaulani Goo, "Government Increasingly Turning to Data Mining", *The Washington Post*, 15 June 2006. http://www.washingtonpost.com/wp-dyn/content/article/2006/06/14/AR2006061402063.html

Molas-Gallart, J., "Government Policies and Complex Product Systems: The Case of Defence Standards and Procurement", *International Journal of Aerospace Management*, Vol. 1, No. 3, 2001, pp. 268–280.

Moores, T., "Do Consumers Understand the Role of Privacy Seals in E-Commerce?", *Communications of the ACM*, Vol. 48, No. 3, 2005, pp. 86–91.

MPHPT, Information and Communications in Japan: *Building a Ubiquitous Network Society that Spreads Throughout the World*, White Paper, Ministry of Public Management Home Affairs Posts and Telecommunications of Japan, Economic Research Office, General Policy Division, Tokyo, 2004. http://www.johotsusintokei.soumu.go.jp/whitepaper/eng/WP2004/2004-index.html

Müller, B., "Equity in Climate Change – The Great Divide", Executive summary, Oxford Institute for Energy Studies with the support of Shell Foundation. http://www.oxfordenergy.org/pdfs/great_divide_executive_summary.pdf

Müller, G., and S. Wohlgemuth (eds.), *Study on Mobile Identity Management*, FIDIS Deliverable D3.3, May 2005. http://www.fidis.net

Murakami, T., "Establishing the Ubiquitous Network Environment in Japan: From e-Japan to U-Japan", NRI Paper 66, Nomura Research Institute, Tokyo, 2003. http://www.nri.co.jp/english/opinion/papers/2003/pdf/np200366.pdf

Naylor, David, & Cyril Ritter, "B2C in Europe and Avoiding Contractual Liability: Why Businesses with European Operations Should Review their Customer Contracts Now", 15 September 2004. http://www.droit-technologie.org

Nissenbaum, H., "Privacy as Contextual Integrity", in *Washington Law Review*, Vol. 79, No. 1, 2004, pp. 101–139.

Norris, P., *Digital Divide: Civic Engagement, Information Poverty, and the Internet Worldwide*, Cambridge University Press, Cambridge, 2001.

O'Brien, T.L., "Identity Theft Is Epidemic. Can It Be Stopped?", *The New York Times*, 24 October 2004.

*OECD Guidelines Governing the Protection of Privacy and Transborder Flows of Personal Data*, Organisation for Economic Co-operation and Development, Paris, 23 September 1980.

*OECD Guidelines on the Protection of Privacy and Transborder Flows of Personal Data*, Organisation for Economic Co-operation and Development, Paris, 2001.

*OECD Guidelines for the Security of Information Systems and Networks: Towards a Culture of Security*, Organisation for Economic Co-operation and Development, Paris, 2002.

OECD, *Emerging Systemic Risks in the 21st Century*, Paris, 2003.

OECD, *Report on Disclosure Issues Related to the Use of Copy Control and Digital Rights Management Technologies*, DSTI/CP(2005)15/FINAL, 2006. https://www.oecd.org/dataoecd/47/31/36546422.pdf

Oertel, B., M. Wölk, L.M. Hilty et al., *Risiken und Chancen des Einsatzes von RFID-Systemen: Trends und Entwicklungen in Technologien, Anwendungen und Sicherheit*, SecuMedia, Ingelheim, 2004.

Ofcom, Online protection: A survey of consumer, industry and regulatory mechanisms and systems, 21 June 2006. http://www.ofcom.org.uk/research/technology/onlineprotection/report.pdf

O'Harrow, R., *No Place to Hide*, Simon & Schuster, New York, 2005.

Olsen, T., T. Mahler et al., "Privacy – Identity Management, Data Protection Issues in Relation to Networked Organisations Utilizing Identity Management Systems", LEGAL IST: Legal Issues for the Advancement of Information Society Technologies, Deliverable D11, 2005. http://193.72.209.176/default.asp?P=369&obj=P1076

Orr, R.J., R. Raymond, J. Berman and F. Seay, "A System for Finding Frequently Lost Objects in the Home", *Technical Report* 99–24, Graphics, Visualization, and Usability Center, Georgia Tech, 1999.

Paciga, M., and H. Lutfiyya, "Herecast: An open infrastructure for location-based services using WiFi, Wireless and Mobile Computing, Networking and Communications", WiMob'2005, IEEE International Conference, 2005, pp. 21–28.

Palmas, G., N. Tsapatsoulis, B. Apolloni et al., *Generic Artefacts Specification and Acceptance Criteria*, Oresteia Deliverable D01, STMicroelectronics s.r.l., Milan, 2001.

Peers, S., and A. Ward (eds.), *The European Union Charter of Fundamental Rights*, Hart Publishing, Oxford, 2004.

Pennington, R., H.D. Wilcox and V. Grover, "The Role of System Trust in Business-to-Consumer Transactions", *Journal of Management Information System*, Vol. 20, No. 3, 2004, pp. 197–226.

Perri 6 and Ben Jupp, *Divided by Information? The "Digital Divide" and the Implications of the New Meritocracy*, Demos, London, 2001.

Pfitzmann, A., "Anonymity, unobservability, pseudonymity and identity management requirements for an AmI world", SWAMI Final Conference, Brussels, 21–22 March 2006.

Pfitzmann, A., and M. Hansen, *Anonymity, Unlinkability, Unobservability, Pseudonymity, and Identity Management – A Consolidated Proposal for Terminology*, Version v0.27, 20 February 2006. http://dud.inf.tu-dresden.de/Anon_Terminology.shtml

Pfitzmann, A., and M. Kohntopp, "Striking a Balance between Cyber-Crime and Privacy", *IPTS Report* 57, EC-JRC, Seville, September 2001. http://www.jrc.es/home/report/english/articles/vol57/welcome.htm

Poulsen, K., "Traffic Hackers Hit Red Light", *Wired News*, 12 August 2005. http://www.wired.com/news/technology/0,1282,68507,00.html

Prins, J.E.J., "The Propertization of Personal Data and Identities", *Electronic Journal of Comparative Law*, Vol. 8.3, October 2004. http://www.ejcl.org

Prins, J.E.J., and M.H.M. Schellekens, "Fighting Untrustworthy Internet Content: In Search of Regulatory Scenarios", *Information Polity*, Vol. 10, 2005, pp. 129–139.

Punie, Y., "The future of Ambient Intelligence in Europe: The need for more Everyday Life", *Communications and Strategies*, Vol. 57, 2005, pp. 141–165.

Punie, Y., S. Delaitre, I. Maghiros and D. Wright (eds.), *Dark Scenarios in Ambient Intelligence: Highlighting Risks and Vulnerabilities*, SWAMI Deliverable D2, A report of the SWAMI consortium to the European Commission, November 2005.

Rannenberg, K., "Multilateral Security: A Concept and Examples for Balanced Security", ACM New Security Paradigms Workshop, September 2000, pp. 151–162.

Reed, Ch., and A. Welterveden, "Liability", in Ch. Reed and J. Angel (eds.), *ComputerLaw*, London, 2000.

Resnick, P., and R. Zeckhauser, "Trust Among Strangers in Internet Transactions: Empirical Analysis of eBay's Reputation System", in Michael R. Baye (ed.), *The Economics of the Internet and E-Commerce*, Vol. 11 of *Advances in Applied Microeconomics*, JAI Press, Amsterdam, 2002, pp. 127–157.

Resnick, P., R. Zeckhauser, E. Friedman and K. Kuwabara, "Reputation Systems: Facilitating Trust in Internet Interactions", *Communications of the ACM*, Vol. 43, No. 12, 2000, pp. 45–48. http://www.si.umich.edu/~presnick/papers/cacm00/reputations.pdf

Richtel, M., "Suddenly, an Industry Is All Ears", *The New York Times*, 4 March 2006.

Roussos, G., and T. Moussouri, "Consumer Perceptions of Privacy, Security and Trust in Ubiquitous Commerce", *Personal and Ubiquitous Computing*, Vol. 8, No. 6, 2004, pp. 416–429.

Sachinopoulou, A., S. Mäkelä, S. Järvinen et al., "Personal video retrieval and browsing for mobile users" in *17th International Symposium Electronic Imaging Science and Technology*, San José, CA, 16–20 January 2005.

Samuelson, P., "Privacy As Intellectual Property?", *Stanford Law Review*, Vol. 52, 2000.

Savidis, A., S. Lalis, A. Karypidis et al., *Report on Key Reference Scenarios*, 2WEAR Deliverable D1, Foundation for Research and Technology Hellas, Institute of Computer Science, Heraklion, 2001.

Schneider, F.B. (ed.), *Trust in Cyberspace*, National Academy Press, Washington, DC, 1999.

Schneier, B., "Risks of Relying on Cryptography", *Communications of the ACM* 42, No. 10, 1999.

Schneier, B., "The Future of Surveillance", *Crypto-Gram News letter*, 15 October 2003.

Schneier, B., "Information security: How liable should vendors be?", *Computerworld*, 28 October 2004. http://www.schneier.com/essay-073.html

Schneier, B., *Secrets & Lies*, Wiley Computer Publishing, New York, 2000.

Schneier, B., "Customers, Passwords, and Web Sites", in *IEEE Security & Privacy Magazine*, Vol. 2, No. 5, 2004.

Schneier, B., "Identification and Security", *Crypto-Gram Newsletter*, 15 February 2004. http://www.schneier.com/crypto-gram-back.html

Schneier, B., "National ID Cards", *Crypto-Gram Newsletter*, 15 April 2004. http://www.schneier.com/crypto-gram-back.html

Schneier, B., "Why Data Mining Won't Stop Terror", *Wired News*, 9 March 2005. http://www.schneier.com/essay-108.html

Schreurs, W., M. Hildebrandt, M. Gasson and K. Warwick, *Report on Actual and Possible Profiling Techniques in the Field of Ambient Intelligence*, FIDIS Deliverable D7.3, 2005. http://www.fidis.net

Schreurs, W., M. Hildebrandt, E. Kindt and M. Vanfleteren, "*Cogitas, ergo sum*. The role of data protection law and non-discrimination law in group profiling in the private sector", to be published in M. Hildebrandt and S. Gutwirth (eds.), *Profiling the European Citizen*, Springer, Dordrecht, 2008 (forthcoming).

Schwarz, J., Statement of John Schwarz, President, Symantec Corporation on Worms, Viruses and Securing Our Nation's Computers, House Government Reform Subcommittee on Technology, Information Policy, Intergovernmental Relations and the Census, Washington, DC, 2003. http://reform.house.gov/UploadedFiles/Schwarz-v5.pdf

Scott, A.O., "A Future More Nasty, Because It's So Near", Film review of "Code 46", *The New York Times*, 6 August 2004.

Sharpe, B., S. Zaba and M. Ince, "Foresight Cyber Trust and Crime Prevention Project: Technology Forward Look: User Guide", Office of Science and Technology, London, 2004.

Singsangob, A., *Computer Software and Information Licensing in Emerging Markets, The Need for a Viable Legal Framework*, Aspen Publishers, 2003.

Solove, D.J., *The Digital Person*, New York University Press, New York, 2004.

Sommer, D., Architecture Version 0, PRIME Deliverable D14.2.a, 13 October 2004, pp. 35–36, 57–58. http://www.prime-project.eu.org

Sorkin, D.E., "Technical and Legal Approaches to Unsolicited Electronic Mail", *University of San Francisco Law Review*, Vol. 35, 2001.

Spiekermann, S., and F. Pallas, "Technology Paternalism – Wider Implications of Ubiquitous Computing", *Poiesis & Praxis*, Vol. 4, No. 1, 2006.

Spiekermann, S., and M. Rothensee, "Soziale und psychologische Bestimmungsfaktoren des Ubiquitous Computing", Institut für Wirtschaftsinformatik, Humboldt-Universität zu Berlin, 2005. http://interval.hu-berlin.de/downloads/rfid/neuste%20forschungsergebnisse/SocioPsychofak.pdf

Stajano, F., and R. Anderson, "The Resurrecting Duckling: Security Issues for Ubiquitous Computing", first *Security & Privacy Supplement to IEEE Computer*, April 2002, pp. 22–26.

Stajano, F., and J. Crowcroft, "The Butt of the Iceberg: Hidden Security Problems of Ubiquitous Systems", in Basten et al. (eds.), *Ambient Intelligence: Impact on Embedded System Design*, Kluwer, Dordrecht, The Netherlands, 2003.

Stout, D., "Data Theft at Nuclear Agency Went Unreported for 9 Months", *The New York Times*, 10 June 2006.

Streitz, N.A., and P. Nixon, "The Disappearing Computer", *Communications of the ACM*, Vol. 48, No. 3, 2005, pp. 32–35.

Sturcke, J., and agencies, "US access to flight data unlawful", *The Guardian*, 30 May 2006.

Subirana, B., and M. Bain, *Legal Programming: Designing Legally Compliant RFID and Software Agent Architectures for Retail Processes and Beyond*, Springer, New York, 2005.

Summers, D., "Bureau admits innocents branded criminals", *The Herald* [Scotland], 22 May 2006.

Sutter, G., "'Don't Shoot the Messenger?' The UK and Online Intermediary Liability", *International Review of Law Computers & Technology*, Vol. 17, No. 1, 2003, pp. 73–84.

SWAMI, "Safeguards in a World of Ambient Intelligence (SWAMI): Policy Options to Counteract Threats and Vulnerabilities – First Results", Report submitted to the participants of the SWAMI conference, Brussels, 21–22 March 2006.

Tuohey, J., "Government Uses Color Laser Printer Technology to Track Documents. Practice embeds hidden, traceable data in every page printed", *PC World*, 22 November 2004. http://www.pcworld.com/news/article/0,aid,118664,00.asp

Upton, M., "Casual Rock Concert Events", June 2005. http://www.crowddynamics.com/Main/Concert risks.htm

[US] Committee on Information Systems Trustworthiness, *Trust in Cyberspace*, National Research Council, National Academies Press, Washington, DC, 1999.

[US] Committee on Radio Frequency Identification Technologies, *Radio Frequency Identification Technologies: A Workshop Summary*, Computer Science and Telecommunications Board, National Research Council, National Academies Press, Washington, DC, 2004. http://books.nap.edu/catalog/11189.html

[US] National Telecommunications and Information Administration (NTIA), *Falling through the Net: Towards Digital Inclusion. A Report on Americans' Access to Technology Tools*, US Department of Commerce, Economics and Statistics Administration, National Telecommunications and Information Administration, Washington, DC, 2000. http://search.ntia.doc.gov/pdf/fttn00.pdf

Venkatesh, V., "Determinants of Perceived Ease of Use: Integrating Control, Intrinsic Motivation, and Emotion into the Technology Acceptance Model", *Information Systems Research*, Vol. 11, No. 4, 2000, pp. 342–365.

Vijayan, J., "ID Theft Continues to Increase. More than 13 million Americans have been victimized, new study reveals", *Computerworld*, 30 July 2003. http://www.pcworld.com/news/article/0,aid,111832,00.asp

Vishwanath, A., "Manifestations of Interpersonal Trust in Online Interaction", *New Media and Society*, Vol. 6, No. 2, 2004, pp. 224 f.

Waelbroeck, D., D. Slater and G. Even-Shoshan G [Ashurst], *Study on the Conditions of Claims for Damages in Case of Infringement of EC Competition Rules*, commissioned by European Commission DG Competition, 2004. http://ec.europa.eu/comm/competition/antitrust/others/actions_for_damages/study.html

Waldo, James, Herbert S. Lin and Lynette I. Millett, *Engaging Privacy and Information Technology in a Digital Age*, Computer Science and Telecommunications Board, National Academies Press, Washington, DC, 2007.

Weis, S.A., S.E. Sarma, R.L. Rivest and D.W. Engels, "Security and Privacy Aspects of Low-Cost Radio Frequency Identification Systems", in D. Hutter, G. Müller et al. (eds.), *Security in Pervasive Computing*, First International Conference, Boppard, Germany, 12–14 March 2003, Springer (Lecture notes in computer science, 2802), Berlin/New York, 2004, pp. 201–212.

Weiser, M., "The Computer for the 21st Century", *Scientific American*, Vol. 265, No. 3, 1991, pp. 94–104.

Weiser, M., "Some Computer Science Issues in Ubiquitous Computing", *Communications of the ACM*, Vol. 36, No. 7, 1993, pp. 75–85.

Weiser, M., and J.S. Brown, "The Coming Age of Calm Technology", in P.J. Denning and R.M. Metcalfe (eds.), *Beyond Calculation: The Next Fifty Years of Computing*, Copernicus, New York, 1997.

Welen, P., A. Wilson and P. Nixon, *Scenario Analysis*, Gloss Deliverable D.9, University of Strathclyde, Glasgow, 2003. http://iihm.imag.fr/projects/Gloss/Deliverables/D9–1.pdf

Whitehouse, O., *GPRS Wireless Security: Not Ready for Prime Time*, Research report, Stake, Boston, MA, 2002. http://www.atstake.com/research/reports/acrobat/atstake_gprs_security. pdf

Wilkinson, L., "How to Build Scenarios", *Wired* 3, Special Issue. http://www.wired.com/wired/ scenarios/build.html

Williams, A., "House of Lords to investigate Net security", *PCPro*, 28 July 2006. http://www. pcpro.co.uk/news/91105/house-of-lords-to-investigate-net-security.html

Wright, D., "The dark side of ambient intelligence", *Info*, Vol. 7, No. 6, October 2005, pp. 33–51. http://www.emeraldinsight.com/info

Wright, David, "Alternative futures: AmI scenarios and *Minority Report*", *Futures*, Vol. 40:5, June 2008 (forthcoming).

Wright, D., et al., "The illusion of security", *Communications of the ACM*, 2008 (forthcoming).

WWRF, *The Book of Visions 2001: Visions of the Wireless World*, Version 1.0, Wireless World Research Forum, 2001. http://www.wireless-world-research.org/general_info/BoV2001-final. pdf

Xenakis, C., and S. Kontopoulou, "Risk Assessment, Security & Trust: Cross Layer Issues", Special Interest Group 2, Wireless World Research Forum, 2006.

Zeller, T. Jr., "For Victims, Repairing ID Theft Can Be Grueling", *The New York Times*, 1 October 2005.

Zetter, K., "TSA Data Dump Leads to Lawsuit", *Wired News*, 14 July 2005. http://www.wired. com/news/privacy/0,1848,68560,00.html

# Contributors

## Editors

**David Wright**
Partner
Trilateral Research and Consulting
London

**Serge Gutwirth**
Professor of Law
Vrije Universiteit Brussel
Brussels

**Michael Friedewald**
Senior Researcher
Fraunhofer Institute of Systems and Innovation Research
Karlsruhe, Germany

**Elena Vildjiounaite**
Researcher
VTT Technical Research Centre of Finland
Oulu, Finland

**Yves Punie**
Senior Scientist
European Commission JRC
Institute for Prospective Technological Studies (IPTS)
Seville

# Authors

Vrije Universiteit Brussel
Faculty of Law, Law Science Technology
and Society (LSTS)
Pleinlaan 2
1050 Brussel
Belgium

Serge Gutwirth
serge.gutwirth@vub.ac.be
Paul De Hert
Wim Schreurs
Anna Moscibroda
Michiel Verlinden


VTT Technical Research Centre
of Finland
Kaitoväylä 1
FIN 90571 Oulu
Finland

Elena Vildjiounaite
Elena.Vildjiounaite@vtt.fi
Petteri Alahuhta
Pasi Ahonen


Fraunhofer Institute for Systems and
Innovation Research (ISI)
Breslauer Strasse 48
76139 Karlsruhe
Germany

Michael Friedewald
m.friedewald@isi.fraunhofer.de
Ralf Lindner


Institute for Prospective Technological
Studies (IPTS)
European Commission JRC
Edificio Expo, C/Inca Garcilaso, s/n
41092 Sevilla
Spain

Yves Punie
Yves.Punie@ec.europa.eu
Ioannis Maghiros
Sabine Delaitre
Barbara Daskala


Trilateral Research and Consulting
22 Argyll Court
82–84 Lexham Gardens
London W8 5JB
United Kingdom

David Wright
david.wright@trilateralresearch.com

# Index